The Complexity Challenge

To Ted

With admiration

and thanks

Don

8/16/99

Science, Technology and the International Political Economy

Series Editor: John de la Mothe

The upheavals of the international political economy during recent decades have fundamentally altered the relationship between firms and states, citizenship and management, social institutions and economic growth. The changing pace of competition, firm performance and geo-economics is shifting the pressures on public policy and corporate strategy alike. As a result, our conceptual frameworks for analyzing key events, emerging trends and driving forces are being challenged. As unclear as the future is, what remains certain is that science, technology and innovation will occupy a central place. By looking at a wide array of issues – ranging from security and foreign affairs, the environment, international institutions, corporate strategy and regional development to research policy, innovation gaps, intellectual property, ethics and law – this series will critically examine how science and technology are shaping the emerging international political economy.

Published titles in the series:

Evolutionary Economics and the New International Political Economy, edited by John de la Mothe and Gilles Paquet

Global Change and Intellectual Property Agencies, by G. Bruce Doern

Systems of Innovation, edited by Charles Edquist

Universities and the Global Knowledge Economy, edited by Henry Etzkowitz and Loet Leydesdorff

Forthcoming titles in the series:

Innovation and the Service-Based Economy, edited by Ian Miles and Mark Boden

Innovation Strategies in Middle Power Countries, edited by John de la Mothe and Gilles Paquet

Regional Innovation, Knowledge and Global Change, edited by Zoltan Acs

Science and Technology and Governance, edited by John de la Mothe

Proposals for books can be sent directly to the series editor:
    John de la Mothe
    Program of Research on International Management and Economy (PRIME)
    Faculty of Administration
    University of Ottawa
    275 Nicholas Street
    Ottawa, Canada K1N 6N5

The Complexity Challenge

Technological Innovation for the 21st Century

Robert W. Rycroft and Don E. Kash

PINTER

London and New York

Science, Technology and the International Political Economy Series
Series Editor: John de la Mothe

Pinter
A Cassell Imprint
Wellington House, 125 Strand, London WC2R 0BB
370 Lexington Avenue, New York, NY 10017-6550

First published in 1999
© Robert W. Rycroft and Don E. Kash 1999

British Library Cataloguing in Publication Data
A catalogue record for this book is available from the British Library
ISBN   1–85567–608–7 (hardback)
         1–85567–611–7 (paperback)

Library of Congress Cataloging-in-Publication Data
Rycroft, Robert W., 1945–
      The complexity challenge: technological innovation for the 21st
century/ Robert W. Rycroft and Don E. Kash.
         p.   cm. -- (Science, technology, and the international
political economy series)
      Includes bibliographical references and index.
      ISBN 1–85567–608–7 (hardcover). – ISBN 1–85567–611–7 (pbk.)
      1. Technological innovations–Economic aspects–United States.
2. Technological innovations–Economic aspects. 3. Organization.
4. Competition, International. I. Kash, Don E. II. Title.
III. Series.
HC110.T4R93   1999
338′.064′0973–dc21   98–37514
                                                                                       CIP

Typeset by BookEns Ltd., Royston, Herts.
Printed and bound in Great Britain by TJ International Ltd, Padstow, Cornwall

To Kim and Betsy

Contents

Figures

Tables

Preface

This book began as a search for an answer to the following question: what, if anything, could national technology policy do to eliminate the United States' trade deficit? The first step in the investigation involved looking at the nature of the deficit. The USA has run a continuous trade surplus with regard to services and it has, since 1976, run a continuous trade deficit with regard to goods. The most attractive way to deal with the nation's trade deficit would be to increase its exports of high-value and high-value-added goods. A large proportion of these are technological products that gain their competitive advantage by repeated innovation.

This study began with a set of implicit assumptions. They were that the actions needed to enhance innovation were generally associated with research and development, adequate investment capital, appropriately trained personnel, and appropriate trade arrangements. Starting from these assumptions, we prepared 350 pages of manuscript. Although the pages were voluminous, what we were saying was not very satisfactory.

In 1993, a student brought one of the authors a copy of Mitchell Waldrop's book *Complexity: the Emerging Science at the Edge of Order and Chaos.* Both of us read it with fascination. The reason was that the book provided us with language that fit much better with what we were finding in our study of technological innovation than did the more traditional language we had been using. Within two months, we threw the existing manuscript away and started over.

This led us to an extensive search into the various definitions of complexity. Ultimately, we chose to divide technologies into two categories – simple and complex – and we chose to identify complex technologies using a concise definition. A technology is complex if it cannot be understood in detail by an individual expert and communicated in detail among experts across time and distance. Using that definition, we then investigated how the goods that represented the top 50 percent in value of all world goods exports would be grouped if we used the simple/complex distinction and applied it to both technological products and technological processes. The findings were striking. The United States does particularly poorly with regard to complex products produced by complex processes, and its competitiveness in this category is continuing to erode.

This pattern was puzzling in the extreme. In an effort to understand how the innovation of complex technologies occurs, we undertook a series of case studies. We did this because we concluded that only such case studies offered the necessary insight into the process of innovating complex technologies.

In total, we started eleven case studies. The effort proved too large for us to manage, and only six of those case studies are used in this book. All the interviewing associated with the six case studies has been completed and we have completed initial versions of the case studies. We plan to turn all the case studies into working papers that will be available from the Institute of Public Policy at George Mason University.

How to use the case studies in the book posed a serious challenge. In total, the case studies represent about 250 manuscript pages. We provide a brief summary of the case studies in Chapter 5. We then use examples from the case studies repeatedly throughout the book with the goal of making them sufficiently knowable to the reader that references to them can be used in a fairly shorthand way.

What follows is an investigation of the process of innovation associated with complex technologies. These complex technologies are becoming increasingly important in the commercial marketplace. We hope this book contributes to greater insight into how the innovation of complex technologies occurs. We also hope that insight will have benefit to those who develop and use corporate strategies and public policy.

Acknowledgments

Development of this book benefited from support provided by the Center for Innovation Management Studies at Lehigh University. We express our appreciation for their support.

Many people have contributed to this book. Among the most important are a large number of people from the companies that were associated with our case studies. We give special thanks to the following: Michael Bagshaw, John R. Carruthers, Michael Chessman, Toshi Doi, Robert Gunstra, Doug Haines, John Hart, Ed Karrer, C. J. Kranzmark, Stan Mansfield, Raymond McIntyre, Barry Melor, Jack Parker, Larry Partain, Neil Paton, Dave Penning, Earl Ross, Brian Rowe, James Sidenstick, Chester Sims, William Spencer, Yoshinori Tanaka, Jim Williams, and George Zdasiuk.

We have both used portions of the evolving manuscript as a part of our teaching for the past four years. We owe a very great debt to our graduate students. Graduate students were especially valuable and important participants in the development of the case studies. In particular, Richard Adams and Stephen Lieberman were involved in repeated interviewing. Adams made two trips to Japan to interview with people at Sony. Robert Schaller read and reread the manuscript, provided the graphics, put the whole package together for the publisher and provided wise council on a continuing basis. Our debt to him is large.

The following people provided detailed comments on all or parts of the manuscript. Vernon Van Dyke read two drafts of the manuscript and provided invaluable comments on both substance and the presentation. Robert Katt provided invaluable editorial and substantive assistance. Stephen Kline, Francis Fukuyama, Roger Stough, Christopher Hill, Theodore Schlie, William Kingsdon, Nicholas Vonortas, Fumio Kodama, and Richard Nelson provided valuable comments.

Rebecca Walter and Jama Mooney provided typing and administrative support of exceptional quality.

Kim and Betsy have been great. We suspect they have great difficulty remembering a world before complexity.

PART I

CHAPTER ONE

The Silent Emergence of Complexity

Managers of successful organizations in both the private and public sectors of advanced countries share a dirty little secret – they don't understand why they are successful. Our technologies, economy, and society are so complex that it is impossible for single individuals to fully understand them.[1] Thus, whatever success organizations achieve occurs despite the lack of comprehensive understanding by any individual.[2]

Although it is popular to think of the corporate chief executive officer (CEO) as a "captain of industry" who, like a ship's captain, commands the behavior that keeps the ship on course, given the ubiquity of complexity, leaders have come to accept their limited ability to control as a fact of life. They have become comfortable operating with a more general level of understanding. Whether they are company presidents, technological entrepreneurs, program managers, or design engineers, the message is the same, success occurs absent detailed understanding by individuals:

- "Hitachi is too complicated for anyone to run it. As president, all I can do is think and talk with people about the future and then communicate those thoughts to others in the company."[3]
- "Intel operates on the Noyce principle of minimum information: One guesses what the answer to a problem is and goes as far as one can in a heuristic way. Thus, rather than mount research efforts aimed at truly understanding problems and producing publishable technological solutions, Intel tries to get by with as little information as possible."[4]
- "There was no way Hewlett-Packard and Philips could know in advance what our relative contributions to the project would be, so we agreed to decide how the profits would be split after the technology was on the market."[5]
- "The Japanese supplier delivered a 97 percent finished product that had been through repeated prototype tests before we furnished them the turbine's specifications."[6]

What is happening? How do corporations, government agencies, and other organizations achieve success despite the limited understanding of those who lead them? The general answer is that success depends heavily on continuously adaptive organizational networks that know how to do more than any individual can understand in detail. These networks manifest patterns that are very different from those of traditional organizations, and much of what follows is a search for those patterns. But one pattern is so compelling that it is evident at the start. *In the realm of complex technologies, organizational networks have blurred the line between the public and private sectors and between company strategies and public policy.*

Success in our complex world is clearly dependent on ever-changing relationships among the organizations that participate in the networks. The assumption that clear and permanent boundaries can be established between organizations located in the public and private sectors does not fit with the reality of contemporary advanced societies. Thus, innovative managers increasingly focus on facilitating interactions among diverse organizations, and all managers — whether located in public or private sector organizations — must be concerned with the operation of networks.

A revolution in organizational structures and the role of managers has occurred as complexity has come to characterize a vast and growing range of activities in advanced societies. At the heart of the growing complexity are fundamentally changed commercial technologies and the organizations that make them.[7] Society is passing through, in Andrew Grove's metaphor, *a strategic inflection point.* "A strategic inflection point is when the balance of forces shifts from the old structure, or the old ways of doing business and the old ways of competing, to the new."[8]

We have all been dazzled by the great technological achievements of the defense and space programs. But these high-profile accomplishments have much less to do with the strategic inflection point to which corporate and government managers must adapt than what has occurred silently with such seemingly prosaic products as automobiles and corn planters.

Consider for a moment the evolution of your car in recent decades. Until the 1970s a car was likely to have two automatic control subsystems: an automatic transmission and an automatic choke in the carburetor. By comparison, today's cars are complex sets of interacting automatic subsystems. For example, the fuel system has incrementally become an intricate linkage of sensors, microprocessors, and controls that govern the fuel injection process with such sensitivity that many young drivers have never known a car to cough and jump when it was cold. One major auto company CEO recently commented on the increasing sophistication of today's automobiles: "The Ford Taurus has more computing power than the original Apollo that went to the moon [in 1969]."[9] With this complexity has come the end of the "shade tree" mechanic, the guy who could fix anything. Even skilled technicians, those that have been formally trained, can only function with specialized tools and diagnostic equipment.

The transition that is taking place has not resulted from a big bang; there has been no great conceptual breakthrough, no great invention. Rather, it has happened silently as technological systems, economic systems, and social systems have become incrementally more complex.[10]

One of the authors owns a farm in Iowa, where the ancient practice of planting provides an illustration. When the farm was acquired in 1971, corn and soybeans were planted using a mechanical planter. Through a series of gears, one of the planter's wheels was linked to a slotted rotating disk located in the bottom of the box that held the seed. As the wheel turned, the slots in the disk lined up with a tube whose outlet was behind a plow that opened a furrow in the ground. Usually, when the slot was aligned with the tube, a seed fell into the furrow.

Twenty-seven years later, a microprocessor monitors every seed planted with a vacuum system that assures the seeds drop through the tube as necessary to achieve the desired planting density. The tractor operator has a liquid crystal indicator for each planter box, which instantly communicates any malfunction. The planting density is controlled by a digital database derived from last year's production record, collected when the crop was harvested with a combine. Soon planting, as well as the application of fertilizer and chemicals, will be controlled with a precision of one meter (three feet) through the use of a satellite-based global positioning system (GPS). The regimens for planting and applying fertilizer and chemicals are calculated to achieve maximum production with minimum fertilizer and chemical residue. The goal is no longer just the most efficient production. To that goal has been added minimum environmental damage.[11]

The ancient act of planting has evolved to a point where it involves a continuous interaction among mechanics, electronics, optics, biotechnology, chemicals, space technology, and environmental science and technology. The evolution of the planter illustrates how a dazzlingly complex technical system silently crept up on us. The system was developed in an uneven series of incremental steps, each involving innovations that enhanced the system's performance. Unlike the leaders of the organizations that produce the planter, those who use the system today are, with rare exceptions, unaware of the strategic inflection point they have been passing through in the past 27 years. What has occurred is viewed as a natural evolution.

In parallel with the development of the planter has been the development of the organizational network (e.g. linked firms, universities, government laboratories) that created, acquired, and integrated the diverse knowledge reflected in today's planting. All complex technologies manifest a process of coevolution between the technologies and the organizational networks that produce and use them.[12] Embedded in these organizational networks is a capacity for creativity and innovation that in earlier times was provided by inventors and entrepreneurs like Edison and Ford. The networks have made success so routine that it is now a pervasive characteristic of life that we enjoy and expect to enjoy ever expanding technological capabilities.[13] The opportunities for economic success and the challenge of management and governance in contemporary organizations and societies are inseparable from the general pattern of accelerating complexity.

A common and sometimes costly misperception is to attribute economic success to "high technology" (i.e. high levels of research and development or large commitments of scientists and engineers) rather than complexity. Cars and planters (the auto and food industries) are not high tech, but they, like most of the products and processes that pervade our lives, have become complex. They are also economically as significant as any high tech industry. Because products and processes have become complex in a silent process, those of us who use them commonly give little thought to the transition that has occurred.

However, those who lead the organizations that produce cars, planters, and other modern products cannot escape grappling with complexity, even though they sometimes do so absent a clear sense of what they are grappling with. Specifically, without detailed understanding they must manage and steer organizations that are participants in continuously adapting organizational networks that know how to do what has not been done before.[14] The complexity integral to most modern products and processes and to the networks that produce them no longer affects just those involved in the production processes; it now permeates every level of advanced societies.

The result is that management at every level, from the company to the country, is increasingly carried out on a day-to-day basis by self-organizing systems that both defy centralized management and have changed the meaning of individual accountability.[15] Uncertainty about how to deal with the next problem, challenge, or opportunity has become a continuing fact of life. When self-organization fails to deliver success, however, managers of organizations are commonly under great pressure to carry out major organizational and institutional adaptations.[16] These are times of especially high risk and high potential for organizations and their managers.

The blurred boundaries between public and private sector organizations mean that managers in the public sector face the same kinds of challenge.[17] As James Metcalfe points out, and as one should expect, this is especially true for those involved in the making of technology policy:

> [T]he policy maker is cast as a behavioralist engaging in adaptive policy making, seeking improvements in the technological performance of the economy in the context of immense micro complexity. Just as individuals operate under the constraints of localised, imperfect and uncertain information, so does the policy maker who must also be content with the limits set down by higher political authority. Options are constrained administratively and politically, policy makers operate with multiple objectives, and one cannot expect the policies which emerge to be independent of the processes by which they are formed.
>
> There is no presumption that any policy maker has a superior understanding of market behavior or technological opportunities, and so technology policy may fail just as readily as the technology strategies of private firms. *The important questions relate to how well policy makers learn and adapt in the light of experience. In short, the scope for policy is not to optimise with respect to some objective function (e.g. social surplus) but rather to stimulate the introduction and spread of improvements in technology. At the core of this approach are complexity, cognitive limitations, and the role of organisations as operators translating individual subjective knowledge into collective outcomes.*[18]

In short, the technology policy process should mirror the complexity and adaptive nature of the innovating firms and other organizations it is attempting to foster. And increasingly, good corporate commercialization strategies and good public policy depend on a common pattern of self-organization that is derived from self-conscious efforts to design "an organizational structure capable of learning and adjusting behavior in response to what is learned."[19]

Thus, although there is a near consensus on the importance of technological innovation and the high priority it should receive in organizations at every level of society, the lack of detailed understanding of how complex technological innovation is accomplished means that those who share the dirty little secret live anxious lives. Andy Grove believes that in a world of continuous technological change that defies detailed understanding, "even those who believe in a scientific approach to management will have to rely on instinct and personal judgement," because in a complex world there are no reliable theories to guide change.[20]

How the life of the manager has changed is suggested by the following story, overheard by one of the authors. In the early 1970s, over drinks one evening following a meeting in the nation's capital, a senior executive of an electrical equipment supplier commented on the terrible choice faced by utility industry executives. Their dilemma, he said, was, "do the perks that flow from high salaries and endless meetings at posh golfing resorts compensate for the pervasive boredom of jobs where the growth in electricity demand and the way to supply it are answered by a universally accepted formula?" In a regulated industry experiencing 7 percent growth in demand, the answer was ever larger facilities that provided economies of scale. Twenty-five years later one is hard pressed to find any such boring management job.

The contemporary challenge faced by managers is uneven, unrelenting change in systems that are too complex for them to understand.[21] Success today can turn into failure tomorrow, followed by success the day after tomorrow. Doubtless this has always been true, but surely never before has the time between success and failure been so short for so many people and organizations. In the 20 years between the mid-1970s and mid-1990s, the huge US automobile industry went full cycle. Although it has recovered, no one believes its future success is a given. In the case of the semiconductor industry, the cycle of success to failure to success took only a little over a decade (1983–94). For many corporate managers, time spans are especially short. In one week in July 1997, what has been called the "revolving door" was experienced by the chairman of Apple Computer and the CEO designate of AT&T. Their tenures were nine and seventeen months, respectively.[22]

The short success-to-failure cycles evident in industry are also evident in governments and in countries. The relative economic and social success of countries appears to be in continuous flux. Over the past two decades, economic leadership has varied greatly among the United States, Japan, and the major developed countries in Europe.[23] In parallel, the capacity of some less industrialized countries to rapidly develop has been both dazzling and followed by precipitous declines.[24] The tradition of metaphorically designating a *century* as, for example, British or American is now quaint. It would take a courageous scholar today to predict a British, American, Japanese, or German decade.

Should we care how complex technological products and processes come into existence and achieve commercial success? After all, if the process is so complicated that even the managers of successful technology-producing companies don't know enough to control the process, why worry about it? Why not just let it happen?

The economic importance of complex technology

The problem with denying the emergence of complexity is that complex technological products increasingly compete in a global market and, even among the industrialized countries, different cultures and societies are not equally successful in nurturing competitive producers of these technologies.[25] As global competition increases, relative success in supplying the markets for complex technological products and processes will become increasingly important to the ability of an advanced society to maintain and improve its standard of living.[26]

Part of the answer, then, is that there may be a potential for improving competitiveness in these market sectors. But along with this carrot there is also a goad. If a society, consciously or inadvertently, impedes the organizational processes required to stay ahead of the competition, it may find itself losing ground over time to those societies that offer a more favorable environment for rapid production of new, complex, high-value products, capable of winning larger shares of the global market.

Export market growth and complexity

Figure 1.1 illustrates the growing importance of complex technologies in the global marketplace. We analyzed the 30 products that had the highest total value as exports in world trade in 1970. The first pie chart in Figure 1.1 shows how these exports divide into categories based on two dimensions of complexity: whether the

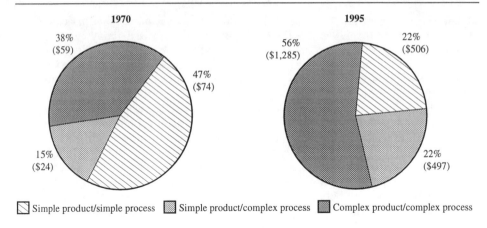

Figure 1.1 Thirty most valuable product exports: a comparison for 1970 and 1995 (in billions of US dollars)

Sources: United Nations, *Yearbook of International Trade Statistics. Vol. II: Trade by Commodity. Commodity Matrix Tables*, New York: United Nations, 1975, pp. 17–19; United Nations, *International Trade Statistics Yearbook. Vol. II: Trade by Commodity. Commodity Matrix Tables*, New York: United Nations, 1996, pp. 3–238.

process by which the product was made is simple or complex, and whether the product itself is simple or complex. In both dimensions, "complex" means that the process or product cannot be understood in full detail by an individual expert sufficiently to communicate all the details of the process or product across time and distance to other experts. A simple process or product is one that can be understood and communicated by one individual.

The second chart in Figure 1.1 shows the same categories applied to the 30 highest-value product exports in 1995, which were not the same 30 as in 1970. The top 30 exports in 1970 represented 48 percent of all goods exported that year; in 1995, the top 30 represented 46 percent of all exported goods. In both years, none of the top 30 products were categorized as complex products produced by a simple process, so that combination does not appear in the charts.

Although the absolute value of each category increased substantially from 1970 to 1995, the relative sizes (relative values) of the sectors changed dramatically in favor of increasing complexity of the process and the product. In 1970, 47 percent of the value of the top 30 exports was in simple products produced by simple processes. By 1995, this category had dropped to 22 percent. The most valuable product in this category in 1995 was crude oil. By comparison, the percentage of export value in complex products produced by complex processes grew from 38 percent in 1970 to 56 percent in 1995. The most valuable product in the category in both years was automobiles, which we described earlier as a complex product, but not a high technology one.

The percentage of total export value in simple products produced by complex processes also increased, nearly doubling from 1970 to 1995. A typical product in this category is industrial chemicals. Chemical plants have undergone increasing integration of sensors, controls, and computers into ever more complex technological processes, an integration that has fundamentally changed the mode of production in most chemical plants.

The Appendix provides the raw data and details of this analysis, but a few points are helpful in illustrating the notion of complexity with which our story begins. Only eleven of the products in the most valuable 30 of 1970 were still among the 30 most valuable in 1995. Even among these eleven holdovers, there were significant modifications in how they were characterized. For instance, "office equipment" in 1970 had become "office equipment and ADP (automated data processing) equipment" in 1995.

Computer software represents an interesting case of category migration over this period. If the database had included computer software, it probably would have been classified for 1970 as a complex product produced by a simple process, because software at that time was generally written by a few individuals. However, by 1995 most of the high-value commercial software products – such as operating systems for large or small general-purpose computers, the suites of application programs for microprocessor-based computers, and the custom software systems developed for a single user-entity in industry or government – entailed complex production processes. Teams of analysts and programmers, often with considerable turnover, develop each product. Additional teams of testers (including experienced users) are needed to debug problems that none of the developers "knew" existed.

Can US technology producers compete in the global market?

The perils of remaining ignorant about factors that promote or hinder successful innovation of complex technologies may already be upon us. Figure 1.2 compares the international trade balances for the United States and Japan for the top 30 technological products in 1980 and the top 30 in 1995. (Values for both years are in

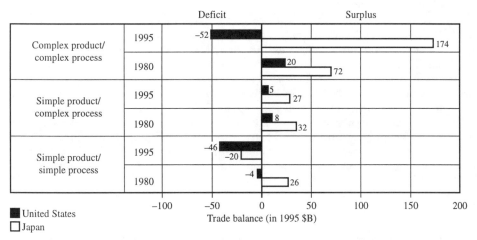

Figure 1.2 International trade balances for the United States and Japan for the top 30 technology products, 1980 and 1995 (in billions of 1995 US dollars)

Sources: United Nations, *Yearbook of International Trade Statistics. Vol. I: Trade by Country*, New York: United Nations, 1985, pp. 482–94, 971–6; United Nations, *International Trade Statistics Yearbook. Vol. I: Trade by Country*, New York: United Nations, 1996, pp. 532–8, 1100–5.

1995 US dollars.) The same categorization of simple versus complex processes and products used for Figure 1.1 was applied here. (See the Appendix for details.)

Japan was used for this comparison for a number of reasons. It is generally recognized as a leading competitor in technological products; that is, it is home to producers that compete successfully with US producers. Japanese production organizations have in the past been frequently cited for their ability to get products to the market faster than their American competitors, even when the scientific knowledge underlying the technology was first "made in America." Second, these competitive successes of Japanese technology producers have often been discussed in relation to cultural or sociopolitical differences between the two countries.[27] Third, the body of this book explores at length the Japanese experience with innovating complex technologies, and the interpretation and explanation offered by a number of observers who compare that experience with US practices.

As Figure 1.2 shows, between 1980 and 1995 Japan's trade surplus of $26 billion of simple products produced by simple processes became a deficit of $20 billion. The USA experienced a decline in this category of similar magnitude, with its deficit increasing from $20 billion to $46 billion. Both of these advanced industrial societies faced stiff competition in these products from newly industrialized countries.[28] In simple products from complex processes, the USA went from a surplus to a small deficit, while the Japanese increased their surplus modestly. The stunning difference, though, is in the category of complex products produced by complex processes. Even in 1980, Japan's surplus in this category was almost three times the US surplus ($72 billion versus $20 billion). Over the intervening period, the value of the yen against the dollar doubled, which made Japanese exports relatively more expensive. And at the end of the period, Japan was experiencing a major recession. Nevertheless, by 1995 Japan had more than doubled its surplus from $72 billion to $174 billion. Meanwhile, The US surplus of $20 billion in the same category reversed into a deficit of $52 billion.

Finding and defending an explanation for this pattern is not easy. Some students of technology innovation and its role in commercial success have argued that facets of Japanese culture – for instance, those which encourage cooperation, trust, and confidence in acting on "tacit knowledge" – play an important role in promoting innovation in complex technologies.[29] The corresponding US norms, they argue, tend to hinder innovation. The validity of these explanations, and what can be done to change the situation, are key issues we will explore in depth. But the patterns in the historical data as shown in Figures 1.1 and 1.2 are a clear warning that *something different is happening, and we had better pay attention.* In a swiftly moving global marketplace, those who refuse to learn from the recent history of commercial successes (and failures) in the rapid evolution of complex technologies may not get a second chance to repeat their mistakes.

General rules

The increasing complexity of advanced societies makes it necessary to reexamine the use in management and decision making of general rules, rules that apply in all or nearly all cases. Certainly in the United States and in Western societies generally, there appears to be a powerful inclination to formulate "universal lawlike" rules that purport to provide understanding and guidance. Formulating simple models of cause and effect relations (a billiard-ball model of causality) doubtless reflects a human interest in abstracting out the controlling features of causal structures. For most of us there is a powerful need to have "a practical range of effective action" that seeks to isolate effective means to our ends.

In a complex society general rules won't take one very far towards management success for at least two reasons. First, cause and effect relationships are difficult to identify in complex systems, and when identified they seldom remain stable for very long because of repeated innovation. Later in the book we discuss a case where the intervention of a regulatory agency into the network innovating a medical technology was seen by those involved in the network as costly in terms of both efficiency and effectiveness. The general rule was that government regulation always costs money. In the end the regulatory agency's requirement that the network convert tacit knowledge to explicit knowledge and maintain records resulted in improved efficiency and effectiveness for the network. Government regulatory participation produced unexpected economic benefits.

Second, complex systems almost always have unique characteristics. In part that is because the innovation of complex technologies almost always requires a pattern of organizational learning that rests heavily on groups solving problems.[30] Several who have studied organizational learning characterize it as local learning: what is learned is in part unique to those involved because it is based on previous accumulated learning that is partly tacit.[31]

Although navigating on an uncharted sea of complexity, where reliance on general rules doesn't work, may seem threatening, it also offers nearly limitless opportunities. Think for a moment of the most fundamental characteristic: the capacity to innovate technologies has released us from many if not most of the limits of scarcity. With the capacity to create technologies we are substantially freed of the constraints of scarce resources. Faced with scarcity we now commonly create a substitute. In the Second World War, for example, it was synthetic rubber; today it is synthetic drugs.

For those decision makers and managers who are willing to experiment and rapidly learn from failure, the future seems limitless. But the opportunities for failure are also limitless. Surely nothing deserves more attention than the pursuit of insight into this increasing complex world, and especially its changing system of production. That is the task of what follows.

Reading the rest of the book

Two sources of information are extensively cited in the following chapters. The first is a combination of two exploding fields of study: the *science of complexity* and *evolutionary economics*.[32] The second is six case studies of technologies that have been experiencing rapid innovation. The science of complexity offers a useful conceptual framework and vision of technological innovation. Especially, it provides a set of ideas and concepts that are useful in the search for insights into how complex organizational systems carry out the innovation of complex technologies. Over time, these ideas have been woven into the field of evolutionary economics, founded on the principles of Joseph Schumpeter. Evolutionary economics has experienced dramatically increasing attention around the world, as the more mainstream schools of economics have been unable to provide an effective assimilation of technological innovation into their economic growth models.[33]

The integration of concepts from the science of complexity and evolutionary economics has proven to be particularly useful in the context of studies of Japanese and other East Asian technological and economic developments. As investigators have looked more closely at this region, a picture of the relationship between technological innovation in the private sector and public policy has emerged that is very different from the traditional view held in the United States.[34] This has led to a reexamination of innovation in the United States. The six case studies that inform this book were carried out as a part of the reexamination, and they make it clear that the innovation of complex technologies does not conform to traditional assumptions. Rather, the case studies show striking similarities between innovation patterns in the USA and those in Japan.

We have entered an era pervaded by complex technologies, and we have neither conceptual maps that are satisfactory for guiding our way nor an adequate language to describe and communicate the new reality. This book is an initial mapping and linguistic effort. The goal is to construct a conceptual map of technological innovation that will offer greater appreciation of this important area of experience by using the language of complexity science and evolutionary economics. The book follows the suggestion of Richard Nelson that understanding of "quite complex causal arguments" can be gained by using *appreciative* stories (i.e. told by those who appreciate the details).[35]

The integration of appreciative stories from the case studies with the literature of complexity science and evolutionary economics appears to offer an important new lens for looking at and developing insights into innovation. The effort begins in Part I with three stage-setting chapters. Chapter 2 addresses the need for fitting management and governance concepts to a new reality characterized by an enormous technical creative capacity. This creative capacity is a double-edged sword for management. The formulation merges recent East Asian experience and (largely) European ideas to provide a set of useful concepts.

Chapter 3 sketches an overview of the historical coevolution of organizations and technologies through three successive production eras: craft production of very simple process and product technologies, mass production of moderately complicated technologies, and the advent of what we call the "synthetic production" of highly complex technologies. For each of the three periods, there is a discussion of the dominant organizational types and the advantages and liabilities of the dominant relations between organizations and technologies.

Chapter 4 considers in detail the concept of complexity. Some nonlinear models of innovation are introduced. Also introduced here are the set of ideas derived from complexity science and evolutionary economics (e.g. self-organization, path dependence) that structure the remainder of the book. The seven subsequent chapters are introduced by a brief summary of the case studies. Chapters 6 to 9 in Part II, are organized to build key concepts from the source disciplines and the case studies into a useful conceptual map. The final three chapters, which make up Part III, pull together the overarching themes of the book and present a set of suggestions for the future.

Although what follows inevitably simplifies and abstracts the "stories" regarding management and innovation, we have sought to remain true to the facts as we understand them. The language and description used in the book allow one to address large portions of the technological landscape (such as the role of tacit knowledge and skills in network self-organization) that are commonly ignored when one uses traditional frameworks (e.g. neoclassical economics). The language developed in the next ten chapters has a much better fit with contemporary technological reality than the older terminology and models. The book builds on the tradition of scholars who have recognized the substantial risks of generalizing from limited case studies, but have argued that, "in something as complex and essentially practical as engineering, theorizing not grounded in factual knowledge is a good deal riskier."[36]

Notes

1. Stephen J. Kline, *Conceptual Foundations for Multidisciplinary Thinking*, Stanford, CA: Stanford University Press, 1995, pp. 32–4; W. Brian Arthur, "Complexity in Economic Theory: Inductive Reasoning and Bounded Rationality," *American Economic Association Papers and Proceedings*, Vol. 84, No. 2, May 1994, pp. 406–11.
2. Ron Sanchez, "Strategic Management at the Point of Inflection: Systems, Complexity and Competence Theory," *Long Range Planning*, Vol. 30, No. 6, December 1997, pp. 939–45; Ralph Stacey, "Management and the Science of Complexity: If Organizational Life is Nonlinear, Can Business Strategies Prevail?" *Research-Technology Management*, Vol. 39, No. 3, May/June 1996, pp. 8–10.
3. Interview with Katsushige Mita, President, Hitachi Ltd, June 15, 1989.
4. Gordon E. Moore, "Some Personal Perspectives on Research in the Semiconductor Industry," in Richard S. Rosenbloom and William J. Spencer, eds, *Engines of Innovation: US Industrial Research at the End of an Era*, Boston: Harvard Business School Press, 1996, p. 168.
5. Interview with John Hart of Hewlett-Packard, September 30, 1994.
6. Interview with GE officials at the Evendale plant in Cincinnati, Ohio, May 18, 1994.
7. Kulwant Singh, "The Impact of Technological Complexity and Interfirm Cooperation on Business Survival," *Academy of Management Journal*, Vol. 40, No. 2, April 1997, pp. 339–67; James Wade, "Dynamics of Organizational Communities and Technological Bandwagons: an Empirical Investigation of Community Evolution in the Microprocessor Market," *Strategic Management Journal*, Vol. 16, Special Issue, Summer 1995, pp. 111–33; Larry D. Browning, Janice M. Beyer, and Judy C. Shetler, "Building Cooperation in a Competitive Industry: Sematech and the Semiconductor Industry," *Academy of Management Journal*, Vol. 38, No. 1, February 1995, pp. 113–51.
8. Andrew S. Grove, *Only the Paranoid Survive: How to Exploit the Crisis Points that Challenge Every Company and Career*, New York: Doubleday, 1996, pp. 27–52.
9. Alex Trotman, Ford Motor Company Chairman and CEO, as reported by Matt Nauman in the *San Jose Mercury News*, September 8, 1997, p. IE.
10. Michael E. McMaster, *The Intelligence Advantage: Organizing for Complexity*, Boston: Butterworth-Heinemann, 1996; Frederick L. Pryor, *Economic Evolution and Structure: the Impact of Complexity on the US Economic System*, New York: Cambridge University Press, 1996; David L. Harvey and Michael Reed, "Social Science as the Study of Complex Systems," in L. Douglas Kiel and Euel Elliott, eds, *Chaos Theory in the Social Sciences: Foundations and Applications*, Ann Arbor, MI: University of Michigan Press, 1996, pp. 295–323.
11. Scott W. Horsley, "Precision Farming: Farmers Using Satellites, Computers, and Soils Tests to Protect Ground Water," *Ground Water Monitoring and Remediation*, Vol. 15, No. 4, 1996, p. 66.
12. Vincent Mangematin, "The Simultaneous Shaping of Organization and Technology within Cooperative Agreements," in Rod Coombs, Albert Richards, Pier P. Saviotti, and Vivien Walsh, eds, *Technological Collaboration: The Dynamics of Cooperation in Industrial Innovation*, Brookfield, VT: Edward Elgar, 1996, pp. 119–41; Richard R. Nelson, "The Coevolution of Technologies and Institutions," in Richard W. England, ed., *Evolutionary Concepts in Contemporary Economics*, Ann Arbor, MI: University of Michigan Press, 1994, pp. 139–56.

13. Andreas Pyka, "Informal Networking," *Technovation*, Vol. 17, No. 4, April 1997, pp. 207–20; Andrew C. Inkpen, "Creating Knowledge through Collaboration," *California Management Review*, Vol. 39, No. 1, Fall 1996, pp. 123–40.
14. Kline, *Conceptual Foundations for Multidisciplinary Thinking*, pp. 171–8.
15. Robert Jervis, "Complexity and the Analysis of Political and Social Life," *Political Science Quarterly*, Vol. 112, No. 4, Winter 1997–8, pp. 569–93; Paul R. Krugman, *The Self-organizing Economy*, Cambridge, MA: Blackwell Publishers, 1996; Woody van Olffen and A. Georges L. Romme, "The Role of Hierarchy in Self-Organizing Systems," *Human Systems Management*, Vol. 14, No. 3, 1995, pp. 199–206.
16. Margaret J. Wheatley and Myron Kellner-Rogers, "Self-organization: the Irresistible Future of Organizing," *Strategy and Leadership*, Vol. 24, No. 4, July/August 1996, pp. 18–24.
17. L. Douglas Kiel, *Managing Chaos and Complexity in Government: a New Paradigm for Managing Change, Innovation and Organizational Renewal*, San Francisco: Jossey-Bass, 1994.
18. J. S. Metcalfe, "Evolutionary Economics and Technology Policy," *Economic Journal*, Vol. 104, No. 425, July 1994, p. 933 (emphasis added).
19. Richard R. Nelson and Sidney G. Winter, *An Evolutionary Theory of Economic Change*, Cambridge, MA: Harvard University Press, 1982, p. 384.
20. Grove, *Only the Paranoid Survive*, p. 35.
21. Margaret J. Wheatley, *Leadership and the New Science: Learning about Organization from an Orderly Universe*, San Francisco: Berrett-Koehler Publishers, 1992.
22. Steve Schiesel, "Leases Get Shorter for Executives," *The New York Times*, July 18, 1997, pp. C1–C6.
23. James A. Belohlav, "The Evolving Competitive Paradigm," *Business Horizons*, Vol. 39, No. 2, March/April 1996, pp. 11–19; Richard A. Bettis and Michael A. Hitt, "The New Competitive Landscape," *Strategic Management Review*, Vol. 16, Special Issue, Summer 1995, pp. 7–19.
24. Linda Y. C. Lim, "Whose 'Model' Failed? Implications of the Asian Economic Crisis," *Washington Quarterly*, Vol. 21, No. 3, Summer 1998, pp. 25–36.
25. Daniele Archibugi and Jonathan Michie, "Technological Globalisation or National Systems of Innovation?" *Futures*, Vol. 29, No. 2, March 1997, pp. 121–37; US Congress, Office of Technology Assessment, *Innovation and Commercialization of Emerging Technologies*, Washington, DC: Government Printing Office, September 1995; US Congress, Office of Technology Assessment, *Multinationals and the US Technology Base: Final Report of the Multinationals Project*, Washington, DC: Government Printing Office, September 1994; Council on Competitiveness, *Competitiveness Index, 1994*, Washington, DC: Council on Competitiveness, June 1994.
26. Robert H. Hayes, "US Competitiveness: 'Resurgence' Versus Reality," *Challenge*, Vol. 39, No. 2, March/April 1996, pp. 36–44; Roy Rothwell, "The Changing Nature of the Innovation Process," *Technovation*, Vol. 13, No. 1, January 1993, pp. 1–2; Jacques de Bandt, "Alternative Approaches to Developing National Technological Policies," *International Journal of Technology Management*, Special Issue on the Increasing Role of Technology in Corporate Policy, 1991, pp. 14–44.
27. Fumio Kodama, *Emerging Patterns of Innovation: Sources of Japan's Technological Edge*, Boston: Harvard Business School Press, 1995; Martin Fransman, "The Japanese Innovation System: How Does It Work?," in Mark Dodgson and Roy Rothwell, eds, *The Handbook of Industrial Innovation*, Brookfield, VT: Edward Elgar, 1994, pp. 67–77; Ken-Ichi Imai, "The Japanese pattern of Innovation and Its Evolution," in Nathan Rosenberg, Ralph Landau, and David C. Mowery, eds, *Technology and the Wealth of Nations*, Stanford, CA: Stanford University Press, 1992, pp. 225–46.
28. Barry P. Bosworth, "Growing Pains: Trade Frictions Corrode the US-Asian Relationship," *Brookings Review*, Winter 1996, pp. 4–9.

29. Ikujiro Nonaka and Hirotaka Takeuchi, *The Knowledge-creating Company: How Japanese Companies Create the Dynamics of Innovation*, New York: Oxford University Press, 1995; Howard E. Aldrich and Toshihiro Sasaki, "R&D Consortia in the United States and Japan," *Research Policy*, Vol. 24, No. 2, March 1995, pp. 301–16.

30. William Lazonick, "Learning and the Dynamics of International Competitive Advantage," in Yuichi Shionoya and Mark Perlman, eds, *Innovation in Technology, Industries, and Institutions: Studies in Schumpeterian Perspectives*, Ann Arbor, MI: University of Michigan Press, 1994, pp. 189–211; W. Mark Fruin and Toshihiro Nishiguchi, "Supplying the Toyota Production System: Intercorporate Organizational Evolution and Supplier Subsystems," in Bruce Kogut, ed., *Country Competitiveness: Technology and the Organization of Work*, New York: Oxford University Press, 1993, pp. 225–46.

31. David T. Lei, "Competence-building, Technology Fusion and Competitive Advantage: the Key Roles of Organizational Learning and Strategic Alliances," *International Journal of Technology Management*, Vol. 14, Nos 2/3/4, 1997, pp. 208–37.

32. For overviews of these fields, see: Ralph D. Stacey, *Complexity and Creativity in Organizations*, San Francisco: Berrett-Koehler Publishers, 1996; George A. Cowan, David Pines, and David Meltzer, eds, *Complexity: Metaphors, Models, and Reality*, Reading, MA: Addison-Wesley Publishers, 1994; M. Mitchell Waldrop, *Complexity: the Emerging Field at the Edge of Chaos*, New York: Simon and Schuster, 1992; Richard R. Nelson, "Recent Evolutionary Theorizing about Economic Change," *Journal of Economic Literature*, Vol. 33, No. 1, March 1995, pp. 48–90; Christopher Freeman, "Critical Survey: the Economics of Technical Change," *Cambridge Journal of Economics*, Vol. 18, No. 5, November 1994, pp. 463–514; Peter Hall, *Innovation, Economics, and Evolution: Theoretical Perspectives on Changing Technology in Economic Systems*, New York: Harvester Wheatsheaf, 1994; and Richard H. Day and Ping Chen, eds, *Nonlinear Dynamics and Evolutionary Economics*, New York: Oxford University Press, 1993.

33. Richard R. Nelson, "What Has Been the Matter with Neoclassical Growth Theory?," in Gerald Silverberg and Luc Soete, eds, *The Economics of Growth and Technical Change: Technologies, Nations, Agents*, Brookfield, VT: Edward Elgar, 1994, pp. 290–324.

34. Martin Fransman, "Is National Technology Policy Obsolete in a Globalized World? The Japanese Response," *Cambridge Journal of Economics*, Vol. 19, No. 1, February 1995, pp. 95–120; Chalmers Johnson, "Comparative Capitalism: the Japanese Difference," *California Management Review*, Vol. 35, No. 4, Summer 1993, pp. 51–67; Robert Z. Lawrence, "Japan's Different Trade Regime: an Analysis with Particular Reference to *Keiretsu*," *Journal of Economic Perspectives*, Vol. 7, No. 3, Summer 1993, pp. 3–19; James P. Womack and Daniel Roos, *The Machine that Changed the World*, New York: Rawson Associates, Macmillan, 1990.

35. Nelson, "Recent Evolutionary Theorizing about Economic Change," pp. 85–6.

36. Walter G. Vincenti, *What Engineers Know and How They Know It*, Baltimore: Johns Hopkins University Press, 1991, p. 200.

CHAPTER TWO

Fitting Concept to Reality

There is a disconnection between our reality and the way we conceptualize it and discuss it. That disconnection is the result of the growing capacity to carry out complex technological innovation by *synthesis*. Innovation by synthesis has become the most dynamic component of our production system, and it has caused fundamental changes in our physical and organizational reality. The organizational ability to routinely produce new and enhanced technological processes and products by combining components and knowledge in ways that deliver *synergism* has created a reality where dramatic change is the normal condition.[1] Two manifestations of that change are evident: the level of complexity is increasing, and so is the rate of change.

By comparison, the concepts we use to try to explain and discuss reality have not experienced the same change. Although a growing number of US business leaders, some scholars, and even a few government officials have adapted their conceptual models and are in continuous search of new concepts that accurately characterize and provide insight into the synthetic reality, they remain a small minority. The majority of Americans, and certainly the majority of those involved in the formulation of company strategies and public policies, continue to conceptualize the world in terms more appropriate for the era of industrial or mass production.

What are the major inconsistencies between the industrial conceptual system and the synthetic reality? The industrial conceptual system: (a) is predominantly linear in its assumptions about interactions; (b) gives major emphasis to the search for and use of cause and effect relationships; (c) celebrates efficiency; and (d) assigns dominant decision making roles to individuals, especially to organizational leaders. Alternatively, the synthetic reality: (a) is increasingly nonlinear in its interactions; (b) gives major emphasis to continuous learning from positive as well as negative feedbacks and to cybernetic adaptations that make identification of cause and effect relationships difficult and less meaningful; (c) celebrates speed to market; and (d) assigns key decision making roles to groups solving problems.[2]

Through an uneven, unpredictable, incremental process, the United States and other advanced countries have developed sophisticated national innovation systems capable of routinely carrying out synthesis.[3] Dynamic national innovation systems include large numbers of continuously learning organizations that create and combine knowledge in different ways in order to repeatedly develop new and enhanced technological capabilities.[4] The spread of these innovation capabilities to an ever larger number of technological sectors and organizations is at the heart of our changed reality. It is the advancing and spreading capability to undertake synthetic innovation that drives the growing complexity evident in our technologies and more broadly in our society.

Viewed historically, the capacity to do innovation by synthesis has been a cumulative process. Today's capabilities stand on the shoulders of patterns of organizational learning that have been accelerating since the Second World War. In the last quarter of the twentieth century, this process has taken us through Andy Grove's strategic inflection point. These shifts involve *changes in substance*, and particularly in the organizational and technological substance of human production systems. The reality of synthetic production systems involves fundamental *self-organized and recurring* changes in what people make, how they make it, and how they think about and react to the world around them when they are doing so.[5]

The capacity to innovate by synthesis has made the industrial conceptual system obsolete as a vehicle for gaining intelligence and guiding the development of corporate strategies and public policies. There is a compelling need for a conceptual system that can offer useful guidance for what is appropriately called *synthetic decision making*.

Problems of decision making in the twenty-first century

Leaders of companies and countries are continuously in search of new concepts, rules, and models that will be useful in dealing with an ever-changing reality. Evidence of how difficult decision making has become is everywhere. Repeated modification of strategies has become a requirement for firms,[6] and the rapid adjustment of public policies has become the norm for governments.[7]

Where the route to success involves doing what has not been done before (innovating), and where complexity makes what is being done today difficult or impossible for individuals to understand in detail, adapting new strategies or policies always entails great risks and uncertainties. Yet leaders in both the public and private sectors are expected to identify the route to success. Thus, when organizational plans, corporate strategies, or national policies don't work, there is often a reflex suspicion that leaders are either incompetent or corrupt.[8]

The challenges and dilemmas posed by the disconnection between concepts and reality were illustrated during an interview when the authors were searching for firms that would cooperate in the development of our case studies. Several interviewees noted that their company had developed three different business plans in the past six years, and they implied the ever changing business plans raised doubts about the competence and motives of their leaders. One interviewee said: "we assume the people at the top are playing some kind of corporate power struggle game, and although we say the words they want to hear, we just continue doing what we have always done. We pay no serious attention to the changing business plans."

Given the character of the synthetic reality, it appeared that everyone in the company was missing the boat. Leaders who hand down business plans from the top that are seen as unrelated to the activities of those in the organization clearly do not appreciate the implications of complexity. Alternatively, the interviewees failed to appreciate the importance of the need to modify company strategies in the face of changing reality. Clearly some of the interviewees continued to believe that their management should know the path to success, and that the path should remain relatively constant over time.

The capacity to innovate technologies that generate explosive economic growth and profits is a well known phenomenon. Bill Gates and Microsoft are among the best known examples. In less than two decades, Gates has become twice as rich as John D. Rockefeller was.[9] The nearly universal view is that Gates brings a unique genius to Microsoft. That is clearly the view reflected in *Business Week*'s finding that "most observers agree that if something happened to Gates Microsoft's stock would go into a tailspin."[10]

The conventional perception of Gates as a throwback to the older entrepreneurial tradition of the industrial era doesn't hold up, however, when Microsoft's development is subjected to close examination. Instead, chance and history (*path dependence*, in the language of complexity science) appear to have played major roles in Microsoft's evolution:

> It's well known that the Microsoft Corporation's dominating influence on software got its start by pure chance. When IBM decided to create its personal computer, the PC, the group in charge of its development first approached a company called Digital Research about providing the PC's operating system. When Digital Research put IBM off, the group interviewed Bill Gates and his still-small company, Microsoft. Recognizing what a tremendous opportunity it was, Gates did everything he could to convince IBM that Microsoft would be the right choice, but the ultimate selection of Microsoft came down at least in part to a personal connection: IBM chairman John Opel had served on the board of United Way with Gates's mother and thought it would be nice to do business with "Mary Gates's boy's company." The operating system that Microsoft developed, MS-DOS, became the industry standard – not so much on its own merits as because it was part of the IBM PC package – and Gates was on his way to becoming a multibillionaire.[11]

How are we to interpret the dominance of Microsoft when we add to the above the fact that MS-DOS was clearly inferior to Apple Computer's MacIntosh OS system throughout at least the 1980s and the first half of the 1990s? Microsoft's triumph would appear to rest in part on a fundamentally flawed decision by IBM, good old-boy/girl politics, and a key mistake by Apple in pursuing a strategy that resisted licensing its operating system to others.[12]

Part of the emphasis on Gates's role in this series of events reflects the dominant conceptual system. At a minimum, that system has little room for the notion of path dependence. In fact, appreciating the role of history and of chance turns out to be absolutely necessary for gaining insight into the innovation of complex technologies.[13]

The conceptual limits faced by those who make strategic decisions in companies when changes in the mode of production occur is suggested by now-commonplace articles in the business press about yesterday's "high flying" firms struggling to find a new strategy that works. The August 4, 1997, issue of *Business Week* illustrates the theme. The cover story focused on the Silicon Graphics Corporation. It began by summarizing the situation as follows: "Back in July 1995, no computer maker was flying higher. Dubbed the 'gee-whiz company' by *Business Week* three years ago, SGI is scrambling to stay off technology's long list of has beens."[14]

In another article in the same issue, the venerable, 118-year-old, Eastman Kodak Company was characterized as having experienced a nearly 30 percent drop in its stock value in six months. The article emphasized that this followed immediately on the heels of an all time high stock price in February 1997, which had been produced by a two-year-old recovery strategy that involved restructuring and cutting 14,700 jobs. Behind the precipitous drop in the price of Kodak's stock was a highly successful market challenge by Fuji, a challenge the recovery strategy had not anticipated.[15]

Like company strategies, national public policy can become obsolete at dazzling rates. The track record of US semiconductor policies provides a good example. In 1980, companies like Apple Computer, Hewlett-Packard, Intel, Motorola, Varian, and Eaton exemplified the American dream. They dominated the production of computers, semiconductor chip making, and the manufacture of the equipment used to produce chips. Public policy had played an indirect and unplanned role in the early advance of this industry during the 1960s and 1970s by providing large and long-term markets in the space and defense industries. These government markets gave small companies the incentive to invest in new products and factories.

By 1982, however, Japanese semiconductor companies, with government assistance, produced more "memory chips" than American companies. Three years later, Japan surpassed the USA in total semiconductor production, while managing to keep its own market (by then the world's largest) virtually closed to international competition. Some observers speculated that the semiconductor industry would go the way of consumer electronics.

By 1986, US public policy had changed in a very fundamental way. Under heavy pressure from domestic industry, the US government forced the Japanese to open their market to foreign firms and to put a floor under prices. A year later, the US government supported – at a level of $100 million per year, matched by industry contributions – a new chip-making R&D consortium, Sematech (Semiconductor Manufacturing Technology), to enhance American corporate competitiveness.[16]

By 1994, it was clear the US semiconductor and equipment manufacturing industries had regained their competitiveness against the Japanese. The industry members of Sematech decided to no longer take government money. In less than a decade public policy had gone full cycle, from hands off, to intimate involvement, to substantial decoupling. Both the relationships within the industry and the industry's relationship with government had been fundamentally redefined. A level of cooperation existed that would have been inconceivable in 1980.[17] And the pattern of collaboration continues to become more complex. For example, on September 11, 1997, three of the most important companies in the chip industry announced the formation of the largest US commercial partnership between firms and government. Intel, Motorola, and Advanced Micro Devices announced a new joint venture with three US national laboratories (Lawrence Livermore, Sandia, and Lawrence Berkeley), in which the companies will contribute some $250 million to the government laboratories in a project aimed at the further miniaturization of microprocessors. The organizational framework and decision rules developed for this initiative (i.e. the provision of corporate funds to pay the salaries of government researchers, the creation of a limited liability company able to license technology created by the partnership to chip manufacturers, giving the new company's stakeholders first access to any new manufacturing equipment that results from licenses) mirror the complexity of chip technology. Very complex technologies demand very complex strategies and decision making capabilities.[18]

The context of synthetic decision making

Insight into the transition toward fitting concept to reality – to engaging in synthetic decision making – requires looking at the process of synthesis associated with the innovation of complex technologies. Synthetic production has been added to and has become economically more important than the industrial and craft production systems that dominated most of the twentieth century. Chapter 3 investigates the emergence of synthetic production in some detail, but a brief description of the synthetic process and some of its implications for synthetic decision making is necessary at this point.

A key element in the innovation of a complex technology is the specification of the desired performance criteria (e.g. weight, speed of function) for the components, the subsystems, and the entire technological system. These criteria are always beyond the current state of the art; that is, they involve producing something for the first time. And these criteria must be combined and integrated – *synthesized* – in order for the entire technological system to perform as designed. Three patterns are normally evident in the synthesis of these performance criteria:

> First, the initial performance criteria are continually adjusted and readjusted; second, some subsystems are unable to meet the performance standards initially specified; and third, some subsystems are able to develop performance capabilities that are far superior to those initially defined. [Innovations], then, involve an extremely complex process of trial and error in multiple organizations, so the development process must be susceptible to continuous and rapid change.[19]

The critical characteristic of synthesis is the ability to combine ever changing and diverse knowledge and capabilities and to produce complex products and processes with previously unavailable performance characteristics. Synthesis requires the development of distinctive network organizational arrangements.[20] When broad-based organizational capabilities for carrying out synthesis exist, societies can be freed from the constraints of limited inputs or factors of production. That is, the capacity to create through synthesis allows companies and countries to escape what were traditionally thought to be finite limits established by labor, capital, and natural resources. Organizational adaptations can be substituted for these traditional factors of production. A widely used illustration of this capability is the finding in the influential MIT-based study of the automobile industry, *The Machine that Changed the World*, that the Japanese were producing autos with vastly less capital, people, factory space, and inventory than US producers.[21] The consequences of synthesis are far reaching: they offer companies and countries ways to by-pass capital shortages, for instance.

For those involved in developing company strategies or national policies, it is important to keep at least three consequences of the synthetic reality in mind. Together they are central to appreciating both the opportunities and the constraints associated with strategy and policy. The capability for synthesis means that: (a) the capacity exists to create, in a nonlinear way, almost anything on demand; (b) the boundaries between activities and organizations will be blurred and often made indistinguishable; and (c) the organizational networks that innovate technologies are characterized by organizational learning and dynamic self-organization.

Nonlinear creative capacity

The capacity to create on demand has not only significantly expanded the boundaries of the traditional factors of production (i.e. capital, labor, resources), it has resulted in a bewildering variety of products tailored to specialized customer desires. For example, even something as simple as the bicycle can be had in more than eleven million design variations, with the chosen combination delivered within two weeks.[22] Organizational networks are now able to "articulate" demand – convert vague wants into well-defined ones – by "fusing" existing technological capabilities (e.g. by combining electronic, crystal, and optics technologies for liquid crystal displays in pocket calculators).[23]

A network was created that put people on the moon. Materials producers presently make plastics that are stronger than steel. The agricultural system will one day develop perennial corn. Our parents assumed the world of tomorrow would be only a variation of the world of today; our children will be shocked if the world of tomorrow is not dramatically different. In our parents' case, change appeared linear. In our children's case, *changes are nonlinear.*

Nonlinear creativity is a major source of *unknowability*, in the sense of knowing based on linear, reductionist traditional science. Innovating complex technologies may feature a dynamic in which heretofore distinct sectors fuse and spin off entirely new families of technologies in unpredictable ways. With these emerging technologies may come new risks (e.g. environmental, health, and safety hazards) that seem certain to multiply in the twenty-first century.[24] In order to minimize risks and maximize opportunities, managers and policy makers will have to embrace both rapid technological and organizational change. Responding to the unexpected will require paying attention to patterns and being able to accommodate; that is, to change even more. This means that both company strategies and public policies will have to be dynamic, always subject to improvement, and never final.[25]

Unless the synthetic reality becomes part of our conceptual system, our metaphors, and even our rhetoric, corporate managers and public policy makers will be in constant jeopardy from their constituents and stakeholders, who will continue to behave as if change can be controlled because they assume it is linear and mechanical.

Blurred boundaries

Western societies, and especially the United States, express, implement, and maintain their views of reality by establishing and preserving boundaries. As we enter the twenty-first century, the traditional physical, ideological, and organizational borders that have been used to structure American beliefs, behavior, and approaches to defining reality are being challenged everywhere. In our companies, our communities, and our public decisions some boundaries disappear, some shift, but across the board the old conceptual and relational outlines of society and the world are being undermined by complexity.[26] This is because a central attribute of synthesis is interdependence, a merging of parts. Complex systems have amorphous boundaries.

For Americans who have grown up in the culture of modern science, where analysis – dividing and subdividing a complex whole into simple component elements – is the assumed path to understanding, boundaries that ebb and flow are extremely disorienting. The ability to identify boundaries is fundamental to the traditional division-of-labor approach to management and policy; it is a pervasive expectation of Americans. But complex systems routinely change their internal structures, and complex human systems, such as the organizational networks that innovate complex technologies, do so by a process of self-organization.[27] The modification of boundaries is a consistent outcome, if not always the intent, of complex organizational development.[26]

The most important implication for policy and corporate strategy of continuously changing boundaries is that it has become dysfunctional to maintain the traditional walls of separation in the American system of management and governance. Think for a moment about our faith in profit and cost centers and the associated organizational mandates. Within the arena of complex technological innovation, the time-honored walls between different activities such as research, development, and manufacturing have become barriers to efficacious strategies and policies. Most complex products are no longer created in a research laboratory and "tossed over the wall" to manufacturing and marketing expertise. Instead, teams of experts drawn from every commercialization activity work concurrently to innovate new technologies. In the synthetic reality these teams increasingly include suppliers and customers as partners – anyone who can provide valuable knowledge and skills.[29]

One result is an increase, even in the United States, of interactions between government and the private sector aimed at fostering innovation. The growing pattern of launching consortia like Sematech reflects the increasingly important role of linkages between public agencies and for-profit firms, a phenomenon much more advanced in Japan and Europe.[30]

The simultaneous blending of skills and know-how, such as those held by research scientists (often in universities), corporate or government design and development engineers, shopfloor workers, customers, and others, has another notable consequence: the blurring of cause and effect. For instance, the old debate about the relative relevance of "technology push" versus "market pull" in delivering new products and processes has become an anachronism. In many cases one cannot say with confidence that either breakthroughs in research "cause" commercial success or that the generation of successful products or processes was a predictable "effect" of having the capability to read user demands or other market signals accurately. Interdependence means that managers and policy makers cannot be expected to formulate programs that control effects by manipulating causes. Blurred boundaries mean that even the most enlightened technology strategies and policies cannot minutely control the rate or course of innovation.[31]

Dynamic organizational systems

Organizational networks provide the basic means of coping with complexity because they effectively connect individuals and groups that possess the expertise and capabilities essential to innovation.[32] Although most individuals and groups involved in the innovation of complex technologies are located in firms, they are often intimately connected to government and university experts, as well as people in intermediate organizations, such as professional or trade associations, think tanks, or advocacy groups. Whatever their makeup, these networks have unique adaptive capabilities.[33] The ability to create networks that can modify themselves quickly is the key to innovative success in a growing number of complex technology sectors.[34]

Networks pose a major challenge for corporate managers, and an even greater challenge for public policy, because they make it hard to identify the targets for regulations, incentives, and sanctions. Public policy in the United States generally focuses either on macro variables such as interest rates or on distinct organizational units such as companies or sectors. However, in complex systems it is often difficult to identify a discrete unit to which our traditional reductionist, analytical toolkit can be applied. To appreciate the challenge, one only needs to look at the difficulties associated with attempting to establish domestic content standards for foreign-owned automobile companies. Fifty percent domestic content may only mean that the low-value, commodity parts of a car will be made in the United States, while the high-value-added, non-commodity components will be imported.

Similarly, complexity often makes it inappropriate to focus policy on a particular product technology. Because networks are so important for high-value-added innovation, the components and subsystems that comprise complex products are often synthesized by widely dispersed, rapidly evolving, and often obscure organizations.

In much the same way, complexity makes it difficult to target the linkages between or the relationships among organizations in a network. For example, it was once possible to focus on corporate interactions, whether done secretly or specified in written contracts, that raised questions about antitrust or intellectual property rights violations. Network relationships are more complicated, involving not just diverse kinds of formal contracts and licenses but also many informal tacit information exchanges.[35] Interaction in networks often requires high levels of reciprocity and trust so that communication and learning can take place rapidly. Concerns about intellectual property for the parties involved may be outweighed by the benefits of rapidly and continuously sharing tacit knowledge.[36] Networks may include large numbers of elaborate links. The linear, reductionist US policy system is not well equipped for participation in such complex arrangements.

Synthetic decision making

Any examination of the disconnect between reality and today's dominant concepts generates hopes for a synthetic conceptual system. If only a new Copernicus or Einstein would offer a simple route to understanding and management. Absent that possibility, what are the likely responses of decision makers to the new synthetic reality? Some directions are suggested by looking at what they do in the United States, not what they say. Other routes are implied by investigating the Asian experience. Still other pathways are suggested by conceptual formulations occurring at the margins of economics, engineering, and science.

US action versus rhetoric

Nothing reflects the pressures generated by synthetic reality better than the growing advocacy in the American business and technology communities for direct, self-conscious, and supportive national policy aimed at making US commercial technologies more competitive globally. This emerging view reflects a growing belief that US companies need an active and supportive public sector if they are to compete with foreign companies backed by their national governments.[37] But of equal or greater importance as an indicator of change is the growing pattern of traditional business competitors developing intimate cooperation in areas where they previously competed. Increasingly, this cooperation among competitors is facilitated by government. We found such intimate cooperation in three of the four US-based case studies.

One reflection of this changing climate was the rapid relaxation during the Reagan administration of antitrust actions by the Department of Justice. Another was the white paper on commercial technology issued by the 1992 Clinton presidential campaign. Consistent with this campaign rhetoric, the White House sketched a broad outline of "new directions" for commercial technology policy in February 1993, and followed that with a "progress report" in November.[38] The new administration made major changes in the budget for research and development (R&D). A new cabinet-level body, the National Science and Technology Council (NSTC), established strategic planning guidelines for federal agency budgets which emphasized improving the nation's commercial technological capabilities.[39]

Although the Clinton initiatives had growing support within the internationally oriented business community, they immediately became a major focus of opposition when the Republicans won a majority in Congress in the 1994 election, and that opposition has continued. It is based primarily on ideology – the belief that government should have no direct and self-conscious role in commercial activities.[40] The views generally articulated by the opponents of direct government participation in networks aimed at commercial innovation reflect the industrial conceptual system. Clearly, major divisions exist concerning the appropriate role of government in the commercial technology arena, but equally clearly, many of the factors that put the issue of commercial technology policy on the national agenda remained unchanged throughout the 1990s.[41]

Robert White, who served as Undersecretary of Commerce for Technology, has articulated a view held by many involved in internationally competitive businesses:

> The process of innovation is a delicate ecosystem. Most agree that the federal government should maintain an environment conducive to innovation. This Congress must avoid undermining the scientific and technological enterprise – and its collaborative and entrepreneurial nature – that drives our economic expansion. What makes this so challenging is that any one member of Congress has control over only a small piece of the mosaic. Each member must look beyond the piece of federal science and technology under his or her committee and assess the impact on the innovation process as a whole.[42]

This view is given impetus by the fact that, even during one of the longest periods of continuous economic growth in the nation's history, the competitiveness of US companies in the world market as measured by the trade balance remains a source of worry. More than two decades after the USA first entered the era of large and continuing trade deficits, and more than a decade after the devaluation of the dollar, there is little prospect of fixing the trade imbalance with the USA's largest technological competitor, Japan. More broadly, the nation's trade deficit for 1998 was $168.7 billion. In the key arena of manufactured goods, the 1998 trade deficit was $197.2 billion.[43]

The fact that the increasing trade deficit is occurring in an otherwise positive economic situation is not easily explained. Diagnoses of the deficit, which are legion, include badly structured macroeconomics, an inadequately trained workforce, too many remaining trade barriers, badly outdated manufacturing, a loss of moral fiber, and the irrelevance of the entire issue.[44] Perhaps the only compelling explanation is that there are no simple explanations.

Continuing to debate explanations that cite individual variables as a cause for the trade deficit, or debating any other issue related to the innovation of complex technologies, offers little insight. If debates to inform policy and business decisions are to be fruitful, they will need more organic and systematic approaches. In search of such approaches, it is useful to examine, first, Asian experiences with successful technological innovation, and, second, some conceptual developments in economics, engineering, and science. These concepts have emerged from *a merger of evolutionary economics and complexity science.*

Asian experience

The commercial technological successes of Japan and the newly industrializing countries of East Asia that first became evident in the 1970s have been repeatedly documented.[45] Initially, many Americans disregarded the Japanese successes, or invented special circumstances to account for it. It was common in the 1970s and 1980s to attribute Japan's success to unique and transitory factors; for example, the two oil crises of the 1970s.[46]

More than two decades later a growing number of students of innovation take a different view. They argue that the success of Japan and some of the other East Asian countries results from the existence of *national systems of commercial technological innovation that involve overtly supportive public policies, systems that are vastly different from that which traditionally characterized the American experience.* The Asian systems have their origins in very different economic systems, different cultural orientations, and even quite different styles of capitalism.[47] At their center are organizational arrangements that rely in substantial part on cooperative relationships, including collaboration between industry and governments. Some scholars argue not only that the Asian experience is transferable across national boundaries in principle, but that in practice parts of the experience will inevitably be transferred because of the new reality created by technological innovation.[48] Proponents of this view have concluded that the traditional American conceptual model of technological and economic development is inappropriate to the new reality.[49]

In fact, over the past two decades it is evident that both the United States and Europe have made significant modifications in their national innovation systems based on lessons derived from Japan. Increasingly the networks that successfully innovate complex technologies in the United States have emphasized experience and not theories, in much the same way as the Japanese. Perhaps no part of the lesson drawn from experience is more evident than the emphasis on production and especially on process technologies. In Japan and many of the other Asian nations production, not consumption, the traditional US emphasis, has been the primary national priority. One illustration of the national differences in purpose is that Japanese companies have consistently emphasized R&D on the process technologies that underpin modern "lean" or "agile" manufacturing, while American companies traditionally focused on products.[50]

The emphasis on process innovation helps explain why Japan was the first to emphasize the importance of organizing people and machines into synthetic production systems on a large scale. The Japanese have consistently paid more attention than Americans to the interdependence of human and organizational elements in production. Until quite recently, for example, US companies sought to automate production with the goal, framed in the monstrous doublespeak of scientific management, being "to integrate people out of the system."[51]

   Another distinct lesson derived from Japan is that long-term technological goals require government to play a major role in setting economic policies. In the United States, such involvement is approached with great caution, and many Americans still see government participation in the innovation process as introducing inefficiencies into markets, and thus as ultimately costly. But the relatively successful history of powerful governments in East Asia has led to their being perceived as both competent and legitimate participants in sector-specific economic activities.[52] Even with the financial meltdown that began in 1997, there was little indication of a move away from the perception that government had a central role in commercial technological success.

   To the substantial regret of many Americans, few East Asians (and Europeans as well) share the belief in arm's length, adversarial relationships between competitor companies and between government and business. Industries in most countries not only enjoy supportive relationships with financial institutions and other companies, but also consider a supportive government as a given. Government is assumed to be an essential actor in shaping markets and supporting commercialization in the national interest – a perspective still hard for Americans to accept.[53] Yet a growing number of industrial leaders in the USA see no alternative to active government participation when their foreign competitors have that kind of participation.

   One thing is clear: *all governments seek national economic advantage.* As competition in the global economy increases, the pursuit of national economic advantage becomes even more significant. As the belief grows that direct government participation is useful, aggressive technology policies developed in cooperation with industry are likely to become even more common around the world. In the years to come, self-conscious and explicit technology policies will likely take on even greater importance in all advanced countries.[54]

   As technologies compete in a world market, that market is increasingly affected by the fact that East Asian nations have less trust in market mechanisms than Americans have. From the Asian perspective, the unpredictability of markets means they should not be trusted to make big decisions (e.g. how a society should be run, what direction an economy should take). In Japan, for instance, it is quite common for company representatives as well as government officials to speak negatively of "excessive competition" or "confusion in the market," and to advocate reshaping markets in the national interest. The market-defining policies undertaken by the Japanese have included restricting foreign investment and foreign exchange, weakening enforcement of antitrust, increasing industry concentration, and forming cartels during bad economic times. These overt market-shaping actions are reinforced by more subtle managing of market dynamics by organizational arrangements like the "societies of business," or *keiretsu*, which often use mutual shareholding, interlocking directorates, and close buyer–supplier relationships to engage in exclusionary behavior.[55]

   By comparison, intrinsic market uncertainty has been precisely the key to the American view of economic life. Of course, both public and private organizations in the United States also mold markets, but this is generally camouflaged as market failure or excused as vital to national security. The idea that organizations should systematically seek to shape markets through the use of strategy and public policy has traditionally been foreign to discussions of innovation and management in the United States. It seems clear that a convergence is occurring between US views and those of other countries, and the convergence involves movement from both directions.

As technologies become more complex and as the recognition grows that success rests on trial and error experience, networks wherever they are located seem likely to do what works, regardless of whether it fits with theory. The body of theory that has dominated throughout the industrial era is clearly no longer adequate.

New concepts

The inconsistency between the industrial conceptual system and the new reality has stimulated a number of European and American scholars and practitioners to search for new concepts. The increasing merger of complexity science and evolutionary economics is one of the results. Unlike neoclassical economic theory, the merger focuses attention on what has long concerned students of technological innovation: "how to improve the generation and exploitation of innovative opportunities; the properties of the institutions supporting technological change; the most adequate forms of corporate organization; and the effects on innovation of different public policies."[56]

Evolutionary economic theory has four general principles:

- The term "evolutionary" ought to be reserved for theories about *dynamic time paths*, theories that attempt to explain how things change over time (about disequilibrium) and how selection takes place.
- Evolutionary models contain both *systematic* and *random* elements. In most instances, the systematic elements act to "winnow" the random ones; winnowing implies a selection for *fitness*.
- Evolutionary economics features *learning dynamics*, in which individuals, firms, etc., adapt their plans, strategies, or behaviors as a result of both positive and negative feedback from the consequences of what has been tried.
- Evolutionary learning is *imperfect* (mistake-ridden) and involves *discovery*, but of a discontinuous type: rates of learning and adaptation change.[57]

In the abstract, the application of these principles to technological and organizational change is straightforward. Because learning is the key, and because learning is *path-dependent*, market forces alone do not suffice to select optimal learning. Some selection of the learning critical to technological innovation must therefore be done self-consciously by the organizations doing the innovation, as they gather information and reach out to link to new capabilities to solve technological problems. In sum, organizations do much more than respond to external, market, stimuli. They seek to influence markets by choosing innovation options based on their accumulated capabilities and their search for new knowledge.

When learning leads to adaptation and new organizational forms (termed *self-organization*) that solve technological problems, the organizations have attained greater fitness. This pattern occurs in the development and evolution of networks that successfully innovate complex technologies. It is important to note that solving a given technological problem does not imply a linear progression of ever greater fitness. That is, a given technological solution may result in an organization (e.g. a network) making itself less capable of making the changes needed to achieve greater fitness in the future. But as a general rule, organizational and technological fitness *coevolve* from a combination of external (e.g. market) and internal organizational variables.[58]

These principles of evolutionary economics are compatible with a good deal of what is known about technological change, and they help put the Asian experience in perspective. Almost every study of technological innovation notes a high degree of risk and uncertainty, a constant sense of novelty, a drive to solve new problems, and, above all, a lot of trial-and-error searching and nonlinear learning.[59] Knowledge is the new competitive resource and, because it resides in people and organizations, it is a renewable resource. The knowledge needed normally includes both tacit and explicit components.[60]

The Japanese in both the public and private sectors have made the development of needed human resources and the organizations that mobilize them a major priority of both company strategies and national policy. In Japan, for instance, companies treat employees as their most important assets and give priority to providing opportunities for employee growth. Combined business and government funding for workforce training in Japan has been twice as high as in the USA.[61]

Networks of highly trained workers develop and exist in a symbiotic relationship with the complex technologies they produce. These networks are *learning organizations* capable of integrating explicit and tacit knowledge and skills, embedding them in equipment (increasingly by way of software), and applying them to problem solving, experimentation, and commercial innovation.[62]

The Japanese *keiretsu*, for example, make sense when viewed through the conceptual lens of evolutionary economics. For instance, the constant shaping of markets by these networks through interorganizational relationships and public policy would be expected if, as evolutionary economics asserts, organizational learning, adaptation, and self-organization are as important to the coevolution of organizations and technologies as are market forces. Successful *keiretsu* should be expected to develop and act upon market-defining strategies.[63]

The essentials

Given the interdependence between complex organizations and complex technologies, understanding the patterns associated with successful networks offers valuable insights for managers. A clear priority is information on how expertise and capabilities must be linked to produce the desired technological synthesis. When organizational capabilities are widely dispersed (among firms, government agencies, and universities), the most productive linkages can only be established empirically. That is, organizational networks are built and adapted in significant part using learning that accumulates from continual trial and error. There is a Japanese saying that the only way to ford a river is to step in and feel for the stones. Clearly, those who have forded many streams become better at it. The same is true for those who wish to build and sustain organizational networks that innovate complex technologies. An empirical approach is the only option, because no one has a reductionist conceptual or theoretical model that predicts how the innovation of complex technologies will happen.

How, then, does one create innovative organizations without an explicit theory explaining how complex technological innovations occur? The beginning step is to recognize in this process that management is heavily dependent on *metaphors*. Metaphors are in many ways the currency of complex systems.[64] Brian Arthur, one of the architects of the Santa Fe Institute (SFI), where the links between evolutionary economics and the science of complexity are emerging, articulates the value of metaphors:

It turns out that an awful lot of policy-making has to do with finding the appropriate metaphor. Conversely, bad policy-making almost always involves finding inappropriate metaphors. For example, it may not be appropriate to think about a drug "war," with guns and assaults.

So from this point of view, the purpose of having a Santa Fe Institute is that it, and places like it, are where the metaphors and a vocabulary are being created in complex systems. So if somebody comes along with a beautiful study on the computer, then you can say, "Here's a new metaphor. Let's call this one *the edge of chaos*, or whatever." So what the SFI will do, if it studies enough complex systems, is to show us the kinds of patterns we might observe, and the kinds of metaphors that might be appropriate for systems that are moving and in process and complicated, rather than the metaphor of clockwork.[65]

Through metaphors our imaginations are free to twist and turn in complex ways, to construct, reconstruct, and make sense of the complex reality through which we live our lives.[66] Ikujiro Nonaka says that metaphors have been essential for the conversion of tacit knowledge into explicit knowledge in Japanese firms. He argues that metaphors provide "a way for individuals grounded in different contexts and with different experiences to understand something intuitively through the use of imagination and symbols without the need for analysis or generalization."[67] By way of metaphors, groups of people can put together what they know, both tacitly and explicitly, in new ways, and begin to communicate new knowledge.

The *trajectory* is a particularly valuable metaphor in our pursuit of insight into the innovation of complex technologies and the structure and behavior of the networks that coevolve with them. A trajectory refers to a pathway of organizational and technological coevolution. As indicated in Figure 2.1, the most common way of illustrating a trajectory is the S-shaped curve, relating additional performance (i.e. technological capabilities) over time. A curved line linking two dimensions of the innovation of a complex technology simplifies reality a great deal. In fact, a trajectory is rarely unambiguously defined on any dimension at any point in time. The precise character of technological trajectories can only be outlined in hindsight.[68] None the less, a trajectory is a powerful metaphor. This is because

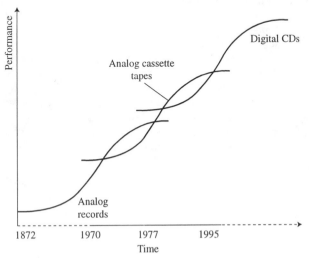

Figure 2.1 Audio innovation trajectories

much of the experience with complex technologies and the new concepts derived from complexity science and evolutionary economics can be synthesized within the imagery of a trajectory.

Figure 2.1 uses the three historically dominant audio technology trajectories to illustrate one pattern of innovation associated with complex technologies. The first trajectory (analog records) was launched with Edison's innovation of the phonograph. Incremental innovations along that trajectory took the technology from a cylinder to a long-playing, stereophonic record. A trajectory transition took place with the introduction of the magnetic cassette tape, which also went through a series of incremental innovations. The third trajectory, the digital compact disc (CD) has experienced the same pattern of incremental innovations.

Both the launching of new trajectories and the movement to trajectory transitions or transformations involves creating or fundamentally restructuring the organizational network, while incremental innovations normally involve minor adaptation in the network. In all cases, however, there is a process of coevolution occurring between the evolving technology and the network that produces it. For complex technologies, especially for those experiencing rapid change, the process of coevolution is often so organic and seamless that it is difficult to distinguish between the organizations and the technologies. In Chapter 6 we identify five levels of organization associated with the innovation process: work groups, core actors (e.g. firms, government agencies, university laboratories), networks, complexes, and national innovation systems. Each of these is a system with intermingling of social and technical parts. For the purpose of launching trajectories and innovating along them, the network is the dominant sociotechnical system.

Insight into how networks are linked to the innovation of complex technologies is facilitated by looking in some detail at the process of self-organization. Network self-organization involves three sets of factors: (a) network resources; (b) constraining and focusing forces; and (c) emerging innovation patterns. Network resources include existing core capabilities, complementary assets, and organizational learning. Constraining and focusing forces include potential core capabilities, complementary assets, organizational learning opportunities, path dependencies, and the selection environment (largely markets). A trajectory is the dominant way of expressing how all these factors emerge as patterns of complex technological innovation.

The general importance of the trajectory metaphor is evident when one appreciates how far the pervasiveness of complexity has taken us from America's dominant concepts about how our physical reality operates. Americans overwhelmingly use analytical metaphors and mechanistic models. These worked well enough in the simpler industrial, or mass-manufacturing, reality of the past; they are inappropriate in today's more complex, dynamic reality. As Arthur notes, our simple metaphors are seventeenth-century assumptions about the world as "clockwork." Ours is increasingly a world of synthetic, self-organizing systems.

The next chapter traces the evolution of production from the craft mode through the emerging synthetic mode. It provides a basis for appreciating the historical roots of today's complex network organizations and their role in technological innovation.

Notes

1.   Peter A. Corning, "Synergy and Self-organization in the Evolution of Complex Systems," *Systems Research*, Vol. 12, No. 2, June 1995, pp. 89–121.

2. Michael D. McMaster, *The Intelligence Advantage: Organizing for Complexity*, Boston: Butterworth-Heinemann, 1996, pp. ix–xxiv; Robert U. Ayres, "Toward a Non-linear Dynamics of Technological Progress," *Journal of Economic Behavior and Organization*, Vol. 24, June 1994, pp. 35–69.
3. Chris Freeman, "The 'National System of Innovation' in Historical Perspective," *Cambridge Journal of Economics*, Vol. 19, No. 1, February 1995, pp. 5–24; Bengt-Ake Lundvall, "Introduction," in Bengt-Ake Lundvall, ed., *National Systems of Innovation: towards a Theory of Innovation and Interactive Learning*, New York: Pinter Publishers, 1992, pp. 1–19.
4. Jacqueline Senker, "National Systems of Innovation, Organizational Learning and Industrial Biotechnology," *Technovation*, Vol. 16, No. 5, May 1996, pp. 219–29.
5. Michael Storper and Robert Salais, *Worlds of Production: the Action Frameworks of the Economy*, Cambridge, MA: Harvard University Press, 1997, p. 12.
6. Ralph D. Stacey, "Management and the Science of Complexity: If Organizational Life Is Nonlinear, Can Business Strategies Prevail?" *Research-Technology Management*, May/June 1996, pp. 8–10; David Levy, "Chaos Theory and Strategy: Theory, Application, and Managerial Implications," *Strategic Management Journal*, Vol. 15, Summer 1994, pp. 167–78.
7. J. S. Metcalfe, "Technology Systems and Technology Policy in an Evolutionary Framework," *Cambridge Journal of Economics*, Vol. 19, No. 1, February 1995, pp. 25–46; Keith Smith, "Innovation Policy in an Evolutionary Context," in P. Paolo Saviotti and J. Stanley Metcalfe, eds, *Evolutionary Theories of Economic and Technological Change: Present Status and Future Prospects*, Reading, PA: Harwood Academic Publishers, 1991, pp. 256–75.
8. Charles R. Morris, "It's *Not* the Economy, Stupid," *Atlantic Monthly*, Vol. 272, No. 1, July 1993, pp. 49–62.
9. Allan Sloan, "The New Rich," *Newsweek*, August 4, 1997, p. 49.
10. John A. Byne, Jennifer Reingold, and Richard A. Melcher, "Wanted: a Few Good CEOs," *Business Week*, August 11, 1997, p. 66.
11. Robert Pool, *Beyond Engineering: How Society Shapes Technology*, New York: Oxford University Press, 1997, p. 20.
12. James Wade, "Dynamics of Organizational Communities and Technological Bandwagons: an Empirical Investigation of the Evolution of the Microprocessor Market," *Strategic Management Journal*, Vol. 16, Special Issue, Summer 1995, pp. 111–33.
13. Nathan Rosenberg, *Exploring the Black Box: Technology, Economics, and History*, New York: Cambridge University Press, 1994, pp. 9–23; W. Brian Arthur, *Increasing Returns and Path Dependency in the Economy*, Ann Arbor, MI: University of Michigan Press, 1994.
14. Robert D. Hof, Ira Sager, and Linda Himelstein, "The Sad Saga of Silicon Graphics," *Business Week*, August 4, 1997, p. 66.
15. Geoffrey Smith, Brad Wolverton, and Theresa Palmer, "A Dark Kodak Moment," *Business Week*, August 4, 1997, p. 30.
16. Larry D. Browning, Janice M. Beyer, and Judy C. Shetler, "Building Cooperation in a Competitive Industry: Sematech and the Semi-Conductor Industry," *Academy of Management Journal*, Vol. 38, No. 1, February 1995, pp. 113–51; Peter Grindley, David C. Mowery and Brian Silverman, "SEMATECH and Collaborative Research: Lessons in the Design of High-technology Consortia," *Journal of Policy Analysis and Management*, Vol. 13, No. 4, Fall 1994, pp. 723–58.
17. "Winning through Cooperation: an Interview with William Spencer," *Technology Review*, Vol. 100, No. 1, January 1997, pp. 22–7; William J. Spencer and Peter Grindley, "SEMATECH after Five Years: High-technology Consortia and US Competitiveness," *California Management Review*, Vol. 35, No. 4, Summer 1993, pp. 9–32.
18. Elizabeth Corcoran, "US Tech Firms Seek Tinier Chip: Bomb Labs Will Handle Research," *Washington Post*, September 11, 1997, pp. A1 and A23.
19. Don E. Kash, *Perpetual Innovation: the new World of Competition*, New York: Basic Books, 1989, p. 151.

20. Richard N. Osborn and John Hagedoorn, "The Institutionalization and Evolutionary Dynamics of Interorganizational Alliances and Networks," *Academy of Management Journal*, Vol. 40, No. 2, April 1997, pp. 261–78.
21. James P. Womack and Daniel Roos, *The Machine that Changed the World*, New York: Rawson Associates, Macmillan, 1990.
22. Trudy E. Bell, "Bicycles on a Personalized Basis," *IEEE Spectrum*, Vol. 30, No. 9, September 1993, pp. 32–5.
23. Fumio Kodama, "Technology Fusion and the New R&D," *Harvard Business Review*, Vol. 70, No. 4, July/August 1992, pp. 32–5.
24. Bjorn Walstrom, "Avoiding Technological Risks: the Dilemma of Complexity," *Technological Forecasting and Social Change*, Vol. 42, No. 4, December 1992, pp. 351–65.
25. C. Dyke, "Expectation and Strategy in a Nonlinear World," *Systems Research*, Vol. 7, No. 2, 1990, pp. 117–25.
26. Donald N. Michael, "Governing by Learning: Boundaries, Myths, and Metaphors," *Futures*, Vol. 25, No. 1, January/February 1993, pp. 81–2.
27. Ralph D. Stacey, *Complexity and Creativity in Organizations*, San Francisco: Berrett-Koehler Publishers, 1996, pp. 72–106.
28. Deborah K. Schaff, "The New Evolutionary Paradigm," *Futurics*, Vol. 16, 1992, p. 54.
29. Morgan L. Swink, J. Christopher Sandvig, and Vincent A. Mabert, "Customizing Concurrent Engineering Processes: Five Case Studies," *Journal of Product Innovation Management*, Vol. 13, No. 3, May 1996, pp. 229–44; Otis Port, "Moving Past the Assembly Line," *Business Week*, No. 3289, Special Issue, October 23, 1992, p. 178.
30. Andrew Tylecote, "Managerial Objectives and Technological Collaboration: the Role of National Variations in Cultures and Structures," in Rod Coombs, Albert Richards, Pier P. Saviotti, and Vivien Walsh, eds, *Technological Collaboration: The Dynamics of Cooperation in Industrial Innovation*, Brookfield, VT: Edward Elgar, 1996, pp. 34–53; Roy Rothwell, "Successful Industrial Innovation: Critical Factors for the 1990s," *R&D Management*, Vol. 22, No. 3, July 1992, pp. 232–3.
31. Michael, "Governing by Learning," pp. 83–4.
32. Kulwant Sing, "The Impact of Technological Complexity and Interfirm Cooperation on Business Survival," *Academy of Management Journal*, Vol. 40, No. 2, April 1997, pp. 339–67.
33. Anders Lundgren, *Technological Innovation and Network Evolution*, New York: Routledge, 1995, pp. 77–102.
34. Jacqueline Senker and Margaret Sharp, "Organizational Learning in Cooperative Alliances: Some Case Studies in Biotechnology," *Technology Analysis and Strategic Management*, Vol. 9, No. 1, 1997, pp. 35–51.
35. Andrew C. Inkpen, "Creating Knowledge through Collaboration," *California Management Review*, Vol. 39, No. 1, Fall 1996, pp. 123–40.
36. Yasunori Baba and Ken-ichi Imai, "A Network View of Innovation and Entrepreneurship: the Case of the Evolution of the VCR Systems," *International Social Science Journal*, Vol. 45, No. 1, February 1993, pp. 26–7.
37. Robert H. Hayes, "US Competitiveness: 'Resurgence' Versus Reality," *Challenge*, Vol. 39, No. 2, March/April 1996, pp. 36–44; Richard R. Nelson, "Why Should Managers Be Thinking about Technology Policy?" *Strategic Management Journal*, Vol. 16, No. 8, November 1995, pp. 581–8; Hedrick Smith, "Biting the Hand that Feeds: If Commerce Isn't an Ally, Competing Globally Isn't an Option," *Washington Post*, August 6, 1995, p. C5; Eugene B. Skolnikoff, "Evolving US Science and Technology Policy in a Changing International Environment," *Science and Public Policy*, Vol. 22, No. 2, April 1995, pp. 74–84; John S. McClenahen, "Now Do We Need an Industrial Policy?," *Industry Week*, March 18, 1991, pp. 36–62.
38. President William J. Clinton and Vice President Albert Gore, Jr, *Technology for America's Economic Growth, a New Direction to Build Economic Strength*, Washington, DC:

Executive Office of the President, February 22, 1993; President William J. Clinton, *Technology for Economic Growth: President's Progress Report*, Washington, DC: Executive Office of the President, November 1993.

39. Irwin Goodman, "New Cabinet-level Council to Shape Clinton Science Policy and Budgets," *Physics Today*, Vol. 47, No. 1, January 1994, pp. 35–7.

40. David J. Hanson, "Advanced Technology Program: Victim of Congressional Fervor?," *Chemical and Engineering News*, Vol. 73, No. 34, August 21, 1995, pp. 27–31; Gene Koprowski, "Does High Technology Need Fed Funds?" *Forbes ASAP*, April 10, 1995, pp. 88–9, 91; E. J. Dione, Jr, "The Elections: No Cure for What Troubles Us," *Washington Post*, December 27, 1994, p. A15.

41. Rose M. Ham and David C. Mowery, "Enduring Dilemmas in US Technology Policy," *California Management Review*, Vol. 37, No. 4, Summer 1995, pp. 89–107; Martin Fransman, "Is National Technology Policy Obsolete in a Globalized World? The Japanese Response," *Cambridge Journal of Economics*, Vol. 19, No. 1, February 1995, pp. 95–120; Daniel F. Burton, Jr, "Competitiveness: Here to Stay," *Washington Quarterly*, Vol. 17, No. 4, Autumn 1994, pp. 99–109.

42. Robert M. White, "A Message to Congress," *Technology Review*, Vol. 100, No. 10, October 1997, p. 5.

43. International Trade Administration, US Department of Commerce, *Monthly Trade Update*: December 1998, Washington, DC: US Department of Commerce, February 19, 1999.

44. Council on Competitiveness, *Competitiveness Index, 1996*, Washington, DC: Council on Competitiveness, 1996; Maria Papadakis, "The Delicate Task of Linking Industrial R&D to National Competitiveness," *Technovation*, Vol. 15, No. 9, November 1995, pp. 569–83; Paul Krugman, "Competitiveness: a Dangerous Obsession," *Foreign Affairs*, Vol. 73, No. 2, March/April 1994, pp. 28–44.

45. Barry P. Bosworth, "Growing Pains: Trade Frictions Corrode the US-Asian Relationship," *Brookings Review*, Winter 1996, pp. 4–9; Lawrence G. Franko, "The Japanese Juggernaut Rolls On," *Sloan Management Review*, Vol. 37, No. 2, Winter 1996, pp. 103–9; James Fallows, *Looking at the Sun: the Rise of the New East Asian Economic and Political System*, New York: Pantheon Books, 1994; Alfred Balk, ed., "Asiapower," *IEEE Spectrum*, Vol. 28, No. 6, June 1991, pp. 24–66.

46. "The Fight over Competitiveness: a Zero-sum Debate?" *Foreign Affairs*, Vol. 73, No. 4, July/August 1994, pp. 186–203.

47. Chalmers Johnson, "Comparative Capitalism: the Japanese Difference," *California Management Review*, Vol. 35, No. 4, Summer 1993, pp. 51–67; David J. Teece, "The Dynamics of Industrial Capitalism: Perspectives on Alfred Chandler's *Scale and Scope*," *Journal of Economic Literature*, Vol. 31, No. 1, March 1993, pp. 199–225; Stewart R. Clegg and S. Gordon Redding, "Introduction: Capitalism in Contrasting Cultures," in Stewart R. Clegg and S. Gordon Redding, eds, *Capitalism in Contrasting Cultures*, New York: Walter de Gruyter, 1990, pp. 1–28.

48. Richard Florida and Martin Kenney, *Beyond Mass Production: the Japanese System and Its Transfer to the United States*, New York: Oxford University Press, 1993.

49. Hedrick Smith, *Rethinking America*, New York: Random House, 1995, pp. xvii–72; Lane Kenworthy, *In Search of National Economic Success: Balancing Competition and Cooperation*, London: Sage Publications, 1995, pp. 154–96.

50. Joseph C. Montgomery and Lawrence O. Levine, eds, *The Transition to Agile Manufacturing: Staying Flexible for Competitive Advantage*, Milwaukee, WI: ASQC Quality Press, 1996; James P. Womack and Daniel T. Jones, "From Lean Production to the Lean Enterprise," *Harvard Business Review*, Vol. 72, No. 2, March/April 1994, pp. 93–103; John H. Sheridan, "Agile Manufacturing: Stepping beyond Lean Production," *Industry Week*, Vol. 242, No. 8, April 19, 1993, pp. 30–46; Christopher T. Hill, "New Manufacturing Paradigms – New Manufacturing Policies?" *The Bridge*, Vol. 21, No. 2, Summer 1991, pp. 15–24.

51. John A. Alic, "Computer-assisted Everything? Tools and Techniques for Design and Production," *Technological Forecasting and Social Change*, Vol. 44, 1993, pp. 359–61.
52. Hisatoshi Yamamoto, "Complementary Competition in Japan," *Research-Technology Management*, Vol. 37, No. 2, March/April 1994, pp. 49–54.
53. Kosaku Yoshida, "New Economic Principles in America – Competition and Cooperation: a Comparative Study of the US and Japan," *Columbia Journal of World Business*, Vol. 26, No. 4, Winter 1992, pp. 30–44.
54. Alan Tonelson, "The Perils of Techno-globalism," *Issues in Science and Technology*, Summer 1995, pp. 31–8.
55. Robert Z. Lawrence, "Japan's Different Trade Regime: an Analysis with Particular Reference to *Keiretsu*," *Journal of Economic Perspectives*, Vol. 7, No. 3, Summer 1993, pp. 3–19.
56. Giovanni Dosi, "Perspectives on Evolutionary Theory," *Science and Public Policy*, Vol. 18, No. 6, December 1991, p. 338.
57. Giovanni Dosi and Richard R. Nelson, "An Introduction to Evolutionary Theories in Economics," *Journal of Evolutionary Economics*, Vol. 4, No. 3, 1994, pp. 153–72.
58. Richard R. Nelson, "The Coevolution of Technologies and Institutions," in Richard W. England, ed., *Evolutionary Concepts in Economics*, Ann Arbor, MI: University of Michigan Press, 1994, pp. 139–156.
59. Senker, "National Systems of Innovation, Organizational Learning and Industrial Biotechnology," pp. 219–29; Patricia A. Meyers, "Non-linear Learning in Large Technological Firms: Period Four Implies Chaos," *Research Policy*, Vol. 19, No. 2, April 1990, pp. 97–115.
60. E. B. Grant and M. J. Gregory, "Tacit Knowledge, the Life Cycle and International Manufacturing Transfer," *Technology Analysis and Strategic Management*, Vol. 9, No. 2, 1997, pp. 149–61.
61. Sheridan, "Agile Manufacturing: Stepping beyond Lean Production," p. 44.
62. Ashoka Mody, "Learning through Alliances," *Journal of Economic Behavior and Organization*, Vol. 20, No. 1, February 1993, pp. 151–70; Knut H. Sorenson and Nora Levold, "Tacit Networks, Heterogeneous Engineers, and Embodied Knowledge," *Science, Technology, and Human Values*, Vol. 17, No. 1, Winter 1992, pp. 13–35.
63. H. Kevin Steensma, "Acquiring Technological Competencies through Inter-organizational Collaboration: an Organizational Learning Perspective," *Journal of Engineering and Technology Management*, Vol. 12, No. 4, January 1996, pp. 267–86; Georges Romme, "The Formation of Firm Strategy as Self-organization," in Christopher Freeman and Luc Soete, eds, *New Explorations in the Economics of Technical Change*, New York: Pinter Publishers, 1990, pp. 38–54.
64. August Tepper, "Controlling Technology by Shaping Visions," *Policy Sciences*, Vol. 29, No. 1, February 1996, pp. 29–44; Craig L. Pearce and Charles P. Osmond, "Metaphors for Change: the ALPs Model of Change Management," *Organizational Dynamics*, Vol. 24, No. 3, Winter 1996, pp. 23–35; Anthony J. N. Judge, "Metaphor and the Language of Futures," *Futures*, Vol. 25, No. 3, April 1993, p. 275.
65. Quoted in M. Mitchell Waldrop, *Complexity: the Emerging Science at the Edge of Order and Chaos*, New York: Simon and Schuster, 1992, p. 334.
66. Gareth Morgan, "More on Metaphors: Why We Cannot Control Tropes in Administrative Science," *Administrative Science Quarterly*, Vol. 28, No. 4, December 1983, p. 603.
67. Ikujiro Nonaka, "The Knowledge-creating Company," *Harvard Business Review*, Vol. 69, No. 6, November/December 1991, p. 100.
68. Jens F. Christensen, "Asset Profiles for Technological Innovation," *Research Policy*, Vol. 24, No. 5, September 1995, p. 743.

CHAPTER THREE

The Evolution of Technological Innovation

The historical patterns of coevolution among production processes, organizations, and technological products have helped create and reconfigure America's decision making landscape. In this chapter, we examine these patterns by comparing three different production eras: craft, mass manufacturing, and synthetic.[1]

- Craft production involves highly skilled workers making customized products for individual consumers.
- Mass manufacturing involves the division of a product into its component parts, which are standardized, and then making and assembling the parts under conditions where efficiency increases with scale.
- Synthetic production involves teams of multiskilled people using flexible, increasingly automated machines to design and make a large variety and relatively high volume of products on the same production line.

Because the dominant characteristics of these eras are so different, observers often overlook an important point: each era has been built on the accomplishments of the past. Craft production was important to and an integral part of the success of mass production, and both craft and mass production have been indispensable in the rise of today's synthetic production. Indeed, analysts of scientific and technological change have noted that real world economies are always a mixture of different production types.[2]

Computer software technology provides a good example of the kind of interplay that repeatedly takes place among craft, mass, and synthetic production. Michael Cusumano identifies the intertwining of three paths in the evolution of computer software: (a) full customization (i.e. craft production), where each software product is unique and highly skilled technicians write programs to meet very specialized customer requirements; (b) full standardization (i.e. mass production), where the objective is to design and manufacture commodity-type software that maximizes application for average user needs; and (c) semi-customization/semi-standardization (i.e. synthetic production), where a balance is struck between delivering unique product characteristics and maintaining the flexibility to reconfigure designs in ways that enable software to be integrated with larger systems.[3] At any given time, a combination of these three production pathways is likely to characterize the development of software technology.

The new production reality

Insight into the new production reality is facilitated by noting that technological innovation historically has generated Janus-like challenges for society: it has routinely presented us with obstacles embedded in opportunities, and vice versa. For example, although automobiles have been critical to international competitiveness and economic growth, they have threatened the global environment. The response often has been to seek another technological fix – for instance, to pursue the innovation of a vehicle that simultaneously is competitive and produces little or no pollution.[4] But experience suggests this technological fix will also have unanticipated consequences. Such is the nature of technological change.

On another dimension the contemporary innovation process has created permanent disequilibrium for both technologies and society. To illustrate, the capacity to innovate continuously and rapidly has dramatically altered considerations of time and cost. Speed to market is critical to success.[5] Product cycles are shrinking everywhere, while niche markets for specialized products proliferate. Traditional cost considerations often become secondary to market share, for example, when large "families" of automobiles and parts, rather than specific cars, become the basis for assessing production efficiencies and profits. Automobile production and assembly have become global in scope, as new collaborative arrangements are worked out across national boundaries. For the automobile industry, temporal and financial boundaries have become blurred and difficult to assess.[6] The overall effect of the capacity to innovate in an unremitting fashion has been to threaten with obsolescence many existing beliefs about how society operates.

Many people see these innovation-driven changes as chaotic, beyond governance. Evolutionary economics and the science of complexity appear to offer a less disturbing picture, one which suggests we look for patterns in this seeming chaos. The capacity to identify patterns offers a valuable new perspective on decision making with regard to complex innovation.[7]

Innovation in an evolutionary context

The search for patterns encourages a historical look at the coevolution of technology and organizations. One pattern is clear: contemporary technology did not spring full-blown from the foreheads of individual inventors. The accelerating changes in the world's physical boundaries reflect the gradual *evolution* of a production system that has taken us, over the past two centuries, from a world of scarcity, similarity, and highly constrained choices to one of seemingly limitless abundance, diversity, and constantly expanding options. Table 3.1 sketches the evolution from simplicity through an intermediate stage to complexity for production (the processes whereby knowledge, materials, and other inputs are converted into products), organization (the structures whereby expertise and capabilities are mobilized and linked in order to carry out technological innovation and production),[8] and outputs, increasingly technological products.

Table 3.1 summarizes the changes associated with the evolution from craft production through the system of mass manufacturing (or, as it is sometimes termed, "industrial" production) to a newly emerging synthetic mode.[9] Concurrently, the most important production organizations have evolved from ones dominated by

Table 3.1 Complexity in production, organization, and technology

Simple	Intermediate	Complex
Production		
Craft	*Mass Manufacturing*	*Synthetic*
Tacit knowledge; artisan/apprentice expertise; basic materials; multipurpose tools; small scale; innovation by individuals	Explicit know-how; division of labor in expertise; natural resource intensive; single-purpose tools; large scale; innovation institutionalized in R&D unit	Explicit and tacit knowledge synthesized; constant learning; synthetic materials; multi-purpose tools; variable scale & scope; innovation through organization
Organization		
Owner-managed; non-hierarchical; niche creation strategy; innovation as core capability; personal contact as complementary assets; informal links to other organizations	Hierarchical, decentralized management; diversified; strategy of portfolio management; core capability risk control; complementary assets as specialized knowledge; R&D links to other organizations compartmentalized	Flattened, decentralized structure; multifunctional, cross-institutional teams; collaboration as strategy; innovation as core capability; groups as complementary assets; extensive external linkages non-compartmentalized
Technology		
Custom products; variety; low volume; few components; simple architectures; value added by uniqueness	High volume; low variety; many linear-linked components and architectures; value added by efficiency	Complex systems that offer user flexibility; large numbers of components; complex architectures

owner-managers to bureaucratic structures to the more flexible network type.[10] Meanwhile, the dominant outputs of the production system have evolved from handicrafts through mass-produced, standardized commodities, to ever changing high-value-added technological products designed to meet or create varying and diverse customer preferences by delivering some combination of new capabilities, improved quality, enhanced performance, and lower costs.[11] Both products and production processes have evolved toward ever greater complexity. Initially they were composed of a few components (i.e. parts that embody core concepts and perform distinct functions), with architectures that connected them in simple (i.e. linear) fashion. Today a major portion of the most valuable products are technologies composed of many components, with architectures that link them into integrated, coherent wholes which users can adapt to their own changing needs.[12]

The complexity of our new production reality requires different and ever changing patterns of organization. Figure 3.1 shows the time sequence associated with the evolution to the new complex production reality. Until the nineteenth century, craft production dominated. Industrial (mass) production, which was invented in the nineteenth century, soon became the primary mode of production. In the second half of the twentieth century, synthetic production has been supplanting mass production.[13]

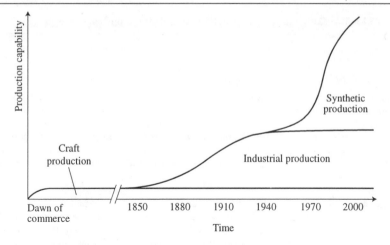

Figure 3.1 Modes of production, past to present

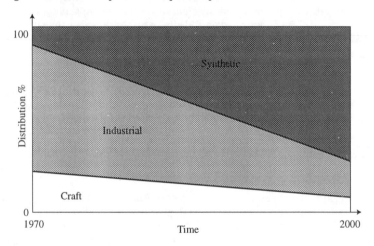

Figure 3.2 Character of processes and products

The accelerating change in production that has occurred in the post-Second World War period can be likened to a rope in which different fibers have been woven. Before 1940, the "production rope" was overwhelmingly composed of two fibers (i.e. craft and mass production). Over the next five decades a new type of fiber (i.e. synthetic products and processes) has been twisted into the rope. Today the rope looks very different from its pre-1940 segment. It still has some of the older fibers, but if one looks only at the two ends, they appear to be different entities altogether. The product and process technologies that, taken together, now constitute the rope are a combination of the three production modes, as illustrated in Figure 3.2.

Production, organization, and product technologies have coevolved toward greater complexity. Before we trace this evolution, it is useful to repeat that what transpired was a *transition from one dominant pattern of production to another.* Each type of production continues to play a role in commercialization, but over time each has given way to an approach better fitted to competitive success. In addition, we note that although the chapter focuses on companies as the major innovative organizations, networks of firms and other organizations have gradually replaced the individual firm as the primary locus of innovation in a growing number of complex technology sectors.

Craft production

Craft production, which has been with us since the dawn of commerce, involves highly skilled workers making customized products for individual consumers. Until roughly 1850, craft production dominated commerce in the United States and elsewhere.

The individual craftworker's skill has always been at the center of the craft production process; simple but flexible tools augment and expand the worker's capacity for productive expression. The craftworker uses tools to embody knowledge in a wide variety of products. Yet the precise relationships between the craftworker and those tools have never been clearly specified by any abstract, codified model. Indeed, in craft production many technical aspects were not and still are not amenable to codification. Instead, they accumulate as tacit knowledge, as the craftworkers become more skilled.[14] Thus, an initial strength of craftsmanship was its pragmatism and flexibility based on tacit knowledge, which was communicated through demonstration and apprenticeship. Eventually, however, this vagueness was craft production's undoing.

It proved easy for advocates of mass production to discredit craft production techniques because, as Piore and Sabel have recounted, while craft production clearly worked in practice, as a model it was "invisible – a practice without a name, by definition incoherent."[15] Alternatively, mass production's greater efficiency and its highly "scientific" and explicit model had all the attributes of being "modern" as understood at the time. These factors eventually made the mass production paradigm almost irresistible in both practice and theory.

The transition away from craft to mass production in the United States was also expedited by the absence of the strong societal belief in craft traditions found in, for example, Great Britain at the time. There is ample evidence, for example, that many British industries and their customers (e.g. production machinery, firearms) were so preoccupied with the values of craftsmanship (e.g. pride in workmanship, individuality, high standards of product quality, technical perfection) that they ignored the commercial advantages of the emerging American system of manufacturers that was the precursor of mass production. Because these craft values had not established such long-term roots in US society, mass production techniques were adopted more uncritically and rapidly. As Nathan Rosenberg has remarked, "the American system of manufacturers was above all, a totally unsentimental approach to the productive process in industry."[16]

By the peak of craft production in the United States, the small entrepreneurial American firms that dominated it were the product of at least three hundred years of (mostly European) organizational evolution away from family- and kinship-based commercial relationships. Many significant modifications were involved in this long process, but perhaps the most important was the change in the location of the workplace from the craftworker's shop to the factory. Rosenberg and Birdzell point out how this transformation set the stage for the mass production era:

At the beginning of the nineteenth century, most finished goods in Europe and the United States still came from workshops in which the owner had not become wholly specialized to a commercial and financial role, but rather had personal knowledge of the production processes and kept a personal hand on production work. In the guild tradition, the workshop owner was called, for example, an ironmaster or a master potter with connotations of applied personal skill that did not become a mere figure of speech until the latter half of the nineteenth century.

Many of the workshops were no more than cottages where an individual worker and his or her family applied their skills to materials supplied by a merchant trader. Nor was this unity of the workplace and the household limited to rural cottage industry. In the towns, under the guild system, it was more typical than exceptional for the master to live and work in the same building and for the apprentices and journeymen to live in this same household. The factory owners who, a little later, supplied housing for their workers (in so-called company towns) were following an earlier guild practice on a larger scale. The degree to which a worker was treated less as a stranger and more as a member of the master's family must have depended partly on the size of the enterprise, as it still does on farms. The social distance between the owner and employees in these workshops was no doubt appreciable from the beginning, but the rise of factories sharply increased the gap, not simply by interposing a hierarchy of foremen and foreladies, superintendents, and managers between worker and owner, but by the differentiation of roles and by separation within the community. The owner no longer knew how to do the employees' many specialized tasks, and most of the employees were even further out of touch with the financial and commercial problems which preempted the owner's attention.[17]

Table 3.2 helps us understand why the owner-entrepreneur and his craft workers began to drift apart. The flexibility associated with craft production was attained at substantial cost-inefficiency. This tradeoff was not only acceptable in simpler times, it was advantageous. Inevitably, however, the autonomy and discretion regarding the design of work that was granted the craftworkers by their owner-entrepreneurs was challenged by the (even then) growing complexity of technological innovation (e.g. new forms of energy, advances in production tools). In this new environment, factories were more efficient than the kinship/family production organization had been. But efficiency did not come without its own significant price – the loss of organizational trust. The operation of the ever larger and more complicated factories demanded more rules. As Francis Fukuyama has observed, craft production was especially vulnerable to the inverse relationship between rules and trust: the more people depend on rules to regulate their interactions, the less they trust each other. On the other hand, retaining trust relationships as part of the proper functioning of the workplace seems to have been a key factor in craft production's survival. In Fukuyama's words, trust relationships were so important to many craftsmen that their demise "could not be compensated by higher wages."[18]

The staying power of trust-based craft relationships is demonstrated by the fact that craft industries have survived and shown a good deal of vitality even in the midst of dominant mass production workplaces. And even in the early factories, craft values and processes were far from eliminated. Workers continued to control much of the pace of work, and their skills still defined many of the details of production.[19] The companies that carried out the craft tradition in its heyday were, by the standard of what was to come, non-hierarchical. For the most part, they still are today. Craft organizations continue to emphasize relatively informal and unobtrusive management. Interpersonal relationships have continued to dominate,

Table 3.2 Innovation in craft and mass production organizations

Craft Production	Mass Production
Strategy: make customized products for individual customer; attain high premiums	**Strategy:** mass production of limited number of commodity products; charge low prices but generate large volumes
Implementation: non-standard inputs; non-standard processes; non-standard outputs; little division and specialization of labor; low level of process automation; relatively high worker skills and discretion; relatively low level of management control; few or no economies of scale; some scope economies based on individual knowledge	**Implementation:** standard inputs; standard processes; standard outputs; high division and specialization of labor; high level of process automation; relatively low worker skills and discretion; relatively high level of management control; high economies of scale; some scope economies based on common components and shared resources or assets
Tradeoff: product–process flexibility over process efficiency	**Tradeoff:** Process efficiency over product–process flexibility

Source: Michael A. Cusumano, "Shifting Economies: from Craft Production to Flexible Systems and Software Factories," *Research Policy*, Vol. 21, No. 5, October 1992, p. 458.

with the consequence that much craft organizational structure remains *ad hoc*. Interactions among workers still depend on a good deal of trust and mutual adjustment.[20]

Very simple self-organization and restructuring has been possible under these circumstances. Indeed, a bewildering array of new forms and interrelationships have been characteristic of craft production. Organizational flexibility has been a requisite, because inputs and work processes have been non-standardized and have required adaptation to customize the craft product, and because there is little or no division and specialization of labor.[21]

As long as the context within which they operated was relatively simple and predictable, uncomplicated and adjustable craft organizations dominated the American economic landscape. Over time, however, these organizations have been limited by the scale and scope of innovative, value-creating activities that the craft owner-entrepreneur could effectively manage, not to mention the increasing speed with which these activities have taken place.

Even though craft organizations have been highly creative, they have had difficulty following through on opportunities. When craft production was at its zenith, fundamental weaknesses began to manifest themselves. Although the craft organization could certainly innovate, it did so by way of individual knowledge, physical skill, and manual labor. Talented craftworkers embodied core capabilities. Value was added, but as we have seen, not in a very efficient way. Inefficiency remains today a major problem for craft organizations. Because craft production takes place serially, at any particular time a good portion of the craftsman's tools are idle. A major reason for the development of mass production was the desire to eliminate or reduce the idleness of craft tools and equipment.[22]

However inefficient the craft organization has been, it also has been relatively self-sufficient, relying on internal know-how. In most cases, the experience and understanding of the craft owner-entrepreneur and those in direct contact with him represent enough expertise and capability to accomplish craft tasks. Thus, there has been little need for craft organizations to engage in extensive search and discovery processes for things like complementary assets.

In fact, there have been strong barriers to engaging in external relationships of any kind, especially when innovation is the objective. Much craft learning has always taken place through apprenticeship, and many craft skills have been quite complex, requiring some time to learn. Formal education often has not been as relevant as learning by doing. Long practice and experience have been required to master tasks which may be ill-defined and based in tacit knowledge. At the end of this time-consuming process, artisans have been valued for their in-depth understanding and talent. Such apprentice-communicated learning has been quite innovative, but it has been difficult to share the knowledge with others, if sharing was ever the objective. Often sharing has not been the goal. Rather, skills acquired after long apprenticeship can be and have been used in a monopolistic way; for instance, to increase prices or restrict employment.[23] Equally damaging, the apprenticeship system has often built in a resistance to newer techniques or methods that might reside in other organizations. For these reasons, craft organizations have tended to be relatively isolated, except for their linkages to small, specialized suppliers or users.

As we have said, however, the craft tradition has shown a great resilience over time and is present in some strength today. The persistence of craft traditions has been impressive. For instance, Edward Nell reminds us that craft production continued to dominate even the American aircraft and shipbuilding industries until the "hot-house pressure of war-time mobilization" triggered a shift to mass production between 1939 and 1940.[24]

Mass production

The conceptual core of mass production is the analytical (i.e. reductionist) model that has structured modern science throughout its three hundred year history. This model posits a finite physical world that can be understood by analysis, by division into component parts, and ultimately by finding the most elemental part. As the model was applied to mass production, its finite boundaries were established by known products. Mass production came to mean the division of each product into its components, which are standardized, and learning how to make and assemble each of these parts in the most efficient way to make the whole. It has been assumed that mass production is (or eventually will be) susceptible to complete rational understanding and management. The strategic implications of these assumptions are shown in Table 3.2.

At the lowest level in the mass production organization, the assembly line tasks, each function is described in detail. Specialization and division of labor are extremely high, and although specialization changes as one moves up the organizational hierarchy, the basic objective does not: generating process efficiency (and, by implication, trading off flexibility). The division of labor assigns to managers and staff experts (i.e. industrial engineers or financial specialists) the responsibility for analysis, while workers are left to concentrate on doing their particular task and nothing more. Work should be organized and conducted systematically and in a logical sequence, under tight supervision. Similarly, communication is tightly controlled and is rigidly hierarchical in both its collection and its dissemination. Ultimately, the overall process efficiency is to be accomplished by achieving perfect efficiency in each segment of the production process.[25]

As was the case with the growth of science, when the mass production system grew in scale and complexity, it was necessary to further divide and subdivide tasks and narrow the scope of the specialists who defined and managed them. It was thought that mass production could escape dependence on tacit knowledge, but this never happened.

The corporate "combine" organization (i.e. the centralized merger of previously entrepreneurial firms) which first undertook mass production (often called "Fordist" because of Henry Ford's initial success) reflected the influence of science and rationality. "Scientific management" and related models dominated this period of innovation. There was considerable variation from one economic sector to another – from Standard Oil to Western Union – but organizational design was always analytical, hierarchical, and characterized by linear processes:

> Linearization of productive activities has been historically considered the main way to increase the specialization of productive assets and to reduce idle-times in transferring parts within the production cycle.
>
> Fordism, as a full application of the scientific division of labor, was the massive linearization of all of the productive activities. It became a way of controlling the internal organization of the plants, but it also became the way to control industry organization.[26]

Indeed, the almost frantic search by corporate combines for new ways to control the production system in the period after 1870 has been termed a "control revolution" in America. This was the beginning of the era of bureaucracies, with the hope that their "rationalized" procedures and rules would lead to efficiency. It was also the beginning of the development of the means of acquiring, storing, retrieving, and analyzing information for the coordination and integration of the means of production.[27]

The Ford Motor Company was the prototype combine in the early twentieth century. As it developed, functional departments such as engineering and purchasing were created and ever more control was exerted over employees by techniques of organization. In combination with assembly line production, Ford was able to operationalize its "five principles of power": accuracy, economy, system, continuity, and speed. These were Henry Ford's key elements of mass production. As they came to be understood by other innovative organizations in the United States and abroad, they changed the world.[28]

Eventually, however, the division of labor and the emphasis on organizational control proved deadly to adaptability and flexibility in the combine. The conservatism of much mass production in the combine era led to what Daniel Boorstin characterized as "frozen modes" of organization.[29] Organizational control of this sort was to become equally difficult for the *conglomerate*, the decentralized, diversified successor to the combine as the dominant mass production organization. Initially appearing in the recovery from the Great Depression and proliferating in response to the post-Second World War economic boom, individual conglomerates have been involved at a given point in time in everything from baking bread to running automobile parking companies to producing high technology defense systems. Strategically, the conglomerate has been primarily concerned with the financial bottom line of its diverse elements, so new mechanisms have been developed for establishing differentiated goals and objectives, as well as techniques for monitoring and collecting various performance indicators from the diverse profit centers. These tools and techniques have been predominantly financial in character, and thus management increasingly moved under the control of financial expertise.

The conglomerate mode of organization provides a way for profit-making corporations rapidly to take on new products and technologies. Frequently this involves the purchase of start-up or entrepreneurial firms. At the same time, conglomerates offer flexibility in disposing of inadequately performing units. Enterprises that do not deliver adequately on the bottom line are usually gone quickly. Not infrequently, the products of such business units have been made obsolete by technological change.

For a time, the conglomerate appeared to provide financial stability in a changing world. In concept, it looked like a conveyor belt; at its front end it could pick up growth companies (frequently created by entrepreneurs pushing state-of-the art technologies) and at its back end it could dump unprofitable operations. Over time, however, the management of eclectic portfolios became increasingly difficult. The decentralized conglomerate, unlike its vertically integrated, centralized combine predecessor, constantly had to juggle differentiated patterns of frequently rapidly accelerating technological innovation, a wide variety of environmental risks and opportunities, and diverse financial performance requirements.

As these disparate and rapidly changing activities became ever more complex, conglomerate management became increasingly difficult. For managers seeking to minimize risk through the exercise of detailed financial control, the changing production environment driven by technological innovation posed continuous threats. Diverse and continuous technological innovation was incompatible with predictability. The conglomerates typically responded by divesting themselves of activities that were not predictable, by emphasizing financial transactions (this pattern took on the label *paper entrepreneurialism*), and by seeking to assure that some large portion of their business was with the government (typically in the form of defense technology programs). William Lazonick has labeled this behavior as the search for "planned coordination of the market."[30] But, on balance, such efforts were wrongheaded and shortsighted. They were wrong because the conglomerates became increasingly risk averse and the search for predictability generated pressures for short-term solutions to what were rapidly becoming long-term technological challenges. Nonetheless, the conglomerate mode was the first US business organization that undertook endogenous change, reorganization, as a matter of conscious and explicit strategy – what we would now call self-organization. Conglomerates did this because they commonly made innovation a much higher priority than combines ever had.[31]

Conglomerates began to see innovation in strategic terms, but even as they altered their view of technological change, their organizational structures began to cause problems. As Lazonick says, "when top executives in US companies were inclined to engage in innovation, they faced increasing uncertainty that their mature organizational structures would be equal to the task."[32]

The largest structural obstacle for conglomerates was their overarching emphasis on linking disparate production activities by the hierarchical processing of financial information. The preeminence of the financial dimension eventually led to an organizational mentality that "began to abandon the idea that corporate activity should be technologically related or linked by common markets."[33]

By the 1970s, many American conglomerates were in serious trouble. As their difficulties multiplied, their concern with the short-term bottom line increased proportionately. Most conglomerates took the path that one study called "the great U-turn," in which they chose not to add to their innovative capabilities but instead to use their financial skills to extract value from existing capabilities. By engaging in unprecedented speculation, mergers, hostile takeovers, etc., conglomerate organizations restructured themselves in ways which eroded the technological capabilities that had previously created value.[34]

As the big conglomerates lost ground in the late 1970s and early 1980s, a popular thesis in the United States was that small entrepreneurial firms, with their typical innovativeness, would carry the day. The explanation (or hope) was that a group of new, creative, business-technical entrepreneurs such as Steven Jobs, one of the founders of Apple Computer, would lead a national rally. It was taken for granted that the United States continued to be the location of the technological frontier in fields like biotechnology and semiconductors. The myth that the "Lone Ranger" companies in places like Silicon Valley could succeed where the conglomerates were having trouble was a widespread but, unfortunately, little investigated tenet.[35]

It quickly became obvious that the context in which entrepreneurial firms of the 1980s had to operate had changed radically from the environment a century earlier. The innovation of complex technologies had come to require teamwork. It demanded the ability to tap and gain synthesis from a wide variety of capabilities and assets. Finally, for firms to succeed over the long term required resources of substantial magnitude. The dream that small US start-up companies would be the equal of Japanese and European megafirms faded in the realization that, while US entrepreneurial organizations were good at radical innovations, they were not equally accomplished at continuous incremental improvements in their process and product technologies.[36]

Instead, the organizational form and behavior required for success in a marketplace structured by increasingly rapid innovation-to-obsolescence cycles had to combine characteristics of craft production with some traits typical of the combine and conglomerate mass production organizations, plus more. Time was now critical. Getting to the market first with a superior product at competitive price was becoming the key to success. By the late twentieth century, innovation required the kind of human knowledge present in the entrepreneurial organization more than ever. Yet the complexity of the most important (and most profitable) technological problems and opportunities meant that it was increasingly groups or teams of talented people, not rugged individuals, that could best mobilize these skills and understanding. These complex problems and opportunities demanded the ability to access talent and capability wherever they were organizationally or geographically located. Size was also important, as was stable, long-term support of the kind provided by the successful combines.[37]

Finally, winning in the new global marketplace required the flat, horizontal organizational linkages pioneered by the innovative conglomerates. But now those linkages had to be much more complex, facilitating information and knowledge flows and synthesis that went far beyond the needs of financial management. Above all, successful technological innovation obliged people to interact with each other over time. It made communication, both horizontal and vertical, an absolute necessity, so that each of the parts of the organization was knowledgeable about and supportive of the others.

The new bottom line for innovation was that no single organization could keep pace in all the areas relevant to commercialization for any extended period of time. Even the largest conglomerates could not simultaneously mobilize a wide variety of innovative capabilities and link them to expertise wherever it resided around the globe. Technological innovation had made existing organizational boundaries obsolete.

By the late 1980s, then, it was obvious to many observers that existing organizational arrangements in the United States were inadequate for the innovation of complex processes and products. Too many American companies were still making tradeoffs to achieve short-term efficiencies that were costly for continuous innovation. Many had begun to seek increased government intervention as a means to making their environment more predictable. To a growing number of students of US commercialization, all these developments suggested the need for a new type of innovative organization. What would it look like, and how would it come into being? How would it evolve?

Entering the synthetic production era

We noted earlier in this chapter that synthetic production involves teams of multiskilled people using flexible, increasingly automated machines to design and make a large variety and relatively high volume of products on the same production line. In the synthetic production mode, competitive advantage is determined by speed to the market, and by the ability to satisfy customer preferences and tastes. The key to success is continuous, intermingled process and product innovation that combines many of the advantages of craft and mass production, while avoiding most of their liabilities.[38]

Whereas mass production was dependent upon high volumes and long production runs to make products, success in synthetic production rests on making rapid innovations in process systems to deliver new capabilities, improved quality, enhanced performance, lower cost products, or some combination of the three.

Some have termed this "lean production," because factories in Japan proved they could develop, produce, and distribute products with half or less the human effort, space, tools, time, and overall expense that had previously been necessary. The idea of lean production originated with the most comprehensive study of the international automobile industry to date. This analysis found lean production had as its goal the achievement of perfection, defined in terms of "continually declining costs, zero defects, zero inventories, and endless product variety."[39]

Others have argued that the new production paradigm goes beyond the idea of lean, to what is termed "agile" production – a broader view that encompasses not only the factory but the entire production enterprise.

> Agility is accomplished by integrating three resources: technology, management, work force, into a coordinated interdependent system. Highly flexible production machinery is a necessary condition for the emergence of agile manufacturing enterprises, but it is not sufficient by itself to bring them about. Achieving short product cycle times – the rapid creation, development, and manufacture of new products – requires linking these technologies to organizational structures that can fully exploit their power.[40]

Watchwords like agile or lean do capture a good deal of the nature of synthetic production, but they are snapshots of a constantly evolving pattern of human activities that is affecting and being affected by social, cultural, economic, and technological conditions in ways that are likely to have broad implications for innovation in the twenty-first century.[41]

We use the label "synthetic" to encompass both lean factories and agile companies that innovate within the context of network organizations. Networks are structured like spider webs: they link the diverse knowledge of producers, suppliers, and users located in different organizations into flat structures that facilitate rapid exchange and decision making.[42] Networks resulted because the innovation of complex technologies has "communication and coordination requirements [that] are often quite stupendous, and in practice the price system does not suffice to achieve the necessary coordination."[43]

Tables 3.3 and 3.4 delineate the basic characteristics of the lean factory and agile company. These tables reflect, again, the key roles the Japanese and East Asian experiences have played in shaping our understanding of the evolution of lean manufacturing, the agile enterprise, and synthetic production networks.[44]

As significant as the international experience has been, there is every likelihood

Table 3.3 Characteristics of the lean manufacturing factory

Element	Mass manufacturing	Lean manufacturing
Workplace organization	Hierarchical Functional/specialized departments Rigid, inflexible	Flat Multi cross-functional teams Flexible
Job design	Narrow, do one job Repetitive/simplified/ standardized – "idiot proof"	Broad, rotate jobs Multiple responsibilities
Employee skills	Specialized	Multi/cross skilled
Workforce management	Command/control systems	Self-management
Communications	Top down/need to know	Widely diffused/big picture
Decision making responsibility	Chain of command	Widely diffused
Direction	Standard/fixed operating procedures	Procedures under constant change
Worker autonomy	Low	High
Performance measurement	Track record measured by management	Self-measurement
Compensation	Seniority by job classification	Pay for knowledge/ skill/experience
Reward systems	Financial	Multidimensional
Employee knowledge of organization	Narrow	Broad
Leaders	Authoritative	Facilitative
Bargaining	Power/rights-based	Interest-based

Table 3.4 Characteristics of the agile company

Organizational resources	Characteristics
Management: full use of corporate capabilities and assets	• Mutual responsibility for success or failure • Problem solving based on mutual trust, cooperation • Localized decision making capacity
Technologies: totally integrated production process	• Seamless information flows among manufacturing, R&D, etc. • Concurrent, rather than sequential, work processes • Simultaneous process and product development • Dynamic reconfiguration of production processes • Enhanced process control by closed loop monitoring, real-time sampling, diagnostics • Intensive computer modeling of processes to eliminate prototyping, pilot stages • Upgradable products – designed for disassembly, recyclability, etc.
Workforce: maximizing the scope for human initiative	• Knowledgeable, highly trained, empowered workers • Continuous worker training and education • "Social contract" between employer and employee

that the evolution of synthetic production has only begun. Probably the various Japanese and East Asian models will metamorphose into something else in the United States. We agree with Michael Borrus and Stephen Cohen, who anticipate the emergence of a uniquely US version of synthetic production, based in networks perhaps quite different from the East Asian or Japanese ones:

> Our hypothesis, then, is that US firms are not reorganizing themselves by copying or adapting the specific linkage structures that defined lean production in the Japanese environment, even though their efforts are often promoted and conceived in that way. Rather, US firms are attempting to develop new linkages that define alternative production organizations. Information technology will serve to rearrange linkages among firms and their suppliers, partners, and customers, as well as between design, engineering, manufacturing, assembly, distribution, and service operations – regardless of where they may lie relative to the boundaries of the firm. Ford, for example, recently announced a major initiative to move design out of specific geographic and corporate locations and into its companywide telecom network.
>
> Network-supported transactions will overturn the conventional economics of production. Increasingly, networking configurations will come to embody more and more of the production process. Some of these network-supported relationships will be "agile," in the current vogue – capable of being rapidly connected and disconnected as production needs change. But some of these relationships, perhaps the vast majority, will be enduring – that is, capable of supporting the long-term and interdependent sharing of data and know-how that underlies technological advance. Network flexibility will then be central to competitive advantage, for that will shape both the ability of a firm to experiment with new forms of organization, and the knowledge it accumulates along the way.[45]

There is a new, evolving conceptual model at the core of the synthetic model of production. First, the synthetic model is *organic*, as opposed to mechanistic.[46] It is the antonym of the industrial system's analytic model. The synthetic model is characterized by combination, integration, and continuous ever changing interaction among parts. The analytic model is characterized by separation and stable linear relations among its parts. The synthetic model does not offer the order and clarity of the analytic model – it does not allow for deduction from the general to the specific. After the fact, however, the conceptual framework for synthetic production is being worked out, as Tables 3.3 and 3.4 help illustrate. A common thread through these tables and a concept central to organic synthesis is that innovative organizations behave much like autonomous living systems. Thus, we should expect that different firms and network organizations in different countries are responding in different ways to the new model of production.[47]

But the network organizations engaged in synthetic production are clearly a different type of "organism." Network organizations are not only capable of learning, they also apply these "learned means" or problem solving capabilities to technological change in ways that not only manipulate the environment for their purpose, such as extracting additional expertise, but actually adapt the environment to the "organism," as in "locking in" a market for a synthetic product.[48] Organizational synthesis, therefore, generates new knowledge and capabilities as a consequence of human intent and action. Moreover, just as with living organisms that are capable of learning, synthetic production is inherently a *self-correcting* process.[49] However, one must not understate the difficulty of learning and self-correction. Collective learning capabilities in synthetic network organizations are far superior to those of mass or craft firms but, as we will see in later chapters, the learning process remains highly imperfect and filled with failure, untapped discoveries, errors, and discontinuous advancement. So learning must be an inherently trial-and-error process.[50]

Second, synthetic innovation has the *combination* and *integration* of technology, people, and the organization as a cornerstone. Synthesis does not place a higher priority on any one component, such as technology or individual expertise. Rather, the focus is on the coherence of all factors.[51]

Of course, organizational integration, like learning, is an imperfect process. Inevitable tensions exist between efforts to blend organizational resources and the vitality that comes from the highly decentralized, often fragmented exploration and search processes that give the synthetic organization its innovative advantage. How these tensions are resolved and a balance achieved is likely dependent on the particular technological community's definition of the relevant problems and patterns of inquiry for each technological trajectory. Integration takes place around these technological guide posts.[52]

Third, the synthetic model rests on the notion that new knowledge and capabilities can be developed in perpetuity, that there can be *infinite improvement in production*.[53] It presumes this even though the players do not understand how the enhancement of production is to be accomplished in the future. The conceptual framework posits that production is improved by cumulative trial-and-error learning, and by continuously experimenting with new organizational combinations of expertise and skills. Such experimentation places a premium on informal organization, and on the involvement of multiple, shifting sets of teams of individuals working to create new knowledge, adapt to new circumstances, and create new strategic directions.[54]

Finally, synthetic production is inherently *complex*. Synthetic production systems have characteristics similar to those of organisms, and their growth patterns are typically rapid and can be exponential. The high level of complexity causes synthetic production to defy reductionist analysis or deterministic predictability. At least to date, this complexity has precluded the development of an explanatory analytic, reductionist theory. Yet this complexity allows, even promotes, rapid adaptation and innovation. As complexity increases, the opportunities for innovation increase because capabilities and expertise from any place in a production system can be tapped for use in any other location.

The flexibility which flows from these complex organic processes often allows movement from one product to another with little or no cost in resources or time. Frequently, the economic consequence is that new products can be introduced without new capital investments in production processes. In the case of mass production, introducing a new product was likely to generate an exponential capital cost curve: R&D costs were small, but manufacturing costs were huge. With synthetic production, the introduction of a new product means additional capital costs may end at the time a satisfactory prototype is developed (often with the aid of computer simulation).

One manifestation of the capital-cost consequences of this new production is reflected in the expenditure pattern of many Japanese corporations, where more money is invested in R&D than on capital improvements. Fumio Kodama refers to this transition as the movement from "producing" to "thinking" organizations.[55]

Conclusions

The synthetic model challenges most of the "truths" traditionally held by US companies: cooperation is less desirable than succeeding on one's own; labor–management relations must be adversarial (indeed, all relations must be contentious); information is power and cannot be shared; trust makes one vulnerable; there are single technological solutions to complex problems; and markets will appear by themselves once better "mousetraps" are invented.[56] The list could go on and on.

The most important cause of this challenge to the standard American view of technological change is that production has moved toward greater complexity. But what does complexity mean, and why is it such an important concept for technological innovation?

Notes

1. Michael J. Piore, "The Revival of Prosperity in Industrial Economies: Technological Trajectories, Organizational Structure, Competivity," in Dominique Foray and Christopher Freeman, eds, Technology and the Wealth of Nations: the Dynamics of Constructed Advantage, New York: Pinter Publishers, 1993, pp. 322–31.
2. Edward J. Nell, "Transformational Growth and Learning: Developing Craft Technology into Scientific Mass Production," in Ross Thomson, ed., Learning and Technological Change, New York: St Martin's Press, 1993, p. 227.
3. Michael A. Cusumano, "Shifting Economies: from Craft Production to Flexible Systems and Software Factories," Research Policy, Vol. 21, No. 5, October 1992, pp. 461–2.
4. President William J. Clinton and Vice President Albert Gore, Jr, Technology for America's Economic Growth, a New Direction to Build Economic Strength, Washington, DC: Executive Office of the President, February 22, 1993, p. 33.

5. George Stalk, Jr, and Thomas M. Hout, *Competing Against Time*, New York: Free Press, 1990.
6. Michael A. Cusumano and Kentaro Nobeoka, "Strategy, Structure and Performance in Product Development: Observations from the Auto Industry," *Research Policy*, Vol. 21, No. 3, June 1992, pp. 265–93.
7. M. Mitchell Waldrop, *Complexity: the Emerging Science at the Edge of Order and Chaos*, New York: Simon and Schuster, 1992, pp. 327–30.
8. Eugene B. Skolnikoff, *The Elusive Transformation: Science, Technology, and the Evolution of International Politics*, Princeton, NJ: Princeton University Press, 1993, p. 14.
9. Don E. Kash, *Perpetual Innovation: the New World of Competition*, New York: Basic Books, 1989, pp. 16–37.
10. Paul L. Robertson and Richard N. Langlois, "Innovation, Networks, and Vertical Integration," *Research Policy*, Vol. 24, No. 4, July 1995, pp. 543–62.
11. Robert H. Hayes and Gary P. Pisano, "Beyond World Class: the New Manufacturing Strategy," *Harvard Business Review*, Vol. 72, No. 1, January/February 1994, pp. 77–86; Steven Goldman and Kenneth Preiss, eds, *21st Century Manufacturing Enterprise Strategy: an Industry-led View, Volume I*, Bethlehem, PA: Iacocca Institute, Lehigh University, 1991, p. 2.
12. Charles R. Morris and Charles H. Ferguson, "How Architecture Wins Technology Wars," *Harvard Business Review*, Vol. 71, No. 2, March/April 1993, pp. 86–96; Rebecca M. Henderson and Kim B. Clark, "Architectural Innovation: the Reconfiguration of Existing Product Technologies and the Future of Established Firms," *Administrative Science Quarterly*, Vol. 35, No. 1, March 1990, pp. 9–30.
13. Richard Florida and Martin Kenney, *Beyond Mass Production: the Japanese System and Its Transfer to the United States*, New York: Oxford University Press, 1993; Michael Piore and Charles Sabel, *The Second Industrial Divide*, New York: Basic Books, 1984, pp. 19–104.
14. Nell, "Transformational Growth and Learning," p. 221.
15. Piore and Sabel, *The Second Industrial Divide*, pp. 47–8.
16. Nathan Rosenberg, *Exploring the Black Box: Technology, Economics, and History*, New York: Cambridge University Press, 1994, p. 120.
17. Nathan Rosenberg and L. E. Birdzell, Jr, *How the West Grew Rich: the Economic Transformation of the Industrial World*, New York: Basic Books, 1986, p. 152 (emphasis added).
18. Francis Fukuyama, *Trust: the Social Virtues and the Creation of Prosperity*, New York: Free Press, 1995, p. 229.
19. Walter Licht, *Industrializing America: the Nineteenth Century*, Baltimore: Johns Hopkins University Press, 1995, pp. 48–50.
20. Charles F. Sabel, "Studied Trust: Building New Forms of Cooperation in a Volatile Economy," in Foray and Freeman, eds, *Technology and the Wealth of Nations*, pp. 340–1.
21. Cusumano, "Shifting Economies," pp. 457–8.
22. Herman E. Daly and John B. Cobb, Jr, *For the Common Good: Redirecting the Economy toward Community, the Environment, and a Sustainable Future*, Boston: Beacon Press, 1989, p. 11.
23. Rosenberg and Birdzell, *How the West Grew Rich*, p. 174.
24. Nell, "Transformational Growth and Learning," p. 222.
25. Hayes and Pisano, "Beyond World-class," p. 86.
26. Patrizio Bianchi, "Structural Change and Strategic Behavior: Moving from Mass Production to Flexibility," *International Journal of Technology Management*, Vol. 6, Special Publication on the Role of Technology in Corporate Policy, 1991, p. 23.
27. Thomas P. Hughes, *American Genesis: a Century of Invention and Technological Enthusiasm, 1870–1970*, New York: Viking Press, 1989, pp. 298–9.
28. David A. Hounshell, *From the American System to Mass Production: 1800–1932. The*

Development of Manufacturing Technology in the United States, Baltimore: Johns Hopkins University Press, 1984, p. 228.

29. Daniel J. Boorstin, *The Americans: the Democratic Experience*, New York: Viking Press, 1973, p. 547.

30. William Lazonick, *Business Organization and the Myth of the Market*, New York: Cambridge University Press, 1991, p. 50.

31. Louis Galambos and Joseph Pratt, *The Rise of the Corporate Commonwealth: Business and Public Policy in the 20th Century*, New York: Basic Books, 1988, pp. 30–3.

32. Lazonick, *Business Organization and the Myth of the Market*, p. 50.

33. Galambos and Pratt, *The Rise of the Corporate Commonwealth*, p. 165.

34. Bennett Harrison and Barry Bluestone, *The Great U-Turn: Corporate Restructuring and the Polarizing of America*, New York: Basic Books, 1988, pp. 3–21.

35. Richard Florida and Martin Kenney, *The Breakthrough Illusion: Corporate America's Failure to Move from Innovation to Mass Production*, New York: Basic Books, 1990, pp. 1–13.

36. Rosenberg, *Exploring the Black Box*, pp. 135–7.

37. Nell, "Transformational Growth and Learning," p. 223.

38. Bianchi, "Structural Change and Strategic Behavior," p. 29.

39. James P. Womack, Daniel T. Jones and Daniel Roos, *The Machine that Changed the World*, New York: Rawson Associates, Macmillan, 1990, p. 14.

40. Goldman and Preiss, eds, *21st Century Manufacturing Enterprise Strategy*, p. 8.

41. Christopher T. Hill, "New Manufacturing Paradigms – New Manufacturing Policies?," *The Bridge*, Vol. 21, No. 2, Summer 1991, pp. 15–24.

42. Anders Lundgren, *Technological Innovation and Network Evolution*, New York: Routledge, 1995, pp. 77–104; Robert B. Reich, *The Work of Nations: Preparing Ourselves for 21st Century Capitalism*, New York: Alfred A. Knopf, 1991, pp. 87–97.

43. David J. Teece, "Competition, Cooperation, and Innovation: Organizational Arrangements for Regimes of Rapid Technological Progress," *Journal of Economic Behavior and Organization*, Vol. 18, No. 1, June 1992, p. 22.

44. James P. Womack and Daniel T. Roos, "From Lean Production to the Lean Enterprise," *Harvard Business Review*, Vol. 72, No. 2, March/April 1994, pp. 93–103; John H. Sheridan, "Agile Manufacturing: Stepping Beyond Lean Production," *Industry Week*, Vol. 242, No. 8, April 19, 1993, pp. 30–46.

45. Michael G. Borrus and Stephen S. Cohen, "Beyond Lean: an Essay," *IEEE Spectrum*, Vol. 30, No. 9, September 1993, p. 68.

46. Geoffrey M. Hodgson, "The Economy as an Organism – Not a Machine," *Futures*, Vol. 25, No. 2, May 1993, pp. 392–403; Roy Rothwell, "Successful Industrial Innovation: Critical Factors for the 1990s," *R&D Management*, Vol. 22, No. 3, July 1992, pp. 228–9.

47. Richard Florida, "The New Industrial Revolution," *Futures*, Vol. 23, No. 6, July/August 1991, pp. 559–76.

48. James Wade, "Dynamics of Organizational Communities and Technological Bandwagons: an Empirical Investigation of Community Evolution in the Microprocessor Market," *Strategic Management Journal*, Vol. 16, Special Issue, Summer 1995, pp. 111–33.

49. Milton D. Lower, "The Concept of Technology within the Institutionalist Perspective," *Journal of Economic Issues*, Vol. 21, No. 3, September 1987, pp. 1147–76.

50. Giovanni Dosi, "Perspectives on Evolutionary Theory," *Science and Public Policy*, Vol. 18, No. 6, December 1991, pp. 353–61.

51. W. Karwowski *et al.*, "Integrating People, Organization, and Technology in Advanced Manufacturing: A Position Paper Based on the Joint View of Industrial Managers, Engineers, Consultants, and Researchers," *International Journal of Human Factors in Manufacturing*, Vol. 4, No. 1, January 1994, pp. 1–19.

52. Giovanni Dosi, "Sources, Procedures and Microeconomic Effects of Innovation," *Journal of Economic Literature*, Vol. 26, No. 3, September 1988, pp. 1125–35.

53. Ikujiro Nonaka and Hirotaka Takeuchi, *The Knowledge-creating Company: How Japanese Companies Create the Dynamics of Innovation*, New York: Oxford University Press, 1995, pp. 5–6.
54. A. Georges L. Romme, "The Process of Self-renewal by Management Teams," *Human Systems Management*, Vol. 13, No. 1, 1994, p. 55.
55. Fumio Kodama, "Technology Fusion and the New R&D," *Harvard Business Review*, Vol. 70, No. 4, July/August 1992, p. 73.
56. Goldman and Preiss, eds, *21st Century Manufacturing Enterprise Strategy*, p. 12.

CHAPTER FOUR

Complexity

As the twenty-first century approaches, contradiction and paradox are everywhere we look. For example, the metaphor of a "Japan Inc." that would dominate the twenty-first century has been replaced by an image of Japan as the "sick man of Asia." Similarly, the image of America in decline has been replaced by the image of "America the boastful."[1] Our traditional frameworks do not provide much guidance. Nowhere are the inadequacies more evident than in the area of governance, the public–private "steering" of society. Yet as much as we are confused by the process of "complexification,"[2] we are also fascinated by its opportunities and challenges. For every ecological or health hazard that suddenly appears, there is the promise of a new information system, energy source, or pharmaceutical.

Complexity, but especially technological complexity, is at the center of the contradictions and paradoxes that pervade our lives. In chapter 1, technological complexity was defined as any technology that could not be understood in detail by an expert individual, but it was also noted that definitions of complexity have proliferated. One commentator distinguishes more than thirty.[3] Many definitions share the idea that complexity is increasingly a characteristic of systems: integrated entities of heterogeneous parts which act in a coordinated way.[4] The system concept, specifically the notion of technological and organizational systems, is explored in this chapter and throughout the rest of the book.

Technological compexity

There are at least three fundamentally different conceptualizations of technological complexity. The simplest is to measure the number of components. Figure 4.1 shows how complexity, measured by components in a range of manufactured products, increased over the 180 years between 1800 and 1980. For example, the musket which Eli Whitney produced for the US government had 51 components. By comparison, the space shuttle has some ten million.

The second conceptualization argues that looking only at components misses a key part of technological complexity, the cybernetic contribution made by architectures which integrate components and subsystems through sophisticated feedback loops.[5] Increasingly, product technologies have self-adjusting and self-correcting attributes. Modern automobiles have sensors and computers that adapt the performance of the engine to temperature, altitude, and various other conditions. The Model A Ford had no such capability. Cybernetic patterns also pervade the process side of technology. Many automobile engines are now developed through

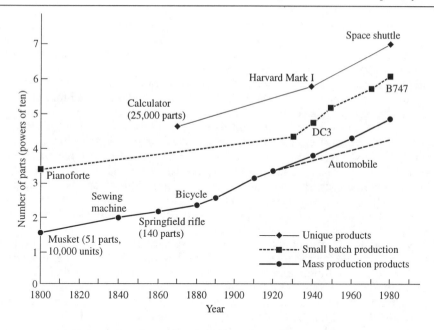

Figure 4.1 Trends in component complexity
Source: R. U. Ayres, "CIM: a Challenge to Technology Management," *International Journal of Technology Management*, Vol. 7, Nos 1/2/3, Special Publication on Strengthening Corporate and National Competitiveness Through Technology, 1992, p. 19.

processes that employ concurrent engineering to increase feedback and interaction in tighter, shorter cycles.[6]

Across the spectrum of commercial technologies, it is now normal for both product and process innovation to emphasize adjustment and adaptation though continuous feedback. By whatever measure of feedback one uses, the trend is toward greater complexity,[7] but there is great variability within that trend. For example, greater complexity in process technology can reduce product complexity. This happened, for example, when changes in Ford's manufacturing system in the early 1990s innovated an engine with 25 percent fewer components.[8]

The third conceptualization of complexity rests on the assumption that, although appreciation of the dynamic interaction between process and product innovation is essential, one must also look closely at the relation between process and product technologies and the organizational systems that innovate them. This perspective highlights the idea of *sociotechnical systems*. Sociotechnical systems feature "coupled social and technical parts which humans erect and operate primarily to control our environment and perform tasks we cannot do without such systems."[9] Using this concept, it can be seen that there are many types of sociotechnical systems in addition to the network organizations that are the focus of this book. National systems of innovation, complexes (i.e. integrated networks, such as the US military–industrial complex), individual organizations (i.e. a modern firm or government agency), and cross-functional teams or work groups are all socio-technical systems. In their most advanced and complex form, sociotechnical systems may involve thousands of highly trained people, very complicated equipment and facilities, and numerous feedback loops. Edward Wenk has said of these systems that they combine hardware, software, and "socialware" in such ways that "the term system is a metaphor for comprehensiveness."[10]

Stephen Kline has sought to gauge the large differences in the level of complexity of sociotechnical systems by formulating an index based on a combination of three measures: (a) the number of ways changes can occur within a technological system; (b) the number of decisions that must be made to design the technological system; and (c) the number of control modes in the technological system, plus those that connect the system to its surrounding environment. "Control modes" refer to feedbacks which result in adaptation. Using Kline's scheme, both technological systems and the organizations that innovate them reflect very large complexity indices.[11] Using this index, Kline has argued that sociotechnical systems are inevitably more complex than the process and product technological systems they innovate.

Again, the notion of technological complexity used in this book is that a simple technology can be understood by an individual expert — can be designed or described in detail by an expert and communicated across time and distance to another expert — while a complex one cannot. The product types summarized in Figure 1.1 are individually identified in Tables 4.1 and 4.2 to illustrate general trends toward complexity from 1970 to 1995. The products and the processes that produce them were assigned to the four cells through consultation with technical experts. These tables distribute the technologies within the same four-cell matrix used in Figure 1.1 (combinations of simple and complex processes and products). With rare exceptions, there was unanimity on the cell in which each product and process type should be located. Where there was disagreement, the product or process was assigned to the simple category, to bias the matrix conservatively with respect to the prevalence of complexity (see the Appendix).

Table 4.1 Most valuable products in world trade, 1970

Simple process/simple product	*Simple process/complex product*
Non-electric machines; crude petroleum; copper; clothing not of fur; iron & steel; power machinery, non-elec.; paper and paper board; organic chemicals; non-cotton woven textiles; ships and boats; textile yarn and thread; meat; coffee; iron and steel shapes; textile and leather machinery; wheat; nonferrous base metal ore; pulp and waste paper; sugar & honey	
Complex process/simple product	*Complex process/complex product*
Petroleum products; plastic materials; machines for special industries; medicinal products	Road motor vehicles; electrical machinery; telecommunications equipment; office machines; aircraft; switchgear for electrical power machinery; instruments, apparatus

Source: United Nations, *International Trade Statistics Yearbook, Volume II: Trade by Commodity: Commodity Matrix Tables*, New York: United Nations, 1975, pp. 17–19.

Table 4.2 Most valuable products in world trade, 1995

Simple process/simple product	Simple process/complex product
Crude petroleum; furniture, parts thereof; aluminum; women's outerwear nonknit; footwear; pearl, prec., semi-prec. stone; meat fresh, chilled, frozen; base metal mfrs NES	
Complex process/simple product	Complex process/compex product
petroleum products, refin.; paper and paperboard; polymerization, etc. prods; medicinal, pharm. product; switchgear, etc., parts NES; non-elec. machine parts, acc. NES; iron, steel univ., plate, sheet; articles of plastic NES; toys, sporting goods, etc.; heating, cooling equipment	Pass. motor veh. exc. buses; transistor valves, etc.; automatic data proc. equip.; motor veh. parts, access. NES; telecom. eqpt, pts acc. NES; office, ADP mch pts, access.; electrical machinery for special indus.; internal combustion piston engines; measuring, controlling instr.; lorries, spcl mtr veh. NES

Source: United Nations, *International Trade Statistics Yearbook, Volume II: Trade by Commodity: Commodity Matrix Tables*, New York: United Nations, 1996, pp. 3–238.
Note: NES = not elsewhere specified.

Table 4.3 Thirty most valuable technological product exports, 1995

Simple process/simple product	Simple process/complex product
$282 billion (14 percent)	
Complex process/simple product	Complex process/complex product
$486 billion (23 percent)	$1321 billion (63 percent)

Source: United Nations, *International Trade Statistics Yearbook, Volume II: Trade by Commodity; Commodity Matrix Tables*, New York: United Nations, 1996, pp. 3–238.

When the data in Figure 1.1 and Tables 4.1 and 4.2 are compared, one result stands out. Fewer than 50 percent of the most valuable products in 1970 are still in the most valuable category in 1995. Moreover, both the complexity of products and the proportion of total value represented by complex products has increased markedly over the two decades (see Figure 1.1). When one considers only the 30 most valuable technological product exports for 1995 (Table 4.3, which excludes nonmanufactured products like crude oil), just 14 percent are simple products produced by simple processes.

The need for a fourth conceptualization of technological complexity became evident when we sought expert advice on locating the technologies in the four-cell matrix. For many of the technologies located in the complex process/complex product cell it is practically impossible to distinguish between process and product innovation. Even Kline's cybernetic formulation is too *analytical* and *mechanistic* to fit the reality of complex technologies. Accounting for system behavior in terms of the functions performed by parts and the interaction among the parts, as was done in helping position the products within the matrix, is useful for identifying growing technological complexity, but it is a too restrictive view of innovation to inform technology strategies and policies for the next century. Rather, improving our knowledge of complexity demands, at a minimum, combining "analytical" and "synthetic" strategies. Analytical strategies involve identifying system components and determining what each does, in order to reconstruct how the system operates as a whole. Synthetic strategies start with the system's behavior and then investigate how a set of component operations might produce that behavior.[12] Our route involved combining both approaches, by examining the network type of socio-technical system using a combination of Kline's analytical formulation and recent work in complexity science and evolutionary economics.

Organizational complexity

The literature on complexity and evolutionary systems shares the emphasis on the inseparability or coevolution of technology and organizations that Kline targets with his definition of sociotechnical systems. Before we examine the linkages between technology and organization, it is useful to revisit the evolution from simple to complex production sketched in Table 3.1. Recall that interaction and interdependence among production, organization, and technology is the historical norm, but these relations have now become so intertwined that they are almost impossible to treat separately.

Contemporary competitive success frequently involves something approaching seamlessness between ever changing technological products and the organizational networks and production processes that innovate them. Some students have emphasized that this merging is essential to "product integrity." Especially for complex technologies experiencing repeated innovation, components, architectures, and subsystems must be integrated so that quality and customer satisfaction are delivered consistently. Integrity requires the synthesis of technologies and organizational systems, because "every product reflects the organizations and the development process that created it."[13]

But it wasn't always so. Neither the entrepreneurial organization of craft production nor the combine or conglomerate organizations of mass production needed integration to innovate. Figure 4.2 suggests their pattern of innovation and why these earlier organizational types could be less concerned about coherence – as long as most valuable technologies were simple, a linear pattern of innovation worked well. As discussed in Chapter 1, for most of the post-Second World War period, the linear model (outlined in Figure 4.2) dominated the literature on organizational innovation.

The linear model in its post-Second World War form assumes research is the precursor of everything else. Prior to the war, the presumption was different. The prevailing view held that invention of the kind associated with Thomas Edison

Research → Development → Design → Manufacturing → Marketing → Services

Figure 4.2 The linear model of innovation
Source: Stephen J. Kline, "Innovation Is not a Linear Process," *Research Management*, Vol. 28, No. 4, July/August 1985, p. 40.

drove later innovation activities. However, both these views of the sources of new ideas and methods shared the assumption that innovation proceeded through steps that were sequential in time and hierarchical in logic and in practice.[14]

Because the prewar version of the linear model saw the heroic entrepreneur-inventor, typified by Edison, as the driver of a linear model of innovation, this view had the happy coincidence for Americans of reinforcing long-held cultural values that stressed the importance of individual effort and enterprise. Many contemporary historians of technology reject the emphasis on the individual. For instance, these historians assert that Edison's well equipped and staffed laboratory was his principal advantage over other entrepreneurs. In other words, by the time Edison and other inventors occupied center stage in the public's perception of US innovation, the organized research laboratory had probably already supplanted their individual entrepreneurial talents.[15]

Scientists doing basic research replaced the inventor-entrepreneur in the postwar formulation of the linear model. Like the myth that was perpetuated about Edison as the source of technological innovation, the preeminence of basic research for innovation is largely a fiction – one that has dominated the conceptualization of innovation during the second half of the twentieth century. The centrality of basic research as the source of innovation has steadily eroded as network organizations have proven superior in the nonlinear and evolutionary processes essential to the innovation of complex technologies.

The implications for organizational networks of the changing patterns of innovation are of major importance for those formulating strategies and making technology policy. The linear model fits well with the organizational pattern integral to most mass manufacturing and to the patterns of many defense and space programs. In this organizational pattern, clear responsibility has been needed for each part of the delivery operation.[16] Unfortunately, the linear model provides little guidance for the organizational complexity needed for much present technological innovation. When research is not at the core of the innovation process and innovation does not take place sequentially or hierarchically, the linear model detracts from effective decision making.

In today's complex processes of technological innovation, the givens are constant risk and uncertainty, multiple feedback loops, surprises and mid-course adjustments, and the like. Success in this context requires users, suppliers, and assemblers to be intimately linked to manufacturing, design, R&D, and servicing. More accurate conceptual models were needed for this kind of innovation, and Figures 4.3 and 4.4 illustrate two that are useful: "chain-linked" and "concurrent" models. Both are nonlinear and reflect a dynamic missing in the linear model. The chain-linked model shows aspects of both nonlinearity and linearity and emphasizes tight linkages. The concurrent model displays the compression of innovation so that activities proceed in parallel, not sequentially.

As with the linear model, both these newer conceptualizations have organizational implications. Both models emphasize the organizational need for *external linkages* among firms, university or government laboratories, other actors, and the market. They also imply the necessity of interorganizational communication.

Yet, even the chain-linked and concurrent models fall short in capturing the information flows integral to the innovation of complex technologies. Whether the purpose is to monitor outside research or assess constantly changing user needs, managing information flows is crucial. When all is said and done, both models are

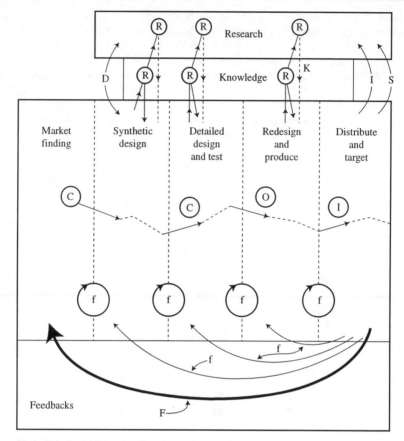

Chain-linked model showing flow paths of information and co-operation.
Symbols on arrows:
C = central chain of innovation;
f = feedback loops;
F = particularly important feedback.
K–R: Links through knowledge to research and return paths. If problem solved at node
        K, link 3 to R not activated. Return from research (link 4) is problematic ---
        therefore dashed line.
D: Direct link to and from research from problems in invention and design.
I: Support of scientific research by instruments, machines, tools, and procedures of
        technology.
S: Support of research in sciences underlying product area to gain information
        directly and by monitoring outside work. The information obtained may apply
        anywhere along the chain.

Figure 4.3 The chain-linked model of innovation
Source: Stephen J. Kline, "Styles of Innovation and Their Cultural Basis," *Chemtech*, Vol. 21,
No. 8, August 1991, p. 472.

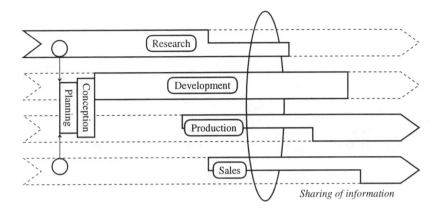

Figure 4.4 The concurrent model of innovation
Source: Ministry of International Trade and Industry, *Issues and Trends in Industrial/Scientific Technology: towards Techno-globalism*, Tokyo: Ministry of International Trade and Industry, September 1992, p. 12.

too analytical in their conceptualization of complex organizational and technological change. Here again evolutionary economics and complexity science offer guidance.

Self-organization

Few concepts are more helpful in providing insight about the network-based sociotechnical systems that are involved in the innovation of complex technologies than *self-organization*. Self-organization refers to the capability of some systems to reorder themselves into ever more complex structures.[17] Nobel Laureate Ilya Prigogine and his colleagues first advanced the concept from their research on the thermodynamic behavior of physical systems (e.g. chemicals) conventionally thought to be "dissipative" (i.e. subject to entropy or increasing disorder). Instead of always finding disordering processes, Prigogine found many examples of "dynamic" systems, experiencing increasing levels of complex organization. Systems far from thermodynamic equilibrium were especially able to counteract entropy by achieving a level of complex self-organization (which Prigogine called "autopoiesis") that enabled further evolution of complex structure.[18]

Later research focused on the role of information exchanges as the basis for self-organizing biological and socioeconomic systems. This insight is especially useful for the study of the sociotechnical systems that innovate technologies, because it fits with much current work in evolutionary economics.[19]

Self-organization would be a key synthetic concept if for no other reason than that it helps explain how some social systems are able to adjust, devise solutions, and create options as their environment changes. Self-organization is especially useful for this book's purposes because it suggests that *sociotechnical systems, especially network organizations, devise technological innovations as ways to overcome obstacles in their environment or create or take advantage of new opportunities*. The increasing complexity of products and processes with the greatest export value (Figure 1.1 and Table 4.3) is linked with self-organizing networks. Such network organizational systems are continuously self-reproducing themselves by developing the more sophisticated skills and structures necessary to innovate technologies that overcome obstacles, or create new pathways.[20]

Today self-organization can be seen as analogous in function to the guiding intelligence offered by the innovator-entrepreneur in earlier times. Self-organization serves the role of 'creative destruction' Schumpeter identified with the entrepreneur. Like Schumpeter's entrepreneur, self-organization challenges orthodoxies.[21] For instance, self-organization strikes at the heart of the assumption made in neoclassical economics that the firm is a "black box."[22] It has long been the conventional wisdom in neoclassical economics that most internal organizational actions are responses to the external environment (e.g. market forces). Thus, for example, organizations have been assumed to have little discretion in their choice of structure.

Increased complexity has made it difficult to maintain this distinction between an internal response and external stimulus. Rather, ideas central to the concept of self-organization provide a better fit with experience. It seems clear that "environmental influences are as much a part of organisations today as are organisational structures, administrative activities or production facilities."[23] Complex organizational systems succeed by a process of self-organization that involves a great many component "agents," including individuals, groups, and suborganizations, being involved in rich interaction with each other and with "outsiders" such as competing organizations.

Organizations that become proficient at monitoring and acting upon the rapid and complex flow of information are the most successful in reforming themselves – by self-organization.[24] Self-organization is dependent upon and central to a continuing learning process. Learning in this context is characterized by what Gareth Morgan calls "systematic wisdom," not an understanding of artificial organizational "causes" and "effects."[25] As used by Morgan, systematic is a synonym for systemic: it pertains to an entire system, as opposed to its parts severally or jointly.

Systematic wisdom makes possible the profusion of temporary networks that quickly unite to exploit a specific technological opportunity – the so-called "virtual corporations." Virtual corporations tap diverse sources of expertise and capabilities for the purpose of achieving a synthesis, and are in perpetual flux, continuously adding and dropping organizational elements. One expert has called this the "Terminator II" organization because it resembles the metal monster faced by Arnold Schwarzennegger in the movie of that title. The monster had the ability to liquefy, then harden again in a new shape: now a man, now a machine, now a knife.[26] Such is the character of self-organizing systems.

Organizational learning

At the heart of self-organization is organizational learning. A learning organization is skilled at developing, accumulating, and transferring knowledge, as well as modifying its behavior and structure to reflect new knowledge and insights.[27] *Self-organization is learning in practice, and synthetic technological innovation is an organizational learning process.*

Aspects of both tacit and explicit knowledge fuel organizational learning. Learning in sociotechnical systems, including organizational networks, is most efficacious when communication is continuous and enhanced by trust and reciprocity. Traditionally, for instance, the critical importance of tacit learning through shopfloor experience has been underestimated.[28] Tacit knowledge is ubiquitous in sociotechnical systems. It resides in individuals and work groups and often provides "connectivity" among bodies of codified knowledge in the learning organizations. In sum, tacit knowledge, teamwork, and group intelligence are central to sociotechnical systems that are successful innovators.[29]

Self-organization based on organizational learning is messy and far from linear rationality. Complex network organizations engage in what Daryl McKee calls "error-embracing" behavior. Many discoveries go untapped, previous experiences must be "unlearned," and mistakes must be viewed as natural by-products of uncertain operating environments.[30] Organizational learning is essential, but imperfect. Network organizations accept that "not knowing" is a constant. As one study puts it: "An effective network can exist only if the organizational thinking advocates that it is not bad not to know, it is only bad not to learn."[31]

The networks that innovate complex technologies normally operate under intense time pressures. Faster product cycles and shrinking ability to capture the benefits of new ideas demand sophisticated collaborative inquiry, self-reflection, and scanning capabilities because agents in networks are involved in an ongoing crisis. Patricia Meyers summarizes the dilemma faced by complex innovative organizations as that of trying to steer innovation in a context of pervasive uncertainties:

> To meet the challenge of technological acceleration firms must learn faster and more effectively because the most successful innovative organizations are also high performance learning systems. Moreover firms must create different ways of learning and of "learning how to learn" under these unfamiliar, dynamic environmental conditions.[32]

In the unpredictable manner of complex systems, the vulnerability conventionally associated with uncertainty frequently becomes a network strength. Faced with uncertainty, the organizational members of networks find the pursuit of fitness requires a reciprocal learning process. An illustration is Chaparral Steel, cited by *Fortune* in the early 1990s as one of the ten best managed factories in the USA. Chaparral, which developed an organic learning network heavily dependent on international linkages, met Dorothy Leonard-Barton's definition of a "virtual research organization." By incorporating expertise from Italy, Germany, Mexico, and Japan, Chaparral can quickly learn how to develop novel specialized steel products.[33]

Critical to appreciating what takes place in learning organizations is recognition that increasingly individual learning is not enough. Rather, continuous learning must occur across the organization. This kind of organizational learning is often said to be one of the advantages Japanese manufacturers have had over their competitors. For instance, in comparing the initially highly touted but ultimately unsuccessful Uddevalla plant of Volvo with the Toyota–General Motors joint venture – the New United Motor Manufacturing, Inc. (or NUMMI) plant in California – Paul Adler and Robert Cole found that differences in the ability to integrate individual learning into system-wide learning were an important factor in the failure of the former and the success of the latter.[34]

Learning among work groups in organizations like NUMMI or Chaparral Steel involves long-term commitments by both workers and companies. Learning both within and among groups involves major emphasis on what some now call the "organizational glue" of networks: good communication. The central advantage of emphasizing teams lies in the reduction of organizational barriers to the communication of knowledge. Freely flowing information is the new "raw material" of innovation. Valuable technologies are now knowledge-intensive, as are the organizational networks that produce them.[35] As complexity increases, the critical knowledge increasingly resides in groups. Maximizing the flow of knowledge and information depends on eliminating fear, fostering a common vision, sense of direction, and understanding of values.[36]

Path dependence

Brian Arthur argues that one of the major differences between natural resource-based, commodity sectors and knowledge-based, high technology sectors is that the latter provide many more opportunities for learning and positive feedback – for applying what was learned to the production of the next iteration of technologies. Arthur says that greater organizational understanding of how to make one product technology can make it easier to innovate products incorporating similar or related technologies.[37]

Learning and positive feedback, then, in combination with high and specialized initial costs, can result in path dependence and "lock-in" and make it very difficult for competitors to displace dominant products and processes. If learning and positive feedback take place rapidly and broadly enough, the first product technology may be the only one of several possibilities that is ever developed. Thus, the choice of technology for use in the initial prototype can be of critical importance.[38]

Alternatively, the first product may lose advantage to later products if the latecomer's innovation features faster and more widespread organizational learning. The most widely cited example of this phenomenon, where positive feedback, increasing returns, and lock-in overcame both a temporal and a technological advantage, is the capture of the video cassette recorder market by a network (led by JVC) producing the VHS format. By most estimates, the VHS format was technologically inferior to Sony's Betamax format. Not only was VHS ultimately the economic winner, the manufacturing and marketing expertise learned and applied in its production also paid off for JVC and its partners when they entered the camcorder market.[39]

Regardless of whether the first innovator or a latecomer ultimately triumphs, it is increasingly the case that path dependence – the history of technological and organizational coevolution – matters. Historical details, often apparently minor at the time, can be amplified by positive feedback and increasing returns, so that once a path has been taken it may become entrenched. In such circumstances, even a crisis may not be enough to dislodge a technology buttressed by strong status quo forces.[40]

Successful organizations continuously engage in purposeful search for and construction of technological capabilities which are built upon their past experiences of success and failure, as well as their future expectations. The advantage goes to organizations that reduce uncertainty by learning and *adapting* through continuous positive reinforcement. In the words of David Teece:

> Successful technological innovation requires complex forms of business organization.
> To be successful innovating organizations must form linkages, upstream and

downstream, lateral and horizontal. Advanced technological systems do not and cannot get created in splendid isolation. The communication and coordination requirements are often quite stupendous, and in practice the price system does not suffice to achieve the necessary coordination.[41]

Although Teece speaks of linkages and coordination rather than networks, the point is the same: *the organizational key to learning and positive feedback is the network* (Figure 4.5). Although they may be supported by other sociotechnical systems, such as national innovation systems, it is networks that connect the diverse expertise in specialties such as design and servicing, connections that are central to complex technological innovation. The groups that hold much of the expertise are linked in all kinds of ways, ranging from face-to-face contact to long-distance communication. Expert groups may reside in a myriad of institutional settings (e.g. government laboratories, corporate manufacturing plants). Finally, links include both formal contracts, licenses, etc., and informal (e.g. personal) relationships. Also, the network is embedded in a larger sociotechnical system, the technology complex.

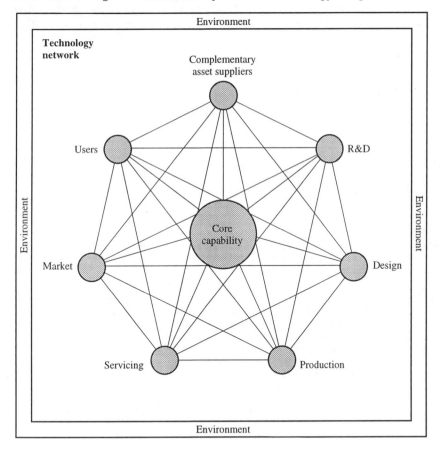

Figure 4.5 The network organizational system
Source: Robert W. Rycroft and Don E. Kash, "Complex Technology and Community: Implications for Policy and Social Science," *Research Policy*, Vol. 23, No. 6, November 1994, p. 619.

Such collaborative connections often appear anarchistic or random. As traditional organizational boundaries erode, distinctions between competitive and collaborative relations in the environment become increasingly turbulent, and some networking seems to be taking place outside the purview of managers. Order is difficult to impose or insure when bonds are informal and cross-organizational. Complexity science suggests that neither chaos nor equilibrium is likely to be found in these systems; to expect either is to miss the final set of key concepts.

Coevolution and emergence

Complex sociotechnical systems and technologies coevolve in the process of technological innovation. Furthermore, these systems generate new emergent properties'[42] as innovation occurs. The synergistic interplay, for example, of networks and complex technologies simultaneously creates new organizational characteristics and new technological capabilities. If the formulations of complexity science are correct in the context of technological innovation, one would expect to see: (a) emergent organizational systems (changing incentives, constraints, and connections); (b) emergent behaviors (new ways of interacting); and (c) emergent concepts (like self-organization).

Examples can be found in the recent emergence of R&D collaborations in biotechnology. These collaborations are fluid networks that are often interorganizational, crossing university and corporate boundaries. Many biotechnology networks begin as informal linkages and then evolve into more formal structures. To date, the predominant explanation for the transformation from casual relationships to more formally organized ones has relied upon the integrating power of the market. Now, however, the concepts of self-organization, learning, and path dependence support emergence as an alternative explanation for cases like the following, from the Danish biotechnology industry:

> [In the beginning] the actors are loosely coupled and their number is variable. Their interaction is free, driven more by accidental opportunities than by precise intentions and organizational strategies. When occasionally shared projects emerge, interactions crystallize into somewhat more durable, committing forms of relationships. On such occasions, elements of structure and order can be recognized, if only temporarily. While they exist, these crystallized relationships act as "centres of gravity," in the sense that they seem to attract more researchers, more often than not resulting in *quite complex crystals of collaboration.* However, it is important to add that first of all many such centres of gravity exist at any point in time, and secondly being part of one such crystal of collaboration does not seem to prevent (in terms of time or loyalty) anybody from participating fully in the current stream of interaction ... The accidental connections described above bring hitherto separate parts of the field to mesh temporarily, reshuffling links of communication and collaboration. Through this, highly unlikely partners sometimes find themselves sharing projects that nobody would consciously have designed.[43]

As this passage suggests, emergence is often the result of a synthesis of "internal" and "external" variables, a merging of organizational and environmental factors. Central to the notion of emergence is the fact that complex networks are not always created either as a function of selection by environmental forces or conscious choices by network members. *Complex network organizations are continually emerging.* A key player in the complexity science community, John Holland, says that these innovative organizations "never get there" in traditional performance terms (e.g. efficiency, optimality) because they are always "in the process of becoming" rather than ever reaching equilibrium for any extended period of time.[44]

As Holland says, there is nothing efficient or optimal about the evolving structures or behaviors of complex organizational networks. Instead, emergence is associated with playing ever changing roles and following constantly evolving rules that facilitate learning and positive feedback. Roles and rules that do not contribute to adaptation must be weeded out if a network is to succeed. Adaptation of this kind must be anticipatory and knowledge-based.

Finally, the process of anticipatory adaptation leading to emergence by any organizational member of a network has the effect of influencing every other organizational member with which it interacts. Each organizational strategy or action aimed at technological innovation alters the context for other organizations and in turn affects their own innovative strategies and actions. This is the process of coevolution, a source of an ever shifting landscape of alliances, rivalries, and supplier–producer–customer relationships.[45] Coevolution even further blurs the distinctions between internally fueled and externally generated organizational change. Taken together, emergence and coevolution help illustrate how self-organization and selection by market forces are two sides of the same coin.

Implications for managers and policy makers

Policy makers and managers at both company and country level have an understandable preference for dealing with simple, linear phenomena under conditions of relative stability, continuity, and testability. For example, US technology policy debates have traditionally simplified physical reality by treating technology in the same manner neoclassical economics treated organization – as a "black box," an exogenous variable, external to the political economy. Arthur has characterized this simplification of technology as follows:

> the notion was that technologies came at random out of the blue, fell from heaven in celestial books of blueprints for making process steel, or silicon chips, or anything like that. And those things were made possible by inventors – smart people like Thomas Edison who sort of got these ideas in their bathtubs and added a page to their book of blueprints.[46]

Defining technology and the organizations that create it in simple terms has allowed highly reductionist analysis to be used in the policy process. Theoretically elegant frameworks were developed, even if they were detached from reality. Technique and analytical procedures came to be emphasized more than conformance with things in the world. The key assumptions of the policy context were equilibrium and stability. Continuity was given much greater significance than change, even in the dynamic area of continual technological innovation.

In part, the emphasis on equilibrium (except for the occasional crisis that could not be ignored) reflected the desire for standardized policy interventions and stable projections in order to reduce political uncertainty and ease concerns about administration and accountability.[47] But above all, simplicity gave primary weight to market forces. In the language of complexity science, the emphasis clearly was on the power of selection acting on the competitive fitness of individuals. There was a good deal of social Darwinism in the policy community's search for simplicity.

Policy models based on simplicity also dovetailed nicely with the dominant American ideology of *laissez-faire*. Simplicity in studying and formulating technology policy guaranteed that for most of the postwar period America's passion for free-market principles would not be overtly challenged. Policy makers put in place a muddled collection of largely macro-level initiatives intended to facilitate the technology selection process (e.g. tax incentives, reduced regulation). An appeal to national security made it legitimate at times to subsidize technologies that had "dual use" (i.e. civilian and military utility), and some of these interventions had results quite consistent with Asian experience and European theory (i.e. evolutionary economics). However, any market intervention of this sort undertaken by civilian US governmental agencies was almost sure to be given the ultimate kiss of death in technology policy: labeled "picking winners."[48]

Slowly but surely the key concepts derived from complexity science have been creeping into the US technology policy debate. The proliferation of complex products in the international marketplace has made it more difficult to continue viewing technological innovation through the lens of simplicity. There are some good studies of the trends toward ever greater complexity, and even a few policy assessments that make explicit reference to complex technologies and organizational networks as part of the changing global marketplace. Few analyses, however, recognize the importance of complexity and translate this into their policy prescriptions for the future, but those that do provide a glimmer of how useful the idea of complexity can be.[49]

Alternatively, the conventional wisdom still suggests that tinkering at the margins of the existing policy apparatus will suffice. The notion that complexity demands radically different policies has little currency. In the words of George Cowan, former president of the Santa Fe Institute, "The moment you depart from the linear approximation, you're navigating on a very broad ocean."[50] In technology policy, America has been unwilling to sail on that sea.

Consider some proposals from the US National Academy of Sciences/National Academy of Engineering system made during the height of interest in considering new national technology initiatives – the year or so after President Clinton was first elected. After making only the most casual mention of increasing complexity, one study emphasizes greater public–private sector cooperation, with the pivotal caveat that "as the federal government seeks to promote technological leadership more actively, it has available only the economic policy levers that permit market forces to play a major role."[51]

Another study mentions complexity in passing, calling for policies to enhance investments in human capital, promote collaboration in "precompetitive" research, and support infrastructure development.[52] A third analysis, the only one to be explicit about growing complexity, suggests the need for "an institutional focus" within the federal government to "monitor, harness and supplement" the existing federal technology programs. Otherwise, the proposals are mostly modifications of traditional market-oriented initiatives (e.g. R&D tax credits, government procurement changes).[53]

These studies, hesitant as they are, pay more attention to complexity than those being done by most of the others involved in the US policy debate. Their weakness flows not from the fact that their prescriptions are too general. In truth, their authors have expended great effort trying to generate specific prescriptions. *A major lesson to be drawn from complexity science is that policies cannot be specified apart*

from the reality in which particular complex systems are interacting and evolving.
To continue Cowan's metaphor of navigation, consider the following comment from
Arthur:

> Actually, you're just the captain of a paper boat drifting down the river. If you try to
> resist, you're not going to get anywhere. On the other hand, if you quietly observe the
> flow, realizing that you're part of it, realizing that the flow is ever-changing and always
> leading to new complexities, then every so often you can stick an oar into the river and
> punt yourself from one eddy to another.
>
> So what's the connection with economic and political policy? Well, in a policy
> context, it means that you observe, and observe, and observe, and occasionally you
> stick your oar in and improve something for the better. It means that you try to see
> reality for what it is, and realize that the game you are in keeps changing, so that it's up
> to you to figure out the current rules of the game as it's being played. It means that you
> observe the Japanese like hawks, you stop being naive, you stop appealing for them to
> play fair, you stop adhering to standard theories that are built on outmoded
> assumptions about the rules of play, you stop saying, "Well, if we could only reach
> equilibrium we'd be in fat city." You just observe. And where you can make an effective
> move, you make a move.
>
> Note that this is not a recipe for passivity, or fatalism. This is a powerful approach
> that makes use of the natural nonlinear dynamics of the system.[54]

Current assessments of national technology policy options in the United States
continue to be built on the "outmoded assumptions" of simplicity. Heavily analytical
and reductionist, these attempts are destined to be futile whether they are presented
in a general form, as in an "institutional focus" that will "monitor, harness, and
supplement" existing programs, or delineated in more specific language (e.g. a
Civilian Technology Corporation that will support development of critical
technologies).[55] Terms like "monitor" or "critical technologies" are useless unless
they are linked to reality – to specific technologies and the organizations that
innovate them.

The four-cell categorization of simple and complex products and processes
(Tables 4.1 and 4.2) illustrates the point. Monitoring the evolution of complex
product technologies is clearly a more demanding task than monitoring changes
in simple ones. Similarly, infrastructure or worker training investments differ
across the simple–complex continuum. And this is just the tip of the iceberg. The
new environment of complex processes and complex products demands, at a
minimum, that policy for complex technologies be fine-tuned to the level of the
"family" of processes and products that together comprise the technological–
economic sector.

It is at the sectoral level that one can observe and "navigate" the complex flow of
organizational and technological evolution. Only at that level is there an opportunity
to be effective, to stick in your policy "oar." Thus, although it may be possible to
successfully develop and implement policies for broad categories of simple
technologies, the appropriate level of analysis for complex technology policy aims
at the individual items displayed in the lower half of Table 4.2 – sectors like plastics
or aircraft – not at lists of "precompetitive" or "critical" technologies. Moreover,
complex technology policy must give at least as much weight to the organizational
dimension of innovation as it does to market selection factors. Again, although it
may be adequate to rely on market forces for the innovation of simple products and
processes, complex technological innovation requires the development of policy

making capabilities to enhance self-organization, learning, positive feedback, and emergence on a sector-specific basis.

A good many, perhaps most, Americans will find this new physical reality discomforting. That is particularly the case given the strong economic performance of the United States in the 1990s, and the widespread belief that the permanent answer to economic success has been found in the market. Unfortunately, this is almost certainly an overly simplistic image of reality. The simple metaphors by which we have lived for so long – the "invisible hand," "the rugged individual" – no longer apply to the commercialization of the most valuable technologies in the global marketplace. There are not yet familiar images to replace these old standbys. Nonetheless, we must change course. Heinz Pagels was on target when he argued eloquently that complexity is the future:

> I am convinced that the societies that master the new sciences of complexity and can convert their knowledge into new products and forms of social organization will become the cultural, economic, and military superpowers of the next century. While there is great hope in this development, there is also the terrible danger that this new salient in knowledge will aggravate the differences between those who possess it and those who do not.[56]

Pagels's warning about the mixture of hope and danger is compelling. Countries that are not able or willing to embrace complexity are very likely to find themselves at great risk in the global political economy. The United States is no exception.

Notes

1. Paul Krugman, "America the Boastful," *Foreign Affairs*, Vol. 77, No. 3, May/June 1998, pp. 32–45.
2. John L. Casti, *Complexification: Explaining a Paradoxical World through the Science of Surprise*, New York: HarperCollins, 1994.
3. John Horgan, "From Complexity to Perplexity," *Scientific American*, Vol. 270, No. 6, June 1995, p. 107.
4. Stephen J. Kline, *Conceptual Foundations for Multidisciplinary Thinking*, Stanford, CA: Stanford University Press, 1995, p. 16.
5. Mike Hobday, "Product Complexity, Innovation and Industrial Organisation," *Research Policy*, Vol. 26, No. 6, February 1998, pp. 694–9; Charles R. Morris and Charles H. Ferguson, "How Architecture Wins Technology Wars," *Harvard Business Review*, Vol. 71, No. 2, March/April 1993, pp. 86–96.
6. David Woodruff and Jonathan B. Levine, "Miles Traveled, More to Go: Western Cars Have Improved a Lot, but Not Enough," *Business Week*, Special Issue, October 15, 1991, pp. 70–3.
7. W. Brian Arthur, "On the Evolution of Complexity," in George A. Cowan, David Pines, and David Meltzer, eds, *Complexity: Metaphors, Models, and Reality*, Reading, MA: Addison-Wesley, 1994, pp. 65–81.
8. Woodruff and Levin, "Miles Traveled, More to Go," p. 71.
9. Kline, *Conceptual Foundations for Multidisciplinary Thinking*, p. 60.
10. Edward Wenk, Jr, *Making Waves: Engineering, Politics, and the Social Management of Technology*, Chicago: University of Illinois Press, 1995, p. 11.
11. Stephen J. Kline, "A Numerical Index for the Complexity of Systems: the Concept and Some Limitations," in *Proceedings of November 1990 Conference, Association for Computing Machinery on Managing Complexity and Modeling Reality*, New York: ACM Press, 1991.
12. William Bechtel and Robert C. Richardson, *Discovering Complexity: Decomposition and*

Localization as Strategies in Scientific Research, Princeton, NJ: Princeton University Press, 1993, p. 18.

13. Kim B. Clark and Takahiro Fujimoto, "The Power of Product Integrity," *Harvard Business Review*, Vol. 68, No. 6, November/December 1990, p. 107.

14. Nick Henry, Doreen Massey, and David Wield, "Along the Road: R&D, Society and Space," *Research Policy*, Vol. 24, No. 5, September 1995, p. 709.

15. John K. Smith, "Thinking About Technological Change: Linear and Evolutionary Models," in Ross Thomson, ed., *Learning and Technological Change*, New York: St Martin's Press, 1993, pp. 67–8.

16. David J. Teece, "Inter-organizational Requirements of the Innovation Process," *Managerial and Decision Economics*, Vol. 10, Special Issue on Competitiveness, Technology, and Productivity, Spring 1989, p. 35.

17. W. Mitchell Waldrop, *Complexity: the Emerging Science at the Edge of Order and Chaos*, New York: Simon and Schuster, 1992, p. 102.

18. Ilya Prigogine and Isabelle Stengers, *Order Out of Chaos*, New York: Bantam Books, 1985; Ilya Prigogine and Peter M. Allen, "The Challenge of Complexity," in William C. Shieve and Peter M. Allen, eds, *Self-organization and Dissipative Structures: Applications in the Physical and Social Sciences*, Austin, TX: University of Texas Press, 1982, pp. 3–39; G. Nicolis and Ilya Prigogine, *Self-organization in Non-equilibrium Systems*, New York: Wiley Interscience, 1977,.

19. Arthur De Vany, "Information, Chance, and Evolution: Alchian and the Economics of Self-organization," *Economic Inquiry*, Vol. 34, No. 3, July 1996, pp. 427–43; Mary E. Lee, "The Evolution of Technology: a Model of Socio-ecological Self-organization," in Loet Leydesdorff and Peter Van den Besselaar, eds, *Evolutionary Economics and Chaos Theory: New Directions in Technology Studies*, New York: St Martin's Press, 1994, pp. 167–79; Jacques Lesourne, "Self-organization as a Process in the Evolution of Economic Systems," in Richard H. Day and Ping Chen, eds, *Nonlinear Dynamics and Evolutionary Economics*, New York: Oxford University Press, 1993, pp. 150–66; John Foster, "Economics and the Self-organization Approach: Alfred Marshall Revisited," *The Economic Journal*, Vol. 103, No. 419, July 1993, pp. 985–7.

20. Michael J. Radzicki, "Institutional Dynamics, Deterministic Chaos, and Self-organizing Systems," *Journal of Economic Issues*, Vol. 24, No. 1, March 1990, p. 82.

21. Joseph A. Schumpeter, *The Theory of Economic Development*, Cambridge, MA: Harvard University Press, 1934.

22. Richard R. Nelson, "Why Do Firms Differ and How Does It Matter?" *Strategic Management Journal*, Vol. 12, Special Issue, Winter 1991, p. 64.

23. A. Georges L. Romme, "The Formation of Firm Strategy as Self-organization," in Christopher Freeman and Luc Soete, eds, *New Explorations in the Economics of Technical Change*, New York: Pinter Press, 1990, p. 40.

24. Ralph D. Stacey, *Complexity and Creativity in Organizations*, San Francisco: Berrett-Koehler, 1996, pp. 107–17.

25. Gareth Morgan, *Images of Organization*, Beverly Hills, CA: Sage Publications, 1986, p. 254.

26. Thomas A. Stewart, "The Search for the Organization of the Future," *Fortune*, Vol. 125, No. 10, May 18, 1992, p. 98.

27. David A. Garvin, "Building a Learning Organization," *Harvard Business Review*, July/August 1993, p. 80.

28. Ikujiro Nonaka and Hirotaka Takeuchi, *The Knowledge Creating Company: How Japanese Companies Create the Dynamics of Innovation*, New York: Oxford University Press, 1995, p. 49; Ikujiro Nonaka, "The Knowledge-creating Company," *Harvard Business Review*, Vol. 69, No. 6, November/December 1991, p. 98.

29. Wendy Faulkner and Jacqueline Senker, *Knowledge Frontiers: Public Sector Research and Industrial Innovation in Biotechnology, Engineering Ceramics, and Parallel Computing*, New York: Oxford University Press, 1995, pp. 200–12.

30. Daryl McKee, "An Organizational Learning Approach to Product Innovation," *Journal of Product Innovation Management*, 1992, pp. 235–40.
31. John B. Bush, Jr and Alan L. Frohman, "Communicating in a 'Network' Organization," *Organizational Dynamics*, Autumn 1991, p. 33.
32. Patricia W. Meyers, "Non-linear Learning in Large Technological Firms: Period Four Implies Chaos," *Research Policy*, Vol. 19, No. 2, April 1990, p. 97.
33. Dorothy Leonard-Barton, "The Factory as Learning Laboratory," *Sloan Management Review*, Vol. 34, No. 1, Fall 1992, pp. 33–5.
34. Paul S. Adler and Robert E. Cole, "Designed for Learning: a Tale of Two Auto Plants," *Sloan Management Review*, Vol. 35, No. 4, Spring 1993, pp. 92–3.
35. Tuomo Alasoini, "A Learning Factory: Experimenting with Adaptable Production in Finnish Engineering Workshops," *International Journal of Human Factors in Manufacturing*, Vol. 6, No. 1, Winter 1996, pp. 3–19.
36. Alan M. Webber, "What's So New about the New Economy?" *Harvard Business Review*, Vol. 71, No. 1, January/February 1993, pp. 20–42.
37. W. Brian Arthur, "Positive Feedbacks in the Economy," in W. Brian Arthur, ed., *Increasing Returns and Path Dependence in the Economy*, Ann Arbor, MI: University of Michigan Press, 1994, pp. 1–12.
38. Robin Cowan, "Tortoises and Hares: Choice among Technologies of Unknown Merit," *Economic Journal*, Vol. 101, No. 407, July 1991, pp. 809–10.
39. Yasunori Baba and Ken-ichi Imai, "A Network View of Innovation and Entrepreneurship: the Case of the Evolution of the VCR Systems," *International Social Science Journal*, Vol. 45, No. 1, February 1993, pp. 23–34; W. Brian Arthur, "Self-reinforcing Mechanisms in Economics," in Philip W. Anderson, Kenneth J. Arrow and David Pines, eds, *The Economy as an Evolving Complex System*, New York: Addison-Wesley Publishing Company, 1989, pp. 10–17.
40. Robin Cowan and Philip Gunby, "Sprayed to Death: Path Dependence, Lock-In and Pest Control Strategies," *Economic Journal*, Vol. 106, May 1996, pp. 521–42.
41. David J. Teece, "Competition, Cooperation, and Innovation: Organizational Arrangements for Regimes of Rapid Technological Progress," *Journal of Economic Behavior and Organization*, Vol. 18, June 1992, p. 22.
42. James F. Crutchfield, "Is Anything Ever New? Consider Emergence," in Cowan, Pines, and Meltzer, eds, *Complexity: Metaphors, Models, and Reality*, pp. 515–33; Richard R. Nelson, "The Coevolution of Technologies and Institutions," in Richard W. England, ed., *Evolutionary Concepts in Contemporary Economics*, Ann Arbor, MI: University of Michigan Press, 1994, pp. 139–56.
43. Kristian Kreiner and Majken Schultz, "Informal Collaboration in R&D: the Formation of Networks across Organizations," *Organization Studies*, Vol. 14, No. 2, 1993, p. 200 (emphasis added).
44. John H. Holland, "Complex Adaptive Systems," *Daedalus*, Vol. 121, No. 1, Winter 1992, p. 20.
45. Stuart A. Kaufman, "Principles of Adaptation in Complex Systems," in Daniel L. Stein, ed., *Lectures in the Sciences of Complexity*, New York: Addison-Wesley Publishing Co., 1989, pp. 675–6.
46. Quoted in Waldrop, *Complexity*, p. 118.
47. L. Douglas Kiel, "The Nonlinear Paradigm: Advancing Paradigmatic Progress in the Policy Sciences," *Systems Research*, Vol. 53, No. 2, 1992, pp. 31–6.
48. Robert W. Rycroft and Don E. Kash, "Technology Policy Requires Picking Winners," *Economic Development Quarterly*, Vol. 6, No. 3, August 1992, pp. 227–40.
49. Ralph D. Stacey, *Complexity and Creativity in Organizations*, San Francisco: Berrett-Koehler Publishers, 1996; James Wade, "Dynamics of Organizational Communities and Technological Bandwagons: an Empirical Investigation of Community Evolution in the Microprocessor Market," *Strategic Management Journal*, Vol. 16, Special Issue, Summer

1995, pp. 111–33; Larry D. Browning, Janice M. Beyer, and Judy C. Shetler, "Building Cooperation in a Competitive Industry: Sematech and the Semiconductor Industry," *Academy of Management Journal*, Vol. 38, No. 1, February 1995, pp. 113–51; L. Douglas Kiel, *Managing Chaos and Complexity in Government: a New Paradigm for Managing Change, Innovation and Organizational Renewal*, San Francisco: Jossey-Bass, 1994.

50. Quoted in Waldrop, *Complexity*, p. 66.

51. Committee on Science, Engineering and Public Policy, National Academy of Sciences/National Academy of Engineering/Institute of Medicine, *Science, Technology and the Federal Government: National Goals for a New Era*, Washington, DC: National Academy Press, 1993, p. 6.

52. Martha C. Harris and Gordon E. Moore, eds, *Linking Trade and Technology Policies: Prospering in a Global Economy*, Washington: National Academy Press, 1993, pp. 8–10.

53. Committee on Technology Policy Options in a Global Economy, National Academy of Engineering, *Mastering a New Role: Prospering in a Global Economy*, Washington, DC: National Academy Press, 1993, pp. 2–6.

54. Quoted in Waldrop, *Complexity*, pp. 330–1.

55. Committee on Science, Engineering and Public Policy, National Academy of Sciences/National Academy of Engineering/Institute of Medicine, *The Government Role in Civilian Technology: Building a New Alliance*, Washington, DC: National Academy Press, 1992.

56. Heinz Pagels, *The Dreams of Reason: the Computer and the Rise of the Sciences of Complexity*, New York: Simon and Schuster, 1988, p. 53.

PART II

CHAPTER FIVE

Summary of Cases Used in Part II

As part of the research carried out in the preparation of this book, case studies of six complex technologies were carried out. The case studies had two purposes. One was to investigate the utility of the central concepts of complexity science and evolutionary economics in providing insight into the innovation of complex technologies. The other was to investigate innovation patterns evident across a range of technologies and over the lifespan of individual technologies.

The six cases were not selected on the basis of a predetermined set of criteria; rather, they represent the first targets of opportunity available that met the complexity standard. That is, each technology is beyond the ability of an individual expert to understand it in detail or to communicate it with precision across time and distance. The search for these targets of opportunity involved interviews associated with technologies other than those investigated in the case studies. In the following chapters, reference is sometimes made to these additional interviews.

The case studies are spread across four generic categories of technology: (a) mechanical; (b) electronic; (c) electronic-mechanical; and (d) electronic-optical-mechanical. The mechanical technology is the blade for high pressure turbines on General Electric jet engines. The electronic technology is the Intel microprocessor. The two electronic-mechanical technologies are the Sony 3.5 inch microfloppy disk drive (MFDD) and the Clinac linear accelerator for cancer treatment innovated by Varian. The two electronic-optical-mechanical technologies are the Sony compact disc (CD) and the Hewlett-Packard cardio-imaging technology. Note also that two of the cases involved Japanese-based technologies: Sony's MFDD and the CD.

Each case study is structured around what experts judge to be significant innovations. In each study the goal was to gain a picture of the processes of innovation associated with the coevolution of the technology and the organizational network. The methodology used was simple and involved two steps. First, the significant technological innovations were identified and described. Second, the structure and processes of the network were described as they existed at the time each significant innovation was introduced into the market. The goal was to get a picture of how the coevolution process occurred by gaining what were snapshot descriptions at the time significant innovations were taken to the market.

Each of the case studies manifested increasing complexity of the coevolving technologies and networks. The pattern of increasing complexity was evident when the innovations and networks were compared with any of the measures of complexity discussed in Chapter 4. Especially striking was the pattern of increasing network complexity. The case studies are replete with examples of the ever greater diversity of organizations involved in innovating these complex technologies.

Nonfirm network participants are particularly conspicuous. Perhaps just as prominent is the wide range of relationships (e.g. informal agreements in addition to formalized commitments) developed by these diverse network members.[1]

Case study narratives

The following are summary narrative descriptions of the six innovation histories reflected in the case studies and graphs of the six technologies' various trajectories. These are accompanied by outlines of significant data for each technology and its coevolving organizational network.

The Clinac: radiation therapy linear accelerators

Varian Associates' Clinac was first used in 1961 to treat cancer patients, and by the mid-1970s there had been a trajectory transition that saw the previously dominant cobalt-60 machines replaced by the new linear accelerator technology. Over the course of the three decades following its initial innovation, the Clinac went through several significant incremental innovations along the trajectory. In the late 1980s a new trajectory was launched. This involved a synthesis of the previously physics-based Clinac technology with computer-based information technology. The result was the evolution of two parallel Clinac trajectories during the 1990s.

In the Clinac network, Varian is the holder of the core capabilities. These capabilities initially included the capacity to innovate critical hardware subsystems and carry out systems integration. From the beginning, the network has had significant participation by lead users located in the health care system. They have supplied critical complementary assets including such things as knowledge about latent needs. Varian's core capabilities have also been intimately intertwined with complementary asset suppliers, located both in other parts of Varian and in outside organizations such as those that have provided the magnetrons and klystrons that

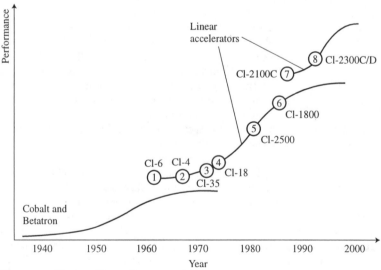

Figure 5.1 Varian Clinac linear accelerators

Table 5.1 Varian Clinac linear accelerators

Time frame	Product/technology	Capability	Network	Public policy
1940s to 1960s	Cobalt-60, Betatron electron beam accelerators	First and primary means of radiation therapy for three decades, precursors to linear accelerator technology	Stanford University, Stanford U. Hospital, specialized suppliers	
1961	CL-6: 6 MV (million volts) X-rays	First fully isocentric (360°) commercial radiotherapy accelerator built in the USA	Stanford U. Hospital, NEC manufacturing license agreement, Clinac user's group	International Atomic Energy Commission, state suggested regulations (advisory roles); federal procurements
1968	CL-4: 4 MV X-rays	Effective cobalt replacement, sealed-off standing wave (SW) guide	Los Alamos Laboratory	
1972	CL-35: 10 & 25 MV X-rays/6–30 MeV (millions of electron volts)	Wide range X-ray/electron beam capability enabled advanced radiotherapy, 25 MW SLAC klystron provided very high energy and dose rate capability	Sponsored cancer research at universities	National Cancer Institute study of radiotherapy requirements
1973	CL-18: 10 MV X-rays/6–18 MeV	Low-cost mid/high-energy unit (low voltage gridded electron gun) with dual mode capability and improved control of output beam		FDA assumes regulatory authority for radiation therapy linear accelerators
1981	CL-2500: 6 & 24 MV X-rays/6–22 MeV	Energy switch enabled high-quality dual X-ray beams from high energy SW guide, extended X-ray and electron energy ranges beyond CL-18 – suitable for advanced therapy at major institutions		
1988	CL-2100C: 6 & 18 MV X-rays/6–20 MeV	Replaced CL-1800, established computerization of the product line, enabled Clinac to become part of integrated system network and viable platform for dynamic radiotherapy	Increased involvement with information management systems organizations	
1992	CL-2300C/D: 6 & 20 MV X–rays/6–22 MeV	Improved treatment versatility and potential effectiveness, extended dynamic conformal therapy capabilities	Decreased number of suppliers, but very intimate relationships remain (e.g. EEV)	

are the sources of the microwave and X-ray power. With the launching of the new trajectory the network has expanded to include computer and software capabilities and the increasingly important health care managers, who in the 1990s are key decision makers as a result of the recent changes in the US health care delivery system.

Cardio-imaging technology

Hewlett-Packard's (HP) development of the ultrasound-based cardio-imaging technology (CIT) began in the early 1970s and the technology trajectory dominated by the early 1980s. Over the course of the decade and a half following its initial innovation, the CIT went through five significant incremental innovations along the ultrasound-based trajectory. In the early 1990s development of a new magnetic resonance imaging (MRI) based trajectory was undertaken. By 1995 a prototype of the MRI-based CIT had been successfully demonstrated and two CIT technology trajectories were in existence.

The ultrasound-based CIT network had HP as the holder of its core capabilities, including: (a) phased array transducers; (b) signal processing; and (c) systems integration. The network has been heavily intertwined with lead users located in the health care system who have supplied critical complementary assets such as knowledge about latent needs. HP's core capabilities have also been intimately intertwined with complementary asset suppliers located both in HP and in other firms, such as those supplying video capabilities and microprocessors.

With the launching of the MRI-based trajectory the network was reconfigured. HP joined forces with the Dutch firm Philips, under arrangements where each held core capabilities in the new network. Philips was the holder of most of the MRI hardware capabilities, while HP was the holder of the electronics, systems

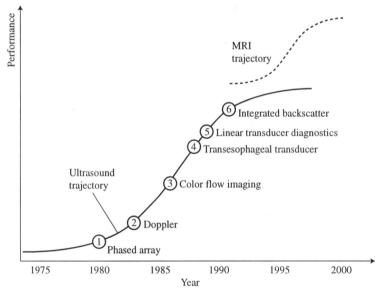

Figure 5.2 HP cardio-imaging technology

Table 5.2 HP cardio-imaging technology

Time frame	Product/technology	Capability	Network	Public policy
1980	Phased array: 64 channel transducer; sweep signal over 90° arc	Transducer, signal processing, system integration	HP Labs, HP Andover, Stanford University	Health care policies, high performance medical technology
1983	Doppler: measures blood flow velocity	Enhanced signal processing	SRI, Houston Memorial Hospital	FDA regulations
1986	Color flow: two-dimensional doppler image	Enhanced signal processing	Duke University Medical Center, NOAA	Uncertainty regarding government/industry cooperation
1988	Transesophageal: locates transducer in esophagus	Improved access	Oldelft, University of Aachen	
1989	Linear array: diagnosis of artery blockage	New transducer	University of Massachusetts, Duke University	
1991	Integrated Backscatter: distinguishes among tissue types		Washington University (St. Louis), U. of Iowa, Stanford Univ.	
Future	MRI: three-dimensional image of heart	MRI-based system	Philips	Uncertainty regarding US health care policy

integration, and marketing capabilities. When the new trajectory had been demonstrated in prototype form, a corporate decision in HP resulted in its withdrawal from the network, leaving the capabilities accumulated during the initial innovation phase with a network that had Philips as the holder of its core capabilities.

Micro floppy disk drive

Advances in floppy disk technology have occurred in increments along a single trajectory since IBM introduced the 8 inch diameter floppy disk drive in 1972. Sony's 3.5 inch micro floppy disk drive (MFDD) was introduced in 1980 and by 1987 it was the industry-wide standard. Sony's initial effort to enter the data storage market was the result of two failed and related initiatives: (a) an attempt to use the magnetic tape storage capability of the Betamax video cassette; and (b) an effort to develop a new word processing system. The MFDD design offered three enhancements over existing floppy disk technology: reduced energy use, increased storage capacity, and a hard plastic case with a cover over the disk access window. Thus, the MFDD drove the then-dominant floppy disk designs and their innovators from the market.

The MFDD network was critical in achieving industry success. The network's core

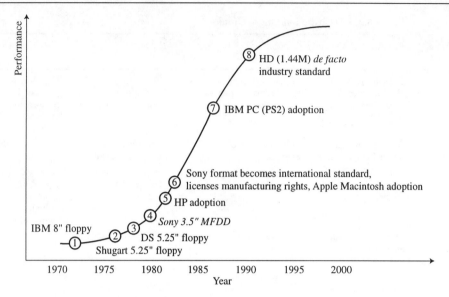

Figure 5.3 Sony 3.5 inch micro floppy disk drive

Table 5.3 Sony 3.5 inch micro floppy disk drive

Time frame	Product/technology	Capability	Network	Public policy
1972	8″ diameter "floppy" disk	Lower cost, portable media for smaller office automation systems	IBM	Public policy played little to no role through-out the evolution of the MFDD
1976	5.25″ floppy	Increased storage capacity	Shugart	
1978	5.25″ Double-density floppy	Increased storage capacity	Several	
1979	400 MB capacity Betamax cassette	Alternative to magnetic tape storage (ultimately failed)	Sony/DEC joint venture	
1980	3.5″ micro floppy disk drive (MFDD)	New 3.5″ floppy format within hard plastic cover, increased storage capacity and reliability	Result of Sony's failed word processing system joint venture, "Series 35"	
1981	3″, 3.25″ MFDD	Competitive products with hard plastic covers (Dysan's 3.25″ has soft jacket)	Hitachi/Matsushita/ Maxell/Dysan	
1982	5.25″ double-sided (DS) disk drive	Doubles 5.25″ capacity	Tandon	
1982	3.5″ MFDD	Major computer company adopts Sony format	Hewlett-Packard/Sony	

Table 5.3 continued

Time frame	Product/technology	Capability	Network	Public policy
1982–3	3.5″ format accepted as industry standard	Sony 3.5″ MFDD adopted after considering four formats; Sony licenses manufacturing rights	US Standards Committee	
1983	3.5″ MFDD	Apple adopts Sony format for new Macintosh computer	Apple Computer	
1987	3.5″ MFDD	IBM adopts Sony format for PS2 PC, ensures industry-wide adoption for IBM PC "clones"	IBM	
1988–9	3.5″ high-density (HD)	HD capability becomes industry *de facto* standard	Several	

capabilities, all located within Sony, included: (a) the disk drive adapted from video recording; (b) media materials derived from experience with magnetic storage; (c) the plastic shell derived from experience with cassettes; (d) the motor from the company's electronics components; and (e) LSI technology from its semiconductor group.

Sony's ability to synthesize a diverse set of in-house capabilities, combined with its desire to increasingly involve a set of complementary asset users greatly assisted in the innovation process. Users from the computer industry provided critical requirements of which Sony had little knowledge. These users included, at various points in time, DEC, HP, Apple, and IBM. In addition, the Sony network was able to win a design competition ultimately judged by an *ad hoc* standards committee established by the previously dominant US industry, in part to keep Japanese companies from the floppy disk market. Also, Sony ensured industry-wide adoption of its design by selling manufacturing licenses to other companies.

Compact disc

Sony's audio compact disc (CD) was initially introduced to the market in 1982 and by 1984 the technology had become the single world standard. The CD trajectory represents the output of an innovation effort initiated in 1977 when Sony and two other companies first demonstrated digital audio disc (DAD) technology. The CD innovation was the result of a self-conscious effort to develop an alternative to the then-dominant analog magnetic recording technology. By 1990 CD sales exceeded cassette tape sales and by the early 1990s they were the dominant medium in the audio recording industry.

The CD network during the critical 1979–81 period when the technology format was being developed had its core capabilities held by two companies: Sony and the Dutch electronics firm Philips. Sony's capabilities were in audio technology and computer simulation and Philips's capabilities were in optics and lasers. The CD network was linked into an international *ad hoc* DAD committee formed by over 50 companies to exchange information about the technology. In 1980 the DAD committee served as the judge in a competition among three candidate formats

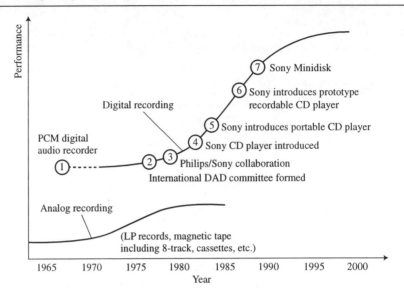

Figure 5.4 Sony CD player

Table 5.4 Sony CD player

Time frame	Product/technology	Capability	Network	Public policy
1967	PCM (pulse code modulation) digital audio recorder	First digital technology proof-of-concept	NHK Technical Research Institute	Public policy played little to no role throughout the evolution of the CD player
1977	Digital audio disc (DAD)		Sony, Mitsubishi, Hitachi; *ad hoc* int'l DAD committee representing 50–70 companies	
1979			Philips, Sony formal collaboration on DAD design standard	
1980	Three candidate formats considered by DAD group: Philips/Sony, JVC, Telefunken		Philips/Sony, JVC, Telefunken	
1980–1	Multichannel digital audio stationary head (DASH) technology	Collaboration on audio sampling rate and other prof. studio recording requirements	Sony, CBS-Sony, Polygram	
1982	Compact disc (CD) player	First commercial introduction based on Philips/Sony format	Sony	

Table 5.4 continued

Time frame	Product/technology	Capability	Network	Public policy
1982–4	Portable CD player	Key industry players cut prices of CD players, Sony introduces portable CD player	Sony, Philips, CBS-Sony, Polygram	
1987	Prototype CD recorder	First product with digital recording capability	Sony	
1989	Sony "Minidisc"	First commercial recordable digital disc	Sony	

concerning which would be the world standard. The Sony/Philips design won. During the 1980–1 period the network included intimate links with the audio production firms CBS-Sony and Polygram, as part of the network's effort to carry the format to commercialization.

Some of the critical technological subsystems necessary to the development of the CD were provided by Sharp, Olympus, and CBS-Sony. The initial commercial success of the CD lasted for a year, at which point sales dropped rapidly. To stimulate sales, prices were cut by two-thirds. Also during this period Sony developed a superior low-cost optical pick-up subsystem which allowed Sony not only to reduce its production costs, but also to become the chief supplier of this required device to most of its CD competitors.

Turbine blade

General Electric's (GE) innovation of blades for high pressure turbines on jet engines began during the Second World War. Initial work focused on the forged turbine blade trajectory launched by the British and the Germans prior to GE's involvement. By the mid-1950s, however, a new cast turbine blade trajectory had been launched and all the significant turbine blade innovations since have taken place along that trajectory. Over the course of almost five decades since GE began incrementally innovating cast turbine blades, three significant innovations have occurred along the trajectory. Further, within each of these innovations many smaller innovations have occurred. For example, at least sixteen different alloys have been developed in the pursuit of ever higher operating temperatures. Between 1950 and 1990, alloy operating temperatures increased from 1550° F (about 850° C) to nearly 2000 °F (about 1090° C).

The turbine blade network began with GE as the holder of both the core capabilities and many of the important complementary assets. Initially, GE followed a philosophy of having all the core capabilities and critical complementary assets in-house. The core capabilities remain today as they were initially: blade design, materials (e.g. alloys) development, and fabrication. Beginning at a fairly early stage, complementary assets were increasingly accessed from other organizations. For example, when GE began using cast versus forged blades, these were acquired from specialized firms. Also, from the beginning, the US military has been a key source of complementary assets. It has worked closely with the network in defining future needs, has provided development funding, and has provided an assured market. In

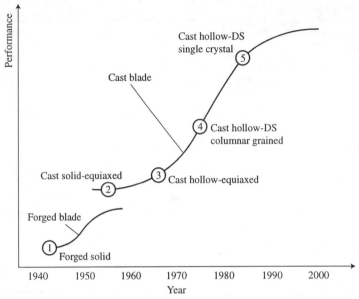

Figure 5.5 GE turbine blade

Table 5.5 GE turbine blade

Time frame	Product/technology	Capability	Network	Public policy
1940s to late 1950s	Forged solid blades: vitallium, nickel-based superalloys	1400–1700 °F operating temperatures; used in engines, J47, J73, J79	Technology transfer from British Royal Air Force to GE via US Army Air Corps	Large federal government procurements, major support of R&D, construction of labs/T&E facilities, DOD and FAA performance standards
Late 1950s to late 1960s	Cast solid-equiaxed blades: austenal process, vacuum furnace (VIM)	1700–1800 °F operating temperatures; used in engines, J85, TF39	Increasing use of subcontractors (casting firms such as Howmet and PCC), commercial aircraft manufacturers	Increased emphasis on monitoring of federal contracts including subcontractors
1960s to mid-1970s	Cast hollow-equiaxed blades: investment casting, mono-shell mold, grainex, microcast-X methods	1800–2300 °F operating temperatures; used in engines, CFM56	Learning multiplier through casting firms shared by competitors (GE and Pratt & Whitney)	Major change in procurement policy toward formalization (due to contracting abuses)

Table 5.5 continued

Time frame	Product/technology	Capability	Network	Public policy
Mid-1970s to mid-1980s	Cast hollow-DS columnar grained blades: CAD/CAM, directional solidification (DS)	2300–2600 °F operating temperatures; used in engines, C58, CF6	DOD contracting reforms cause more "arm's length" relationships with key suppliers	Airline deregulation, disbanding of CAB reduced assured market opportunities
Mid-1980s to present	Cast hollow-DS single crystal blades: hot isostatic pressing, electron beam processing	2600–2800 °F operating temperatures; used in engines, CJ805, GE90	Tighter linkages with major customers (Boeing 777) and suppliers (IHI), cost/profit sharing and other changes in supplier arrangements	DARPA creates UES to facilitate software development of computer prototyping of new turbine blades

the 1990s the network involves a diverse set of complementary asset suppliers and users. What began as a network largely located within GE is today one composed of a very diverse set of organizations.

The microprocessor

Intel's microprocessor was initially introduced in 1971 and by 1978 lock-in had occurred when IBM chose Intel's x-86 format for its personal computer (PC). Over the course of the two decades since the technology trajectory was established, seven significant incremental innovations have occurred using the x-86 format. Each incremental innovation has involved a roughly fourfold increase in capacity derived from a process that involves miniaturization and increased chip size. The next innovation, expected in 2000, will involve a microprocessor that combines both the previous format and a different (i.e. RISC) format on the same chip. Some believe this to be the first step in the launching of a transition to a new technological trajectory.

The microprocessor network has had Intel as the holder of its core capabilities from the beginning. These capabilities have included design, systems integration, and fabrication. The network has always included a diverse set of suppliers, software producers, and users. This is most evident with the symbiotic linkage that has existed with Microsoft, the primary developer of the operating systems for PCs. Over time the network has become ever more diverse as it has become intertwined with potential competitors and with the federal government through the SIA, the SRC, and Sematech. Both the expansion of the network and increased intimacy of relationships were triggered, in part, by a Japanese competitive challenge in the early 1980s. Network intimacy is continuing to accelerate as the complexity and cost of each innovation accelerate. For example, the next microprocessor, the 64-bit P-7 (Merced), is being produced by a network involving both Intel and HP as holders of core capabilities. HP brings to the network its capabilities in RISC technology along with vital sharing of significant fabrication costs. Also, the Intel/HP cooperation is a conscious effort to limit the number of new trajectories competing for the post x-86 market.

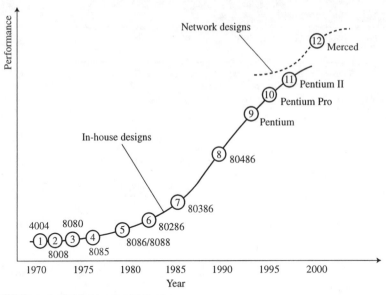

Figure 5.6 Intel microprocessor

Table 5.6 Intel microprocessor

Time frame	Product/technology	Capability	Network	Public policy
1971	4004: 4 bit; 2.3K transistors; 108 KHz speed; 0.06 MIPS (million instructions per second); 10μ (microns) device feature size	First microprocessor on a chip; special purpose application	Intel/Busicom collaboration	Public support via R&D funding and DoD/space market
1972	8008: 8 bit; 3.5K transistors; 200 KHz; 0.06 MIPS; 10μ; silicon gates	Microprocessor for general purpose calculators, bottling machines	Intel disbands design group	
1974	8080/Z-80: 8 bit; 6K transistors; 1.5 MHz; 0.64 MIPS; 6μ	Intel instruction set developed; usage includes first PC (Altair)	Intel, Zilog spin-off	
1976	8085: 8 bit; 6.5K transistors; 5 MHz; 0.37 MIPS; 3μ	Industrial usage broadens to include Toledo scale	Intel/Toledo collaboration	
1978–79	8086/88: 16 bit; 29K transistors; 5–10 MHz; 0.33–0.75 MIPS; 3μ	IBM/Microsoft adopt Intel instruction set for PCs	Intel/IBM/Microsoft	DARPA funds VHSICP for high speed processors
1982	80286: 16 bit; 134K transistors; 6–12 MHz; 0.9–2.66 MIPS; 1.5μ	Movement to specialized capability	Process technology increases from Japan; SRC created	Relaxed view of antitrust; MCC created

Table 5.6 continued

Time frame	Product/technology	Capability	Network	Public policy
1985	80386: 32 bit; 275K transistors; 16–33 MHz; 2.5–11.4 MIPS; 1.5–1.0μ	Shift to process driven innovation; desktop computing takes off; IBM "clones" appear	Chip crisis with Japan	Semiconductor Trade Agreement (STA) ratified
1989	80486: 32 bit; 1.2–1.4M transistors; 25–100 MHz; 20–70.7 MIPS; 1.0–0.6μ	Specialized training; used in high-end desktops, servers	Japan dominates process technology; Sematech created	Half of Sematech support comes from government
1993	Pentium: 32 bit (64 bit data bus); 3.1–3.2M transistors; 60–120 MHz; 100–203 MIPS; 0.8–0.35μ	Increasing importance of packaging and testing	SRC funds $30 million for universities	Limited US support for process technology, STA renewed
1995	Pentium Pro: 32 bit (64 bit data bus); 5.5M transistors; 100–200 MHz; 150–250 MIPS; 0.6–0.25μ		SIA Semiconductor Roadmap developed, Intel begins collaboration with HP (June 94) on next-generation 64-bit chip	
1997	Pentium II: 32 bit (64 bit data bus); 7.5M transistors; 233–333 MHz; 200–400 MIPS; 0.35–0.25μ	Higher-end workstations and network servers	SIA Semiconductor Roadmap updated	Intel funds national labs to advance E-beam photolithography R&D
2000	Merced (P7): 64 bit; 10M+ transistors; 900 MHz-1 GHz; 1000+ MIPS; 0.18μ–0.13μ	High-end workstations, TBD		

Note

1. Rod Coombs, Albert Richards, Pier P. Saviotti, and Vivien Walsh, "Introduction: Technological Collaboration and Networks of Alliances in the Innovation Process," in Rod Coombs, Albert Richards, Pier P. Saviotti, and Vivien Walsh, eds, *Technological Collaboration: the Dynamics of Cooperation in Industrial Innovation*, Brookfield, VT: Edward Elgar, 1996, pp. 1–17.

CHAPTER SIX

Self-organization

For most Americans, the idea that much technological innovation comes from self-organizing networks and other sociotechnical systems is a radical concept. Yet in an era of increasingly complex technologies only a capacity for self-organization makes technological advance possible. Self-organization in the era of synthetic production is the guiding intelligence of most complex technological innovation.

What has happened is suggested by the comment made by the president of Hitachi, quoted in Chapter 1. The Japanese corporation is too complex for an individual to direct. Self-organization is a concept that the Japanese interviewees in our case studies found quite congenial. It is, however, a dramatic departure from the notions of how innovation takes place that have traditionally guided US thinking. The principal view in the United States has been heavily influenced by economic theories that see organizational adaptations associated with technological innovation as linear responses controlled by external forces, in particular responses determined by classical "iron laws" of market supply and demand (see Chapter 2).

A growing body of research, including the case studies developed for this book, indicates that contemporary organizational behavior involves patterns that are at odds with the traditional view. The organizations that are continuously successful in innovating complex technologies are dependent on a capacity for reordering themselves into more complex structures and for using more complex processes. For networks, the evolution of these processes and structures toward greater complexity depends on the interactions and relationships among the network members. For these interactions and relationships to lead to new behaviors (e.g. new innovation patterns), the collection of network members must be self-determining; that is, they must be able to set goals, make choices, and carry through on decisions. Market forces certainly form part of the environment within which the configuration of network participants interact, but those forces do not determine how the interactions evolve.

Self-organization is increasingly carried out through cybernetic (i.e. information feedback) processes.[1] These processes are integral to accessing, creating, and moving the knowledge essential to innovation. When organizations at one level of self-organizing complexity interact with others in the context of emerging technologies, their mutual adaptations with the technologies can lead to another level of self-organizing complexity. Thus, the self-organization of network members at one level creates the next level of complex organization, the network itself. The self-organization of networks, in turn, may have broad societal consequences; for example, scientific disciplines may be modified or new ones may come into existence, or new bodies of law or regulation may be developed.[2] When effective self-organization alters the broader societal factors appropriately, the processes of self-renewal, technological development, and market selection are enhanced.[3]

As mentioned earlier, one of our case studies, the evolution of the Clinac (Varian's linear accelerator for cancer treatment), provides an example of self-organization altering a network's context in ways that enhanced technological innovation and success in the marketplace. The US Food and Drug Administration (FDA), a regulatory agency, entered and participated in the Varian network in ways that contributed to altering the market for the Clinac.

Few of the participating organizations in the Clinac network were desirous of FDA regulatory involvement when it began in 1976. Those initial concerns were reinforced when it became obvious that the FDA did not have enough knowledge of the technology to develop good regulations. Faced with this problem, the agency decided to emphasize the documentation of manufacturing practices, with the goal of learning how to guarantee the production of safe and efficacious treatment machines. The regulatory-driven documentation of the network's manufacturing turned out to be important for the evolving self-organization of the network, because it resulted in a significant conversion of tacit knowledge into explicit knowledge, from which the entire network could quickly learn. Safety regulation had the effect of institutionalizing information feedback mechanisms, which previously had been informal, throughout the network. Partly as a consequence of this FDA focus on manufacturing, the Clinac network was able to improve manufacturing performance. Thus, self-organization involving new participation by a government agency contributed to improvements that made the Clinac more competitive.

The concept of self-organization

Self-organization has become something of a "buzzword" as analysts from numerous perspectives struggle to understand the progressive evolution of complex systems. Although Nobel Laureate Ilya Prigogine's landmark work on thermodynamic systems far from equilibrium is everyone's starting point,[4] more recent research on social systems is of the greatest utility for our purposes.[5] Margaret Wheatley's description of self-organization, at the company level, is particularly useful:

> Companies organized around core competencies provide a good example of how an organization can obtain internal stability that leads both to well-defined boundaries and to openness over time. A business that focuses on its core competencies identifies itself as a portfolio of skills rather than as a portfolio of business units. It can respond quickly to new opportunities because it is not locked into the rigid boundaries of preestablished end products or businesses. Such an organization is both sensitive to its environment, and resilient from it. In deciding on products and markets, it is guided internally by its competencies, not just the attractiveness or difficulty of a particular market. The presence of a strong competency identity makes the company less vulnerable to environmental fluctuations; it develops an autonomy that makes it unnecessary to be always reactive ... These companies highlight a principle that is fundamental to all self-organizing systems, that of *self-reference*. In response to environmental disturbances that signal the need for change, the system changes in a way that remains consistent with itself in that environment. The system is autopoietic, focusing its activities on what is required to maintain its own integrity and self-renewal. As it changes, it does so by referring to itself; whatever future form it takes will be consistent with its already established identity. Changes do not occur randomly,

in any direction. They always are consistent with what has gone on before, with the history and identity of the system.[6]

Wheatley's emphasis on the centrality of *core competencies* to the self-organization of firms holds also for networks organized to innovate technologies. For some time, students of business organization and management have focused on the concept of core competencies (or core capabilities) as the key to an organization's identity. These interrelated sets of expertise, skills, and understanding must be embodied in an organization's evolving structure and behavior.[7] All the elements of core capabilities must be tied closely enough together to ensure self-organization. Otherwise, the network will not be creatively responsive (i.e. innovative) in the face of environmental changes (i.e. external forces).

Core capabilities are what innovative organizations "know how to do uniquely well," and those capabilities provide "a better-than-average degree of success over the long term."[8] An example is the systems integration knowledge central to Hewlett Packard's (HP) cardio-imaging technology (CIT) network. In the CIT case, proficiency in systems integration allowed HP to become adept not only at meshing a variety of other internal core capabilities in fields like digital electronics, signal processing, and medical transducers, but also at linking these to other network competencies (e.g. Sony's video capabilities).

Core capabilities are derived from many sources, and the stimuli for their development may be diverse. On one point there is a near consensus among students of technological innovation: market mechanisms are not sufficient by themselves to create and maintain core capabilities.[9] The factor usually cited as undermining the power of the "invisible hand" to determine core capabilities is the pervasive *uncertainty* innovative organizations face today.

Technological uncertainty is ubiquitous in complex technological sectors, and the risk associated with that uncertainty is important in inducing collaborative and integrative initiatives that often lead to network formation, as shown in Figure 6.1. This indicates how networks may be a response to uncertainties about changes in technologies and appropriability. Networks become more attractive organizational options as innovation moves away from standard and stable technologies and as property rights become less clear. Faced with unpredictable and complex technological environments, networks help member organizations coordinate actions (e.g. learning processes) in ways that share risks. As David Teece notes, "There is no arena in which uncertainty is higher and the need to coordinate greater than in the development and commercialization of new technology."[10]

At the root of the success of the network is its superior capacity to foster collaborative, mutually enhancing interactions among its components. These interactions, in turn, enhance the ability of the network to self-organize and adapt in the face of great uncertainty and risk.

Both risk reduction and rapid learning, for example, were integral to the Sony–Philips joint initiative to develop a format for audio compact discs (CDs). This year-long cooperative effort occurred in an environment where the audio industry recognized that a transition from the dominant analog tape technology trajectory to a digital technology trajectory would take place shortly. In an effort to accelerate learning among more than fifty companies from around the world, the audio industry established the Digital Audio Disc (DAD) Committee to facilitate the sharing of digital information relevant to the audio CD. DAD resulted from the

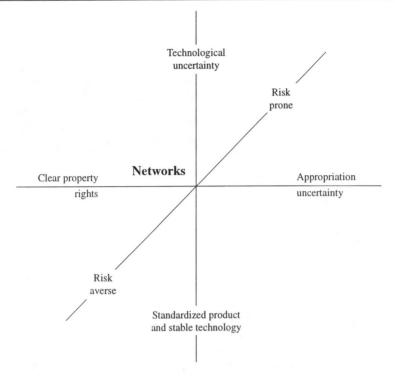

Figure 6.1 Networks, uncertainty, and risk
Source: Chris DeBresson and Fernand Amesse, "Networks of Innovators: a Review and Introduction to the Issue," *Research Policy*, Vol. 20, No. 5, October 1991, p. 365.

recognition that there were benefits to be had for the industry as a whole from reaching agreement on a single digital format. The experience with the competition between the Betamax and VHS formats in the video cassette recorder (VCR) business was important to the CD decision. Specifically, the costs Sony paid by seeking to control the VCR format proved to be very high, and most of the audio CD industry did not wish to take the risks of having to bet on a format that might lose in market competition. Japan's Ministry of International Trade and Industry (MITI) was an important behind-the-scenes actor in supporting this view. As a result, three industry consortia, including the Sony–Philips network, were formed to submit alternative formats to the DAD. Participants agreed, in advance, that the winning format would be the world standard.

A caveat is in order at this point. The focus in this chapter on networks as the key sociotechnical systems must not obscure the broader self-organizing context within which complex technologies are commercialized. Networks are one of an interlinked set of organizational types associated with the innovation of complex technologies. An appreciation of the spectrum of these organizations can be had by examining five categories: (a) work groups; (b) core actors, such as firms, universities, or government laboratories; (c) networks; (d) complexes; and (e) national innovation systems (NIS). Each of these organizational types, which are outlined in Table 6.1, represents a sociotechnical system as defined in Chapter 4. That is, each couples

Table 6.1 Self-organization in sociotechnical systems

Sociotechnical system	*Locus of self-organization*
National innovation system	Social institutions (e.g. communication, education, industrial relations systems)
Complex (i.e. integrated networks)	Technological systems (e.g. groups of complementary, interrelated processes and products)
Network (i.e. integrated formal organizations, work groups, and informal relationships)	Process and product technologies
Core actors (e.g. firm, university, government laboratory)	Core capabilities and complementary assets
Work group/team (i.e. integrated individual skills and knowledge)	Knowledge and skills

multiple social and technical parts into a system which humans erect and operate primarily to control their environment and perform tasks that cannot be done without such systems.

The smallest of the self-organizing sociotechnical systems is the work group. Examples include the constantly evolving multiskilled, multitask production teams associated with concurrent engineering and lean or agile manufacturing. At the work group level, self-organization is driven by the creation and acquisition of new knowledge (both tacit and explicit) and skills.[11]

Next are the firms, university or government laboratories, etc., that normally hold the work groups. These self-organizing sociotechnical systems we refer to as *core actors* because they generally are in possession of a mix of core capabilities and complementary assets which together comprise the major resources underpinning the self-organization required for complex technological innovation.[12] These resources are constantly evolving through a combination of self-renewal and mutual adaptation. The network, in turn, is usually composed of firms and other core actors whose interactions make the network a self-organizing system. As we have seen, most networks have at least some informal (i.e. social, relational) elements, and it is quite common for networks to contain autonomous work groups or even key individuals.[13] A level above the network is the complex. Complexes connect several networks working in the same general technological area.[14] Complexes are roughly bounded by the range of technologies utilized in, for example, agriculture or defense.[15] Finally, a NIS connects complexes, networks, core actors, and work groups with broad sets of social institutions (e.g. educational systems, labor–management relations) that provide the most general context for all technological innovation.[16]

It is important to emphasize that the boundaries of each type of sociotechnical system are likely to be continuously changing and each of the first four types will have multiple linkages to each other. For example, within dynamic self-organizing networks there are usually any number of self-referencing firms, university research institutes, government agencies, and other types of core actors that, in turn, are composed of self-organizing teams of individuals. Similarly, a network innovating,

Table 6.2 A framework for network self-organization

Network resources	Constraining and focusing forces	Emerging innovation patterns
Core capabilities	Organizational learning	Coevolution
Complementary assets	Path dependencies	Technological communities and trajectories
Organizational learning	Complementary assets	
	Selection environment	

Source: Modified from B. Bowonder and M. Miyake, "Creating and Sustaining Competitiveness: an Analysis of the Japanese Robotics Industry," *International Journal of Technology Management*, Nos 5/6/7, 1994, p. 587.

for instance, telecommunications technologies, may become part of a defense complex, or an automobile network may be linked into a more elaborate transportation complex. And at the next level, a medical complex may be connected to broader social institutions like an education system.

But exactly how do sociotechnical systems evolve? In particular, what factors foster network self-organization? Table 6.2 suggests a framework useful for gaining insight into this process. The framework provides reference points used in the discussions that follow in the book. As the table shows, network self-organization involves a continuous interplay among the three sets of factors: network resources, constraining and focusing factors, and emerging patterns of innovation.

Network resources

Any network involved in the innovation of complex technologies has at least three sets of resources: existing core capabilities (or competencies); already internalized complementary assets; and completed organizational learning. Of these, learning is the key, because it is the process by which new capabilities and assets are identified, acquired, shared among network participants, and continuously updated or discarded to give the network as a whole competitive leadership in a particular technological sector.

A successful network must hold some core capabilities; that is, it must excel in some particular aspects of innovation. These aspects may be difficult to learn because of their complexity and tacitness. As we have noted above, among the most difficult capabilities to learn (or to imitate) are those having to do with integrating complex technologies – what is often called systems integration. Given that there are many different ways to organize the designing, prototyping, manufacturing, and marketing of a complex technology, it is obvious that the ability to conceptualize the technology as a whole at an early point in time and carry it through to commercialization represents a powerful, often dominant, capability. The design of a modern airplane, for instance, demands the ability to understand the problems and opportunities involved in integrating advanced mechanical techniques, digital information technology, and new materials, to cite only three of the specialized sets of technologies involved.

Engineering design teams in the aircraft industry typically contain about a hundred technical specialties. Thus, integrating the design activity alone requires a systems capability that may itself constitute a temporary knowledge monopoly built on some of the most complex kinds of organizational learning. Moreover, in something as complex as the design of an airplane, the systems integration competence involves the ability to synthesize participation from a range of network partners (i.e. core actors). There is no way to achieve analytical (i.e. scientific) understanding and control of this sort of complex integration – the competence is, in part, experience-based, experimental, and embodied in the structure and processes of the network. Some have called complex systems integration a type of "organizational technology" that "sits in the walls."[17]

The specific configuration of network resources (e.g. gaps or advantages in complementary assets, high quality or deficient learning of a particular type) is important in determining whether and how the network's members cooperate.[18] An example of how the configuration of network learning evolves and how gaps may appear is presented in Box 6.1.

Box 6.1

The Intel microprocessor case features network learning structured around what is known as "Moore's Law." Articulated first by Gordon Moore, one of Intel's founders, this principle says there will be a four-fold increase in the capacity of semiconductors every three years. Thus, three years has become the rough innovation-to-obsolescence cycle time of the microprocessors innovated by the network centered around Intel as it has moved along the dominant technological trajectory. Acceptance of Moore's Law by the network has provided selection criteria for the information and knowledge that has been sought, created, assessed, and used in the innovation process. As such, Moore's Law has helped structure network organizational learning. And the network's success has been dazzling. Yet network members worry that the dominant pattern of learning may keep them from acquiring the knowledge necessary to adapt to a new technological trajectory in the future.

"Intel's Andy Grove, Inside, " *Newsweek*, September 2, 1996, p. 63.

Constraining and focusing forces

For any network, its history comprises a path dependency that both restricts and amplifies the learning possibilities and the potential for accessing new complementary assets (i.e. sources of knowledge outside the network). The organizational learning that has taken place in the past is a good indicator of where learning is likely to take place in the future. Most networks, therefore, tend to learn "locally," by engaging in search and discovery activities close to their previous learning "neighborhood." Localized learning thus tends to build upon itself and can become a major source of positive feedback, increasing returns, and lock-in. Similar self-reinforcing feedback loops can be created by market selection processes that simultaneously constrain and focus the network's choices about what learning to undertake and what complementary assets to pursue. A network's path dependencies and selection environment thus both restrict and amplify the self-organization process.[19]

A history of flexible and adaptive learning relationships within a network (e.g. with suppliers, customers) provides a participant with formidable sources of competitive advantage. Alternatively, allowing linkages to atrophy or having too narrow a focus on the market can lead to results that are costly. For example, too much weight placed on the short-term orientation of capital markets can kill self-organization and innovation, whereas adaptations that are sensitive to longer-term market forces can contribute to self-organization that is efficacious.[20]

The consequences of rigidity in interorganizational relationships and an excessive emphasis on short-term profits were both evident in several of our US-based case studies. In each instance, however, the networks overcame the problems in significant part through organizational adaptation. Perhaps the clearest example is in the microprocessor case, where an inadequate focus on manufacturing and a lack of cooperation among members of the industry and between the industry and government contributed to the network's inability to respond rapidly to a Japanese market challenge in the early 1980s. When the challenge became a crisis, cooperative industry initiatives through the Semiconductor Industry Association (SIA), created in 1977, not only moved US companies toward closer collaboration with government (e.g. the Semiconductor Trade Arrangement, the Sematech consortium) but also gave the industry a forum capable of undertaking intelligence gathering and coordination (e.g. the generation of strategic industry roadmaps for the future).[21] Thus, initiatives that improved the capability of, and the opportunities for, participants to interact in mutually beneficial ways led to this industry network becoming more "adaptive."

Decisions about augmenting existing resources by manipulating some combination of the constraining and focusing forces are the domain of network strategy. Any network that is successful in continuous innovation is constantly updating its assessments of the mix of opportunities and obstacles that are present in its environment. Strategic choices inevitably affect organizational structure.[22] Thus, evolving alliances with suppliers, users, or competitors mandate changes in structure that most often lead to higher levels of interconnectedness. Box 6.2 illustrates how two traditionally fierce US competitors made major adaptations in their strategies and structures to promote complex innovation.

Box 6.2

Cooperation between General Electric (GE) and Pratt and Whitney (PW) in the development of simulation tools for testing prototype turbine blades represented a fundamental strategic adaptation for both firms. The cooperation was facilitated by the US Air Force, a participant in the jet engine networks of both GE and PW. It was obvious to both engine-producing companies that software which could simulate tests of turbine blade prototypes saved time and money, but effective development of the software required them both to make proprietary information available to a software firm. The Air Force, acting in a marriage broker role, brought GE and PW together with the software producer and turbine blade casting companies. Together they established a network, supported with Air Force funding, that developed the simulation tools.

Network members continuously evaluate their performance in terms of the degree to which self-organizing collaborative processes have constrained or enhanced their organizational and technological resources. If a member company, government laboratory, or university team encounters more problems than opportunities, it will usually exit the network. Decisions to decouple from network relationships are as key to self-organization as decisions to initiate new linkages. On the other hand, linkages associated with network self-organization can have unexpectedly powerful, reinforcing, "bandwagon" effects that take the form of increasing returns.[23] A widely known example is the linkage between Intel's microprocessor and Microsoft's software that was established when IBM chose the two companies to be the primary suppliers of these capabilities for its early personal computers.[24]

Emerging innovation patterns

Self-organizing networks are the source of constantly emerging patterns of innovation. The broadest type of emergent innovative behavior is the coevolution of the network and its technology. Within general patterns of network–technology coevolution, innovation can be seen to emerge in the more focused development of specific technological communities and trajectories.

Coevolution, in which the network organization shapes the process of technological innovation, and that technological innovation shapes changes in the network, is the major emergent property of complex innovation. The key focus of evolutionary economics is on "the properties of economic systems whose dynamics are fueled by the persistent emergence of innovations in products, production processes and forms of organisation."[25] It is the simultaneous evolution of technology and organization that creates novelty, variety, and performance in products and processes *and networks*. The ultimate success of innovation is as much the "selection" of organizational characteristics as that of technological ones.[26]

As a generic concept coevolution involves the interaction of a technological community and an evolving technology moving along a path. The technological community is comprised of those individuals, groups, and organizations that share a particular model of problem-solving for a specific technology path. That is, the members of the community share a common, experienced-based, body of heuristics (i.e. how to do things, where to search) and have broad agreement on the key technological and organizational obstacles and opportunities likely to be encountered in the future evolution of the trajectory. The community will have some consensus regarding how to advance the state of the art.[27] A technological community may be quite small, confined to one firm or even to a work group within a firm, especially following a radical breakthrough, but in most cases of complex technological innovation the community encompasses multiple organizations and networks. Eventually, in the very mature phases of technological advance, the community may expand to include complexes of networks or even broad collections of social institutions (e.g. education systems, legal regimes) at the level of the NIS.[28]

The technological trajectory, illustrated by Figure 2.1, traces the activity of technological advance according to the organizational and technological tradeoffs made in the process of coevolution. Trajectory evolution is the consequence of carrying out, in a particular way, the shared views of the members of the network. Movement along a trajectory is seldom smooth or uniform; typically the process involves encountering barriers and overcoming them in a "bumpy" fashion.[29]

Networks moving along a trajectory will often self-organize by obtaining new resources (e.g. engaging in new learning activities, acquiring new complementary assets) in order to overcome technological barriers. The self-organization to access new complementary assets is so common that it has been suggested that an appropriate metaphor for a rapidly evolving technological trajectory is a collection of constantly "oscillating" assets.[30]

Our case studies suggest that the innovation of complex technologies occurs under three sets of circumstances: (a) relatively predictable, incremental improvements by an established network and technology coevolving along an established trajectory; (b) less predictable movement to a new trajectory by a coevolving established network and technology; and (c) highly uncertain launching of a new trajectory by the coevolution of a new network and technology. In the first case, there is relative confidence among members of the technological community regarding the next two or three advances to be made. In the latter two cases, there is no similar confidence. In these cases, networks must be highly adaptable and their self-organizing capacities are at a premium.

Among students of technological innovation there is growing awareness of the role of self-organization, and especially the coupling of contemporary organizational choices and history. The networks involved in innovation increasingly engage in patterns of interaction that are self-referential.[31] Indeed, these sociotechnical systems *cannot* enter into relationships that are not in part based on the pattern of actions that define them today, and have defined them over the course of their history.

Has self-organization always been present in innovation? If self-organization has always existed, how much of it took place at earlier points in time?

Self-organization in historical perspective

When the conceptual "lens" of self-organization is used to view US history from about 1800 to the 1970s, it is evident *there has always been self-organization associated with technological innovation, and in recent years both have been increasing rapidly.* This finding is evident in the work of a number of historians of technology, economics, and business,[32] but the work of William Lazonick has been particularly informative.[33]

Lazonick's key findings can be summarized in a few sentences. First, there was a time and place where environments (e.g. markets) structured innovation. In the late nineteenth century in Great Britain, the entrepreneurial firm relied almost exclusively on markets to structure all forms of commerce. By the turn of the century, however, growing competition from the United States and other countries had begun the process by which business organizations, in part, superseded markets; that is, organizations partially controlled markets. Change was driven by technological innovation, and as firms and industries sought the "privileged access" to finance, labor, etc. that was necessary for commercial success, they overrode and ignored markets.

During the initial period of these changes, intrafirm reorganization dominated in America as various centralization and decentralization structures were tried. With increased international competition following the Second World War, however, interfirm and interorganizational relationships emerged in growing numbers. This was especially the case as the benefits of the Japanese pattern of industrial cooperation attracted attention.[34] The evolution from markets to "planned coordination" by cooperating business firms and other organizations was aimed less at maintaining high prices or creating barriers to entry (the traditional concerns associated with monopolies and oligopolies) than at *enhancing the capabilities of participating enterprises.*

Key to understanding the historical progression toward interorganizational cooperation is an appreciation that contemporary economies increasingly create value through a process of technological innovation that involves the synthesis of diverse knowledge. Lazonick uses the term "planned coordination" to characterize the more cooperative pattern of relationships among organizations that began following the Second World War. His use of this term corresponds closely to the concept of mutually supporting collaboration that is basic to the self-organization of the networks that have emerged. Whatever the label, continually changing structures and processes became a major characteristic of the dominant US companies in the postwar period. In Lazonick's words:

> Underlying the growth of these dominant corporations was the planned coordination of their specialized divisions of labor – what Alfred D. Chandler, Jr., has aptly described as the "visible hand." Through managerial coordination, industrial corporations were able to develop the combined productive capabilities of human and physical resources in ways that market coordination, with its unplanned interaction of specialized producers, was unable to do. *The more technologically complex the process or product and the less it relied on existing external resources, the greater the corporation's need for the organizational capability to plan and coordinate in order to generate returns.*[35]

If the term "managerial coordination" is replaced with language that is more dynamic and evolutionary, this is a description of self-organization today. However, the dominant US policy debate continues to characterize innovation as over-whelmingly a result of market forces. This formulation sees atomistic organizations being coordinated by the invisible hand of the market. It is a formulation, however, that is now under sustained attack. The attack rests in part on a growing perception that self-organizing networks are the sources of complex commercial technological innovation around the world.[36]

Network self-organization today

Modern self-organizing networks offer the capacity to flexibly and intimately connect technical expertise (e.g. engineering design, prototype development) with social capacities (e.g. political, legal, or financial skills).[37] The innovation of complex technologies increasingly requires the ability to link the technical capabilities of people located predominantly in corporations, universities, and government laboratories with social skills typically found in government agencies, consulting firms, and not-for-profit organizations (e.g. think tanks, professional associations).

General trends

Through cooperative, collective relationships, self-organizing networks are able to influence the shape of their environments and markets. In fact, it is becoming difficult to specify where many network boundaries end and their environment begins. As one assessment of learning in network organizations concludes, "the concept of network may enable us to overcome the artificial division between the economic unit and its environment."[38] None of our case studies illustrates the blurred boundary phenomenon better than the Varian Clinac network, as described in Box 6.3.

Box 6.3

The network centered on Varian and the innovation of the Clinac began in 1950 with a request from a doctor at the Stanford Medical Center to develop a linear accelerator as an alternative to the cobalt-60 cancer treatment technology. Over the years, the Clinac's incremental innovation was intimately tied to one environmental factor – the evolution of medical practice (e.g. the development of new medical specialities, such as radiation oncology, medical physics, and radiation technicians). However, in recent years the capabilities provided by the fusion of the linear accelerator have been increasingly intertwined with the ability of health managers in hospitals and HMOs to exercise increasing influence on how the medical community uses Clinacs. Today, some observers suggest that the technology's present capabilities allow for the development of more efficacious treatment programs than those that can be designed by medical doctors. Even the role of the MD versus the machine is changing. Thus, the line between the network and the medical community is now difficult to delineate.

The blurring of boundaries between the network and its environment is a major reason why cooperative, self-organizing network relationships demand multilateral, "soft" forms of governance (e.g. less arm's length contracting and more flexible relationships).[39] More flexible governance also responds to the need for networks to effectively engage in the synthetic learning through interaction and knowledge creation that has become central to the innovation of complex technologies. Frank-Jurgen Richter says "corporate alliance networks" are able to self-organize because they develop mutual trust and informal relationships:

> cooperative alliances appear as networks of relationships, and demand the creation of particular structures. If they should be enduring, strategic alliances have to be run in an atmosphere of mutual trust that offers conditions for the formation of informally structured networks between sometimes only loosely coupled companies. The companies are no more considering the corporate environment as an absolutely limiting atmosphere to which they have to react and adapt, than they are creating their own corporate environment. This process must be seen as arising from within the corporate system, since the companies are creating the cooperative networks on their own.[40]

Trust and reciprocity are essential for self-organization in networks, and the generation of *increasing returns* is a striking illustration of how reliance on trust-based relationships in networks can lead to successful innovation. For example, the diffusion of credible information among holders of complementary assets and between them and the holders of core capabilities is much more rapid and accurate when they are characterized by high levels of confidence in source integrity and solid faith that knowledge transferred will be returned in kind. Trust leads to cooperative patterns of behavior that, in turn, increase the productivity of knowledge, and thus generate increasing returns.[41] In part, this is because much of what must be communicated and used is tacit. The transfer and diffusion of tacit knowledge often demands sophisticated, intimate and long-term interorganizational arrangements.[42] Of course, the factor underpinning the willingness of many organizations to undertake the fundamental changes in governance necessary for the innovation of complex technologies is the growing realization that the economic benefits can be enormous.[43]

This pattern was especially evident in the Intel microprocessor case. The linkage, for example, between Intel and one of its major suppliers, Applied Materials Corporation, appears long-term, intimate, and rapidly sensitive to both new technological opportunities and changes in the selection environment (e.g. market). The interfirm relationships occur at every level from the production floor to vice presidential meetings to cooperation in the development of the semiconductor industry roadmaps produced under the aegis of the SIA and Sematech.[44]

In a specific instance, Intel and Applied Materials vice presidents meet four times a year to share projections of where they believe their respective technologies will be going over the next five years. At these meetings there is sharing of information that is considered proprietary in the extreme. Only this kind of trust and cooperation allows the network to continuously adapt to the rapid changes that are taking place in the semiconductor industry. To suggest how deeply these trust relationships are now embedded in the network, Intel is considering renting the chemicals used in the fabrication of its microprocessors. That means a chemical company would handle all aspects of chemical use and thus its personnel would be integrated into the day-to-day production activities in Intel's fabrication facilities. In truth, the mixing of Intel personnel with those of suppliers of complementary assets is already so advanced that the only distinction in many cases is the color of their work badges.

The centrality of trust to innovative success was evident in every case study. Particularly impressive is the compelling role trust plays even among the fiercest and most suspicious competitors. Trust interacts with self-interest. Perhaps nothing more effectively illustrates the changes being driven by complex technological innovation than the growing pattern of selective trust, cooperation, and networking among competitive organizations.[45]

The more a network expands, the more pressing is the need for a shared sense of trust, reciprocity, and community among members. Trust allows those involved to transcend interorganizational rivalry and minimize the need for constant monitoring and sanctions to lessen opportunistic behavior. As one study puts it, by creating and maintaining the connectability of social interactions in network organizations, "*trust absorbs complexity.*"[46] With trust, individual and organizational efforts can be focused on the learning process – the acquisition and incorporation of new insights and knowledge. Recognizing that any technology is somewhat path dependent (i.e. heavily influenced by how things were done in the past), shared trust and reciprocity allow the network to rapidly reorder itself by combining and recombining existing core capabilities with new skills, technology, know-how, and expertise.

Often reciprocal network relationships begin as informal linkages and then evolve toward more formal structures. Substantial informality persists, however, even in the most highly structured commercial collaborations (e.g. organized around licensing arrangements, subcontracts). Interpersonal relationships of obligation, common experience, or shared cultural or educational background are important.[47] In fact, Christopher Freeman says that "behind every formal network, giving it the breath of life, are usually various informal networks."[48]

The United States, with its historical emphasis on formidable "walls of separation" between institutions and organizations, creates a hostile climate for self-organizing commercial bonds. Until very recently, for instance, US antitrust law and policy was a major barrier to collaboration among American firms, even to the extent of permitting certain types of information exchange only after a merger of the organizations. This approach was one of many relics of an earlier era when oligopolistic industries operating in largely domestic markets engaged in damaging anti-competitive behavior.[49]

A particularly striking illustration of the antitrust legacy was described to us (see Box 6.4) by an executive of a company we sought to use as a case study. Ultimately, the company decided the risks of loss of proprietary knowledge were too high to participate in our study. One way around the anti-trust restraint that appears several times in our case studies is the initiation of a network by a government organization or the early participation of the government in the network. A clear example is Sematech, which was initially conceptualized by industry but was launched with a high level of Department of Defense involvement and support.

Box 6.4

The company developed a new technology for producing four-color magazine page proofs that ultimately represented a trajectory transition. The transition was from a process that utilized standard photographic technology (e.g. Kodak) to one that used a computer linked to a laser printer that utilized sophisticated software. In the course of the innovation process the company worked closely with other organizations. When the new technology was marketed its network included 25 complementary asset suppliers. Twenty-one of these suppliers were located outside the United States. When asked whether US-based companies could have supplied the assets the answer was, yes. The reason US suppliers were not used was that the company's lawyers suggested there might be antitrust problems since some of the US companies were competitors in other product areas. Cooperating on an informal and intimate basis with foreign companies apparently posed less danger of antitrust action by the US government. The company's attorneys emphasized that there was little threat of antitrust action by the government, but they saw their job as proposing the lowest risk route.

Reforms in antitrust and other areas have reduced some of the obstacles to cooperation in the USA, and as a consequence analysts have begun to pay greater attention to interfirm alliances.[50] However, as Teece understates the problem, studies designed to understand technological innovation in networks "have been somewhat remiss" in analyzing linkages among a wider variety of organizations.[51] For instance, there has been a distinct lack of interest in US networks that have core actors such as government or university laboratories as members. The reasons for the blind spot with regard to interorganizational networks are doubtless multiple.

One appears obvious, however. The dominant ideology in the United States views commercial innovation as the province of companies. In truth, this ideology continues to view coordination and interaction efforts of any kind with great suspicion, including those among competing firms.[52] Given the importance of trust and close cooperation in networks there is instructive value in examining the Japanese track record, where relatively transparent, self-organizing, cooperative relationships have a longer tradition.

The Japanese experience

Japan has made a major contribution to the understanding of self-organization.[53] As networks based in Japan proliferated, they were subjected to considerable evaluation. Lane Kenworthy's comprehensive study of economic cooperation in Japan found the developed world's most extensive cooperation structures and behaviors. Central to this system were innovative networks. The study also found that Japan led the world in economic performance between 1960 and 1990, while the United States and the United Kingdom were much lower in economic performance and last in cooperation. Since much of the Japanese cooperation was a consequence of intentional governmental actions, Kenworthy concluded that "cooperation is a key determinant of economic success."[54] The rapid period of Japanese growth generated a growing body of findings like Kenworthy's.[55] The complex reality of what was taking place is suggested by Ken-ichi Imai:

> During the "rapid growth period" of 1955 to 1964, Japanese firms laid the foundation of inter-firm cooperation which creates a positive-sum game theoretic situation among participating firms. Japanese industries have often developed cooperative vertical (and sometimes horizontal) relationships among firms. The *Keiretsu*, a group of cooperative (and often subcontracting) firms, is an example. A long-term semi-fixed relationship between user and suppliers, or between affiliated firms, subcontractors, vendors, and others enables the participants to share information about the nature of technology and the product involved. The long-run transaction involved in such relationships includes not only an economic component, but also a social one in which trust, loyalty and power are transacted.[56]

As Imai says, the Japanese network organizations succeeded in large degree because of their mutuality, trust, and long-term interactions. Many of the "relational contracts" in Japan establish bonds that routinely transfer the most recent technological knowledge.[57] But make no mistake about it, these factors are balanced by a very hard-nosed approach to business that combines a good deal of discipline with trust and loyalty.[58]

If the Japanese national innovation system encompassed only these interfirm linkages it would be remarkable enough. But there is much more to it. One fundamental idea guides self-organization in Japanese cooperative relationships: government often has been a trusted participant in technological innovation. In fact, government funds and coordinates much commercial collaboration on a regular basis. Public sector funding appears to be a major factor in focusing Japanese cooperative efforts.[59] Government bodies like MITI have induced coordination in this way, but they have also facilitated coordination independent of funding decisions. In fact, the facilitator role may be replacing the funding role. According to Imai, MITI has "coordinated industrial networks by interfacing micro-information in each firm and macro-information of an industry and economy as a whole."[60] Therefore, the proactive shaping of markets by interorganizational networks (either directly or indirectly influenced by government policy) is a socially legitimate commercialization role.[61]

The Japanese approach to shaping markets is illustrated by an examination of the automobile industry. Over a period of about 20 years (1948–68), Japanese automobile companies engaged in a rapid and comprehensive organizational learning process that began with a failed effort by MITI to reduce the number of companies by consolidation. Following that, the policy objective moved sequentially to focusing on manufacturing skills, design, marketing, and servicing expertise. Despite the remarkable upgrading of core competencies in an effort to shape the market, however, Japan's auto production has been path dependent – the long history of making small models with high fuel efficiencies, for example, has locked Japanese producers into certain patterns. Even as learning and self-organization have enabled the companies to continuously improve both process and product technologies and at the same time expand into new product lines, the focus on size and efficiency has remained a dominant orientation.[62] The constraints flowing from path dependency are suggested by the initial success and then erosion of high-end Japanese cars (e.g. Lexus) in the US market. There is substantial evidence to suggest that the American taste for the "speed, power, and status" of the German high-end automobiles remains dominant and the Japanese cars do not satisfy it.[63]

By the early 1980s, as the automobile industry became increasingly global, companies like Nissan, Toyota, and Mitsubishi moved aggressively into strategic alliances with other manufacturers, including many non-Japanese ones (e.g. Mazda–Ford). The central rationale for entering into these interfirm alliances was self-organizational:

> Strategic alliances can help in co-operation and competition simultaneously so that both can win, since an expanding market will offer gains to both partners. Because of strong organizational learning, the Japanese automobile manufacturers, through alliances, increased competencies in which they were weak, much more than their western counterparts. A strong internal parts manufacturing segment and alliances with external firms, together helped Japanese firms to create competitiveness and exploit the world market more effectively.[64]

Coexisting modes of competitive and cooperative behavior, perhaps the most adaptive characteristic of Japanese commercial practice, rest in part on a pattern of intimate government–corporate collaboration. The commercialization roles of public organizations like MITI include helping manage the tradeoff of benefits from fierce competition among Japanese firms against the advantages of cooperation against outside market threats. This balancing process is sometimes called "complementary competition."[65] Thus, after failing to bring off a consolidation of Japan's dozen or so major automobile producers, MITI encouraged them to aggressively seek competitive advantage over each other. At the same time MITI used protectionism, R&D, education, capital accumulation, and many more policy tools to enhance the competitiveness of Japanese cars in international trade.

Throughout its national innovation system, the Japanese government has been and continues to be a major force in enhancing each of the sets of factors in our framework for self-organization (Table 6.2). By supporting complementary competition, the Japanese government has aided in the development of strong and resilient network relationships that have generated new resources, such as core competencies and organizational learning. These networks are also linked to multiple sources of information about new complementary assets and learning opportunities. And Japanese institutions constantly reshape markets and other parts of the selection environment. A result of these system-wide efforts is constant coevolution, as a wide range of technological communities are linked to state-of-the-art information about the movements of existing technological trajectories and the possible fusion of new ones. More than in any other national innovation system, in Japan the government has actively supported the types of self-organization initiatives necessary for contemporary synthetic production.

Conclusions

Both the general literature and our case studies indicate that self-organization is becoming an increasingly prominent pattern in the innovation processes within the United States. An excellent example is furnished by an evaluation of the creation and evolution of Sematech consortium:

> the SEMATECH case contributes to fleshing out the concept of self-organization by showing (1) how systematically members searched the industry for the best practices to use internally and as models for the industry and (2) how members and suppliers were willing to give their knowledge to this cooperative effort ... Our results showed that the founders of SEMATECH came to recognize that a new order was required in their industry to avoid its demise. Their solution showed how open they were to radical change. They decided to do what they had never done before − to found a new organization form, previously unavailable to them because of legal restrictions, that would facilitate cooperation in solving common problems. They backed that decision up with substantial commitments of their own financial resources.
>
> Not all the members of the founding group envisioned much of what happened subsequently. Thus those events were, in accordance with complexity theory, unintended to a degree. Three of the major unintended consequences were (1) a large portion (almost half) of the consortium's resources were used to help the supplier industry through SEMI/SEMATECH [Semiconductor Equipment and Materials Institute/Semiconductor Manufacturing Technology] rather than used directly to help SEMATECH member companies, (2) the consortium developed more commitment and cooperation than many members expected because free riding behaviors became discredited as both counter-normative and inimical to gaining full benefits from membership, and (3) the consortium's life was extended beyond its initial five years because of its members' perception of its success.[66]

Despite the Sematech illustration and many other examples, both our case studies and the broader literature drive home the point that while self-organization is increasingly represented by the behavior of firms and other organizations in the pursuit of complex technological innovation, it is not an acceptable concept in the context of the US policy debate. In our US-based complex technology cases government played important roles at various times and in a variety of ways. However, only in the jet engine turbine blade case did industry people see the combined public–private sector shaping of the market and the network in terms similar to Imai's description of Japanese innovation. In our other cases, interviewees identified important government contributions, but they generally doubted whether the government had a role in shaping markets. Our cases indicate little conscious appreciation of the role government has played or might play in the process of self-organization.

There are many reasons self-organization is incompatible with the culture and ideas that have generally framed policy-making in the USA, but one stands out: the traditional, mass production view of organizations as highly controlled machines is still firmly lodged in our minds. As knowledge has become the most important factor in creating and sustaining competitive advantage in the synthetic production era, however, Americans are being forced to adjust to the notion that a machine is no longer an appropriate organizational metaphor.[67] More dynamic, fluid organizations are needed to create, access, and integrate a wide variety of knowledge-based competencies and assets; thus the explosive growth in numbers and types of network organizations. Those networks capable of self-organization are the focus of the next chapter.

Notes

1. Gareth Morgan, *Images of Organization*, Beverly Hills, CA: Sage Publications, 1986, pp. 84–7.
2. Giovanni Dosi and Bruce Kogut, "National Specificities and the Context of Change: the Coevolution of Organization and Technology," in Bruce Kogut, ed., *Country Competitiveness: Technology and the Organization of Work*, New York: Oxford University Press, 1993, pp. 249–62.
3. Peter A. Corning, "Synergy and Self-organization in Human Evolution," in Bryanna Brady and Linda Peeno, eds, *New System Thinking and Action for a New Century*, Louisville, KY: International Society for Systems Science, 1994, pp. 1–61.
4. Ilya Prigogine and Isabelle Stengers, *Order out of Chaos*, New York: Bantam Books, 1985; Gregoire Nicolis and Ilya Prigogine, *Self-organization in Non-equilibrium Systems*, New York: Wiley Interscience, 1977.
5. Paul R. Krugman, *The Self-organizing Economy*, Cambridge, MA: Blackwell Publishers, 1996; Jose A. Scheinkman and Michael Woodford, "Self-organized Criticality and Economic Fluctuations," *American Economic Association Papers and Proceedings*, Vol. 84, No. 2, May 1994, pp. 417–21; Jacques Lesourne, "Self-organization as a Process in the Evolution of Economic Systems," in Richard H. Day and Ping Chen, eds, *Nonlinear Dynamics and Evolutionary Economics*, New York: Oxford University Press, 1993, pp. 150–66; John Foster, "Economics and the Self-organization Approach: Alfred Marshall Revisited," *Economic Journal*, Vol. 103, No. 419, July 1993, pp. 975–91; Michael J. Radzicki, "Institutional Dynamics, Deterministic Chaos, and Self-organizing Systems," *Journal of Economic Issues*, Vol. 24, No. 1, March 1990, pp. 57–102.
6. Margaret J. Wheatley, *Leadership and the New Science: Learning about Organization from an Orderly Universe*, San Francisco: Berrett-Koehler Publishers, 1992, pp. 93–4 (emphasis added).
7. David J. Teece, Gary Pisano, and Amy Shuen, "Dynamic Capabilities and Strategic Management," *Strategic Management Journal*, Vol. 18, No. 7, August 1997, pp. 509–33; David T. Lei, "Competence-building, Technology Fusion and Competitive Advantage: the Key Roles of Organizational Learning and Strategic Alliances," *International Journal of Technology Management*, Vol. 14, Nos 2/3/4, 1997, pp. 208–37; Gary Hamel and C. K. Prahalad, *Competing for the Future*, Boston: Harvard Business School Press, 1994, pp. 199–211; George Stalk, Philip Evans, and Lawrence E. Shulman, "Competing on Capabilities: the New Rule of Corporate Strategy," *Harvard Business Review*, March/April 1992, pp. 57–69; David J. Teece, "Profiting from Technological Innovation: Implications for Integration, Collaboration, Licensing and Public Policy," *Research Policy*, Vol. 15, No. 6, October 1986, pp. 385–405.

8. Mark R. Gallon, Harold M. Stillman, and David Coates, "Putting Core Competency Thinking Into Practice," *Research-Technology Management*, Vol. 38, No. 3, May/June 1995, p. 20.

9. Gary Hamel, "Competition for Competence and Inter-partner Learning within International Strategic Alliances," *Strategic Management Journal*, Vol. 12, Special Issue, 1991, p. 83.

10. David J. Teece, "Competition, Cooperation and Innovation: Organizational Arrangements for Regimes of Rapid Technological Progress," *Journal of Economic Behavior and Organization*, Vol. 18, No. 1, April 1992, p. 17.

11. Morgan L. Swink, J. Christopher Sandvig, and Vincent A. Mabert, "Customizing Concurrent Engineering Processes: Five Case Studies," *Journal of Product Innovation Management*, Vol. 13, May 1996, pp. 229–44; Tom Kiely, "Innovation Congregations," *Technology Review*, Vol. 97, No. 3, April 1994, pp. 54–60; James P. Womack and Daniel T. Roos, "From Lean Production to the Lean Enterprise," *Harvard Business Review*, Vol. 72, No. 2, March/April 1994, pp. 93–103; A. Georges L. Romme, "The Process of Self-renewal by Management Teams," *Human Systems Management*, Vol. 13, No. 1, 1994, pp. 49–55.

12. Anders Lundgren, *Technological Innovation and Network Evolution*, New York: Routledge, 1995, pp. 93–5.

13. Andreas Pyka, "Informal Networking," *Technovation*, Vol. 17, No. 4, April 1997, pp. 207–20; Richard N. Osborn and John Hagedoorn, "The Institutionalization and Evolutionary Dynamics of Interorganizational Alliances and Networks," *Academy of Management Journal*, Vol. 40, No. 2, April 1997, pp. 261–78.

14. Jane Mareau, "Clusters, Chains, and Complexes: Three Approaches to Innovation with a Public Policy Perspective," in Mark Dodgson and Roy Rothwell, eds, *The Handbook of Industrial Innovation*, Brookfield, VT: Edward Elgar, 1994, pp. 3–12.

15. Don E. Kash, *Perpetual Innovation: the New World of Competition*, New York: Basic Books, 1989, pp. 50–2.

16. Richard R. Nelson and Nathan Rosenburg, "Technical Innovation and National Systems," in Richard R. Nelson, ed., *National Innovation Systems: A Comparative Analysis*, New York: Oxford University Press, 1993, pp. 3–24.

17. Gunnar Eliasson, "Spillovers, Integrated Production and the Theory of the Firm," *Journal of Evolutionary Economics*, Vol. 6, No. 2, 1996, p. 131.

18. H. Kevin Steensma, "Acquiring Technological Competencies through Inter-organizational Collaboration: an Organizational Learning Approach," *Journal of Engineering and Technology Management*, Vol. 12, No. 4, January 1996, pp. 267–86.

19. Arthur De Vany, "Information, Chance, and Evolution: Alchian and the Economics of Self-organization," *Economic Inquiry*, Vol. 34, No. 3, July 1996, pp. 427–43.

20. Vincent Mangematin, "The Simultaneous Shaping of Organization and Technology within Cooperative Agreements," in Rod Coombs, Albert Richards, Pier P. Saviotti, and Vivien Walsh, eds, *Technological Collaboration: the Dynamics of Cooperation in Industrial Innovation*, Brookfield, VT: Edward Elgar, 1996, pp. 119–41.

21. "Winning through Cooperation: an Interview with William Spencer," *Technology Review*, Vol. 100, No. 1, January 1997, pp. 22–7; Peter Grindley, David C. Mowery, and Brian Silverman, "SEMATECH and Collaborative Research: Lessons in the Design of High-technology Consortia," *Journal of Policy Analysis and Management*, Vol. 13, No. 4, 1994, pp. 723–58.

22. Ralph D. Stacey, "The Science of Complexity: an Alternative Perspective for Strategic Change Processes," *Strategic Management Journal*, Vol. 16, Special Issue, Summer 1995, pp. 477–95.

23. James Wade, "Dynamics of Organizational Communities and Technological Bandwagons: an Empirical Investigation of Community Evolution in the Microprocessor Market," *Strategic Management Journal*, Vol. 16, Special Issue, Summer 1995, pp. 111–33.

24. W. Brian Arthur, "Increasing Returns and the New World of Business," *Harvard Business Review*, Vol. 74, No. 4, July/August 1996, p. 102.

25. Giovanni Dosi, "Perspectives On Evolutionary Theory," *Science and Public Policy*, Vol. 18, No. 6, December 1991, p. 354.
26. Gordon R. Foxall and John R. Fawn, "An Evolutionary Model of Technological Innovation as a Strategic Management Process," *Technovation*, Vol. 12, No. 2, April 1992, pp. 193–4.
27. Mario Cimoli and Giovanni Dosi, "Technological Paradigms, Patterns of Learning and Development: an Introductory Roadmap," *Journal of Evolutionary Economics*, Vol. 5, No. 3, 1995, pp. 243–68; Peter Hall, *Innovation, Economics and Evolution: Theoretical Perspectives on Changing Technology in Economic Systems*, New York: Harvester Wheatsheaf, 1994, pp. 28–30; Loet Leydesdorff, "New Models of Technological Change: New Theories for Technology Studies?," in Loet Leydesdorff and Peter Van den Besselaar, eds, *Evolutionary Economics and Chaos Theory: New Directions in Technology Studies*, New York: St Martin's Press, 1993, pp. 186–9; Walter Vincenti, *What Engineers Know and How They Know It*, Baltimore: Johns Hopkins University Press, 1990.
28. Leonard H. Lynn, N. Mohan Reddy, and John D. Aram, "Linking Technology and Institutions: The Innovation Community Framework," *Research Policy*, Vol. 25, No. 1, January 1996, pp. 91–106.
29. Robert U. Ayres, "Toward a Non-linear Dynamics of Technological Progress," *Journal of Economic Behavior and Organization*, Vol. 24, June 1994, pp. 35–69.
30. Jens F. Christensen, "Asset Profiles for Technological Innovation," *Research Policy*, Vol. 24, No. 5, September 1995, pp. 727–45.
31. Frank-Jurgen Richter, "The Emergence of Corporate Alliance Networks – Conversion to Self-organization," *Human Systems Management*, Vol. 13, No. 1, 1994, pp. 19–26.
32. Thomas P. Hughes, *American Genesis: a Century of Invention and Technological Enthusiasm, 1870–1970*, New York: Viking Press, 1989; David A. Hounshell, *From the American System to Mass Production, 1800–1932: the Development of Manufacturing Technology in the United States*, Baltimore: Johns Hopkins University Press, 1984; Louis Galambos and Joseph Pratt, *The Rise of Corporate Capitalism: US Business and Public Policy in the Twentieth Century*, New York: Basic Books, 1988.
33. William Lazonick, *Business Organization and the Myth of the Market Economy*, New York: Cambridge University Press, 1991, pp. 1–19.
34. William Lazonick, "Organizational Integration in Three Industrial Revolutions," in Arnold Heertje and Mark Perlman, eds, *Evolving Technology and Market Structure: Studies in Schumpeterian Economics*, Ann Arbor, MI: University of Michigan Press, 1990, p. 85.
35. Lazonick, *Business Organization and the Myth of the Market Economy*, pp. 28–9 (emphasis added).
36. Robert M. Grant, "Prospering in Dynamically-competitive Environments: Organizational Capability as Knowledge Integration," *Organizational Science*, Vol. 7, No. 4, July/August 1996, pp. 375–87; Mary E. Lee, "The Evolution of Technology: a Model of Socio-ecological Self-organization," in Leydesdorff and Van den Besselaar, eds, *Evolutionary Economics and Chaos Theory*, pp. 167–79.
37. Boelie Elzen, Bert Enserink and Wim A. Smit, "Socio-technical Networks: How a Technology Studies Approach May Help to Solve Problems Related to Technical Change," *Social Studies of Science*, Vol. 26, No. 1, February 1996, pp. 95–141; Wayne E. Baker, "The Network Organization in Theory and Practice," in Nitin Nohria and Robert G. Eccles, eds, *Networks and Organizations: Structure, Form, and Action*, Boston: Harvard Business School Press, 1992, pp. 397–429.
38. Chris DeBresson and Fernand Amesse, "Networks of Innovators: a Review and Introduction to the Issue," *Research Policy*, Vol. 20, No. 5, October 1991, p. 367.
39. Michelle K. Bolton, Roger Malmrose, and William G. Ouchi, "The Organization of Innovation in the United States and Japan: Neoclassical and Relational Contracting," *Journal of Management Studies*, Vol. 31, No. 5, September 1994, pp. 653–79.
40. Richter, "The Emergence of Corporate Alliance Networks – Convertion to Self-organization," p. 20.

41. Niles Hansen, "Competition, Trust, and Reciprocity in the Development of Innovative Regional Milieux," *Papers in Regional Science*, Vol. 71, No. 2, 1992, pp. 103–4.
42. Knut H. Sorensen and Nora Levold, "Tacit Networks, Heterogeneous Engineers, and Embodied Technology," *Science, Technology, and Human Values*, Vol. 17, No. 1, Winter 1992, pp. 26–7.
43. Christopher Freeman, "Critical Survey: the Economics of Technical Change," *Cambridge Journal of Economics*, Vol. 18, No. 5, October 1994, pp. 469–71.
44. Semiconductor Industry Association, *The National Technology Roadmap for Semiconductors*, San Jose, CA: Semiconductor Industry Association, 1994.
45. Brian Bremer, *et al.*, "Keiretsu Connections: the Bonds Between the US and Japan's Industry Groups," *Business Week*, July 22, 1996, pp. 52 and 54.
46. Cristel Lane and Reinhard Bachmann, "The Social Constitution of Trust: Supplier Relations in Britain and Germany," *Organization Studies*, Vol. 17, Issue 3, 1996, pp. 367–8.
47. Keith Dickson, "How Informal Can You Be? Trust and Reciprocity within Co-operative and Collaborative Relationships," *International Journal of Technology Management*, Vol. 11, Nos 1/2, 1996, pp. 129–39.
48. Christopher Freeman, "Networks of Innovators: a Synthesis of Research Issues," *Research Policy*, Vol. 20, No. 5, October 1991, p. 503.
49. Thomas M. Jorde and David J. Teece, "Innovation, Cooperation, and Antitrust," *High Technology Law Journal*, Vol. 4, No. 1, Summer 1989, p. 3.
50. Geert Duysters and John Hagedoorn, "Internationalization of Corporate Technology through Strategic Partnering: an Empirical Investigation," *Research Policy*, Vol. 25, No. 1, January 1996, pp. 1–12; John W. Medcof, "Challenges in Managing Technology in Transnational Multipartner Networks," *Business Horizons*, Vol. 39, No. 1, January/February 1996, pp. 47–54; Anna Grandori and Guiseppe Soda, "Inter-firm Networks: Antecedents, Mechanisms and Forms," *Organization Studies*, Vol. 16, No. 2, 1995, pp. 183–214.
51. David J. Teece, "Inter-organizational Requirements of the Innovation Process," *Managerial and Decision Economics*, Vol. 10, Special Issue on Competitiveness, Technology, and Productivity, Spring 1989, p. 35.
52. John D. Aram, Leonard H. Lynn, and N. Mohan Reddy, "Institutional Relationships and Technology Commercialization: Limitations of Market-based Policy," *Research Policy*, Vol. 21, No. 5, June 1992, pp. 409–21.
53. Caroline F. Benton and Kyoichi Kijima, "Maintaining Foreign Subsidiaries' Ability to Self-organize in the Japanese Market," *Systems Research*, Vol. 13, No. 4, December 1996, pp. 447–56; Fumio Kodama, *Emerging Patterns of Innovation: Sources of Japan's Technological Edge*, Boston: Harvard Business School Press, 1995; Yasunori Baba and Ken-ichi Imai, "A Network View of Innovation and Entrepreneurship: the Case of the Evolution of the VCR Systems," *International Social Science Journal*, Vol. 45, No. 1, February 1993, pp. 23–34; Ikujiro Nonaka and Teruo Yamanouchi, "Managing Innovation as a Self-renewing Process," *Journal of Business Venturing*, Vol. 4, No. 5, September 1989, pp. 299–315; Ikujiro Nonaka, "Creating Organizational Order out of Chaos: Self-renewal in Japanese Firms," *California Management Review*, Vol. 15, No. 3, Spring 1988, pp. 57–73.
54. Lane Kenworthy, *In Search of National Economic Success: Balancing Competition and Cooperation*, London: Sage Publications, 1995, p. 180.
55. Robert H. Hayes, "US Competitiveness: 'Resurgence' versus Reality," *Challenge*, Vol. 39, No. 2, March/April 1996, pp. 36–44; Lawrence G. Franko, "The Japanese Juggernaut Rolls On," *Sloan Management Review*, Vol. 37, No. 2, Winter 1996, pp. 103–9.
56. Ken-ichi Imai, "The Japanese Pattern of Innovation and Its Evolution," in Nathan Rosenberg, Ralph Landau, and David C. Mowery, eds, *Technology and the Wealth of Nations*, Stanford, CA: Stanford University Press, 1992, p. 228.
57. Bolton, Malmrose, and Ouchi, "The Organization of Innovation in the United States and Japan," p. 672.

58. Rajan R. Kamath and Jeffrey K. Liker, "A Second Look at Japanese Product Development," *Harvard Business Review*, Vol. 72, No. 6, November/December 1994, pp. 154–70.
59. Howard E. Aldrich and Toshihiro Sasaki, "R&D Consortia in the United States and Japan," *Research Policy*, Vol. 24, No. 2, March 1995, p. 314.
60. Imai, "The Japanese Pattern of Innovation and Its Evolution," in Rosenberg, Landau, and Mowery, eds, *Technology and the Wealth of Nations*, p. 244.
61. James Fallows, "What Is an Economy For?" *Atlantic Monthly*, Vol. 273, No. 1, January 1994, pp. 76–92.
62. Michael A. Cusumano and Kentaro Nobeoka, "Strategy, Structure and Performance in Product Development: Observations from the Auto Industry," *Research Policy*, Vol. 21, June 1992, pp. 453–80.
63. Alex Taylor III, "Speed! Power! Status! Mercedes and BMW Race Ahead With a New Generation of Cars to Lust For," *Fortune*, June 10, 1996, pp. 47–58.
64. B. Bowonder and T. Miyake, "The Japanese Automobile Industry: an Analysis of Building Competitiveness," *World Competition*, 1992, p. 62.
65. Hisatoshi Yamamoto, "Complementary Competition in Japan," *Research-Technology Management*, Vol. 37, No. 2, March/April 1994, pp. 49–54.
66. Larry D. Browning, Janice M. Beyer, and Judy C. Shetler, "Building Cooperation in a Competitive Industry: Sematech and the Semiconductor Industry," *Academy of Management Journal*, Vol. 38, No. 1, February 1995, p. 142.
67. Geoffrey M. Hodgson, "The Economy as an Organism – Not a Machine," *Futures*, Vol. 25, No. 2, May 1993, pp. 392–403.

CHAPTER SEVEN

Network Self-organization

Self-organizing networks are a response to the inability to innovate complex technologies with yesterday's simpler, rigid, and hierarchical organizational structures and processes. The spontaneous formation of networks marks an acceptance of exploding costs, accelerating time pressures, and ever more complicated technical systems as givens in the pursuit of commercial success.[1] Innovative networks respond to and create change by developing and modifying their mix of core capabilities and complementary assets. Observers of these activities have applied labels like "virtual corporation",[2] "virtual alliance",[3] or "international *keiretsu*"[4] to this new organizational form. Whatever the label, the self-organizing networks share a set of common characteristics, but they also manifest great diversity. A shared characteristic is the ability of networks to provide a structure for organizational learning that transcends the learning of their component organizations. John Mathews sees networks as having a capacity to "accelerate inter-organizational learning."[5] Network diversity appears in many ways. For example, some networks are informal and some are formal. Some exist for only a few weeks, others appear permanent.[6]

Box 7.1

In the innovation of the GE 90 engine, self-organization took the form of network linkages that were adapted so that both knowledge and risk were more fully shared between GE and suppliers of complementary assets. An example of self-organization in this adaptation involved a Japanese company that supplied the GE 90's low pressure turbine, an important complementary technology. In order to facilitate risk-sharing, the Japanese supplier used its own funds for the development of the turbine in return for a guaranteed share of the market.

Knowledge-sharing was based on the Japanese company's advanced prototyping abilities. Through close interaction with GE and other members of the turbine subsystem network, the Japanese supplier was able to deliver a low pressure turbine that had been taken through an extensive set of prototype tests and was very close to being in final form before the final design specifications were provided by GE. Thus a significant complementary innovation was delivered rapidly because of the self-organizing capacity of producer–supplier knowledge relationships.

Self-organization, then, is about a wide variety of webs of firms, government agencies, and universities acquiring knowledge not previously available and grafting it onto existing organizational capabilities.[7] How this works is illustrated by the GE turbine blade case (Box 7.1).

The rapid growth of self-organizing networks reflects both the increasing complexity of technological innovation and the fact that it is impossible to understand such innovation in advance. The uncertainty generated by complexity has required organizational and managerial adaptations. The extent of these changes is suggested by comparing the management rhetoric of ITT's Harold Geneen, one of the best known corporate managers during the 1960s and early 1970s, with the dominant contemporary management perspective. Almost no story about Geneen failed to give attention to his overriding credo: "No surprises."[8] In Geneen's day, a period when assembling diverse conglomerates was the focus of much attention, organizations and their managers sought to analyze all activities, with the purpose of eliminating surprises and uncertainties. In the contemporary world of complex networks and synthetically produced technologies, such rhetoric would be the object of ridicule. The expectation of surprises and the capacity to adapt and benefit from them are key reasons for the development of self-organizing networks. *But how does the network self-organization process work and how do complex networks coevolve with technologies?*

Self-organization and network evolution

Self-organization in networks is best seen by looking at the three sets of resources identified in the preceding chapter: core capabilities, complementary assets, and learning. Insight into self-organization requires examining how these resources are linked, modified, and utilized by network strategies and how these linkages are manifested in network structures.

A network's core capabilities (or competencies) are the knowledge and skills that give it the ability to commercialize technologies uniquely well – better than or equal to competitors. Core capabilities are the most critical ingredient of competitive leadership.[9] A network core capability may be as broad as the mastery of systems integration or miniaturization, or as focused as the ability to conduct R&D in a particular field or manufacture a highly specialized product.[10]

Complementary assets are the supplementary bodies of knowledge and skill that must be accessed by networks to take full advantage of core capabilities.[11] For example, where systems integration is a core capability, distribution or marketing abilities might be required complementary assets. Figure 7.1 characterizes core capabilities as being at the center of a network's innovative capacity, while complementary assets are arrayed at the periphery. If one uses an image of a network as a spider's web, the core capabilities would be located in the middle of the web, while the complementary assets would be located in nodes distributed along the web's filaments.

Creating and enhancing core capabilities is dependent upon a network's learning capacities, especially the accumulation of insights derived from ongoing self-organization among participants.[12] Network core capabilities are continually modified by a range of learning processes and the reshaping of core capabilities and complementary assets in pursuit of solutions to problems.[13] Everything represented in Figure 7.1, then, is subject to change through the process of self-organization.

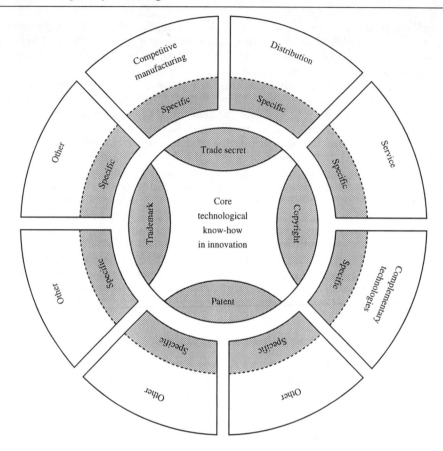

Shaded area represents the less imitable portion of the value chain. Outer segments
represent complementary assets; inner circle segments represent know-how.

Figure 7.1 Core capabilities and complementary assets
Source: David J. Teece, "Strategies for Capturing the Financial Benefits from Technological
Innovation," in Nathan Rosenberg, Ralph Landau, and David C. Mowery, eds, *Technology and
the Wealth of Nations*, Stanford, CA: Stanford University Press, 1992, p. 184.

Strategy is composed of a network's objectives and the shared views of its
members about how to pursue them.[14] Strategy thus requires deciding what core
capabilities to create and maintain over the long term, what complementary assets to
access, and what learning processes to undertake. Holders of core capabilities
commonly play the lead role in conceptualizing and articulating strategies when
networks are being created or when trajectory changes are taking place. For
example, Intel's chief executive officer, Andrew Grove, played a key role in the mid-
1980s when the Intel network moved from a focus on memory chips (e.g. DRAMs and
EPROMs) to microprocessors. Alternatively, strategy for established networks and
trajectories usually evolves through the shared vision of the broader technological

community (e.g. the assumptions underpinning the semiconductor industry's roadmaps) or the common intelligence of the network's participants.

Structure is the design or architecture that a network has at any point in time. The relationships and interactions among existing network resources (i.e. core capabilities, complementary assets, organizational learning) are embedded in network structure (e.g. routines, standards). A part of the process of self-organization involves a continuous interplay between strategy and structure. For example, any existing structure will reflect previous strategies. Thus, strategic modification is always constrained by structure. Modifications in strategy that require changes in the character of core capabilities and complementary assets usually require significant and often difficult changes in structure.[15]

Embedded in structure is substantial prior self-organization and learning that can facilitate and is often critical to the adjustment of the mix of core capabilities and complementary assets. Network learning can and probably must provide the base for network self-renewal and evolution. The ongoing challenge for self-organization is the determination of what learning to reject and what to create or access. Again, the GE turbine case illustrates this interplay (Box 7.2).

Box 7.2

The GE turbine blade evolution has involved ever more sophisticated innovations. Recent innovations have been possible in part because of the availability of computer-aided design (CAD) technologies. The use of CAD, in turn, has required that the tacit knowledge held by the casting companies be integrated into turbine blade designs at a very early stage. Integration of this kind converts tacit to explicit knowledge.

The casting companies were only willing to provide their tacit knowledge if they were assured of follow-on casting work. For many years, a barrier to such cooperation was the requirement by the Department of Defense (DOD) that the choice of a casting company had to be made through an arm's length process where GE provided detailed specifications and the casting firms submitted bids, with the lowest cost bidder winning the production contract.

To deal with the need for early cooperation between blade designers and casting companies, the DOD contracting requirements were changed so that the casting contractor could be chosen in advance of initial design. Two learning patterns associated with self-organization were evident in these adaptations. First, on the technical side, the blade design and casting learning had to be integrated early to synthesize the desired product. Second, the need for technical synthesis required learning on the social side with with regard to contracting arrangements. Faced with a tangible technical need, contracting was adapted so that cooperation could replace competition.

Core capabilities

Network core capabilities have both organizational and technological dimensions. The technological dimension tends to get the most attention because it offers a tangible link to the artifacts (e.g. processes and products) that appear in the marketplace.[16] For instance, R&D has been a commonly identified technological core capability. But focusing primarily on the technological dimension of core capabilities offers only limited insight into network self-organization. A more useful picture is offered by viewing core capabilities as *a set of problem-defining and problem solving insights, based on network-specific patterns of learning and resource accumulation, that are translated into competitive product and process technologies.*[17] Core capabilities are better conceptualized as those network capacities that make it possible to acquire, create, and use combinations of technological and organizational knowledge in ways that produce winners in competitive markets.

Core capabilities have been the focus of growing attention within the business community and among students of technological innovation. Until very recently, however, the creation and maintenance of *network* core capabilities has received little attention. The increasing interest in network core capabilities and more broadly in self-organizing networks reflects several characteristics of contemporary complex technologies. First, creating core capabilities has become an extremely complex process, well beyond the capacities of individual actors. Not even the largest firm can develop and integrate all the specialized knowledge and experience necessary for a new or significantly modified complex technology:

> The fundamental challenge that firms face in commercializing complex technology is developing the multiple competencies required. As complex technologies are systems of many closely coordinated components, firms that independently develop these technologies must possess the ability to manufacture and coordinate many dissimilar components. Though some complex technologies combine components that draw on similar knowledge bases, most complex technologies combine components that draw from different knowledge bases.
>
> Most firms, however, have limited abilities to develop broad sets of competencies. Drawing from a knowledge base to construct and refine a component is a complicated and uncertain process, and organizations must develop routines specialized to each technology or knowledge base. Even when complementary, the knowledge bases and associated routines are often dissimilar and are often best maintained in separate organizations. Organizations are also constrained in their ability to rapidly learn and implement competencies and routines and to effectively perform more than a narrow range of tasks.[18]

Second, developing a new core capability has become increasingly costly. Individual actors can no longer take the risks associated with covering all the costs of creating and maintaining core capabilities. Third, the pressures for accelerating the pace of innovation have escalated and networks often have proven superior to single firms or other actors in the rapid development and integration of core capabilities.[19] Therefore, networks have offered attractive solutions to the problems of complexity, cost, and speed; and the key to their success has been the creation and maintenance of appropriate core capabilities. Embedded in the core capabilities of successful self-organizing networks are two elusive, overlapping, and critical capacities: dynamic network routines and reservoirs of tacit knowledge and know-how.

Dynamic organizational routines

At the heart of networks are what Nelson and Winter have called *organizational routines*. It is roughly accurate to say that routines hold key elements of the "core technological know-how in innovation," which Teece has located at the center of Figure 7.1. These routines are inseparable from the network core capabilities that are critical to the synthetic processes of innovation associated with complex technologies.

Faced with solving problems in the process of carrying out innovations, networks learn and incorporate part of what they learn in routines – in "patterns of interactions which represent successful solutions to particular problems and which are resident in group behavior."[20] Two types of routine have been identified by David Teece and his colleagues:

> *Static routines* embody the capacity to replicate certain previously performed tasks. Needless to say, such routines are never entirely static, because with repetition routines can be constantly improved. The presence of standard learning curve economies often indicate the operation of static routines. *Dynamic routines* are directed at learning, and new product-process development. Thus R&D activity proceeds through the employment of routines to ascertain where to probe, how to probe, and how much to probe.[21]

Networks that continuously self-organize as they innovate complex technologies are especially dependent upon core capabilities that have dynamic routines embedded within them. Such routines are commonly critical to guiding processes of trial-and-error problem solving and learning. For example, a network confronted with an especially difficult technical problem in an otherwise incremental advance along a trajectory may have developed routines that guide it to initially probe lead-users and other sources of market knowledge first, before embarking upon more expensive and long-term search processes like R&D.[22] These dynamic routines are essential to network self-organization because they commonly contain the potential for modifying themselves: they can be "routine-changing routines."[23] If, for example, the most successful knowledge acquisition repeatedly comes from lead-users, over time R&D may be significantly downgraded as a knowledge source for network innovation.

All but the most static routines are difficult to articulate and understand because they have a significantly tacit character. Tacit knowledge often is especially evident in dynamic routines, where it accumulates as the unwritten "know-how" (Figure 7.1). Tacit know-how can often be understood only with experience, and thus many of the most dynamic routines are based on extensive technological experience. This pattern was repeatedly evident in the case studies. One illustration is offered by the Intel microprocessor network's use of task forces as routinized problem solving/ learning vehicles. The way these task forces are created and dismantled is explicit. But the selection of participants and the processes whereby problems are solved and learning occurs are far from explicit. When asked, for example, how task force members know the appropriate solution and why a consensus develops, the answer was: "The solution just emerges and we all know." Thus, the network has come to depend on the highly tacit routines by which task forces converge on emergent solutions.

Marion Sobol and David Lei have observed that the tacitness of many dynamic routines makes them an especially powerful source of core capabilities:

> Within organizations, tacit knowledge and skills are often the result of sustained learning and accumulated experience by individuals and teams where the skills become so deeply ingrained or embedded that it becomes difficult for outsiders to imitate or copy them. Dynamic routines, embedded in different task-, product-, or process-oriented

groups, often serve as the repository of tacit, organization-embedded knowledge. It is these routines that ... lay the foundation for building new sources of insights, experiences, and competences.[24]

Tacit knowledge, in whatever form, tends to be path dependent, in that it is intertwined with the evolution of particular networks and technological trajectories. Taken together, path dependency and the difficulty of diffusing tacit knowledge mean that many routines are network-specific – they rely on the unique patterns of interaction among participants in specific networks.

Thus, in conceptualizing network core capabilities it is useful to think of them as being located both in specific member organizations and in the interactions among those member organizations. The creation and maintenance of these unique collections of core capabilities and their linkages to complementary assets provide the foundation for the collaborative learning and resultant self-organization that determine whether a network succeeds or fails. When one appreciates that much of a network's collection of core capabilities may flow from embedded routines and tacit knowledge that are shared yet inherently elusive, one can begin to appreciate why there are major differences in the overall technological performance of networks within the same product sectors.[25]

The major problem with dynamic routines as repositories of knowledge is that they tend to become static. When this happens, when *core rigidities* develop, the competitiveness of a network erodes. When rigidity develops, modifying core capabilities may require a tangible external threat.[26] A good example is how the Japanese challenge to the US automobile industry in the 1970s and 1980s finally led to a reduction in rigid routines in companies like Chrysler.

Another difficulty in maintaining the evolution and vitality of routines embedded in core capabilities is inherent in network learning itself. Even very innovative networks tend to establish learning routines (e.g. R&D search and discovery rules and procedures) designed to ignore or downplay knowledge that seems irrelevant to current core capabilities. This is perfectly illustrated by Intel's use of minimum information, as articulated by "Noyce's Principle."[27]

As a consequence of localized learning routines a network can become trapped within outdated models of innovation (i.e. rigid routines for shared learning) that inhibit further evolution of core capabilities.[28] It is this concern that is the focus of Andrew Grove's book *Only the Paranoid Survive.*[29]

Know-how and tacit knowledge

The earliest identification of and most widely recognized role of know-how in core capabilities was in connection with process technologies. For instance, complex process technologies (e.g. computer-integrated manufacturing) typically incorporate collections of intricate technical skills deeply embedded in people, equipment, and software. The microprocessors innovated by the Intel network, for example, are manufactured in state-of-the-art facilities that are designed by Intel engineers to incorporate core capabilities in areas of process technology such as etching and assembly.[30]

Although less obvious, the embedding of tacit knowledge in products is as pervasive as it is in processes. Thus, the innovation of microprocessors involves a continuous interchange among groups of experts with experience in both chip design and fabrication.[31] As a further illustration, in seeking to categorize the 30 most valuable technology exports into the matrix in Chapter 1, we found that drawing the line between the innovation of complex process and complex product technologies was often impossible. In many cases, the know-how and tacit knowledge underpinning innovation in complex processes has become inextricably intertwined with the tacit know-how for innovating complex products.

A curious convergence has come from the growing importance of tacit knowledge and know-how to the innovation of complex technologies. Complexity has required ever more diverse organizational and, at the same time, ever more intimate relationships among network participants. Yet a continuing concern has been that, through these diverse and intimate relationships, those who hold core capabilities would involuntarily transfer their knowledge to potential competitors. Intimacy and trust have come to be regarded as both a necessity and a threat. In practice, however, when complex innovation is highly dependent upon core capabilities with significant tacitness, network relationships of all kinds are often much less risky. Even entering into a network with competitors in the same technological sector may become less threatening, since core capabilities based on tacit know-how are more resistant to involuntary transfer.[32]

The Sony–Philips collaboration in developing the CD format nicely illustrates the role of tacit capabilities in fostering a new network. The two companies shared their most intimate knowledge concerning design, and learned together under conditions of trust and reciprocity. Cooperation was open and transpired without even a formal agreement. Two factors appear to have contributed to this process. The first was their shared desire to establish a common global format for the CD. Thus, the two firms entered into the network relationship with the intent that, should their design be chosen, they would make it available to their competitors at low cost. The second factor was that Sony and Philips expected their economic benefits to be generated from adding the tacit knowledge and know-how each would acquire during the design collaboration to their existing, quite dissimilar, tacit-based core capabilities in producing and marketing audio technology. Each company expected payoffs from augmenting their unique core capabilities through tacit learning by interaction.

That Sony and Philips cooperated in very intimate ways without a formal arrangement is not surprising, given the difficulties in determining the exact value of specific kinds of tacit knowledge and know-how in the context of innovation. Their cooperation reflects the near impossibility, during the process of innovation, of defining appropriate methodologies or metrics for valuing what cannot be written down or explained, except perhaps after the fact. The reality is that assuring the flow of tacit knowledge often depends on facilitating close ties among practitioners who have direct experience with the innovation process. Thus, exchanging tacit knowledge often demands informal organizational practices that resemble traditional bartering, as Wendy Faulkner and Jacqueline Senker discovered:

> There are a range of tacit elements in the knowledge which companies use in the course of innovation, and this is acquired through recruitment, RD&D [research, design, and development], and networking. Networking is used to access tacit knowledge relating to both existing knowledge and new knowledge generated by research. By its very nature, tacit knowledge is transferred in person-embodied rather than written form; we therefore suspect that tacit knowledge flows are a very important element of networking in innovation. Networking for tacit knowledge takes place within firms

as well as with external sources. More specifically, informal interaction and barter is a significant channel for transferring tacit knowledge between organizations, and this includes other companies as well as PSR [public sector research].[33]

Building and maintaining core capabilities laced with tacit know-how typically does not permit a simple, additive process of creating and integrating knowledge. Networks must be prepared to engage in more disorderly and trial-and-error activities (e.g. trust-based negotiations) in which the utility of various types of knowledge is treated as a perpetually open question. In the end, tacit knowledge or know-how must often be evaluated by those who have been most closely involved in the innovation.[34] In the case of the cooperation between HP and Philips on the innovation of the MRI-based CIT, there was agreement in advance that those involved would, after the fact, evaluate the relative contributions of the two organizations as the basis for determining the division of profits.

Complementary assets

Core capabilities and complementary assets are closely interconnected in networks, but their patterns of interactions as they undergo self-organization vary significantly. In their relation to core capabilities, complementary assets can be either exploitive or enabling. Exploitive assets are those needed to extract the commercial advantages of existing core capabilities. Enabling complementary assets are those required to bring about technological innovation.[35]

Both exploitive and enabling complementary assets can be either generic or specialized. Generic assets are those that do not need to be tailored for a particular innovation process. Specialized assets must fit with and be integrated into the overall design of the particular innovation. Thus, specialized complementary assets have a high degree of interdependence with the core capabilities, whereas generic ones do not.[36] Distinctions among complementary assets are important because of their implications for network self-organization, especially the relationships among the two categories of complementary asset holders: suppliers and users.

Supplier and user complementarities

Specialized assets are more difficult for competitors to imitate than are generic ones. This fact in part accounts for the different patterns of interaction manifested in the self-organization process by supplier and user complementary asset holders. For example, generic assets are commonly accessed by short-term, arm's length contracting, in which the organization holding core capabilities uses detailed product or process specifications (e.g. performance standards) and suppliers are chosen on the basis of price. Here, interaction is relatively predictable, with the supplier given little latitude for innovation or self-organization. The norm is a one-way flow of mostly explicit knowledge from the supplier to the holder of the core capabilities.

A different pattern emerges where the holders of core capabilities require highly specialized assets. Here the holder of core capabilities often performs the role of strategic coordinator, rather than trying to control specific transactions. Innovation responsibility is dispersed throughout the network to the suppliers of specialized assets. Self-organization and spontaneous improvements in complementary assets can occur more easily when key elements of core capabilities (e.g. design, manufacturing) are shared with valued suppliers over a longer time frame. Gradually the flows of both explicit and tacit knowledge become more symmetrical, trust-based relationships evolve, and the patterns of self-organization become more dense.

Conventional contracts may still be an option with suppliers of specialized assets, but the contracts normally will be for longer terms and will attempt to provide a reassuring background structure for relationships, rather than just mandating specific behavior. Collective problem solving and greater sharing of tacit knowledge are often requisites for accessing specialized complementary assets.[37] Only very flexible contracting can meet these requirements.

The GE turbine blade study provides an illustration. Casting turbine blades remains in part what the industry calls a "black art." It is in every sense a specialized asset. Casting the most sophisticated blades is so specialized that only two companies in the United States do it. The result is a pattern of great mutual dependence between GE and the casting companies. This mutual dependence results from the fact that any new blade design by GE requires early and continuing interaction with the casting company. Because casting is an irreplaceable complementary asset, GE shares a great deal of proprietary tacit knowledge with the casting companies. Sharing is based on trust that the casting firms will not communicate this knowledge to any other jet engine producer. Both GE and the casting companies benefit from this intimate relationship, since everyone learns on a broader front and much faster.

The GE case shows how specialized *suppliers* of complementary assets can have a powerful impact on network relationships. The same kinds of influence can be exercised by organizations that possess *user or buyer complementarities*. Teece provides the distinction between the two types of holders of complementary assets:

> there are buyer complementarities. A "product" can be thought of as the totality of what a customer buys. It is not only the physical device or service from which the customer gets direct utility but includes a number of other factors, products and services that makes the innovation desirable, useful, and convenient. Thus computer hardware must have software available, autos must have gasoline, textbooks must have examination copies, and copiers need copier paper and service.[38]

Frequently, users of process or product technologies possess enough technical and/or organizational knowledge to suggest relevant improvements to the holders of core capabilities. The "lead" or "advanced" users (i.e. the first to employ a new technology) often are especially expert in generating productive modifications. Not only may the use of an innovation by experienced buyers generate new information about user requirements, it may suggest routes to product improvement.[39] The complementary assets embodied in lead users' experience (again, much of it tacit) can be invaluable, especially when user–producer linkages facilitate constant and rapid processes of self-organization.

User complementarities of this sort are one of the most common themes in the case studies. For example, a doctor at the Stanford Medical School initially proposed the Clinac technology and worked with the initial network (centered at the Stanford Physics Department) to develop the first experimental machine. Throughout the incremental innovation of both the linear accelerator and the cardio-imaging technology, medical doctors who were lead users were constantly suggesting practical changes, and thus were major sources of network learning and self-organization.

Organizational learning

Learning through collaboration and effective self-organization requires that network members have a "window" on their partners' capabilities and assets.[40] Network learning thus is inseparable from the evolving interactions among holders of core capabilities and complementary assets that are an ongoing part of network self-organization. The learning that is essential to building core capabilities and to linking them with complementary assets involves at least three collaborative activities: (a) searching for new problem solving knowledge and procedures (e.g. heuristics); (b) experimenting with and redefining the problems; and (c) modifying the technological trajectory.

Searching for new problem solving knowledge and procedures

In successful networks, core capabilities involve *being good at learning certain things* as much as they involve being good at doing certain things. A successful network is characterized by patterns of self-organization that enhance its ability to configure and reconfigure its resources (e.g. capabilities, assets, learning), structures, and strategies in ways that deliver competitive technologies.[41] Because process and product innovation involves solving problems, self-organization is always about a continual search for knowledge and procedures that will contribute to problem solving. Networks that are accomplished at learning can rapidly identify needed problem solving knowledge and procedures wherever they may be located. Faulkner and Senker characterize this search capability as "learning about learning," or "knowledge of knowledge."[42] Learning, therefore, is in part aimed at identifying new core capabilities and complementary assets, and targeting new network members that possess these capabilities and assets.

Successful search processes rely heavily on *heuristics*, the sets of learned "technological guide posts" (e.g. Where do we go from here? Where should we explore? What sort of knowledge should we draw upon?) that emerge from insight gained from collective experience.[43] A set of heuristics exists somewhere on a continuum between a problem that has only vaguely defined boundaries and a problem that has been fully formulated and defined. Heuristics provide enough structure to focus and guide search activities while still allowing enough flexibility to keep open the consideration of a variety of plausible modifications in these activities.[44]

Because much network learning involves tacit knowledge, heuristics often make use of *metaphors*. Metaphorical language is especially useful in expressing visions that provide direction but are not too specific. According to Nonaka and Yamanouchi, "The metaphor provides novel and equivocal meanings or contradictions that depend on indefinite networks of ideas and images. A challenging but equivocal vision encourages people to search for new meanings in which to integrate various interpretations and contradictions."[45] Useful metaphors and heuristics commonly become embedded in the organizational routines which help define core capabilities and are integral to self-organization. Thus, altering heuristics typically means altering routines. Flexible heuristics, in turn, benefit from experimentation in the activities they inform.

Experimentation and problem redefinition

Experimentation is about searching for and testing unorthodox ideas. Individuals and groups involved in experimentation usually have to be willing to suspend their attachment to existing procedures and methods for a while. William Starbuck has described the necessary mind set for experimentation as follows:

> People who see themselves as experimenting are willing to deviate temporarily from practices they consider optimal in order to test their assumptions. When they deviate, they create opportunities to surprise themselves. They also run experiments in ways that reduce the losses failures would produce. For instance, they attend carefully to feedback. They place fewer personal stakes on outcomes looking successful, so they can evaluate outcomes more objectively. They find it easier to alter their beliefs and methods to allow for new insights. They keep on trying for improvements because they know experiments rarely turn out perfectly.[46]

The possibility of failure is inherent in experiments. Implicit in learning from experimentation is a recognition that the more unconventional the concepts and approaches being tested, the riskier the experiments. Experimentation is most beneficial when it takes place in a context that recognizes that *failure plays a large role in building knowledge.* Leonard-Barton says that successful organizations are skillful at incorporating the positive lessons of "intelligent failure."[47] One positive lesson frequently involves *unlearning;* that is, modifying current definitions of problems, methods, and procedures that influence how evidence is interpreted.

How experimentation is done and who does it within a network depend on many factors. An especially important consideration is the state of the knowledge about the technology of concern. For example, if there is a high degree of explicit knowledge, experimentation can be formal, "scientific," and done in a laboratory setting. If, however, the technology is characterized by a high degree of tacitness, experimentation is likely to be defined by an accumulated set of heuristics and other problem-definition procedures. Tacit experiments, which often use "rule of thumb" guidelines, are typically most valuable when carried out as close to actual operations as possible.[48] Recognition of the value of proximity has led to viewing "the factory as learning laboratory." For example, the importance of proximity is one reason for Intel's traditional pattern of spreading its best PhD researchers throughout the operating organization, rather than locating them in an R&D structure.[49]

Experiments that depend on tacit know-how have been most obvious in the advances of core capabilities associated with process technologies. For instance, in many sectors incremental improvements in manufacturing flexibility and quality have come from sustained experiments on the shopfloor. Many lean production capabilities (e.g. just-in-time inventory systems) that first emerged in Japan evolved through the aggregation of numerous small-scale, trial-and-error refinements. Indeed, the Japanese have a term, *kaizen,* that refers to continuous improvement resulting from sustained, but controlled, experimentation.[50] Successful experimentation eventually leads to the creation or acquisition of new shared knowledge that is incrementally embedded in a network's heuristics and routines. In the case of many rapidly evolving technologies, network self-organization benefits from a constant interplay between heuristics and experimentation. This interplay helps refine existing core capabilities and complementary assets, and it contributes to accessing or creating new ones.[51]

Modifying trajectories and communities

Networks that are continually experimenting and learning sometimes develop new routines that result in trajectory changes, where the technologies, the network, and even the broader technological communities are altered. This happened in the case of the Varian Clinac network when experiments that involved the fusion of the traditional machine and the computer were carried out. Individuals who were involved repeatedly emphasize the fundamental changes required when people with expertise in software were brought into the network. Merging the heuristics and routines of players whose backgrounds were in physics-based hardware with those whose backgrounds were in software involved major network adaptation.

Although collaborative learning and self-organization can create entirely new trajectories, networks, and communities, especially when the results of experiments are unexpected,[52] the more typical learning occurs when knowledge acquired in the process of incremental learning along an existing trajectory is integrated into the network. Here the normal pattern involves evolutionary changes in the core capabilities and complementary assets held by existing network participants, or it involves integrating new participants or decoupling old ones.

Strategy

As noted above, at the most general level, network strategy identifies innovation goals and ways to achieve them. The overarching strategic objective is attaining a mutually reinforcing *fit* among network resources (i.e. core capabilities, complementary assets, and organizational learning) in order to create a unique competitive position. In Michael Porter's words: "Competitive strategy is about being different. It means deliberately choosing a different set of activities to deliver a unique mix of value."[53] Core capabilities are at the heart of any competitive mix of value-generating activities, because they tend to bound learning potential and thus the search for complementary assets. *Even though all resources matter in an integrated network, core capabilities matter more – they represent a "strategic resource."* Network strategy must pay special attention to providing a framework for guiding the selection, development, and application of core capabilities.[54] However, a successful network's strategy must do much more than nurture a few critical core capabilities. It must also involve a dynamic vision about how to integrate core capabilities and other resources by manipulating some combination of constraining and focusing forces (i.e. potential core capabilities and complementary assets, organizational learning opportunities, path dependencies, and the selection environment). Viewing strategy as visionary and dynamic is important because it highlights the centrality of self-organizing processes that continuously enhance network capabilities according to self-referential views of what the network already excels in doing and what it wants to do better than its competitors.

Network strategies, then, must give priority to gathering a broad range of intelligence about resources, as well as constraining and focusing forces. A key part of intelligence gathering includes continuous monitoring of promising technological trends.[55] When a market is driven by short cycles from innovation to obsolescence, early identification of commercial opportunities is critical. Thus, one strategic priority is to establish effective communication linkages to possible sources of expertise about where potentially relevant technologies are going. The broad monitoring patterns of successful networks are part of what makes them a source of intelligence far beyond the capabilities of any individual member.[56]

Network strategy, therefore, means something very different from "strategic management" as traditionally taught in business schools. Traditional strategic management has assumed linear models of behavior. Network strategies must reflect the fact that complex relations among member firms and other organizations never reach a stable equilibrium. Ralph Stacey puts it this way:

> Causal links between specific actions and specific organisational outcomes over the long term disappear in the complexity of interaction between people in an organisation, and between them and people in other organisations that constitute the environment – small changes can escalate to have unforeseeable outcomes. It follows that specific long-term outcomes cannot be foreseen and hence cannot be intended by people in an organisation – creative and innovative outcomes can only emerge. Members of an organisation, no matter how intelligent and powerful, will be unable to predict the specific long-term outcomes of their actions. They may specify any long-term state they wish to, they may have any dream, fantasy or vision they like, but they will never be able to determine the sequence of actions required to actualize it. Only when their organisation is operating in the stable zone, only when they are conducting ordinary management to reinforce what they already do well, will they be able to intend long-term outcomes and then only if rivals stay stable enough for long enough. The conclusion is clear: we can actualize intended long-term outcomes only by chance.[57]

Although complexity constrains long-range forecasting, short-term behavior is more predictable. This is because the coevolution of complex networks and technologies is not primarily governed by an external selection process (e.g. market dynamics) but by a self-organizing process that is highly *cooperative*. For instance, all our case studies found that participants in networks moving along an existing trajectory shared a rough consensus on what the next incremental innovations were likely to be.

The microprocessor case illustrates the coordination and learning role of a shared short-term vision. For the microprocessor network the vision has had at least four clearly identifiable parameters guiding innovation and therefore facilitating network learning. The first has been Moore's Law: there will be a fourfold increase in capacity every three years. The second has been that the capacity increases must occur within the x-86 microprocessor format and the software that has run on previous x-86 microprocessors must run on those to be innovated. The third has been that the capacity increase will be accomplished through component miniaturization and increased chip size. The fourth has been that the material used will be silicon.

Strategic coordination

Complexity, the importance of shared tacit learning, and rapid innovation have made cooperation a key element of the network strategies that guide self-organization. US-centered networks appear to have had, at least until very recently, more limited cooperative strategies than their Japanese counterparts.[58] Most cooperation on the innovation of technologies among US commercial networks has involved firms from the same industrial sector utilizing formally established structures to pursue basic research or other forms of "precompetitive" knowledge.

Cooperation on commercialization has not been much in evidence. By contrast, Japanese networks have traditionally involved more nonfirm players (e.g. government agencies), have linked different industrial sectors, have emphasized strategic and structural flexibility (much of it informal and personal in nature), and have often focused on developing commercial processes and products.[59]

Although there are doubtless many explanations for the more expansive Japanese cooperative strategies, the case studies of the two Sony networks are striking in terms of their involvement of a wide range of potential competitors in the early commercial design phase. Indeed, the Japanese have frequently engaged in so much and such stable collaboration that their economic system has been termed "alliance capitalism." Central to Japanese capitalism are strategies that emphasize long-term network relationships with diverse organizations that operate in a variety of sectors.[60]

The fact that many Americans still view collaborative ties in terms of the cartels that dominated key periods of US history is a vestige that constrains the development and evolution of strategies that encourage cooperative self-organizing networks. This view contributes to lower levels of trust and a continuing emphasis on opportunistic behavior. Nevertheless, in fact, if not in rhetoric, the importance to innovation of limiting opportunism and emphasizing cooperative strategies is changing perspectives around the world.[61] The movement away from opportunism and toward cooperation was a very powerful trend in all four of our US-based case studies. Similar trends were identified in a recent Canadian analysis of cooperation in technological innovation:

> Not all uncertainties and risks can be eliminated by networks, but some can be greatly reduced: secondary market uncertainties, behavioral uncertainties resulting from opportunism, and technological uncertainties, in particular those related to systems configurations and interface. Durable networks drastically reduce opportunistic behavior. From an agreed upon initial *modus vivendi*, mutually credible commitments are made in networks on the basis of compatible preferences and goals, which can eventually evolve into a mutual dependency and bondage resulting in positive reciprocity, the development of common language, mutual understanding, and, sometimes, trust. Although blind trust cannot be bought there can be a continuum of states of cooperation leading to guarded trust, either within the firm or between firms.[62]

Clearly, Japanese networks commonly reflect a level of trust and cooperation that goes far beyond a "guarded" state. At first glance Japanese networks appear to reflect almost "blind trust," but any careful investigation demonstrates that "blind" is a grossly inappropriate adjective. Rather, cooperation and trust rest on informal but powerful social contracts that emphasize openness, communication, foresight, *and discipline*. Moreover, this trust isn't "bought," at least in the economic sense of individual transactions. It resides in part in a set of cultural values that place great emphasis on common interest and on the need to rely on others in uncertain, high-risk situations. Japanese network organizations emphasize the value of what many students of innovation refer to as *strategic coordination*. That is, complex organizational relationships (e.g. linkages among producers, suppliers, users; making network connections to competitors) must continuously evolve in order to access necessary complementary assets and create core capabilities.

The growing focus on the importance of strategic coordination is now seen by many observers as being intertwined with increasing returns. For instance, Teece describes strategic coordination as follows:

Because of fundamental weaknesses in the system of intellectual property law, leakage and free riding are commonplace. Moreover, because of the use of strategic trade and industrial policies by some nation states, strategic coordination either by firms or governments is often necessary if innovating firms are to capture value from technology. Strategic coordination can thus enhance the public as well as private interests.

Strategic coordination is often desirable to ensure that capacity levels in an industry are matched to the level of residual demand, to ensure that beneficial standards are adopted, and *to ensure that economies and advantages associated with increasing returns are attained.* Unfortunately, in the United States, strategic behavior is often uncritically viewed as anticompetitive, with negative effects on economic welfare assumed.[63]

As Teece points out, sometimes strategic coordination is carried out by government, sometimes by firms, and sometimes by combinations of both, but by definition it is concerned with networks. Regardless of the locus of coordination, the strategy must ensure timely linkage of core capabilities and complementary assets within a context of network learning. And regardless of how these linkages are constructed, *strategic coordination represents self-organizing behavior.*

Our case studies indicated several instances where strategic coordination was at work during periods of trajectory change, when there is commonly no consensus vision. In an effort to reduce uncertainty, the existing networks in the case studies repeatedly responded by fusing themselves to a previously separate network. Such linkages appear to have had at least three benefits. First, the new fused network has vastly expanded knowledge. Often the new knowledge base is more than the sum of the two previous networks – fusion appears to provide some synergistic effects for knowledge creation. Second, the linkage provides a new learning structure. Finally, and most significantly, *strategic coordination can limit and sometimes eliminate the need for market competition in selecting the next trajectory.*[64] An example of strategic coordination of this type is presented in Box 7.3.

Box 7.3

The 64-bit Intel (Merced) network and an HP network have entered a joint venture to innovate the P7 microprocessor, the next microprocessor after the state-of-the-art Pentium family. This innovation is seen by some as launching the transition to a new format that will include the x-86 plus what is known as RISC (reduced instruction set computing) technology. From Intel's vantage point, it gains access to substantial RISC knowledge held by HP, and the combining of two networks offers a new learning pathway. In addition, the new network holds the possibility of limiting the number of new trajectories that will be competing in the market because the combination of two such prominent firms and their associated networks is intimidating to potential competitors. This is especially the case because a similar combination of IBM and Motorola networks has already staked out a major competitor trajectory. In sum, the two largest computer manufacturers and the two largest microprocessor producers may be dividing the world into two competing trajectories that look much like the pattern of the past two decades, where the Intel and Motorola microprocessors have dominated the market.

Structure

Structure is the design, form, or architecture a network adopts at any point in time. Structure is the operational manifestation of past strategy and collaborative learning. As used here, "structure" is a metaphor. The structure of a network is usually represented as a set of nodes, with communications channels among them. Structure is not adopted or imposed in one bounded action; it emerges incrementally as nodes join or leave the network, as channels of communication are established and terminated, and as the nodes themselves evolve in response to network interactions. Nelson and Winter provide a succinct portrayal of the strategy–structure connection in a company, although their points hold just as well if "network" is substituted for "firm" in the following passage:

> Strategies differ from firm to firm, in part because of different interpretations of economic opportunities and constraints and in part because different firms are good at different things. In turn, the capabilities of a firm are embedded in its organizational structure, which is better adapted to certain strategies than to others. Thus, strategies at any time are constrained by organization. But also a significant change in a firm's strategy is likely to call for a significant change in its organizational structure.[65]

Structure, therefore, reflects prior self-organization and is the base for further self-renewal and evolution. For a long time, the desired traits of organizational structure to foster technological innovation were thought to be stability and predictability. The emphasis was on negative feedback loops that maintained the organization's integrity. In networks this is no longer the case. The goal is to simultaneously maintain a coherent character while changing form:

> Part of their viability comes from their internal capacity to create structures that fit the moment. Neither form nor function alone dictates how the system is constructed. Instead, form and function engage in a fluid process where the system may maintain itself in its present form or evolve to a new order. The system possesses the capacity for spontaneously emerging structures, depending on what is required. It is not locked into any one form but instead is capable of organizing information in the structure that suits the present need.[66]

If a key to technological success is the ability to take advantage of the intimate self-renewing relationship between strategy and structure, then what specific structural arrangements are required? Lazonick argues that the distinctive structural features of networks today are: (a) the organizational integration of a number of distinct firms in pursuit of a common strategy; (b) the long-term integration into the enterprise of personnel below the managerial level (e.g. shopfloor workers); and (c) the cooperation of the state in shaping the social environment to reduce uncertainties.[67]

With regard to the first feature, where complex technological processes and products are concerned, the network structure almost certainly must include elements of several companies plus perhaps government agencies and organizations located in the nonprofit sector (e.g. universities). Not only must the level of integration be extraordinarily high, but these production networks must include all the organizational elements that contribute to the conceptualization, design, development, manufacturing, sales, and servicing of a product. The integration of all these skills, moreover, cannot be static. Innovative networks must be in perpetual flux; that is, organizational elements must be continuously dropped and added.

Similarly, individual elements are likely to be experiencing a continual, shared learning process.

As to the second structural feature, the integration of all levels of personnel, the case studies suggest that the building blocks of network structures are teams or work groups. Processes like concurrent engineering are increasingly used by network structures to integrate expertise from everywhere in the organization.[68] As the complexity of technologies increases, networks must develop ever greater capabilities to use teams and work groups to generate the requisite amount of communication (both tacit and explicit) needed to carry out innovation.[69]

The third structural feature – public–private sector cooperation – has been addressed in previous sections. But it is important to note that governments can and do participate in and even promote the first two structural features. Government can perform many "marriage broker" roles (e.g. providing financial and other incentives) to induce multiple firms to enter a network. And government can facilitate the integration of network personnel by, for instance, supporting the development and diffusion of advanced design or manufacturing technologies that underpin processes like concurrent engineering.[70]

Structure and strategy

Self-organizing networks usually have what Gianni Lorenzoni and Charles Baden-Fuller call a "strategic center," which has an ability *to undertake simultaneous structuring and strategizing.* By this they mean that innovation networks succeed in large part because the organization at the strategic center, usually the holder of many of the core capabilities, is constantly altering the form of its "web of alliances" to incorporate partners' new core capabilities and complementary assets. Thus, when the competencies of other network members are critical to the objectives of the strategic center, "the winners are building strategy and structure simultaneously whereas the losers are signing agreements without changing their organizational forms to match them."[71]

The structure of any adaptive network can thus be seen as coevolving with its strategy as the core organization (the strategic center) reconfigures, always in reference to itself, sets of core capabilities and complementary assets. These capabilities and assets may be already available in the network or exist beyond its current boundaries.

Lorenzoni and Baden-Fuller refer to the network as a "web," and this metaphor is consistent with Robert Reich's generic description of a network structure:

> Instead of a pyramid, then, the high value-enterprise looks like a spider's web. Strategic brokers [e.g. core organizations, strategic centers] are at the center, but there are all sorts of connections that do not involve them directly, and new communications are being spun all the time. At each point of connection are a relatively small number of people – depending on the task, from a dozen to several hundred. If a group was any larger, it could not engage in rapid and informal learning. Here individual skills are combined so that the group's ability to innovate is more than the simple sum of its parts. Over time, as group members work through various problems and approaches, they learn about one another's abilities. They learn how they can help another perform better, who can contribute what to a project, and how they can best gain more experience together. Each participant is on the lookout for ideas that will propel the group forward. Such cumulative experience and understanding cannot be translated

into standard operating procedures easily transferable to other workers and organizations. Each point on the "enterprise web" represents a unique combination of skills.[72]

Organizations structured as webs *evolve dynamic emergent properties* such as the synthesis of economically valuable information through the interaction of network elements. An appropriately structured network can, by virtue of its "interconnectedness," generate dynamic knowledge flows that solve particular problems or suggest new opportunities within a technological trajectory.[73]

Although the variety of network structures is large, they can be grouped into three categories. Some have a low degree of interdependence between partners (e.g. customer–supplier relationships, subcontracting, single-transaction cooperation). Others have a high degree of partner interdependence (e.g. joint ventures, cooperative R&D agreements, consortia, licensing, long-standing trust relations).[74] In the third group are combinations, or "hybrids" of these first two categories.

All three structural categories can use either formal or informal (or a mix of both) linkages for collaboration, although the tendency in the United States is toward formal relationships. Similarly, all the categories can be organized for either general purpose innovation or innovation-specific purposes. Within the case studies only one general purpose network appeared, Sematech.

Finally, the lifespan of networks varies. Many operate for short periods of time; examples are the many "virtual corporations." These are temporary networks of companies and other organizations that come together to exploit specific, fast-changing opportunities, within a transitory (informal) structure. An example is the Sony–Philips linkage established to develop the format for the CD, where each partner contributed core capabilities with the promise of creating a "best-of-everything" network that would, by prearrangement, dissolve when the goal driving cooperation had been achieved.[75] In contrast, many networks exist for long periods of time. Many Japanese *keiretsu* have had long lifetimes, although in all cases their structural composition has been repeatedly modified by the forces of self-organization.

Summary

Networks have become the dominant sociotechnical systems in the innovation of complex technologies because of their self-organizing abilities. Dynamic self-organizing networks demonstrate that organizations are not simply agents of the market; rather, market forces and other aspects of the selection environment cannot be understood without reference to the core capabilities, complementary assets, and learning capacities of networks. This chapter has depicted the innovation of complex technologies as a set of self-reinforcing activities in which network resources, strategy, and structure are integrated to the extent that they have become almost inseparable, with feedback everywhere. Everything is important in such a systems perspective, but *network learning* is absolutely critical to complex innovation in a period of synthetic production.

Network learning fuels the process of self-organization, and it is to the dynamics of learning that we turn in the next chapter.

Notes

1. Frank-Jurgen Richter, "The Emergence of Corporate Alliance Networks – Conversion to Self-organization," *Human Systems Management*, Vol. 13, No. 1, 1994, pp. 22–3.
2. John A. Byrne, Richard Brandt and Otis Port, "The Virtual Corporation," *Business Week*, No. 3304, February 8, 1993, pp. 98–102.
3. Henry W. Chesbrough and David J. Teece, "When Is Virtual Virtuous? Organizing for Innovation," *Harvard Business Review*, Vol. 74, No. 1, January/February 1996, pp. 65–73.
4. Brian Bremer, *et al.*, "Keiretsu Connections: the Bonds Between the US and Japan's Industry Groups," *Business Week*, No. 3485, July 22, 1996, pp. 52–3.
5. John Mathews, "Organizational Foundations of Economic Learning," *Human Systems Management*, Vol. 15, 1996, p. 113.
6. Margaret J. Wheatley and Myron Kellner-Rogers, "Self-organization: the Irresistible Future of Organizing," *Strategy and Leadership*, Vol. 24, No. 4, July/August 1996, pp. 19–20.
7. Andrew C. Inkpen, "Creating Knowledge through Collaboration," *California Management Review*, Vol. 39, No. 1, Fall 1996, p. 124.
8. Anthony Sampson, *The Sovereign State of ITT*, New York: Stein and Daly Publishers, 1973, pp. 73–100.
9. Gary Hamel and C. K. Prahalad, *Competing for the Future*, Boston: Harvard Business School Press, 1994, pp. 197–9.
10. Kumiko Miyazaki, *Building Competences in the Firm: Lessons from Japanese and European Optoelectronics*, New York: St Martin's Press, 1995, pp. 11–38.
11. David J. Teece, "Profiting from Technological Innovation: Implications for Integration, Collaboration, Licensing and Public Policy," *Research Policy*, Vol. 15, December 1986, pp. 285–9.
12. H. Kevin Steensma, "Acquiring Technological Competencies through Inter-organizational Collaboration: an Organizational Learning Perspective," *Journal of Engineering Technology and Management*, Vol. 12, No. 4, January 1996, pp. 275–6.
13. Giovanni Dosi and Luigi Marengo, "Some Elements of an Evolutionary Theory of Organizational Competences," in Richard W. England, ed., *Evolutionary Concepts in Contemporary Economics*, Ann Arbor, MI: University of Michigan Press, 1994, pp. 147–178.
14. Richard R. Nelson, "Why Do Firms Differ, and How Does It Matter?" *Strategic Management Review*, Vol. 12, Special Issue, Winter 1991, p. 67.
15. Richard R. Nelson and Sidney G. Winter, *An Evolutionary Theory of Economic Change*, Cambridge, MA: Harvard University Press, 1982, p. 37.
16. Mark R. Gallon, Harold M. Stillman, and David Coates, "Putting Core Competency Thinking Into Practice," *Research-Technology Management*, Vol. 38, No. 3, May/June 1995, pp. 21–2.
17. David Lei, Michael A. Hitt, and Richard Bettis, "Dynamic Core Competences through Meta-learning and Strategic Context," *Journal of Management*, Vol. 22, No. 4, 1996, pp. 551–2.
18. Kulwant Singh, "The Impact of Technological Complexity and Interfirm Cooperation on Business Survival," *Academy of Management Journal*, Vol. 40, No. 2, April 1997, p. 343.
19. Richter, "The Emergence of Corporate Alliance Networks – Conversion to Self-organization," pp. 19–26.
20. David J. Teece, Richard Rumelt, Giovanni Dosi, and Sidney Winter, "Understanding Corporate Coherence: Theory and Evidence," *Journal of Economic Behavior and Organization*, Vol. 23, No. 1, January 1994, p. 15.
21. Teece, Rumelt, Dosi, and Winter, "Understanding Corporate Coherence," p. 15.
22. Gary S. Lynn, Joseph G. Morone, and Albert S. Paulson, "Marketing and Discontinuous Innovation: the Probe and Learn Process," *California Management Review*, Vol. 38, No. 3, Spring 1996, pp. 8–37.
23. Nelson and Winter, *An Evolutionary Theory of Economic Change*, pp. 256–8.

24. Marion G. Sobol and David Lei, "Environment, Manufacturing Technology, and Embedded Knowledge," *International Journal of Human Factors in Manufacturing*, Vol. 4, No. 2, April 1994, p. 168.
25. Gary P. Pisano, "Knowledge, Integration, and the Locus of Learning: an Empirical Analysis of Process Development," *Strategic Management Journal*, Vol. 15, Special Issue, Winter 1994, pp. 85–6.
26. Dorothy Leonard-Barton, *Wellsprings of Knowledge: Building and Sustaining the Sources of Innovation*, Boston: Harvard Business School Press, 1995, pp. 29–38.
27. Gordon E. Moore, "Some Personal Perspectives on Research in the Semiconductor Industry," in Richard S. Rosenbloom and William J. Spencer, eds, *Engines of Innovation: US Industrial Research at the End of an Era*, Boston: Harvard Business School Press, 1996, p. 168.
28. Caroline F. Benton and Kyoichi Kijima, "Maintaining Subsidiaries' Ability to Self-organize in the Japanese Market," *Systems Research*, Vol. 13, No. 4, December 1996, pp. 447–8.
29. Andrew Grove, *Only the Paranoid Survive*, New York: Doubleday, 1997.
30. Sobol and Lei, "Environment, Manufacturing Technology, and Embedded Knowledge," p. 175.
31. G. Dan Hutcheson and Jerry D. Hutcheson, "Technology and Economics in the Semiconductor Industry," *Scientific American*, Vol. 274, No. 1, January 1996, pp. 54–5.
32. Sidney G. Winter, "Knowledge and Competence as Strategic Assets," in David J. Teece, ed., *The Competitive Challenge: Strategies for Industrial Innovation and Renewal*, Cambridge, MA: Ballinger Publishing Company, 1987, pp. 170–80.
33. Wendy Faulkner and Jacqueline Senker, *Knowledge Frontiers: Public Sector Research and Industrial Innovation in Biotechnology, Engineering Ceramics, and Parallel Computing*, New York: Oxford University Press, 1995, p. 211.
34. Knut H. Sorensen and Nora Levold, "Tacit Networks, Heterogeneous Engineers, and Embodied Technology," *Science, Technology, and Human Values*, Vol. 17, No. 1, Winter 1992, p. 27.
35. Jens F. Christensen, "Asset Profiles for Technological Innovation," *Research Policy*, Vol. 24, No. 5, September 1995, pp. 727–8.
36. David J. Teece, "Profiting from Technological Innovation: Implications for Integration, Collaboration, Licensing and Public Policy," in Teece, ed., *The Competitive Challenge*, pp. 191–3.
37. Christel Lane and Reinhard Bachmann, "The Social Constitution of Trust: Supplier Relations in Britain and Germany," *Organization Studies*, Vol. 17, No. 3, 1996, pp. 365–95; W. Mark Fruin and Toshihiro Nishiguchi, "Supplying the Toyota Production System: Intercorporate Organizational Evolution and Supplier Subsystems," in Bruce Kogut, ed., *Country Competitiveness: Technology and the Organizing of Work*, New York: Oxford University Press, 1993, pp. 225–46.
38. David J. Teece, "Strategies for Capturing the Financial Benefits from Technological Innovation," in Nathan Rosenberg, Ralph Landau, and David C. Mowery, eds, *Technology and the Wealth of Nations*, Stanford, CA: Stanford University Press, 1992, pp. 183–5.
39. Jan Fagerberg, "User–Producer Interaction, Learning, and Comparative Advantage," *Cambridge Journal of Economics*, Vol. 19, No. 1, February 1995, pp. 243–56; Eric von Hippel and Marcie J. Tyre, "How Learning by Doing Is Done: Problem Identification in Novel Process Equipment," *Research Policy*, Vol. 24, No. 1, January 1995, pp. 1–12.
40. Inkpen, "Creating Knowledge through Collaboration," p. 123.
41. Dosi and Marengo, "Some Elements of an Evolutionary Theory of Organizational Competences," pp. 165–77.
42. Faulkner and Senker, *Knowledge Frontiers*, p. 37.
43. Mario Cimoli and Giovanni Dosi, "Technological Paradigms, Patterns of Learning and Development: an Introductory Roadmap," *Journal of Evolutionary Economics*, Vol. 5, No. 3, 1995, p. 246; Giovanni Dosi, "Sources, Procedures, and Microeconomic Effects of

Innovation," *Journal of Economic Literature*, Vol. 26, No. 3, September 1988, p. 1127.

44. Winter, "Knowledge and Competence as Strategic Assets," in Teece, ed., *The Competitive Challenge*, pp. 166–9.
45. Ikujiro Nonaka and Teruo Yamanouchi, "Managing Innovation as a Self-renewing Process," *Journal of Business Venturing*, Vol. 4, No. 5, September 1989, p. 306.
46. William H. Starbuck, "Unlearning Ineffective or Obsolete Technologies," *International Journal of Technology Management*, Special Publication on Unlearning and Learning, Vol. 11, Nos 7/8, 1996, p. 729.
47. Leonard-Barton, *Wellsprings of Knowledge*, pp. 118–19.
48. Pisano, "Knowledge, Integration and the Locus of Learning: an Empirical Analysis of Process Development," p. 89.
49. Moore, "Some Personal Perspectives on Research in the Semiconductor Industry," in Rosenbloom and Spencer, eds, *Engines of Innovation*, p. 168.
50. Lei, Hitt, and Bettis, "Dynamic Core Competences through Meta-learning and Strategic Context," p. 558.
51. Hamel, "Competition for Competence and Inter-partner Learning within International Strategic Alliances," pp. 83–4.
52. Leonard H. Lynn, N. Mohan Reddy, and John D. Aram, "Linking Technology and Institutions: the Innovation Community Framework," *Research Policy*, Vol. 25, No. 1, January 1996, p. 103.
53. Michael E. Porter, "What Is Strategy?" *Harvard Business Review*, Vol. 74, No. 6, November/December 1996, p. 64.
54. Robert H. Hayes and Gary P. Pisano, "Beyond World-class: the New Manufacturing Strategy," *Harvard Business Review*, Vol. 72, No. 1, January/February 1994, p. 86.
55. W. Bradford Ashton, Bruce R. Kinzey, and Marvin E. Gunn, Jr, "A Structured Approach for Monitoring Science and Technology Developments," *International Journal of Technology Management*, Vol. 6, Nos 1/2, 1991, pp. 91–111.
56. Alexander Gerybadze, "Technology Forecasting as a Process of Organisational Intelligence," *R&D Management*, Vol. 24, No. 2, April 1994, pp. 131–40.
57. Ralph Stacey, "Emerging Strategies for a Chaotic Environment," *Long Range Planning*, Vol. 29, No. 2, April 1996, p. 187.
58. Fumio Kodama, "Technology Fusion and the New R&D," *Harvard Business Review*, Vol. 70, No. 4, July/August 1992, pp. 70–1.
59. S. K. Subramanian and Yeswath Subramanian, "Managing Technology Fusion through Synergy Circles in Japan," *Journal of Engineering and Technology Management*, Vol. 8, No. 4, December 1991, pp. 332–3.
60. Michael L. Gerlach and James R. Lincoln, "The Organization of Business Networks in the United States and Japan," in Nitin Nohria and Robert G. Eccles, eds, *Networks and Organizations: Structure, Form, and Action*, Boston: Harvard Business School Press, 1992, pp. 491–520.
61. Richard N. Osborn and John Hagedoorn, "The Institutionalization and Evolutionary Dynamics of Interorganizational Alliances and Networks," *Academy of Management Journal*, Vol. 40, No. 2, April 1997, pp. 261–78; Nirmalya Kumar, "The Power of Trust in Manufacture–Retailer Relationships," *Harvard Business Review*, Vol. 74, No. 6, November/December 1996, pp. 92–106.
62. Chris DeBresson and Fernand Amesse, "Networks of Innovators: a Review and Introduction to the Issue," *Research Policy*, Vol. 20, No. 5, October 1991, p. 368.
63. David J. Teece, "Competition, Cooperation, and Innovation: Organizational Arrangements for Regimes of Rapid Technological Progress," *Journal of Economic Behavior and Organization*, Vol. 18, April 1992, pp. 14–15 (emphasis added).
64. Charles W. L. Hill, "Establishing a Standard: Competitive Strategy and Technological Standards in Winner-take-all Industries," *Academy of Management Executive*, Vol. 11, May 1997, pp. 12–14.

65. Nelson and Winter, *An Evolutionary Theory of Economic Change*, p. 37.
66. Margaret J. Wheatley, *Leadership and the New Science: Learning about Organization from an Orderly Universe*, San Francisco: Berrett-Koehler Publishers, 1992, pp. 90–1.
67. William Lazonick, "Organizational Integration in Three Industrial Revolutions," in Arnold Heertje and Mark Perlman, eds, *Evolving Technology and Market Structure: Studies in Schumpeterian Economics*, Ann Arbor, MI: University of Michigan Press, 1990, p. 80.
68. Morgan L. Swink, Christopher Sandvig, and Vincent A. Mabert, "Customizing Concurrent Engineering Processes: Five Case Studies," *Journal of Product Innovation Management*, Vol. 13, May 1996, pp. 229–44.
69. Tom Kiely, "Innovation Congregations," *Technology Review*, Vol. 97, No. 3, April 1994, pp. 55–60.
70. Alfred Rosenblatt and George F. Watson, "Concurrent Engineering," *IEEE Spectrum*, July 1991, pp. 22–3.
71. Gianni Lorenzoni and Charles Baden-Fuller, "Creating a Strategic Center to Manage a Web of Partners," *California Management Review*, Vol. 37, No. 3, Spring 1995, p. 157.
72. Robert B. Reich, *The Work of Nations: Preparing Ourselves for 21st Century Capitalism*, New York: Alfred A. Knopf, 1991, p. 89.
73. Yasunori Baba and Ken-ichi Imai, "A Network View of Innovation and Entrepreneurship: the Case of the Evolution of the VCR Systems," *International Social Science Journal*, Vol. 45, No. 1, February 1993, pp. 24–5.
74. Stig Larsson, "New Dimensions in Organizing Industrial Networks," *International Journal of Technology Management*, Vol. 8, Nos 1/2, Special Issue on New Technological Foundations of Strategic Management, 1993, pp. 49–50.
75. Samuel E. Bleecker, "The Virtual Organization," *Futurist*, Vol. 28, No. 2, March/April 1994, pp. 9–14.

CHAPTER EIGHT

Network Learning

Keeping pace with the complexity of technological progress requires that networks repeatedly learn about, integrate, and apply a wide variety of knowledge and know-how. The evolution of the computer industry, for instance, has depended on the rapid synthesis of knowledge from a number of scientific disciplines (e.g. solid state physics, mathematics, language theory), and combining this synthetic science with a bewildering array of hardware and software capabilities (e.g. architectural design, chip manufacturing). In such a complex technological environment, no single organization, not even the largest and most sophisticated firm, is likely to succeed if it embarks on a "go it alone" strategy (e.g. relying on its own production experience or R&D). Thus, there is increased dependence in complex technological sectors on self-organizing networks that behave as learning organizations. Networks have proven especially capable of know-how learning (e.g. tacit appreciation of how sets of technologies might be made to work together).[1]

Network learning involves identifying, accessing, creating, diffusing, and continuously updating knowledge to provide commercial technological leadership. Knowledge in both explicit and tacit forms is useful; information and data are not necessarily so.[2] In the process of solving problems, new knowledge is normally integrated into and diffused through the entire network. Network learning is characterized by constant experimentation and the development of new or redefined heuristics; it is associated with an evolving network configuration. New knowledge is essential to network self-organization and the reshaping of technological trajectories that provide the basis for sustainable competitive advantage.[3]

Networks are synergistic: they continuously learn more than the sum of their constituent parts. Networks also learn faster than their constituent parts.[4] Rapid, synergistic network learning processes often depend on trial-and-error activities that are guided by the dynamic routines embedded in network structures. The case studies support the idea that *the greatest advantage a network can have is the ability to learn quickly.* Learning has become so important that the capacity to learn quickly is a strategic objective of many networks.[5] In the innovation of complex technologies, networks prosper only if the interactions of core capabilities, complementary assets, strategy, and structure facilitate rapid learning.

Although the interdependence of network learning and the commercialization of complex technologies is a popular theme, we are only beginning to get a sense for how such learning evolves. Complex network learning is certainly nonlinear, heterogeneous, incomplete, often crisis-oriented, and as dependent on forgetting as on remembering.[6] Much network learning is unplanned and serendipitous, but a critical part results from purposefully "learning how to organize to learn." In Intel, for example, network learning is facilitated by a concerted attempt to reward the sharing of information and capability. To promote sharing, some areas of the company assign high-level technical people the role of full-time communicators.

Fast and continuous learning must quickly recognize and act upon errors, that is, on the differences between the network's expectations and the actual results. Learning from mistakes, which has been called "error-embracing" behavior, can be a source of valuable knowledge. As Akio Morita, one of Sony's founders, has said:

> If the causes of the mistake are clarified and made public, the person who made the mistake will not forget it and others will not make the same mistake. I tell our people, "Go ahead and do what you think is right. If you make a mistake, you will learn from it. Just don't make the same mistake twice."[7]

Network learning is a social and collective activity. Although individual expertise is necessary, it is the collaborative nature of learning that distinguishes networks. Integral to collaboration is flexible communication. Strategies and structures that facilitate rapid communication and learning are essential to the innovation of complex technologies.[8]

Deficiencies in strategy and structure were evident in the failure of the first major organizational effort to deal with innovation after the Second World War – the development of conglomerates. On the strategic side, inertia led to continued emphasis on investment approaches appropriate to mass production – such as investing in equipment rather than in people – but not to synthetic production. Factory workers continued to be treated as inferior learners. To the extent that collective learning was recognized, it was seen as applying only to salaried management personnel. As Lazonick notes, "as workers gained more collective power, American managers became all the more determined to take and keep skills off the shop floor."[9] On the structure side, the conglomerates continued to rely on hierarchical organizations that emphasized specialization, compartmentalization, and rigid authority relations.[10] These approaches to strategic and structural factors remain a barrier to network learning in many sectors in the United States. Thus a quick look at the history of organizational learning in the United States is a useful starting point.

Organizational learning: a brief tour

Throughout the industrial era the dominant focus of organizational learning was *production learning*, the "learning by doing" that results from repetition.[11] Studies of production learning in this era generally shared two assumptions: (a) it is a free good; and (b) it occurs at the same rate for all production, given parallel rates of output. Most investigators rejected the view that production learning might be affected by organizational choices such as different investments in training.[12] Instead, production learning was assumed to result primarily from improvements in individual worker ingenuity, skill, and dexterity associated with repeated practice.

The earliest modifications in this perspective came from studies of sectors experiencing very rapid innovation, such as electronics. Analysts identified sets of internal organizational capabilities that appeared to enable the absorption of information and learning from the external environment. These organizational capabilities, which came to be known as *absorptive capacity*, increased attention to improved production technologies and enhanced techniques for coordinating production processes.[13] However, the idea that deliberate encouragement of internally generated learning could improve production remained foreign to the dominant perspective.

Both production learning and absorptive capacity assumed mechanistic, and thus static, modes of organizational learning. These modes sit well with mass manufacturing and its linear, mechanical model of innovation and static concept of organization. Static concepts, however, are serious problems for the dynamic learning processes integral to networks that innovate complex technologies, because, as Geoffrey Hodgson has observed, "information, learning and knowledge are difficult to incorporate into a mechanistic scheme."[14]

Mechanistic conceptualizations go hand-in-glove with analytical, reductionist approaches to understanding. That is, they lend themselves to understanding and managing by dividing and subdividing into parts and ignoring complex interactions that are not reducible to the linear action of one part on another. Complex systems, however, demand organic conceptualizations and synthetic insights. The transition to organic concepts has been made more difficult by the cultural preferences of Americans for analytical reductionism as the basis for understanding and for individual competition as the basis for societal improvement. These preferences have generated especially serious obstacles to the collaboration needed to create synthetic knowledge. Given the history of mass production, this culture, and the influence of analytic approaches, it is not surprising that network learning has received little attention[15] and that organizational learning generally has been characterized as a "black box" that was not worth studying.[16]

Network learning opportunities

Only recently has this situation begun to change, driven in part by the recognition that organizational arrangements played some part in a variety of Japanese innovation triumphs. Not only did the Japanese success stories involve quite complicated and highly visible networks (e.g. the *keiretsu*); Japanese network learning seemed to feature processes driven at least as much by internal organizational factors, such as strategy and structure, as by external, market forces.[17]

There have been two major consequences of the increased attention to the role of Japanese networks in innovating complex technologies. First, as the body of research on learning organizations in the US and abroad has expanded dramatically,[18] greater attention has been paid to networks as the dominant type of learning organization.[19] Second, once the organizational "black box" was opened, new patterns of network learning were discerned.[20] Table 8.1 summarizes these patterns, and the next section is ordered around these learning opportunities.

Learning by doing

Recent studies of learning by doing have focused on the processes of creating and diffusing new knowledge. These studies argue that innovations in the production process may be a consequence of conscious experimentation and organizational adaptation rather than a simple production function controlled by a standard learning curve.[21] In each of the case studies, creating new knowledge through learning by doing was a common occurrence for those involved.

Table 8.1 Network learning opportunities

Type of learning	Source of learning
Learning by doing	In-house production experience
Learning by using	User experience and competence
Learning from advances in science and technology	Monitoring and forecasting scientific and technological developments
Learning from spillovers	Involuntary leakage or voluntary exchange of useful knowledge
Learning by interaction	Cooperative relationships
Learning from formalized inquiry	Research and development

Sources: Wendy Faulkner, "Conceptualizing Knowledge Used in Innovation: a Second Look at the Science–Technology Distinction and Industrial Innovation," *Science, Technology, and Human Values*, Vol. 19, No. 4, Autumn 1994, pp. 425–58; Franco Malerba, "Learning by Firms and Incremental Technological Change," *Economic Journal*, Vol. 102, No. 413, July 1992, pp. 845–59.

The importance of more dynamic learning by doing was initially recognized in studies of knowledge creation and dissemination in Japanese factories. Japanese successes with process technology focused investigators on what was happening on the shopfloor.[22] Investigations of Japanese manufacturing facilities documented a pattern in which teams of engineers and production personnel experimented by changing technological parameters, such as temperature or pressure settings, and organizational relations (e.g. configurations of work teams) during ongoing manufacturing activities. Rapid improvements in performance often followed these process experiments because they produced more effective knowledge transfer among the teams of engineers and production personnel.[23]

Other analyses have shown that learning by doing is not limited to experimenting with established manufacturing processes. For example, in complex production systems it is often impossible to design optimal technologies in advance of their installation and operation. Learning by doing has been especially evident in the trial-and-error methods used to install and modify computer-based production technology. Labels such as "learning by trying" have been coined to characterize the experimentation needed to make complex combinations of process technologies work well. In some situations so much learning by doing is needed that each organization winds up with a unique computer-aided production system.[24]

Often experimentation with different organizational and technological experiments involves failures. The failures, however, may prove to be significant innovation opportunities. In John Bessant's words, even failed experiments can facilitate learning, "since they reveal the complexity and uncertainty in the innovation process."[25]

The importance of learning by doing and the patterns of its occurrence appear to vary among sectors. Eric von Hippel and Marcie Tyre found that, in the computer manufacturing industry, learning on the factory floor really does require "doing." In that sector, even if knowledge is available before production begins, modern production processes are so complicated that it is unrealistic to expect learning without doing.[26]

Much of the difficulty of learning without doing in complex sectors can be traced to the tacit nature of much of the knowledge previously acquired through learning by doing. Tacit learning by doing is difficult to transfer from any particular phase of the evolution of process technologies to the next phase without actually moving experienced people or providing some mechanism by which the knowledge can be converted to an explicit form.[27] The case studies underline the centrality of tacit knowledge in the process of innovating complex technologies. In the turbine blade case, learning by doing has been critical for the casting companies. When asked how this happens, a senior manager replied that when his casting firm needs to meet a new performance standard, the old timers get together and synthesize from experience. As he admitted, such synthesis is a guess, but one based on 200 person-years of production experience.

Learning by doing is also important for simple technological sectors, but its significance clearly declines as the knowledge required for innovation becomes more explicit. For example, when Gary Pisano examined the biotechnology industry, he found that most knowledge is accessed prior to manufacturing and that substantial redesign of organizational and technological processes often occurs based on what he calls a "learning before doing" experience. In his words:

> The state of prior knowledge about the process technology determines the appropriate strategies for acquiring the requisite feedback. In environments where prior knowledge is weak, high-fidelity feedback requires experiments in the actual production environment ("learning by doing"). In contrast, when reliable theoretical models and heuristics exist [as in the biotechnology industry], laboratory experiments, simulation, and other forms of "learning-*before*-doing" can be productively harnessed.[28]

Learning by using

In some technological areas, significant network learning happens when products are used or when potential users contribute their unique knowledge to the innovation process. The innovation of complex technologies almost always requires "debugging," because attaining synthesis of multiple, complexly interdependent systems and subsystems is difficult in advance. This explains the importance of trial-and-error experimentation in the innovation process. For complex technologies, the process of incremental innovation along a trajectory is often partly spurred by efforts to correct deficiencies identified while using the previous product generation. Incremental learning by using may be anything but smooth and predictable. Because product deficiencies are unpredictable and how users may adapt to or modify product technologies is uncertain, incremental learning by using is typically a "lumpy" or episodic process.[29]

The networks in some sectors have established innovation procedures and mechanisms that are designed to remove some of this unpredictability and take advantage of expected learning in a more systematic way. Sometimes the mechanism involves identifying and working closely with *lead-users*: users who have a history of being early and successful adopters of product technologies and have established their ability to develop innovation-demanding specifications and standards.[30] Often these lead users become members of innovation networks. This has been the case in the US aircraft industry, as aircraft manufacturers and airline companies have developed tight and long-standing relationships.[31]

Another way to seek user-driven innovation more systematically is to involve government agencies intimately in network activities. Again, innovation in the aircraft industry has benefited from participation by the National Transportation Safety Board and the Federal Aviation Administration, both of which systematically document industry experience with airplanes and provide this information to the producer networks. Even with advanced simulation techniques, the flight experience of test pilots and military pilots (lead-users), disseminated through government oversight programs, remains essential to learning whether aircraft have desired properties and where deficiencies may occur.[32]

In other areas, learning by using is a necessity because the performance goals exist in part as tacit knowledge; that is, the desired performance of the technology cannot be explicitly defined. The Varian Clinac case repeatedly illustrates the role of learning by using, especially by lead-users. The initiative for the first use of linear accelerators in cancer treatment came from a doctor at the Stanford Medical School who sought to improve the existing treatment provided primarily by machines using radioactive cobalt (cobalt-60). The doctor used existing experience with these cobalt-60 machines to conceive a better piece of equipment.

As innovation has evolved along the Clinac trajectory, the network has continued deliberate, organized efforts to tap the knowledge of its user community. An example is the annual conference Varian has with a group of users invited for the purpose of identifying future innovations. Central to this process has been the repeated need to convert the often tacit knowledge of the users into explicit knowledge that can be used by the producers. Users have often expressed their needs in use-oriented terms like the following: "We need beam control that will allow us to adjust the energy level as the beam revolves around the patient." Or "We need a capacity to track the precise location of an organ in the body as it changes between treatment visits."

The same pattern of capturing users' knowledge was evident in the cardio-imaging case. That is, the tacit knowledge of diagnosticians was often converted into explicit knowledge that was integrated into the technology. An illustrative input from a diagnostician might be: "I need a picture that provides a clearer boundary between the blood and the flesh in the heart." This conversion process often entails trying out a technology change on the user, to see if it meets an expressed need. Successful innovation happens when the user says: "Yes, that level of clarity will allow me to make a better diagnosis."

These cases are consistent with broader research into sectors like scientific instruments. The evolution of scientific instruments has featured substantial "user innovation" from scientists who identify a new use for existing instruments and so begin the process of designing and developing new types of instrumentation.[33]

But user innovation is not limited to complex sectors. For example, in the construction industry, "user-builders" have been the source of more innovations than manufacturers. Sarah Slaughter found:

> User-builders created most of the innovations in this study; they draw upon their extensive construction experience to create new elements which they then employ. This reservoir of past learning appears to provide opportunities for these users to create innovations which are both inexpensive and rapidly deployed. In addition, these innovations explicitly address problems associated with integrating disparate components into a well-functioning whole unit. In contrast, the innovations commercialized by panel manufacturers only change the product and not its connections to other building equipment.[34]

A key implication of Slaughter's research and other examinations of user innovation is that, in some industrial sectors, users may move well beyond mere incremental adjustments to create entirely new systems, components, or processes. This radical innovation is particularly likely where technologies must be integrated with other systems quickly. User innovations can be a rich source for developing a technology, and possibly they are indispensable in connecting separate technologies into an operational whole. In fact, more sectors now systematically link innovation to user communities. In software manufacturing, for instance, selected lead-users are supplied with new products in the expectation that they will help producers learn where "bugs" or deficiencies occur in how the software performs, and thereby enable the producers to correct or improve the programs.[35]

Increasingly, intimate interaction between users and producers in networks is seen as essential to the learning needed for successful commercialization. Although the pattern is widespread, learning by using appears to have had especially high payoff when technologically advanced users were tightly tied to producers of advanced, complex technology.[36]

Learning from advances in science and technology

One of the most obvious ways networks learn is by producing their own science and technology (S&T). Networks aggressively support a wide variety of R&D programs designed to generate state-of-the-art scientific and technological knowledge. Yet in many sectors one of the most striking adaptations is the extent to which both participant companies and networks have moved away from the "not invented here" syndrome. The commercialization of complex technologies increasingly requires that networks not only produce at least some of the S&T underlying their processes and products but also monitor and acquire relevant knowledge from the broader scientific and technological community.

Synthesizing S&T-based learning from both within and outside the network requires not just promoting internal R&D programs but also investing in intelligence about external R&D initiatives and the status of existing and emerging technology.[37] Monitoring and forecasting S&T usually entails paying attention to more than just explicit knowledge, such as scientific breakthroughs or emerging process and product technologies. It demands a capacity to participate in largely tacit trends, such as the ability to assimilate research techniques and equipment, and to gain experience with new engineering design or prototyping methods.[38] Network learning directed toward monitoring the evolving S&T must also be concerned with organizational factors. Examples include gaining access to information about key technical personnel, new projects, and R&D budgets.[39]

Advances in explicit scientific knowledge are tempting targets for networks, and there is abundant evidence that progress in science has, over time, created an international "pool of knowledge" that has been a significant source of technological opportunities. Biotechnology is only the most recent example. However, the linkage between the stock of scientific understanding and technological advance is seldom simple, direct, or rapid. The connections typically are very complicated and subtle, featuring complex feedback loops and relatively long time lags. In the words of Alvin Klevorick and his colleagues:

A number of studies have documented that, for the most part, scientists and engineers engaged in industrial R&D employ science as a set of tools and stock of knowledge to be tapped in problem-solving. *Used this way, old science may be as useful as more recent developments, and the relation between technological advance and the current scientific frontier may be remote.* The evidence is overwhelming that most applied R&D efforts start with a need or objective and then reach back to science to enable the goal to be achieved. In general, the science employed will be in the mind of the researcher or otherwise easily accessible, as through consultation with other workers. Some industrial R&D scientists will be more up to date than others, and as scholars like Allen have shown, these often serve as "inside consultants." *It is rare that the stimulus for an applied R&D effort comes from an appreciation of new basic scientific findings, and the search for relevant science carries no presumption in favor of recent science.*[40]

In the mass production era, monitoring within a particular technological sector was sufficient to remain current with the state of the art. But increasing complexity demands a much broader reconnaissance using more sophisticated techniques, which may be both costly and time-consuming. Consequently, in some sectors networks have been created whose central tasks are monitoring and trend analysis.

The Japanese have led the way in advanced monitoring of S&T. Networks comprising firms, industry associations, government agencies, and other organizations have developed a reconnaissance capability that is cited by some observers as a major element in the innovation success of Japanese industries. Central to successful organizational monitoring is the ability to clarify technological trajectories and to realize that the knowledge acquired is fraught with uncertainties. Some observers believe many Japanese networks are successful because they follow a "learning to learn" approach to monitoring; they are particularly adept at learning from others' earlier mistakes.[41]

The microprocessor case study is an example of network learning from advances in S&T. The semiconductor industry established the Semiconductor Research Corporation (SRC) on the premise that it had to create new knowledge while simultaneously tapping into worldwide S&T advances. The SRC has provided funds that have been used not only to support research but also to train new scientists and engineers. The training program has been designed to access the university community, and the university researchers associated with the SRC have become a component of its worldwide monitoring system as they pursued their research. The microprocessor and semiconductor network thus has vastly increased its S&T reconnaissance system by expanding academic participation in the Sematech and SRC communities.

Learning from spillovers

Spillovers are the involuntary leakage or voluntary exchange of useful knowledge, whether or not the creator of the knowledge wants to prevent its leakage or exchange.[42] A patent disclosure is a typical voluntary exchange, while frequent involuntary leakages of knowledge follow from the use of "reverse engineering" (i.e. purchasing a competitor's product, inspecting it, and figuring out how it works and how it was made).[43] Both inter- and intraindustry spillovers are sources of network learning, but due to the greater similarities in technological opportunities and processes, intraindustry spillovers seem to occur with more frequency and magnitude. Commonly identified forms of spillovers include not only patent disclosures and reverse engineering, but also acquisition of technical knowledge developed by competitors through licensing, publications or technical meetings, the movement of key people, and informal, interpersonal communication.[44]

Spillover learning has always pervaded technological innovation, but as networks have moved away from the "not invented here" syndrome, the rate of spillover learning has accelerated. Often patterns of spillovers are quite unpredictable. For example, spillover from the scientific instrument industry to the chemical industry, and from chemical products to the non-electrical portion of the machinery industry, has been documented.[45] Given this unpredictability, in the context of complex technologies, it is nearly impossible to protect against spillovers; attempts to do so may backfire by creating barriers to rapid learning.

Why is it so hard for organizations to control access to information about their new product and process technologies? Richard Nelson provides some answers:

> In the first place, the very staking of claims involves the release of information. This is one of the intents of the patent system, and where patents are effective in protecting an innovation they also reveal it. In industries where patents are not particularly effective, but aggressive use of a head start advantage is, companies have strong incentives to stake their claims through advertising, open meetings and a wide variety of other ways, in addition to patenting. They need to attract customers, and this means they need to tell them a lot about their new wares.[46]

While formal sources of spillover such as patent disclosures have been studied a great deal, informal, interpersonal channels have been underestimated until recently. Informal channels appear to be especially significant for the transfer of tacit knowledge.[47] For instance, Faulkner and Senker found that, in the biotechnology, ceramics, and parallel computing industries, technical personnel quite frequently communicated with their counterparts in competitor organizations:

> opportunities to do so arise, for example, when technical people come together at government or industry meetings to agree and establish standards. They are well practised at focusing such discussion on technical areas of common concern – including the largely tacit knowledge related to research and design instrumentalities – at the same time avoiding disclosure of proprietary information. We would therefore suggest that some types of tacit knowledge are quite extensively shared through informal interaction between competitors.[48]

Patterns of spillovers appear to be closely linked to the decisions of firms and other organizations regarding cooperative or non-cooperative approaches to innovation. Thus, symmetric intraindustry spillovers are associated with firm strategies that emphasize collaboration.[49] In fact, spillovers have become such pervasive sources of network formation and learning that the interdependence of network members may be defined to some degree by spillover patterns. Gunnar Eliasson, for instance, argues that networks often coalesce around "technological spillover systems," the pattern of knowledge diffusion (typically with a high tacit content) that emerges from integrated sets of dominant competencies and know-how in a particular industry. According to this analysis, shared recognition of the existence of a pattern of spillovers may be a major incentive for network formation or expansion.[50]

Learning by interaction

A major objective of network interaction is to learn more about the technical and organizational capabilities of network members, but there are also opportunities to enhance competence in collaboration itself. Successful interactive learning commonly triggers further cooperation.[51] The work of Johannes Pennings and his colleagues suggests that firms that succeed at networking may become not only more adept at learning about the technological dimensions of collaboration, but also more skilled in organizational dynamics. For example, companies experienced in collaborative ventures frequently become better at resolving conflicts in organizational governance.[52] This learning is critically important to the processes of effective self-organization that are essential to networks that innovate complex technologies.

The innovation of complex technologies requires an interactive process; as complexity increases, so do the interactive processes. As cooperation evolves, networks and their member organizations are rewarded by branching out and establishing new collaborative interactions. But the precise configurations of these interactions vary widely. For instance, cooperative relationships among organizations can differ in structure (e.g. vertical or horizontal linkages) or duration (e.g. varying from short term to long term).

Whatever the nature of the cooperative relationships, valuable knowledge can be created and transferred through repeated information-exchanging interactions. These collaboration-generated information exchanges have been called the dynamic factor in the creation of information needed to resolve problems.[53]

Interactive learning, sometimes called "learning by collaboration," happens, for example, when producers, suppliers, and users are linked in ways that foster codevelopment of products. Employing suppliers and users as full collaborators in the innovation process means producers must learn *with* them, rather than *from* them.[54] Trust and reciprocity are crucial to this relationship, as is defining the interactions in terms of mutual benefit and abandoning the dogma that commercialization must be a zero-sum game.[55] But this is easier said than done in the United States. A recent study concludes:

> The approach of the central firms we studied is to develop a sense of trust and reciprocity in the system. This trust and reciprocity is a dynamic concept and it can be very tight. This aspect has similarities to contracts in the sense that obligations are precisely understood. *But Anglo-Saxon contracts are typically limited in the sense that partners are not expected to go beyond the contract. In contrast, in a network perspective, the behavior is prescribed for the unknown, each promising to work in a particular manner to resolve future challenges and difficulties as they arise.* This means that each partner will promise to deliver what is expected, and that future challenges will also be addressed positively. If there are uncertainties and difficulties in the relationships, these will be resolved after the work is done. If one party goes beyond (in the positive sense) the traditional contract, others will remember and reciprocate at a later date.[56]

Not surprisingly, the demands of complex technology are engendering efforts to resolve the contradiction between the needs for open-ended, trust-based cooperation and the demands of a legalistic culture. An illustration from our case studies is the agreement between HP and Philips under which the MRI-based cardio-imaging technology was innovated. The agreement started with the assumption that the development effort would be divided roughly evenly between the two companies.

The agreement recognized, however, that this probably would not be the case in practice. Thus, once the technology was on the market, the companies agreed they would meet to evaluate their relative contributions, with that evaluation determining how the profits would be divided. Those involved in developing the agreement indicated that this arrangement for dealing with future profits was accepted because they assumed that the relationship would be one that would continue for the foreseeable future.

Learning from formalized inquiry

Networks engage in formal processes of inquiry aimed at generating knowledge. The best known of these processes is in-house R&D. Most in-house R&D probes "locally," meaning that the R&D is focused on familiar areas. The fact that prior learning has been embodied in organizational routines reinforces this tendency to explore familiar technological trajectories.[57]

R&D-based learning commonly produces two benefits: new knowledge and an enhanced ability of the network to exploit existing information. Formal R&D is a way for a network to "keep its hand in" ongoing scientific and technological developments. Very often, organizations invest in R&D because interindustry spillovers encourage exploration of topics and problems closely related to the spillover knowledge.[58] An example is the initial innovation of the cardio-imaging technology, which explored possibilities presented by major advances in radar technology and digital electronics. These external developments stimulated the evolution of the phased array transducer, a technology that made possible a complete sweep of the heart with sound waves from a single location, with the echo signals processed to give a useful image of the heart muscle.

One point seems clear: network learning from formalized inquiry has the highest payoff when it is fully integrated into the overall network learning process. None of the case studies suggested that the learning opportunities from formalized R&D were a higher priority than any other type of network learning.

Learning, unlearning, and relearning

Unlearning or loss of background knowledge is the opposite side of the coin for all six categories of network learning opportunities. Unlearning is an idea as old as the learning curve itself. Some of the earliest studies of production learning explained variations among companies in part by postulating that organizational forgetting was hampering the otherwise automatic learning curve. The most common explanations for unlearning have been: (a) high turnover rates of experienced production workers who were replaced with inexperienced workers; (b) management–labor conflicts that led to strikes or other work interruptions; and (c) loss of organizational records that conveyed key elements of know-how or routines.[59] This early literature saw unlearning as an unambiguously negative factor, and there is still some accuracy in the argument today. Networks that engage in learning of any type suffer if useful knowledge is not incorporated into organizational routines or otherwise stored. Some forgetting is dysfunctional, so relearning often has to take place. As a consequence, complex networks often feature what might be called "relearning by doing" or "relearning by interaction" at the same time new learning is under way.[60]

More recent work has come to see unlearning more positively as an opportunity to remove obstacles to change. For example, one can find studies today arguing that getting rid of workers for the purpose of unlearning can be positive, if the resultant unlearning is the first step toward new organizational behavior.[61] A more common interpretation, however, is that unlearning, as the giving up of old assumptions, is inextricably intertwined with learning. From this viewpoint, unlearning has more to do with modifying organizational strategy, structure, core capabilities, and complementary assets than it does with the loss of individual workers.

For example, Patricia Meyers found in her detailed case study of Xerox Corporation's copier business in the mid-1970s that, when the company faced a crisis and loss of market, it had to unlearn the assumption that it knew its customers better than its competitors did. Xerox had to learn that revisiting its unquestioned assumptions and unlearning some or all of them was not a one-time event – it had to unlearn continuously.[62]

Richard Bettis and C. K. Prahalad found much the same thing in their investigation of IBM's computer troubles in the early 1980s. Before IBM could respond to the challenge presented by producers of personal computers, it had to unlearn its assumption of the supremacy of mainframes. They concluded:

> The need to unlearn may suggest why new competitors often displace experienced incumbents in an industry when major structural change occurs (e.g. the personal computer revolution). The new entrants are starting with a clean sheet of paper and do not have the problem of having to run down an unlearning curve in order to be able to run up a learning curve.[63]

In the context of self-organizing networks, the variety of learning opportunities and demands for unlearning old habits and old assumptions commonly occur in combinations. As an example, an organization seeking to enter a new technological arena will often undertake a variety of external learning endeavors, including collaboration, monitoring of intraindustry spillovers, and translating foreign research documents. Networks usually have diverse organizations as members because different organizations typically have different kinds of knowledge. Private firms tend to be better sources of tacit technological know-how, while universities are more capable generators and translators of explicit, codifiable knowledge. The increasing need for a variety of knowledge sources and learning capabilities helps explain why network organizations increasingly include corporate, university, and government components.[64] Moreover, the various learning categories are intertwined. Learning from formalized inquiry, for example, can be and is combined with learning by interaction when collaborative R&D projects are undertaken. But how do networks actually learn? What are the network learning processes that are put into place to try to take advantage of learning opportunities?

Network learning processes

In Chapter 7 the discussion focused on learning as a resource in the process of network self-organization (i.e. searching for new problem solving knowledge and procedures, experimenting with and redefining problems, modifying technological trajectories and communities). Thus far, this chapter has emphasized learning opportunities as a factor in "constraining and focusing" the self-organization of networks (see Table 6.2). However, learning opportunities by themselves are only

Table 8.2 Search and discovery processes

Search mode	Learning opportunity	Discoveries
Internal-tacit	Learning by doing	In-house manufacturing modifications
Internal-explicit	Learning from formalized inquiry	In-house experimental and test data; experience with instruments
External-tacit	Learning by using Learning from spillovers	User experience and competence Information from hiring personnel or from reverse engineering
	Learning by interaction	Practical experience of suppliers, customers, or other organizations
External-explicit	Learning by using Learning from science and technology advances	User requirements and demands Published experimental and test data; information about procedures and instruments
	Learning by interaction	Information from licensing agreements or collaborative R&D

Sources: Wendy Faulkner, "Conceptualizing Knowledge Used in Innovation: a Second Look at the Science–Technology Distinction and Industrial Innovation," *Science, Technology, and Human Values*, Vol. 19, No. 4, Autumn 1994, pp. 425–58; Franco Malerba, "Learning by Firms and Incremental Technical Change," *Economic Journal*, Vol. 102, No. 413, July 1992, pp. 845–59; Giovanni Dosi, "Sources, Procedures, and Microeconomic Effects of Innovation," *Journal of Economic Literature*, Vol. 26, No. 3, September 1988, pp. 1120–71.

part of the constraining and focusing dynamic. To grasp how learning serves to dampen or enhance self-organization, one must examine how processes of network learning are carried out. Three interrelated processes appear to be critical to the actual conduct of network learning: (a) search and discovery; (b) transformation; and (c) application.

Search and discovery processes

Ikujiro Nonaka and Hirotaka Takeuchi have provided a valuable conceptual scheme for investigating the search and discovery processes in network learning.[65] Table 8.2 summarizes their analysis and places it in the larger context of the organizational learning literature. The first column categorizes the search process according to whether the source of the knowledge is internal or external to the network and whether the knowledge is tacit or explicit. The second column identifies the types of learning opportunity that are the usual targets of each search process category. The third column lists examples of specific discoveries that often result from different searches and learning opportunities.

Internal-tacit search and discovery

Internal-tacit search processes are especially important to the learning by doing commonly associated with incremental innovation in manufacturing. A frequently cited example of internal-tacit learning in the United States is Chaparral Steel. Chaparral has used trial-and-error innovations in its production facilities to cultivate sophisticated experience-based knowledge that is so embedded in its routines that competitors can tour the steel plant and be shown everything but acquire little knowledge.[66]

Much the same pattern was evident in our turbine blade case. The casting company's plant was open to visitors. In this instance, the internal-tacit learning had led to capabilities that have been called "black art" knowledge. Because production learning is so organic, it normally can only be comprehended as a whole and through hands-on experience. It cannot be easily transplanted piecemeal. The seamless integration is illustrated by the following observation, made during a visit to the casting factory. After touring a production plant that had advanced robots and precision measuring instruments, one of the authors walked by an employee who had a finished turbine blade in a vice. Attached to the thin, curved edge of the blade was a pair of adjustable pliers that had a piece of metal welded to each jaw. After checking a measuring instrument, the employee tapped the metal welded to the jaws of the pliers with a hammer. When asked what he was doing, the man said: "I'm adjusting the shape. Sometimes the blade comes out of production just a little off. I fix them. You have to be careful; you can't hit them too hard or it changes the granular structure of the alloy, and that will cause the blade to fail." This is learning based on internal-tacit search and discovery.

The balance between two sets of factors seems to separate "factories as learning laboratories" from the traditional view of manufacturing as rote repetition. First, core process capabilities that partially define network learning boundaries must be continually evolving, so they don't become static barriers to further learning. For example, Chaparral's understanding of basic manufacturing technology (e.g. electric arc furnaces, casters, rolling mills) has been constantly subjected to testing and experimentation. Modification on the factory floor has been encouraged, and equipment and processes have been constantly redesigned and improved. To foster learning, machines have often been designed in-house rather than purchased from machine-tool builders. To further stimulate internal-tacit learning, contracting with other firms for goods and services has often been rejected in favor of doing the work internally. Even when Chaparral buys from the outside, what is purchased is often modified before or during use. Some modifications have been so fundamental that they have resulted in Chaparral patents. In a few cases (e.g. rolling mill technology) the redesign has so exceeded original capabilities that the original vendor has tried to purchase the modified equipment.[67]

Second, there must be a balanced recognition that, although major advances in technology and know-how can result from internal-tacit search and discovery, there is danger in pushing the state of the art too far, too fast. An attempted advance can be especially dangerous if it requires integrating major technological components or major elements of tacit knowledge acquired from external sources. Networks must be careful not to "push the envelope" on too many frontiers of tacit knowledge at the same time. This is what is meant by the assertion that network learning is both a "constraining" and a "focusing" factor. Again, Chaparral provides an example.

Between 1985 and 1989, Chaparral tried to develop an electric arc saw for cutting steel beams. Dorothy Leonard-Barton and her colleagues described what happened:

> Chaparral wanted to find a faster and more efficient way to cut the steel it produced and discovered that the aerospace industry was using an intensely hot electric arc to cut stainless steel. But the aerospace industry had tried neither to cut sections thicker than eight inches nor to cut through high volumes of material with this process, which

is what Chaparral wanted to do. But Chaparral employees, who time and time again had figured out how to get equipment to perform in ways never intended, were undeterred. They discovered, however, that they lacked the knowledge of physics and electromagnetics necessary for the project to succeed. Even with the help of an outside consultant versed in the required physics, the project was beyond Chaparral's ken.[68]

This experience illustrates the importance of organizational history in internal-tacit searches. *Path dependence* bounds what a network can learn rapidly; the organization's experience, embodied in routines, always constrains search and discovery. If too many technological parameters are changed at the same time, if too many aspects of a network's learning environment are altered together, rates of learning are likely to diminish.[69] Even though Chaparral drew upon its core capabilities in process improvement, it was unable to find or create the tacit knowledge necessary to make the electric arc saw project a success. The venture was terminated, at an expense of some US$1.5 million.

But this termination illustrates another important point: no one was singled out for blame. Rather, Chaparral's approach communicated to its workers that internal-tacit search and discovery is risky and "a certain amount of risk is a concomitant of knowledge acquisition."[70]

Internal-explicit search and discovery

The major internal-explicit search and discovery process is intramural R&D, which is generally seen as having two advantages over extramural R&D: better integration within the network; and fewer knowledge leaks, or spillovers.[71] Spillovers of explicit knowledge are a major concern because, unlike tacit knowledge, explicit knowledge can often be transferred to and exploited by competitors. Intramural R&D has the added benefit of enhancing a network's capacity to recognize, evaluate, negotiate for, and adapt to knowledge from outside sources.

An estimated 75 percent of the intramural R&D performed by US companies focuses on enhancing existing technologies and operates within the learning boundaries of established trajectories. The remainder aims at identifying new opportunities by seeking to expand or change the learning boundaries. Firms routinely invest only small amounts in fundamental research because its potential contribution to productive search and discovery is so uncertain. Industry's underinvestment in fundamental research has led, in the USA, to the federal government being its primary funding source. In effect, government "underwrites the long-term interests of industry by conducting an open-ended and speculative search on its behalf."[72]

The interviews for the case studies were striking in the consistency with which interviewees expressed the importance of government support for fundamental research. This view was asserted even by those who said that fundamental research had contributed little to incremental innovation along their own technological trajectories. Behind this seeming discrepancy appears to be the belief that fundamental research becomes critical when trajectory changes occur. It is also the case that fundamental research in universities is the training ground for future technical and scientific personnel.

Like internal-tacit search, most internal-explicit search activities build on prior network knowledge. When internal-tacit searches are disconnected from ongoing innovation, they seldom contribute to the network's competitive advantage. When internally conducted R&D does not fit with established network routines, commercializing it becomes difficult. Gordon Moore suggests that patterns of this kind were major factors that kept Fairchild Corporation from remaining at the forefront of the semiconductor industry in the late 1960s. Because they relied on existing routines that had led to previous successes, Fairchild's production units resisted applying new knowledge provided by internal R&D.[73]

Alternatively, Corning International is widely noted for its success in using the internal-explicit search mode to maintain industry leadership. Working in one of the oldest manufacturing sectors, Corning's core capabilities in materials have been steadily amplified by R&D. Over time, these core capabilities have evolved from light bulbs and dishes to fiber optics, liquid crystal displays, and new forms of composite materials. Throughout its history, Corning has used explicit knowledge derived from in-house R&D to continue expanding its core technological base.[74]

External-tacit search and discovery

Although internally generated knowledge predominates in the innovation of complex technologies, the experience of potential suppliers and users can be an important external source of learning. An external-tacit search and discovery process leading to a fusion of previously separate core capabilities took place in every case study of a network that underwent a trajectory change. The microprocessor network, for instance, added the RISC capabilities of Hewlett Packard to its core capabilities as it began work on the P7 chip.

More common, however, is the pattern associated with external searches to augment a network's *tacit complementary assets*. Because external-tacit knowledge and skills are often embodied in processes, they usually are integrated into a network's production routines in ways that link participating organizations in tight, long-term relationships. A good example is Sony's experience with the CD. Sony first tried to develop the critically important laser diode in-house. When this initiative failed, Sony established a linkage to Sharp, which then became the supplier of this vital complementary asset.

The search by networks for external-tacit knowledge has become ever more deliberate as the complexity of technologies has increased and complementary assets of all kinds have become more widely dispersed around the world. Two patterns of search are evident. One involves searching for knowledge from new suppliers and users. The other involves searching for knowledge from competitors. In both cases, because the transfer of tacit knowledge is difficult, social and geographic proximity is often an important factor.[75] In both the microprocessor and Clinac case studies, interviewees repeatedly emphasized the value of having immediate access to the tacit knowledge available in Silicon Valley.

Accessing tacit complementary assets held by suppliers or users demands new kinds of organizational arrangement. Distant, formal, and competitive "arm's length" relationships are often dysfunctional when transfer of tacit knowledge is the objective. The initial accounts of the benefits to external-tacit learning that flow from close, continuing relationships were studies of Japanese successes in innovation. These accounts showed how the Japanese preference for long-term, cooperative ties fostered the transfer of external tacit knowledge. Some observers have characterized the Japanese pattern as "relational contracting," in which the continual sharing of tacit (as well as explicit) knowledge is institutionalized through lengthy and very intense bonding mechanisms such as partial equity ownership.[76]

Although first recognized in Japanese examples, external-tacit search processes occur globally. For example, Subtronics, a small Norwegian company, succeeds by cultivating a diverse network of tacit knowledge sources. In Box 8.1 there is a characterization by Knut Sorensen and Nora Levold of the Subtronic network's search processes.

Box 8.1

The most striking feature [of the company, Subtronics] is the impressive heterogeneity of the business, particularly with respect to technical aspects. The in-house competence is concentrated in the field of subsea instrumentation, mainly related to electronics and computer science. However, developing subsea instruments demands a much broader spectrum of knowledge and experience. The company is consequently dependent on quite a substantial network of different organizations, several of which are subcontractors ... In addition, even the customers of Subtronics are important suppliers of problems, knowledge, and skills. Subtronics often sends its engineers to work with customers to learn from them and to try out and make changes in the company's products to satisfy the customer's needs. Such work periods may last for several weeks, and they are important in several respects. While Subtronics has considerable expertise in designing and building custom electronic measurement systems, the firm lacks knowledge about the conditions under which its products are to be employed. Such knowledge is not always transferable in terms of specifications because the customer lacks knowledge about the relevant properties of Subtronic's products. Consequently, specifications are constructed as a collaborative effort in which engineers from Subtronics and engineers employed by the customer negotiate, experiment, and design. The relationship is simultaneously development, design, marketing, and learning. It is a good example of the tacit nature of technology, even in a so-called science-based, high-tech area. Instruments working well under laboratory conditions may have to be rebuilt in order to withstand the pressures of real off-shore conditions. A stormy North Sea is difficult to move inside a laboratory ... Subtronics produces new combinations. Compared to scientific work, the engineers of Subtronics are not doing much to develop new knowledge about general characteristics of nature. They collect existing knowledge either in the traditional mental form or materialized in electronic components, computer programs, mechanical parts, and so on. But exactly in this production of new combinations, they are very sensitive to the nature of the infrastructure within which they work. Without access to the knowledge and experience of customers and suppliers, consulting firms, and research institutes, they would not be able to make these combinations ... The very tacit nature of technological knowledge complicates the transfer of knowledge and demands the mobility of engineers. Even top-notch specialists have to be willing to bring a screwdriver with them into the North Sea to adjust their designs, so that they will function according to specifications.

Knut Sorenson and Nora Levold, "Tacit Networks, Heterogeneous Engineers, and Embedded Knowledge," *Science, Technology, and Human Values*, Vol. 17, No. 1, Winter 1992, pp. 26–8.

Network routines are often critical to the search for external-tacit knowledge because they can compensate for more formal exchange mechanisms (e.g. arm's length contracting) that can be obstacles. Because the role of routines is still not well appreciated, their role in stimulating collaborative efforts (e.g. joint ventures) has probably been underestimated.[77]

External-explicit search and discovery

Recently there has been a rapid increase in networks searching for external sources of explicit knowledge. In part, this increase reflects a recognition by the holders of core capabilities that generating sufficient explicit knowledge internally is impossible. The search methods include company-to-company partnering, multi-company alliances, and university–government–corporate cooperation.[78] Most activity emphasizes access to complementary assets.[79]

Although a rapid increase in external-explicit collaboration has taken place only recently in the United States, such relationships have been common far longer in Europe and Japan. Access to explicit knowledge appears to be the major incentive for forming many cooperative alliances, consortia, and joint ventures, but benefits from learning tacit knowledge are also expected. Recognition that the two kinds of knowledge are to some extent inseparable is now the norm in many technology sectors.[80] The Japanese in particular have taken the inseparability of tacit and explicit knowledge as a given.

One US company that has successfully used external-explicit search through strategic alliances is Eastman Kodak, the world's largest producer of chemical-based films for use in consumer photography, medical imaging (e.g. X-ray photography), and industrial-commercial processes (e.g. typesetting and advertising). Kodak has defined its core capabilities as capturing, recording, transferring, and enhancing images. The company therefore developed a strategy designed to dominate the technologies underlying these imaging processes, no matter what the form of imaging is or who the end user might be.

As part of this strategy, Kodak has highlighted digital-imaging technologies as key to enhancing its core capabilities. To pursue this enhancement, it has built a network whose members include holders of what previously were external complementary assets. For example, Kodak formed a strategic alliance with Silicon Graphics, a leading producer of visual display microprocessors and workstations, to learn more about digital technology. The striking results have been documented in a recent study:

> By linking up with Silicon Graphics, Kodak is able to blend electronics-based knowledge and skills with developments from its own renowned laboratories to create and manipulate new forms of images. The lifelike dinosaurs that thrilled millions of viewers in the blockbuster movie *Jurassic Park* were based on the new imaging technologies resulting from the merged Silicon Graphics and Kodak technologies. Through this alliance, Kodak gains a venue to learn new insights for applying its growing skills and capabilities in advanced forms of imaging. If it continues to pursue emerging opportunities to refine its core imaging competence, it should be able to fully compete in the multimedia market in the next century.[81]

Conversion processes

In addition to search and discovery, the network learning process also frequently requires converting the new knowledge to fit with the knowledge base of the network. For instance, Kodak needed to *convert the explicit knowledge of digital electronics gained from Silicon Graphics into forms that could be assimilated into its partially tacit manufacturing processes.* This difficult explicit-to-tacit conversion process often requires much trial-and-error experimentation before groups immersed in a body of existing tacit know-how can "internalize" new explicit knowledge.

The most obvious and easiest conversion process involves the ability to *change new explicit knowledge to a form compatible with existing explicit knowledge.* Because explicit knowledge can be conveyed in language, written or verbal, or in some other codified form such as blueprints, mathematical expressions, or computer algorithms, its reconfiguration is usually straightforward. Even highly complex explicit knowledge can usually be comprehended over distance and time by anyone who understands the system of knowledge representation.

The most striking reconfigurations in our case studies involved the *conversion of tacit knowledge to explicit knowledge.* The explosion in applications for computers and sophisticated information systems is pressuring the conversion of more and more tacit knowledge to explicit knowledge. A particular accelerated instance happened when computer-aided design (CAD) technology was applied to designing sophisticated jet engine turbine blades. Effective use of CAD for this purpose required that the tacit knowledge held by the casting companies be converted into explicit knowledge that could be represented in the CAD system. A similar change occurred later, when the Air Force funded a software company to develop simulation tools capable of testing prototype turbine blades. Prototype testing had previously required that the casting companies produce prototype blades and physically test them. The computer simulations had to convert substantial quantities of tacit knowledge about blades to explicit knowledge that could be represented in software programs and sets of test data.

As Nonaka states it, converting tacit to explicit knowledge involves finding a way to express the inexpressible. *Metaphors* are one of the most important means to achieve this metamorphosis because they can communicate experiences that cannot be expressed yet in literal description, such as scientific terminology.[82] Literal language is inherently reductionist. It abstracts and segments experience in order to identify elements and their relationships as constituent components of a whole. The resulting knowledge is highly stratified; relationships such as cause and effect, means to ends, or part to whole, are sought at ever deeper levels. By contrast, metaphorical language can convey flexible connections (implicit analogies) from areas of shared experience to the unshared experiences of tacit knowledge; these first links are particularly important when conversion of tacit to explicit knowledge is just getting started. Metaphors may provide initial understanding that creates the shared background of meaning required for literal description.[83] An example of how metaphors are useful devices in converting tacit knowledge into explicit knowledge is provided in Box 8.2.

Converting tacit knowledge to tacit knowledge is of major importance, but it is also the most difficult mode to diffuse through a network. Because tacit knowledge cannot be adequately communicated or translated through word descriptions or other explicit forms of knowledge representation, communicating it across time and

Box 8.2

The process by which Honda designed its "City" car shows how metaphors can be the first step in making the tacit explicit. In 1978, Honda's leadership became convinced that its Civic and Accord models were becoming too familiar and embarked on a project to come up with a product concept fundamentally different than anything they had ever done before. "Let's gamble" was the slogan underpinning the development of the new-concept car. Nonaka describes what happened:

Project team leader Hiroo Watanabe coined another slogan to express his sense of the team's ambitious challenge: Theory of Automobile Evolution. The phrase described an ideal. In effect, it posed the question: If the automobile were an organism, how should it evolve? As team members argued and discussed what Watanabe's slogan might possibly mean, they came up with the answer in the form of yet another slogan: "man-maximum, machine-minimum." This captured the team's belief that the ideal car should somehow transcend the traditional human–machine relationship. But that required challenging what Watanabe called "the reasoning of Detroit," which had sacrificed comfort for appearance.

The "evolutionary" trend the team articulated eventually came to be embodied in the image of a sphere – a car simultaneously "short" (in length) and "tall" (in height). Such a car, they reasoned, would be lighter and cheaper, but also more comfortable and more solid than traditional cars. A sphere provided the most room for the passenger while taking up the least amount of space on the road. What's more, the shape minimized the space taken up by the engine and other mechanical systems. This gave birth to a product concept the team called "Tall Boy," which eventually led to the Honda City, the company's distinctive town car.

Ikujiro Nonaka, "The Knowledge-creating Company," *Harvard Business Review*, Vol. 69, No. 6, November/December 1991, p. 100.

distance is difficult, except through direct interpersonal encounters and shared experience. Thus, even when the importance of converting tacit knowledge is recognized, the conversion often does not occur. But the more common situation probably is that the importance of tacit knowledge is recognized neither by those who possess it nor by those who need to convert it to make it useful.[84]

Moving tacit knowledge from organization to organization within a network is difficult because tacit knowledge is always to some degree idiosyncratic. Converting such knowledge into other forms of tacit knowledge, without a shared language for expressing this knowledge, depends on extralinguistic activities such as observation, imitation, and practice. These activities, in turn, normally require personal proximity and interaction over time. There are many nuances and organization-specific insights incorporated into tacit knowledge, and these subtleties seldom make sense outside the context of specific experiential settings.[85] Without the shared experiences, individuals and organizations have difficulty understanding the intended meaning of what they observe, grasping which aspects of a demonstrated action are worth imitating, or determining which skills to practice.

Our case studies of Silicon Valley networks (the microprocessor and Clinac studies) repeatedly found tacit-to-tacit conversions to be of central importance. Two factors helped to make these knowledge conversion processes succeed: the shared substantive focus on electronics, and the geographical proximity of the network members.

Application processes

Applying network learning is about solving problems, and the problems faced by networks can be divided into two broad categories: (a) the "normal" obstacles encountered in the continuous incremental innovation along established trajectories; (b) the "extraordinary" challenges that may interrupt progress along an existing trajectory, triggering trajectory changes. These categories represent increasingly complex steps in applying network learning to innovation.

Incremental innovation along an established trajectory requires that a network reject large quantities of knowledge, especially when problem solving must take place rapidly. Fast-moving networks engaged in incremental innovations typically apply knowledge derived primarily from within the existing technological community. The problems encountered in the process of incremental innovation tend to be relatively well structured, and so it is possible to rely mostly on internal search and discovery processes and to study the problems in some depth. Most networks involved in incremental innovation tend to trade off breadth for depth of learning application.[86] Thus, the knowledge applied in incremental innovation usually fits within existing technological expectations. Existing core capabilities are generally sufficient for continued advancement along the trajectory, and any needed enhancements in core capabilities generally can be accessed by drawing upon the largely tacit opportunities provided by learning by doing and learning by using.[87] Current strategies and structures, as embodied in heuristics and routines, work well enough that learning processes are shaped to accommodate them.

Even the most surprise-free incremental trajectories, however, do mandate network adjustments. This is because, as Robert Ayres notes, incremental problem solving inevitably becomes harder as a trajectory evolves. Learning tends to be applied to the most obvious, easiest to solve barriers earlier in the trajectory, with the consequence that more difficult barriers are approached as late as possible. And every trajectory has some unique, "configuration-dependent" limits that must be overcome.[88] These more difficult problems often trigger a more intensive search and discovery process for a new combination of core capabilities and complementary assets and for more serious modification of network routines and heuristics. Sometimes, the barrier will prove so difficult that it has to be approached as a "discontinuity," a major change in the technology design for the network.

Disruptions of an existing trajectory require more than incremental organizational and technological change.[89] Networks that are able to combine elements of continuous and discontinuous learning may be able to overcome even daunting problems and continue to innovate along the same trajectory. Only part of the combination of core capabilities and complementary assets accumulated around the dominant technology is disrupted by overcoming a discontinuous barrier. But the problems associated with discontinuous innovation are much less well structured than those faced in incremental innovation. Solving these problems requires more external search and discovery and at least as much focus on breadth of learning as it does on learning depth. Substantial unlearning may be required when a discontinuity is encountered.[90] Thus, a wider and more complex range of learning opportunities may be pursued (e.g. focusing on intrasectoral spillovers and learning from advances in science and technology), and there may be more fundamental modifications in routines and even knowledge transformation processes. The application of learning is therefore less linear (i.e. less reliance on past problem solving processes) and more complex.[91] This seems to be what has happened a number of times in the semiconductor industry, as once seemingly fundamental barriers (e.g. low production yields for large chips) have been overcome by developing ever more complex learning and problem solving relationships without fundamentally modifying the pattern of the existing trajectory or the boundaries of the technological community.[92]

More radical innovation requires major and sometimes fundamental change in both technology and organization. Scientific breakthroughs and technological fusion are major sources of innovations that create new trajectories, but such innovations may also result from an insurmountable discontinuity encountered in an otherwise established trajectory that has been experiencing incremental innovations. New trajectories generated by radical innovations demand the creation of entirely new networks. The greater uncertainty and urgency associated with discontinuous, radical technological and organizational change induces more external search and discovery as well as elaborate efforts to unlearn routines and heuristics developed in the past. Radical innovation is thus responsible for the creation of many strategic alliances and other types of flexible network relationship that facilitate reframing problems and redesigning problem solving approaches. A higher tolerance for mistakes and misapplications of learning must be accepted. Collaborative learning and problem solving appears especially attractive when the knowledge that must be acquired and applied is tacit, expensive, and time-consuming to develop alone.[93]

Conclusions

Networks learn in many ways. Few are easy, inexpensive, or risk-free; and sustaining adequate learning requires purposeful, continual attention. Although the potential benefits from network learning are great, discovering, transforming, and applying the requisite range of tacit and explicit knowledge can be an intimidating technological and organizational challenge. Yet once learning processes are established that make the repeated innovation possible, a network normally has a sustainable competitive advantage. The dynamic capabilities that result from rapid learning are difficult for competitors to replicate, precisely because they are constantly evolving and emerging.

The networks that are best at learning have strong *path-dependent* tendencies. The next chapter addresses the role of history in self-organization, learning, and the innovation of complex technologies.

Notes

1. Andreas Pyka, "Informal Networking," *Technovation*, Vol. 17, No. 4, April 1997, pp. 207–10.
2. Michael E. McMaster, *The Intelligence Advantage: Organizing for Complexity*, Boston: Butterworth–Heinemann, 1996, p. 83.

3. Andrew C. Inkpen, "Creating Knowledge through Collaboration," *California Management Review*, Vol. 39, No. 1, Fall 1996, p. 123.

4. John Mathews, "Organizational Foundations of Economic Learning," *Human Systems Management*, Vol. 15, 1996, p. 118.

5. Gary Hamel, "Competition for Competence and Inter-partner Learning within International Strategic Alliances," *Strategic Management Journal*, Vol. 12, Special Issue, 1991, p. 99.

6. Daryl McKee, "An Organizational Learning Approach to Product Innovation," *Journal of Product Innovation Management*, Vol. 9, No. 3, 1992, p. 232; Patricia W. Meyers, "Nonlinear Learning in Large Technological Firms: Period Four Implies Chaos," *Research Policy*, Vol. 19, No. 2, April 1990, pp. 98–9.

7. Akio Morita, *Made In Japan*, London: Fontana/Collins, 1987, p. 150.

8. Richard N. Osborn and John Hagedoorn, "The Institutionalization and Evolutionary Dynamics of Interorganizational Alliances and Networks," *Academy of Management Journal*, Vol. 40, No. 2, April 1997, pp. 266–72.

9. William Lazonick, "Learning and the Dynamics of International Competitive Advantage," in Yuichi Shionoya and Mark Perlman, eds, *Innovation in Technology, Industries, and Institutions: Studies in Schumpeterian Perspectives*, Ann Arbor, MI: University of Michigan Press, 1994, p. 203.

10. Diana L. Watts, "Disorder and Contradiction: an Empirical Perspective on Self-organization," *Human Systems Management*, Vol. 9, No. 4, 1990, pp. 239–43.

11. Nathan Rosenberg, *Inside the Black Box: Technology and Economics*, New York: Cambridge University Press, 1982, pp. 120–2.

12. Ashoka Mody, "Firm Strategies for Costly Engineering Learning," *Management Science*, Vol. 35, No. 4, April 1989, p. 496.

13. Linda Argote and Dennis Epple, "Learning Curves in Manufacturing," *Science*, Vol. 247, No. 4945, February 23, 1990, pp. 247–8; Wesley M. Cohen and Daniel A. Levinthal, "Innovation and Learning: the Two Faces of R&D," *Economic Journal*, Vol. 99, No. 397, September 1989, p. 569.

14. Geoffrey M. Hodgson, "The Economy as an Organism, Not a Machine," *Futures*, Vol. 25, No. 2, May 1993, p. 396.

15. Fred Kofman and Peter Senge, " Communities of Commitment: the Heart of Learning Organizations," *Organizational Dynamics*, Vol. 22, No. 2, Autumn 1993, pp. 7–10.

16. Norman Clark, *The Political Economy of Science and Technology*, New York: Basil Blackwell, 1985, pp. 190–3.

17. Ikuhiro Nonaka and Hirotaka Takeuchi, *The Knowledge-creating Company: How Japanese Companies Create the Dynamics of Innovation*, New York: Oxford University Press, 1995, pp. 95–122; William Lazonick, "Learning and the Dynamics of International Competitive Advantage," in Yuichi Shionoya and Mark Perlman, eds, *Innovation in Technology, Industries, and Institutions: Studies in Schumpeterian Perspectives*, Ann Arbor, MI: University of Michigan Press, 1994, pp. 189–211; W. Mark Fruin and Toshihiro Nishiguchi, "Supplying the Toyota Production System: Intercorporate Organizational Evolution and Supplier Subsystems," in Bruce Kogut, ed., *Country Competitiveness: Technology and the Organizing of Work*, New York: Oxford University Press, 1993, pp. 225–56; Charles H. Ferguson, "Computers and the Coming of the US Keiretsu," *Harvard Business Review*, Vol. 68, No. 4, July/August 1990, pp. 55–70.

18. John W. Slocum, Jr, Michael McGill, and David T. Lei, "The New Learning Strategy: Anytime, Anything, Anywhere," *Organizational Dynamics*, Vol. 23, No. 2, Autumn 1994, pp. 33–47; Francesca Chiaromonte, Giovanni Dosi, and Luigi Orsenigo, "Innovative Learning and Institutions in the Process of Development: on the Microfoundations of Growth Regimes," in Ross Thomson, ed., *Learning and Technological Change*, New York: St Martin's Press, 1993, pp. 117–49.

19. H. Kevin Steensma, "Acquiring Technological Competencies through Inter-organizational Collaboration: an Organizational Learning Perspective," *Journal of Engineering Technology and Management*, Vol. 12, No. 4, January 1996, pp. 267–86; Nanette S. Levinson and

Minoru Asahi, "Cross-national Alliances and Interorganizational Learning," *Organizational Dynamics*, Vol. 24, No. 2, Autumn 1995, pp. 50–63.

20. Anders Lundgren, *Technological Innovation and Network Evolution*, New York: Routledge, 1995, pp. 77–102; Gianni Lorenzoni and Charles Baden–Fuller, "Creating a Strategic Center to Manage a Web of Partners," *California Management Review*, Vol. 37, No. 3, Spring 1995, pp. 156–60.

21. McMaster, *The Intelligence Advantage*, pp. 83–6.

22. Tuomo Alasoini, "A Learning Factory: Experimenting with Adaptable Production in Finnish Engineering Workshops," *International Journal of Human Factors in Manufacturing*, Vol. 6, No. 1, Winter 1996, pp. 3–19; Paul S. Adler and Robert E. Cole, "Designed for Learning: a Tale of Two Auto Plants," *Sloan Management Review*, Vol. 35, No. 4, Spring 1993, pp. 85–94.

23. Mody, "Firm Strategies for Costly Engineering Learning," p. 498.

24. James Fleck, "Learning by Trying: the Implementation of Configurational Technology," *Research Policy*, Vol. 23, No. 6, November 1994, pp. 637–52.

25. John Bessant, "The Lessons of Failure: Learning to Manage New Manufacturing Technology," *International Journal of Technology Management*, Special Issue on Manufacturing Technology: Diffusion, Implementation, and Management, Vol. 2/3/4, 1993, p. 200.

26. Eric von Hippel and Marcie J. Tyre, "How Learning by Doing Is Done: Problem Identification in Novel Process Equipment," *Research Policy*, Vol. 24, No. 1, January 1995, p. 1.

27. Linda Argote, "Organizational Learning Curves: Persistence, Transfer, and Turnover," *International Journal of Technology Management*, Special Publication on Unlearning and Learning, Vol. 11, Nos 7/8, 1996, pp. 766–7.

28. Gary P. Pisano, "Knowledge, Integration, and the Locus of Learning: an Empirical Analysis of Process Development," *Strategic Management Journal*, Vol. 15, Special Issue, Winter 1994, p. 86.

29. Marcie J. Tyre and Wanda J. Orlikowski, "The Episodic Process of Learning by Using," *International Journal of Technology Management*, Special Publication on Unlearning and Learning, Vol. 11, Nos 7/8, 1996, p. 791.

30. Eric von Hippel, "Lead Users: a Source of Novel Product Concepts," *Management Science*, Vol. 32, July 1986, pp. 791–805.

31. Roy Rothwell, "Issues in User–Producer Relations in the Innovation Process: the Role of Government," *International Journal of Technology Management*, Special Issue on Technological Responses to Increasing Competition, Vol. 9, Nos 5/6/7, 1994, pp. 636–7.

32. K. H. Habermeier, "Product Use and Product Improvement," *Research Policy*, Vol. 19, No. 3, June 1990, p. 278.

33. William Riggs and Eric von Hippel, "Incentives to Innovate and the Sources of Innovation: the Case of Scientific Instruments," *Research Policy*, Vol. 23, No. 3, June 1994, pp. 459–69.

34. Sarah Slaughter, "Innovation and Learning During Implementation: a Comparison of User and Manufacturer Innovations," *Research Policy*, Vol. 22, No. 1, January 1993, pp. 81–2.

35. Habermeier, "Product Use and Product Improvement," p. 273.

36. Jan Fagerberg, "User–Producer Interaction, Learning, and Comparative Advantage," *Cambridge Journal of Economics*, Vol. 19, No. 1, February 1995, pp. 243–56.

37. Alexander Gerybadze, "Technology Forecasting as a Process of Organisational Intelligence," *R&D Management*, Vol. 24, No. 2, April 1994, pp. 131–40.

38. Wendy Faulkner and Jacqueline Senker, *Knowledge Frontiers: Public Sector Research and Industrial Innovation in Biotechnology, Engineering Ceramics, and Parallel Computing*, New York: Oxford University Press, 1995, pp. 218–19.

39. W. Bradford Ashton, Bruce R. Kinzey, and Marvin E. Gunn, Jr, "A Structured Approach for Monitoring Science and Technology Developments," *International Journal of Technology Management*, Vol. 6, Nos 1/2, 1991, pp. 91–110.

40. Alvin K. Klevorick, Richard C. Levin, Richard R. Nelson, and Sidney G. Winter, "On the Sources and Significance of Interindustry Differences in Technological Opportunities," *Research Policy*, Vol. 24, No. 2, March 1995, p. 189 (emphasis added).

41. B. Bowonder and T. Miyake, "Technology Forecasting in Japan," *Futures*, Vol. 25, No. 7, September 1993, pp. 757–75.

42. Raymond De Bondt, "Spillovers and Innovative Activities," *International Journal of Industrial Organization*, Vol. 15, No. 1, February 1997, pp. 1–3.

43. Joel Miller, "Reverse Engineering: Fair Game or Foul?" *IEEE Spectrum*, Vol. 30, No. 4, April 1993, pp. 64–5.

44. Richard C. Levin, Alvin K. Klevorick, Richard R. Nelson, and Sidney G. Winter, "Appropriating the Returns from Industrial Research and Development," *Brookings Papers on Economic Activity*, No. 3, 1987, pp. 805–12.

45. Thomas M. Jorde and David J. Teece, "Innovation, Cooperation, and Antitrust," *High Technology Law Journal*, Vol. 4, No. 1, Summer 1989, pp. 9–10.

46. Richard R. Nelson, "What Is Private and What Is Public about Technology?" *Science, Technology, and Human Values*, Vol. 14, No. 3, Summer 1989, p. 236.

47. Pyka, "Informal Networking," pp. 209–10.

48. Faulkner and Senker, *Knowledge Frontiers*, p. 206.

49. De Bondt, "Spillovers and Innovative Activities," p. 24.

50. Gunnar Eliasson, "Spillovers, Integrated Production and the Theory of the Firm," *Journal of Evolutionary Economics*, Vol. 6, No. 2, 1996, pp. 125–6.

51. Ashoka Mody, "Learning through Alliances," *Journal of Economic Behavior and Organization*, Vol. 20, No. 1, February 1993, pp. 151–70.

52. Johannes M. Pennings, Harry Barkema, and Sytse Douma, "Organization Learning and Diversification," *Academy of Management Journal*, Vol. 37, No. 3, 1994, p. 633.

53. Yasunori Baba and Ken-ichi Imai, "A Network View of Innovation and Entrepreneurship: the Case of the Evolution of the VCR Systems," *International Social Science Journal*, Vol. 45, No. 1, February 1993, p. 25.

54. Rothwell, "Issues in User–Producer Relations in the Innovation Process: the Role of Government," p. 642.

55. Nirmalya Kumar, "The Power of Trust in Manufacturer–Retailer Relationships," *Harvard Business Review*, Vol. 74, No. 6, November/December 1996, pp. 92–106.

56. Lorenzoni and Baden–Fuller, "Creating a Strategic Center to Manage a Web of Partners," pp. 154–5 (emphasis added).

57. Giovanni Dosi, "Sources, Procedures, and Microeconomic Effects of Innovation," *Journal of Economic Literature*, Vol. 26, No. 3, September 1988, pp. 1120–71.

58. Cohen and Levinthal, "Innovation and Learning: the Two Faces of R&D," pp. 569–96.

59. Argotte and Epple, "Learning Curves in Manufacturing," pp. 921–2.

60. Bjorn Johnson, "Institutional Learning," in Bengt–Ake Lundvall, ed., *National Systems of Innovation: towards a Theory of Innovation and Interactive Learning*, New York: Pinter Publishers, 1992, p. 28.

61. McKee, "An Organizational Learning Approach to Product Innovation," p. 240.

62. Meyers, "Non-linear Learning in Large Technological Firms," pp. 99–106.

63. Richard A. Bettis and C. K. Prahalad, "The Dominant Logic: Retrospective and Extension," *Strategic Management Journal*, Vol. 16, No. 1, January 1995, p. 10.

64. Walter W. Powell and Peter Brantley, "Competitive Cooperation in Biotechnology: Learning Through Networks?" in Nitin Nohria and Robert G. Eccles, eds, *Networks and Organizations: Structure, Form and Action*, Boston: Harvard Business School Press, 1992, pp. 370–2.

65. Nonaka and Takeuchi, *The Knowledge Creating Company*, pp. 56–94.

66. Dorothy Leonard–Barton, "The Factory as a Learning Laboratory," *Sloan Management Review*, Vol. 34, No. 1, Fall 1992, p. 24.

67. Leonard–Barton, "The Factory as a Learning Laboratory," pp. 28–9.

68. Dorothy Leonard–Barton, H. Kent Bowen, Kim B. Clark, Charles A. Hollaway, and Steven C. Wheelwright, "How to Integrate Work and Deepen Expertise," *Harvard Business Review*, Vol. 72, September/October 1994, p. 128.
69. David J. Teece, Richard Rumelt, Giovanni Dosi, and Sidney Winter, "Understanding Corporate Coherence: Theory and Evidence," *Journal of Economic Behavior and Organization*, Vol. 23, No. 1, January 1994, p. 17.
70. Leonard-Barton, "The Factory as a Learning Laboratory," p. 32.
71. Dosi, "Sources, Procedures, and Micro-economic Effects of Innovation," p. 1132.
72. Wendy Faulkner, "Conceptualizing Knowledge Used in Innovation: a Second Look at the Science–Technology Distinction and Industrial Innovation," *Science, Technology, and Human Values*, Vol. 19, No. 4, Autumn 1994, p. 441.
73. Moore, "Some Personal Perspectives on Research in the Semiconductor Industry," in Rosenbloom and Spencer, eds, *Engines of Innovation*, p. 166.
74. Herbert I. Fusfeld, *Industry's Future: Changing Patterns of Industrial Research*, Washington, DC: American Chemical Society, 1994, pp. 30–47.
75. David J. Teece, "Competition, Cooperation, and Innovation: Organizational Arrangements for Regimes of Rapid Technological Progress," *Journal of Economic Behavior and Organization*, Vol. 18, No. 1, June 1992, p. 11.
76. Michele K. Bolton, Roger Malmrose, and William G. Ouchi, "The Organization of Innovation in the United States and Japan: Neoclassical and Relational Contracting," *Journal of Management Studies*, Vol. 31, No. 5, September 1994, pp. 656–7.
77. Bruce Kogut, "Joint Ventures: Theoretical and Empirical Perspectives," *Strategic Management Journal*, Vol. 9, No. 4, July/August 1988, pp. 322–4.
78. Charles F. Larson, "R&D in Industry," in Intersociety Working Group, *AAAS Report XIX: Research and Development, FY 1995*, Washington, DC: American Association for the Advancement of Science, 1994, p. 31.
79. US Congress, Office of Technology Assessment, *Multinationals and the US Technology Base: Final Report of the Multinationals Project*, Washington, DC: Government Printing Office, September 1994, p. 98.
80. Inkpen, "Creating Knowledge through Collaboration," pp. 123–7.
81. Slocum, McGill, and Lei, "The New Learning Strategy," p. 43.
82. Ikujiro Nonaka, "The Knowledge-creating Company," *Harvard Business Review*, Vol. 69, No. 6, November/December 1991, pp. 96–104.
83. Hardimos Tsoukas, "The Missing Link: a Transformational View of Metaphors in Organizational Science," *Academy of Management Review*, No. 3, 1991, p. 567.
84. Marion G. Sobol and David Lei, "Environment, Manufacturing Technology, and Embedded Technology," *International Journal of Human Factors in Manufacturing*, April 1994, p. 171.
85. Hubert Saint–Onge, "Tacit Knowledge: the Key to the Strategic Alignment of Intellectual Capital," *Strategy and Leadership*, Vol. 24, No. 2, 1996, pp. 10–14.
86. McKee, "An Organizational Learning Approach to Product Innovation," p. 238.
87. Christopher Freeman, "Critical Survey: the Economics of Technical Change," *Cambridge Journal of Economics*, Vol. 18, No. 5, November 1994, p. 476.
88. Robert U. Ayres, "Toward a Non-linear Dynamics of Technological Progress," *Journal of Economic Behavior and Organization*, Vol. 24, June 1994, pp. 35–42.
89. Thomas Durand, "Dual Technological Trees: Assessing the Intensity and Strategic Significance of Technological Change," *Research Policy*, Vol. 21, No. 4, August 1992, p. 362.
90. McKee, "An Organizational Learning Approach to Product Innovation," p. 239.
91. Meyers, "Non-linear Learning in Large Technological Firms," p. 99.
92. Ayres, "Toward a Non-linear Dynamics of Technological Progress," pp. 55–62.
93. C. Jay Lambe and Robert E. Spekman, "Alliances, External Technology Acquisition, and Discontinuous Technological Change," *Journal of Product Innovation Management*, Vol. 14, No. 2, March 1997, pp. 107–14.

CHAPTER NINE

Path Dependence

History matters a great deal in the innovation of complex technologies. Past actions taken by innovative organizations may be both creators and destroyers of opportunities in the present and future. When history operates as a destroyer it is because previously available possibilities have been foreclosed by innovations in the past. Most trajectories' wakes are littered with discarded technological and organizational options. When history operates as a creator it is because past innovations have generated new options.[1] Complex technologies are especially path-dependent because they rely so heavily on learning accumulated by the self-organizing networks that carry out their innovations.

The creative and destructive effects of the past go a long way toward answering one of the most important questions in the area of technological innovation: why is it that two economies or firms can be at comparable levels of development at one point in their history and later be at different levels? In the extreme cases, how do economies or companies that once were technological leaders become technological followers? The answer is that relative stagnation or leader–follower reversals occur in major part because of the *inherent path dependencies* induced by past technological choices.[2] Minor details can be amplified by *positive feedbacks* that drive the selection of a technology down an unanticipated path.[3] Once a pathway has been established, coevolving technologies and organizations may continue down it even when superior routes (in terms of efficiency or efficacy) might be available. When it becomes difficult or impossible to move from one path to another, *lock-in* is said to occur.[4]

The importance of the power of history in technological change is clearly indicated by Paul David when he observes: "It is sometimes not possible to uncover the logic (or illogic) of the world around us except by understanding how it got that way." For David, a path-dependent sequence of changes is one in which "important influences upon the eventual outcome can be exerted by temporally remote events, including happenings dominated by chance events rather than systematic forces."[5] Because small historical events can become lasting and even permanent effects, the predictability of path-dependent systems can be very small at certain times (e.g. immediately following the occurrence of a small but ultimately important event) and very high at other times (e.g. predicting near-term increments). An example of unpredictable consequences occurred when Sony's failure to develop a word processing system led to its takeover of the floppy disk storage trajectory with its 3.5 inch MFDD system. Alternatively, the confidence members of networks have in the performance characteristics of the next increment along the trajectory represents the easy predictability case. In sum, path dependency may lead to diverse consequences.

It may lead to inflexibility during some phases of the coevolution of technologies and organizations, and in others act to enhance flexibility.[6] But whatever its consequences, path dependence is a powerful influence on complex technologies.

The development of the microprocessor indicates the impact of path dependence as both a destructive and a creative force. Both Intel and Texas Instruments developed microprocessors in roughly the same period of time. Intel chose to develop silicon gates for its microprocessors, based on its experience with memory chips aimed at the commercial market. Texas Instruments chose instead metal gates on its microprocessors, derived in part from its experience with military electronics. The silicon gates worked well, the metal gates did not. The histories of these two organizations clearly played a key role in their relative success with microprocessors.

Sources of path dependence

What do historical studies tell us about the origins of path dependence in the innovation of complex technologies? What historical factors appear to be associated with the destructive and creative aspects of path dependence? There are at least five major sources of path dependence: culture, organizational learning, technological compatibility, standards-setting processes, and industry strategy and public policy.

Culture and path dependence

Technological advancement is always intertwined with a "cultural evolutionary process." That is, a new technology inevitably is closely interconnected with changes taking place in the norms that influence economic, political, and social institutions.[7] Insight into these processes of change and innovation is facilitated by grouping norms into two categories: *instrumental* or *ceremonial*. Instrumental norms include problem-solving routines and heuristics that are integral to carrying out repeated technological innovations. Instrumental norms are derived from experience with what has produced past successes and failures. Ceremonial norms, alternatively, are more deeply embedded in society and they change more slowly. Ceremonial norms (e.g. perceptions of hierarchy, status, or commitment to an ideology) are society's anchors. Preserving them is itself a cherished societal norm.[8] In advanced societies there is often substantial tension between ceremonial and instrumental norms.

At a given time, the interactions between instrumental and ceremonial norms are likely to exert substantial influence on the path of innovation. For example, the cultural attachment in the USA to the ceremonial norms of individualism and adversarial relationships among organizations impedes development of instrumental norms such as group-based learning and cooperation across organizational boundaries. These instrumental norms are assets for the innovation of complex technologies.[9]

Not even the most powerful ceremonial norms, however, can withstand the pressures that flow from technological change. Over time, ceremonial norms are inevitably modified by the perpetual social, political, and economic alterations that are driven by the coevolution of organizations and technologies. For example, dramatic modifications in ceremonial norms have occurred when the mode of production has changed (e.g. from craft to mass to synthetic production). What actually happens is by no means predictable, however. Ceremonial norms that might have been constraining (i.e. negative feedback) in one era of production may become sources of competitive advantage (i.e. positive feedback) in another era. Thus, Japanese values that support group-oriented innovation and emphasis on tacit knowledge that were liabilities in the mass manufacturing era became strengths in the era of synthetic production.[10] It seems plausible that these ceremonial values may be among the factors underlying the Japanese trade success with regard to complex technologies, discussed in Chapter 1.

Learning and path dependence

Learning and path dependence are mutually reinforcing. As technologies and networks coevolve along trajectories, networks experience local learning, which reinforces path dependence. In the pattern of learning associated with incremental innovations, networks learn only what is needed to solve the next problem, as in the "Noyce principle of minimum information." Thus, success rests on carrying out relatively narrow and constrained search and discovery activities. Such local learning bounds a network's technological course, and thus bolsters path dependence.[11]

David Lei and his colleagues describe both the rewards and the risks of learning-based path dependence. It may produce hard-to-imitate expertise and competitive advantage, but it may also produce inflexibility and loss of competitive advantage by eliminating the dynamic quality of core capabilities. Their insights regarding firms apply just as well to networks:

> The accumulation of skills and insights associated with core competences over time can produce path dependence. Path dependency refers to the idiosyncratic patterns of learning and application of competences resulting from the evolution of skills and historical investments and development. As firms build more specialized skills that also become institutionalized, it may narrow the potential strategic opportunities/ alternatives considered by the firm. Significant specialization can produce expertise that is difficult for competitors to imitate and therefore may offer a competitive advantage. That is, path dependence tends to erect barriers over time to imitability because of the difficulty other firms may have in recreating the historical evolution of the core competence used to produce the competitive advantage. However, such path dependence may also delimit future opportunities by narrowing the strategic alternatives considered. Furthermore, there is a tendency for highly specialized skills to become more stable. That is, there may be a reduction in the learning (a loss of meta-learning expertise) and thus, the core competences may lose their dynamic quality. If firms develop core competences that over time lose their dynamic quality, firms may be less prepared to respond to environmental changes. While path dependence is a basic premise in the resource-based view of the firm (i.e. every firm has an idiosyncratic set of resources and skills that lead to a potentially unique strategy and competitive advantage), it could make the firm less flexible and adaptable to environmental challenges. On the other hand, path dependence can reinforce the firm's pattern of learning through complex social arrangements. As such, it does not necessarily produce inflexibility and loss of dynamic quality in its core competences. Thus, path dependence has both positive and potentially negative implications for firm performance over time.[12]

Figure 9.1 illustrates how a network's familiarity with existing technologies and markets can strengthen learning and reinforce the existing technological path.

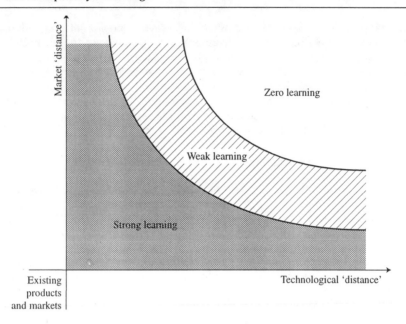

Figure 9.1 Network learning and path dependence
Source: David J. Teece, Richard Rumelt, Giovanni Dosi, and Sidney Winter, "Understanding Corporate Coherence: Theory and Evidence," *Journal of Economic Behavior and Organization*, Vol. 23, No. 1, January 1994, p. 18.

When networks manifest strong external learning, embarking on another technology/market path may be just as rational and feasible as continuing on the established path; alternatively, successful localized network learning reduces the prospect of a change in direction. For example, if a network tries to enter new markets with new technologies, the possibility of failure is high, because the task is likely to be beyond the network's learning range.

Another way in which learning enhances path dependence is through reduction of risk and uncertainty. Network learning cumulatively decreases the costs and risks of innovation, as the organizational learning process evolves along a trajectory. As choices about where and how to engage in search and discovery activities become better defined and routines and heuristics more embedded, the tendency to continue pursuing the existing pathway strengthens. Efforts to reduce uncertainty therefore introduce a certain irreversibility into the evolution of learning-based innovation.[13]

Technological compatibility and path dependence

Technological compatibility involves designs that enable technologies to work together.[14] Sometimes called "interrelatedness," technological compatibility is a major source of path dependence because the value of any single technology in complex systems is dependent upon the availability of other technologies that can be connected or integrated. System interdependence means that a set of technical relationships, once established, becomes a powerful obstacle to embarking on a different technological path.[15]

Two types of technological compatibility are associated with path dependence: substitutability and complementarity. *Substitutes* are systems, subsystems, or components that deliver the same or very similar outputs. For instance, IBM personal computers and IBM-compatible "clones" deliver similar performance capabilities. *Complements* are subsystems or components that produce different outputs, but are capable of being integrated into systems that generate a new combination of outputs. Nathan Rosenberg uses the telecommunications industry as an example of how complements can induce path dependence:

> There are usually several technological options available to a decision-maker, and it is often very difficult and costly to reverse technological decisions once they have been made. This is particularly true in telecommunications where future investments must remain compatible with the currently chosen system, as capital in telecommunications is unusually long-lived.
>
> The ability to evaluate current technological options is complicated by an inability to predict the future evolution of each technology before its adoption. Indeed, future innovations and decisions are dependent on today's choice. The payoff and costs of tomorrow's innovation are dependent on the current adoption decision. Obviously, the potential payoff to an innovation is increased if the innovation is compatible with the current system. Thus, once a system is adopted, innovations that are compatible have higher worth.[16]

Sometimes the paths taken by entire complex systems can hinge on apparently insignificant subsystem or component innovation carried out in response to the need for compatibility. These innovations are referred to as *gateway* technologies: they open and bound pathways that might otherwise not have been taken.[17]

Gateway technologies tend to be found in highly interrelated systems where the development of common specifications and standards is central to innovation. For example, compatibility is essential to the rapid and diverse mix of innovations in microelectronics and computer hardware and software that have characterized trajectories in telecommunications electronics. In this arena digital electronics is a recent case of a gateway technology that has taken the industry along what is now a rapidly growing pathway.

Compatibility among subsystems and components is especially important in *modular systems*. In sectors such as audio electronics, for example, products may be divided into groups of subproducts (modules) that consumers can arrange into various combinations according to their preferences. Modular compatibility allows for the "bundling," "unbundling," and "rebundling" of various product character-istics or attributes to satisfy niche markets. Sometimes, when technologies developed for different markets converge enough, the way will be opened for the development of new trajectories that integrate these previously separate technol-ogies into new modular systems. An example is a stereo system that links and integrates several sound media (e.g. AM and FM radio, compact discs, cassette tapes) by sharing compatible modular amplification and sound production components.[18] An alternative pattern is illustrated in the HP cardio-imaging system, which was designed so that modules that improved performance or added new capabilities could be replaced or added later. Part of the sales strategy for the cardio-imaging system was to develop a product that allowed users to have state-of-the-art capabilities at all times, while never having to replace the whole machine.

Finally, *architectural* innovation can be a very powerful source of path dependence. It is common to illustrate the power of architectural innovation with the complex instruction set computing (CISC) format that is central to PC microprocessor architecture. CISC was chosen by Intel when it developed the microprocessor, later adopted by IBM. This adoption decision created a powerful path dependence.[19]

Standards setting and path dependence

A technological standard is a set of specifications adhered to either informally or as the result of a formal agreement. Informal, or *de facto*, standards may be created through market dominance by one standard over competing options. The CISC microprocessor architecture is an example of an informal standard that emerged from market competition among proprietary alternatives. The competitive advantage that comes from being the sponsor of a winning standard like CISC can be enormous. Those who develop the standard are better positioned to develop products that maximize the standard's capabilities. They are also able to discipline the actions of competitors by modifying the standard.[20]

Formal, or *de jure*, standards are arrived at through agreements reached by voluntary standards setting organizations or by government regulatory agency mandate.[21] Where government plays a role, standards may be established by fiat (e.g. the US Environmental Protection Agency's "technology forcing" standards for air quality), or government may facilitate the implementation of voluntary standards agreed to among affected organizations.[22]

Both *de facto* and *de jure* standards are sources of path dependence closely related to compatibility, since one of their purposes is to assure that technologies work together. Whatever the process involved (e.g. as a result of gateway, modular, or architectural innovation), standards setting adds predictability. It represents a process that reduces uncertainty.

Increasingly, the benefits of path dependence have given strategic importance to standards setting. As *de facto* standards have proliferated, the economic stakes involved have become higher, and it has become obvious that markets alone may not ensure that the best technical option prevails. One result is that many strategic alliances have been formed to promote high quality standards.[23] Robin Mansell says standards have become so interdependent with the various elements of the innovation process (e.g. engineering design, prototype testing, marketing) that they have become the "institutional glue" that links technical and organizational change across national innovation systems.[24]

Mansell's idea of standards as institutional glue is similar to Gregory Tassey's concept of technology infrastructure, or *infratechnology*. Technological infrastructures include the scientific and engineering knowledge that has been embodied in people, organizations, and facilities, plus the economic and political institutions that have been developed to protect intellectual property (e.g. the patent system) and to provide for planning and collaboration among organizations. For Tassey, *standards are the codification of infratechnology.*[25] They facilitate communication and cooperation within and among networks and throughout national innovation systems.

Metaphors like institutional glue also suggest that standards may over time generate path dependence that "hardens" and eliminates flexibility. When the relationships among standards setting institutions and organizations involved in innovation fail to adapt in ways that facilitate innovation, their evolutionary path may ossify:

> Decision-making procedures and technical architectures for equipment, for example, become subject to rigidities arising from the history of investment in technological designs and the weight of accumulated knowledge within a particular technological trajectory. Furthermore, the boundaries between the activities of institutions that are perceived as being competent in certain areas, for example, standards-making, can become "set" in ways that no longer reflect the need to coordinate knowledge accumulation and the flow of information with respect to technique and design, with strategies affecting the commercial potential of products.[26]

Industry strategy, public policy, and path dependence

Path dependence means that early technology choices tend to be reinforced. That reinforcement is linked to industry strategy or public policy in two ways. When path dependence is embedded in company strategies and public policies, those strategies and policies make changing the direction of technology especially difficult. Thus, path dependence bounds not just the technology and organizations directly involved; it also bounds the broader environment of national innovation systems.

Policy and strategy have become ever more important in influencing the particular pathway taken by new technological trajectories. The greatest potential for affecting pathways through use of public policy or industry strategy appears to lie in the area of standards setting. An example is the decision by audio companies to use the DAD committee to select the CD format. Indeed, influencing path dependence by standards setting may become a more important component of policy and strategy because the innovation of many complex technologies demands managed adaptation of standards:

> As technology-based systems become increasingly important and the "windows of opportunity" for making successful investments in the associated markets continues to shrink, *the relevant standards will have to be "managed."* If a standard is fixed, even if it is competitively neutral (an interface standard, for example, rather than a proprietary product element standard), it will eventually act to stifle the introduction of new technology into the system.[27]

Consequences of path dependence

Whether the focus of public policy and corporate strategy is on standards setting or any other significant aspect of innovation, policy makers and managers must inevitably contend with the *effects* of dynamic technological and organizational paths.[28] What are these effects? What is known about the consequences of path dependence? Students of complexity science and evolutionary economics have identified two broad patterns: *increasing returns* and *lock-in*.

Increasing returns

When resource-dependent industries like agriculture and mining were the most important sources of economic and technological advance, it was natural to regard decreasing returns as the norm. These sectors' dependence on finite amounts of land or mineral deposits meant that diminishing returns were a fact of life. Indeed, economic sectors that are based on finite resources are still often significantly constrained by decreasing returns.

In contrast, by the 1920s many observers were realizing that some manufacturing activities were characterized by increasing returns. For example, classical economists noted that particular firms in some manufacturing sectors enjoyed higher returns than predicted from labor and capital invested. The explanation classical economists offered was improved organization. This was the genesis of the idea of increasing returns to scale.[29] The emerging and increasingly powerful neoclassical economic perspective, however, was not receptive to this explanation. Arthur's characterization of the neoclassical position regarding increasing returns is worth recounting at some length:

> In a sense, ideas that made use of increasing returns have *always* been a part of the literature in economics. But in the past they were only partially articulated and were difficult to bring under mathematical control. And they tended to have disturbing implications. As a result many in our profession chose to disregard or dismiss them. This distaste reached its peak in the early 1970s with the broad acceptance in economics that all properly specified economic problems should show a unique equilibrium solution. I was a graduate student about this time, and all results in economics were served to us with the incantation that they were true, "providing there is a sufficient convexity – that is, diminishing returns on the margin." I was curious about what might happen when there were *increasing* returns on the margin, but none of my professors seemed interested in the question or willing to answer it. Examples from increasing returns and nonconvexities were of course mentioned from time to time. But in the main they were treated like the pathological specimens in labeled jars that used to be paraded to medical students – anomalies, freaks, malformations that were rare, but that nevertheless could serve as object lessons against interference in the natural workings of the economy.[30]

Reconsideration of the role of technology in economic advancement was a central factor leading to a resurgence of interest in the concept of increasing returns. Three changes in outlook and approach seem to have been particularly important. First, as noted in the discussion of path dependence, the history of technology and economic development has made a comeback in the newer increasing returns literature.[31] Second, the influences of innovative accidents and serendipity have come to the fore. It is now almost fashionable to take into account the role of chance events in the evolution of technological innovation.[32] Third, the new literature on increasing returns has moved beyond considering firms as the only actors in interorganizational networks.[33] All these trends feature a much deeper probing for path-dependent factors and emphasize the nonlinear processes indispensable to the evolution of technologies.[34]

Under what path-dependent conditions do increasing returns tend to manifest themselves? Four sets of circumstances appear favorable for the emergence of increasing returns: (a) economies of scale; (b) learning effects; (c) coordination benefits; and (d) adaptive expectations.[35]

Increasing returns to scale

We noted earlier that classical economists entertained the idea of increasing returns to scale early in the twentieth century, but interest faded with the arrival of neoclassicism. What has changed is the concept of scale itself. In the dominant neoclassical conceptualization, negative feedback and decreasing returns keep a company from increasing scale beyond some "optimum" level. Beyond an optimum scale of operations, profits decline; this limitation keeps any company from monopolizing a market. Increasing returns to scale based on knowledge intensity, in complex industries like semiconductors, telecommunications equipment, and automobiles, dramatically alter this equilibrium-oriented view of scale. In these sectors, the optimum scale of production may be the entire market. In such situations, being first to the market may translate into an early lead that positive feedbacks magnify into very large-scale market dominance.[36]

Increasing returns from learning

Network learning is perhaps the most powerful way to create increasing returns. Thirty years ago, learning by doing was identified as conducive to positive feedback and increasing returns, and today the entire range of learning opportunities outlined in Chapter 8 (e.g. learning by using, learning from interaction) have been associated with the increasing returns phenomenon.[37]

One of the most dramatic departures from the neoclassical perspective on innovation is the idea that *increasing returns have a much more intimate relationship with learning than had previously been thought*. In fact, Arthur suggests that learning itself may be a process of increasing returns, fed by positive feedback. In his words:

> On first thoughts it may appear that the subjects of learning in the economy and increasing returns have little in common with each other. But in fact there is a strong connection between the two ... Much of learning can be viewed as dynamic competition among different hypotheses or beliefs or actions, with some reinforced and others weakened as fresh evidence and data are obtained. Such competition with reinforcement happens within the brain at the Hebbian neural-synapse level in a literal way – biochemically – when primitive learning takes place. And it happens at a higher level in decision problems when agents choose repeatedly among alternative actions whose consequences are to some degree random. In this case agents emphasize or reinforce the choices that appear most promising as they receive information on their consequences from the environment.[38]

Increasing returns from coordination

This book has emphasized the benefits of network coordination to innovation. Among the many aspects of coordination that produce increasing returns are common standards, languages, or infrastructures and the technical compatibility of interconnected systems. In all these instances, the successful performance of any individual technology is contingent on effective linkages with other technological and organizational elements.

As with the concepts of economies of scale and learning, the idea of externalities from coordination has expanded dramatically as the dynamics of increasing returns have received more attention. Initially, most attention to externalities in networks focused narrowly on how these factors affected the success of competing "dominant designs" or technological standards that were advanced by individual, atomistic firms. Market success was explained largely in terms of efficiency or some aspect of technological superiority. Organization was not an important factor in these assessments. That has changed dramatically, however, with studies of the organizational dynamics that generate coordination benefits from networks. James Wade, for instance, argues that far-flung webs of organizational stakeholders have generated increasing returns in the microprocessor industry. He contends that "in industries with increasing returns, firms cannot be considered atomistically. Competing technologies and standards can usefully be envisioned as separate organizational communities, each supported by a set of interdependent populations."[39]

Increasing returns from adaptive expectations

Finally, there is a dimension of social psychology associated with the generation of increasing returns. In cases where a particular technological alternative is *presumed to be dominant* by a sufficient number of actors (e.g. consumers, suppliers, producers of competing designs), this expectation may become self-fulfilling. A frequently cited example is the widespread assumption, made in the 1980s, that IBM's Disk Operating System (DOS) would become the standard. This expectation reinforced exactly that outcome. Thus, increasing returns are produced when enough expectations about the technological winner amplify (i.e. provide positive feedback to) an existing market advantage (e.g. a small technological lead held by one network or firm).[40]

Lock-in

Sometimes the increasing returns that emerge from path dependence can lead to lock-in. Giovanni Dosi summarizes this dynamic in a situation where the source of increasing returns is organizational learning:

> The exploration of particular technologies and the development of particular problem-solving methods increase the capabilities of firms and industries in these specific directions and thus increase the incentive to do so in the future. These technology-specific forms of dynamic increasing returns tend to "lock in" the processes of technical change into particular trajectories, entailing a mutual reinforcement (a positive feedback) between a certain pattern of learning and a pattern of allocation of resources into innovative activities where learning has already occurred in the past.[41]

Lock-in demonstrates that markets, like organizations, sometimes make selections that do not necessarily represent the best economic or technological outcomes. Early lock-in often turns out to be a costly mistake that is hard to undo. There are at least three potential liabilities of lock-in. First, lock-in can reduce flexibility. For example, an industry can become trapped in obsolete or inferior compatibility relationships or technical standards.[42]

Second, lock-in can be a major barrier to entry by new organizations with a better approach or product (so-called "lock-out").[43] Any time a large number of organizations have moved to support a locked in technology or standard (e.g. many suppliers develop mutually compatible products), the costs of entry for challengers are increased because of the large installed base that would have to be changed.[44] Moreover, a community of suppliers, producers, and users that has adopted a locked in standard, for instance, will have a number of economic weapons they can employ to impede the entry of a challenger. If an outsider (i.e. a company or network that has not adopted the locked in version) develops an improvement, the insider organizations (i.e. those which have already adopted the dominant variant) may render the modification valueless by simply refusing to adopt it. Or the sponsors of the locked in standard may disseminate their technology by licensing it widely in a proactive attempt to deter the development of new potential standards.[45]

Third, early emergence of lock-in increases the economic penalties for hesitancy and mistakes at precisely the time when risk-taking can be most valuable to successful innovation (e.g. during the initial experience with technical designs and performance characteristics, when outcomes of novel approaches are not yet known). In an era of rapid technological change and diffusion, the specter of premature lock-in thus places enormous pressures on networks and firms that are faced with decreasing predictability of outcomes and increasing risk from both stagnation and following the wrong path. These circumstances put a premium on the ability to make strategic decisions.[46]

Whether or not a locked in technology turns out to be technically inferior or superior to its rivals, lock-in can give enormous technological and economic leverage to the organizations that have adopted it. This is especially true when these insider organizations can avoid the pitfalls of premature lock-in outlined above and continue a process of rapid incremental innovation along a technological trajectory. In these instances, a strategy of openness (e.g. sharing technological information with rivals or licensing technology to them) may be pursued to attract new adherents to the dominant technology. Wade describes how this process may unfold:

> Being the sponsor of an open system allows the sponsor to retain a competitive advantage because of the time lag between its implementation of the technology and its diffusion to others. Thus, if the sponsor has core competencies that allow upgradability of components and skills, the sponsor will enjoy transient monopoly positions as it brings upgrades of its technology to market faster than its rivals can imitate.[47]

The idea of a "transient monopoly" resulting from lock-in is useful. To some extent the dynamic evolution of path dependence, increasing returns, and lock-in can lead to an outcome comparable to the legalized monopoly of obtaining patents in more static situations. A transient monopoly maintained by lock-in appears to have happened with Intel's microprocessor technology.

Yet even the strongest lock-in cannot last forever. Even the most dynamic of technological trajectories eventually plays out. Some erosion of lock-in occurs naturally; for example, as organizational learning opportunities are exhausted. Sometimes the complex communities configured around a locked in standard or technology are able to reach a consensus on their own that an alternative standard or technology would be superior − especially if the current commitment is not embodied in expensive, specialized equipment and infrastructure.[48] A consensus change of this sort occurred in the case of the movement from analog magnetic tapes to digital compact discs (CD).

Very often, however, the impulse to "exit from lock-in" comes from outside the community or technological trajectory. A fusing of previously separate technological trajectories is one avenue by which this occurs. A convergence of trajectories can invalidate existing technical standards, demand new compatibility relationships, and generate a range of alternative learning possibilities. This is what happened when the linear accelerator replaced cobalt-60 as the preferred radiation treatment for cancer.

Last, but certainly not least, *lock-in can be terminated by public policy.* Government programs can affect the choice of compatibility criteria (e.g. using government procurement programs as incentives for the development of new technological architectures) or learning opportunities (e.g. public funding of R&D). As we have seen, government is sometimes actively involved in standards setting, both as a facilitator of voluntary standards and as a promoter of public regulations and requirements.

Conclusions

It is not clear how much path dependence, increasing returns, or lock-in occur in a modern economy. Some observers see them as increasingly pervasive phenomena, but others view such claims as overstated. David, for instance, says he has been shocked by the reaction to his case studies. He notes that many of his economist colleagues reacted to his accounts of path dependence and lock-in of the QWERTY typewriter keyboard as if it was "a cute story about the anomalous economics of typewriters," rather than recognizing it as "a metaphor for a class of multiple equilibrium processes."[49]

On this point the authors are in sympathy with David; moreover, we posit that path dependence and increasing returns occur with greater frequency in those complex sectors and trajectories characterized by high levels of connectivity and interdependence (e.g. electronics, telecommunications). That these complex sectors and trajectories happen to be some of the most valuable in world trade seems to us to make even occasional lock-in worthy of discussion and investigation.

With regard to path dependence, we do not defend technological determinism. Instead, what Rosenberg has characterized as "soft determinism" seems more accurate. Soft determinism suggests that "one historical event did not rigidly prescribe certain subsequent technological developments, but at least made sequences of technological improvements in one direction easier."[50]

Notes

1. Michael Storper and Robert Salais, *Worlds of Production: the Action Frameworks of the Economy*, Cambridge, MA: Harvard University Press, 1997, pp. 10–12.
2. Fernando Vega–Redondo, "Technological Change and Path Dependence: a Co-evolutionary Model on a Directed Graph," *Journal of Evolutionary Economics*, No. 1, 1994, p. 61 (emphasis added).
3. Robin Cowan and Philip Gunby, "Sprayed to Death: Path Dependence, Lock-in and Pest Control Strategies," *Economic Journal*, Vol. 106, No. 436, May 1996, p. 521.
4. Peter Hall, *Innovation, Economics, and Evolution: Theoretical Perspectives on Changing Technology in Economic Systems*, New York: Harvester Wheatsheaf, 1994, p. 272.
5. Paul A. David, "Clio and the Economics of QWERTY," *Economic History*, May 1985, p. 332.
6. Alfons Balmann, Martin Odening, Hans-Peter Weikard, and Wilhelm Brandes, "Path–dependence without Increasing Returns to Scale and Network Externalities," *Journal of Economic Behavior and Organization*, Vol. 29, January 1996, p. 160.
7. Richard R. Nelson, "Technical Change as Cultural Evolution," in Ross Thomson, ed., *Learning and Technological Change*, New York: St Martin's Press, 1993, pp. 9–23.
8. Milton B. Lower, "The Concept of Technology within the Institutionalist Perspective," *Journal of Economic Issues*, September 1987, pp. 1153–67; Paul D. Bush, "The Theory of

Institutional Change," *Journal of Economic Issues*, September 1987, pp. 1078–90.

9. Andrew Tylecote, "Managerial Objectives and Technological Collaboration: the Role of National Variations in Cultures and Structures," in Rod Coombs, Albert Richards, Pier P. Saviotti, and Vivien Walsh, eds, *Technological Collaboration: The Dynamics of Cooperation in Industrial Innovation*, Brookfield, VT: Edward Elgar, 1996, pp. 35–53; Lane Kenworthy, *In Search of National Economic Success: Balancing Competition and Cooperation*, London: Sage Publications, 1995, pp. 192–5.

10. Richard Florida and Martin Kenney, "The New Age of Capitalism: Innovation-mediated Production," *Futures*, Vol. 25, No. 4, July/August 1993, pp. 637–51.

11. David J. Teece, Gary Pisano, and Amy Shuen, "Dynamic Capabilities and Strategic Management," *Strategic Management Journal*, Vol. 18, No. 7, August 1997, pp. 522–3; David T. Lei, "Competence-building, Technology Fusion and Competitive Advantage: the Key Roles of Organizational Learning and Strategic Alliances," *International Journal of Technology Management*, Vol. 14, Nos 2/3/4, 1997, pp. 211–13.

12. David Lei, Michael A. Hitt, and Richard Bettis, "Dynamic Core Competences through Meta-learning and Strategic Context," *Journal of Management*, Vol. 22, No. 4, 1996, p. 565.

13. Pari Patel and Keith Pavitt, "The Technological Competencies of the World's Largest Firms: Complex and Path Dependent, but Not Much Variety," *Research Policy*, Vol. 26, No. 2, May 1997, pp. 141–56; Teece, Pisano, and Shuen, "Dynamic Capabilities and Strategic Management," pp. 518–24; David J. Teece, Richard Rumelt, Giovanni Dosi, and Sidney Winter, "Understanding Corporate Coherence: Theory and Evidence," *Journal of Economic Behavior and Organization*, Vol. 23, No. 1, January 1994, pp. 1–30; W. Brian Arthur, "Positive Feedbacks in the Economy," in W. Brian Arthur, ed., *Increasing Returns and Path Dependency in the Economy*, Ann Arbor, MI: University of Michigan Press, 1994, pp. 1–12; Giovanni Dosi, "Sources, Procedures, and Microeconomic Effects of Innovation," *Journal of Economic Literature*, Vol. 26, No. 3, September 1988, p. 1144.

14. Paul A. David and Julie A. Bunn, "The Economics of Gateway Technologies and Network Evolution: Lessons from Electricity Supply History," *Information Economics and Policy*, No. 3, 1988, p. 171.

15. Paul A. David, "Understanding the Economics of QWERTY: the Necessity of History," in W. N. Parker, ed., *Economic History and the Modern Economist*, New York: Basil Blackwell, 1986, pp. 41–3.

16. Nathan Rosenberg, *Exploring the Black Box: Technology, Economics, and History*, New York: Cambridge University Press, 1994, pp. 205–6.

17. David and Bunn, "The Economics of Gateway Technologies and Network Evolution," pp. 165–202.

18. Richard N. Langlois and Paul L. Robertson, "Networks and Innovation in a Modular System: Lessons from the Microprocessor and Stereo Component Industry," *Research Policy*, Vol. 21, No. 4, August 1992, pp. 297–313.

19. James Wade, "Dynamics of Organizational Communities and Technological Bandwagons: an Empirical Investigation of Community Evolution in the Microprocessor Market," *Strategic Management Journal*, Vol. 16, Special Issue, Summer 1995, pp. 118–19.

20. Charles R. Morris and Charles H. Ferguson, "How Architecture Wins Technology Wars," *Harvard Business Review*, Vol. 71, No. 2, March/April 1993, pp. 88–9.

21. Paul A. David and Shane Greenstein, "The Economics of Compatibility Standards: an Introduction to Recent Research," *Economics of Innovation and New Technologies*, Vol. 1, 1990, pp. 4–5.

22. Jennifer Nash and John Ehrenfeld, "Code Green: Business Adopts Voluntary Environmental Standards," *Environment*, January/February 1996, pp. 16–20, 36–45; J. Clarence Davies, "Environmental Regulation and Technical Change: Overview and Observations," in Myron F. Uman, ed., *Keeping Pace With Science and Engineering: Case Studies in Environmental Regulation*, Washington, DC: National Academy Press, 1993, pp. 251–62.

23. Charles W. L. Hill, "Establishing a Standard: Competitive Strategy and Technological

Standards in Winner-take-all Industries," *Academy of Management Executive*, Vol. 11, No. 2, May 1997, pp. 7–25; Bengt-Ake Lundvall, "Standards in an Innovative World," in Richard W. Hawkins, Robin Mansell, and Jim Skea, eds, *Standards, Innovation and Competitiveness: The Politics and Economics of Standards in Natural and Technical Environments*, Brookfield, VT: Edward Elgar, 1995, pp. 7–12.

24. Robin Mansell, "Standards, Industrial Policy and Innovation," in Hawkins, Mansell, and Skea, eds, *Standards, Innovation and Competitiveness*, pp. 213–14.

25. Gregory Tassey, "The Functions of Technology Infrastructure in a Competitive Economy," *Research Policy*, Vol. 20, No. 4, August 1991, p. 357.

26. Mansell, "Standards, Industrial Policy and Innovation," in Hawkins, Mansell, and Skea, eds, *Standards, Innovation and Competitiveness*, p. 214.

27. Gregory Tassey, "The Roles of Standards as Technology Infrastructure," in Hawkins, Mansell, and Skea, eds, *Standards, Innovation and Competitiveness*, p. 169 (emphasis added).

28. Keith Smith, "Innovation Policy in an Evolutionary Context," in P. Paolo Saviotti and J. Stanley Metcalfe, eds, *Evolutionary Theories of Economic and Technological Change: Present Status and Future Prospects*, Reading, PA: Harwood Academic Publishers, 1991, p. 264.

29. James M. Buchanan, "The Return to Increasing Returns: an Introductory Summary," in James M. Buchanan and Young J. Yoon, eds, *The Return to Increasing Returns*, Ann Arbor, MI: University of Michigan Press, 1994, pp. 6–7.

30. W. Brian Arthur, "Preface," in Arthur, ed., *Increasing Returns and Path Dependence in the Economy*, pp. xi–xii.

31. W. Brian Arthur, "Competing Technologies, Increasing Returns, and Lock-in by Historical Events," *Economic Journal*, Vol. 99, No. 394, March 1989, pp. 116–31.

32. Kurt Dopfer, "Toward a Theory of Economic Institutions: Synergy and Path Dependency," *Journal of Economic Issues*, Vol. 25, No. 2, June 1991, pp. 544–7.

33. Yasunori Baba and Ken–ichi Imai, "A Network View of Innovation and Entrepreneurship: the Case of the Evolution of the VCR Systems," *International Social Science Journal*, Vol. 45, No. 1, February 1993, pp. 23–34.

34. W. Brian Arthur, "Increasing Returns and the New World of Business," *Harvard Business Review*, Vol. 74, No. 4, July/August 1996, pp. 100–9.

35. W. Brian Arthur, "Self-reinforcing Mechanisms in Economics," in Philip W. Anderson, Kenneth J. Arrow, and David Pines, eds, *The Economy as an Evolving Complex System*, Redwood City, CA: Addison-Wesley, 1988, p. 10.

36. Richard A. Bettis and Michael A. Hitt, "The New Competitive Landscape," *Strategic Management Journal*, Vol. 16, Special Issue, Summer 1995, p. 11.

37. Richard R. Nelson, "Recent Evolutionary Theorizing about Economic Change," *Journal of Economic Literature*, Vol. 33, No. 1, March 1995, pp. 73–8.

38. Arthur, "Path Dependence, Self-reinforcement, and Human Learning," in Arthur, ed., *Increasing Returns and Path Dependence in the Economy*, pp. 133–4.

39. Wade, "Dynamics of Organizational Communities and Technological Bandwagons," p. 131.

40. David and Greenstein, "The Economics of Compatibility Standards," p. 7.

41. Dosi, "Sources, Procedures, and Microeconomic Effects of Innovation," p. 1148.

42. Joseph Farrell and Garth Saloner, "Standardization, Compatibility, and Innovation," *Rand Journal of Economics*, Vol. 16, No. 1, Spring 1985, p. 71.

43. Carlota Perez and Luc Soete, "Catching up in Technology: Entry Barriers and Windows of Opportunity," in Giovanni Dosi, Christopher Freeman, Richard Nelson, Gerald Silverberg, and Luc Soete, eds, *Technical Choice and Economic Theory*, New York: Pinter Publishers, 1988, pp. 459–60.

44. Shane Greenstein, "Did Installed Base Give an Incumbent Any (Measurable) Advantages in Federal Computer Procurement?" *Rand Journal of Economics*, Vol. 24, No. 1, Spring 1993, pp. 19–39.

45. Wade, "Dynamics of Organizational Communities and Technological Bandwagons," p. 112.
46. Bettis and Hitt, "The New Competitive Landscape," p. 14.
47. Wade, "Dynamics of Organizational Communities and Technological Bandwagons," p. 130.
48. Arthur, "Self-reinforcing Mechanisms in Economics," in Anderson, Arrow, and Pines, eds, *The Economy as an Evolving Complex System*, p. 16.
49. Paul A. David, "Path-dependence and Predictability in Dynamic Systems with Local Network Externalities: a Paradigm for Historical Economics," in Dominique Foray and Christopher Freeman, eds, *Technology and the Wealth of Nations: The Dynamics of Constructed Advantage*, New York: Pinter Publishers, 1993, p. 211.
50. Rosenberg, *Exploring the Black Box*, p. 19.

PART III

CHAPTER TEN

Emerging Patterns

If complexity science and evolutionary economics are to have value to corporate managers and public policy makers who are seeking to foster technological innovation, they must offer usable policy and strategy guidance. That guidance must come from developing insights based on identifying and characterizing different innovation patterns, rather than from a precise understanding of the sources or consequences of particular innovations. The process of identifying and characterizing these patterns continues in this chapter in two steps. First, we name the patterns and provide an overview of their distinctive features. Second, we characterize and compare the patterns, using the concepts developed in Chapters 6 to 9.

Labels and categories

The patterns introduced in Chapter 6 are the conceptual starting point for the search for policy and strategy guidance. Figure 10.1 suggests the relationships among three patterns, which we have labeled as follows.

- *Normal*: the coevolution of an established network and technology along an established trajectory.
- *Transition*: the coevolutionary movement to a new trajectory by an established network and technology.
- *Transformation*: the launching of a new trajectory by a new coevolving network and technology.

The square at the lower left of Figure 10.1 illustrates the kind of fundamental innovation that characterizes the transformation pattern. Innovations in a transformation pattern produce dramatically different technologies; these technologies have fundamentally different characteristics from other technologies. A transforming innovation launches a trajectory; that is, the fundamentally different technology then goes through the series of incremental innovations associated with the normal pattern. The process whereby a transformation pattern settles into a normal pattern is illustrated by the series of incremental innovations at points *a* through *d*. For most complex technologies, the normal pattern is at some point replaced by a transition pattern, illustrated by the triangle at the intersection of the two trajectories. The transition pattern involves an innovation that produces a major change and improvement in the technology. Like the transformation pattern, a transition launches a new trajectory and then settles into the normal pattern illustrated by the series of innovations as points *e* through *g*.

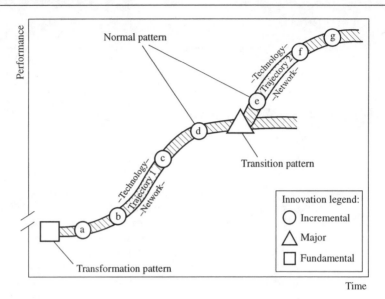

Figure 10.1 Three innovation patterns

The following discussion compares the three patterns in terms of characteristics of their networks, technologies, and trajectories. Special attention is given to the organizational behavior of networks in each of the patterns.

Patterns are potentially valuable to managers and policy makers because they provide insight into relationships that can easily be lost in a welter of details: the complex interactions among networks, technologies, and their environment. If the patterns are to have utility for policy and strategy, every effort must be made to clearly distinguish them. While the discussion emphasizes differences, the innovations associated with all three patterns nevertheless share important attributes. The most significant common trait is that all complex technologies have deep roots in predecessor technologies. Whether normal, transitional, or transformational, innovations of complex technologies arise from a context that conditions them. For this and other reasons, precise boundaries cannot be drawn between the patterns.[1] Rather, the patterns are best seen as dynamic processes that flow into each other. In those regions where the patterns connect, drawing precise distinctions is difficult. The characterization of the three patterns in Figure 10.1 is intended to illustrate both the distinctive features of each pattern and the flow of one pattern into the next.

For differentiating among the three patterns, a key distinction is that between an *established* technology or network and a *new* technology or network. An established technology has the same basic design characteristics before and after an innovation. A new technology features either major modifications in design or the creation of a fundamentally different design as the result of an innovation. As used here, technology designs may refer to processes, products, or both. Similarly, an established network is one that has the same participant organizations holding the same core capabilities and most of the same specialized complementary assets before and after an innovation. Alternatively, new networks have either the same participant organizations or new ones holding new core capabilities and new complementary assets. It is useful to think of both networks and technologies as systems. The linkages among the network members that hold core capabilities and complementary assets are analogous to the linkages among systems, subsystems, and components in complex technologies. The changes in those linkages are highly significant for new networks and new technologies.

Established trajectories, therefore, feature the coevolution of established networks and technologies (the normal pattern). Alternatively, a new trajectory is generated either by an entirely new network and technology (the transformation pattern), or by an established network and technology undergoing a major change (the transition pattern).

Each trajectory corresponds to a particular product and process, and within any technology sector or community there are usually multiple competing trajectories. For example, the coevolving Intel network and its x-86 microprocessor define one trajectory, while the coevolving Motorola network and its 68000 microprocessor represent a competitor trajectory. Often there are also multiple trajectories within the same transition pattern. The transformation pattern appears to feature fewer competing trajectories, and in some cases there may be only one trajectory.

Our case studies provide illustrations of the different dynamics of the three innovation patterns. As reflected in the schematic presented in Figure 10.1, all three patterns may (and often do) emerge during the evolutionary process associated with a technology. Each case study contains examples of more than one pattern.

Each example of a pattern is described in terms of the self-organization framework for networks presented in Chapter 6 and summarized in Table 6.2. This framework includes network resources (existing core capabilities, complementary assets, and organizational learning) and constraining and focusing factors (potential organizational learning and complementary assets, as well as the selection environment and path dependencies).

The normal pattern

The normal pattern is characterized by continuity, represented by the "smooth" curve connecting innovations along its trajectory of incremental changes, in contrast to the sharp discontinuities in the other two patterns. Innovations that occur within the normal pattern are incremental, and even those that must deal with the most difficult barriers or sudden environmental shifts do so largely within the current problem solving model that the coevolving network shares with the established technological community.

Network innovations within the normal pattern have high levels of confidence regarding what problems demand priority and whether the problems can be solved. The dominant short-term uncertainties are about how long the problem solving process will take and how much it will cost. Self-organization occurs in small steps, and strategies and structures can be modified in small steps as each incremental advance occurs.[2] Thus, innovations carried out along an established trajectory as the established network and technology coevolve are less risky than those in the other patterns. When the conditions of greater continuity and surety can be combined with dynamic learning processes, networks have a higher probability of maintaining a competitive advantage. This is the preferred context of operations for most networks, and the one toward which they migrate. The greatest profits tend to

Table 10.1 Typical technological and organizational changes in the normal pattern

Network resources and constraining and focusing factors	Before an incremental innovation	After an incremental innovation
Core capabilities	Established	Established. Some enhancement by way of altered linkages to complementary assets.
Complementary assets	Established	Established, plus any or all of the following: • reconfiguration of existing assets; • upgrading of existing assets (e.g. from generic to specialized; from specialized to synthesis into established core capabilities); • linkages to new assets.
Organizational learning	Local	Local. Often more focused than prior to the increment.
Path dependence	Strong	Strong. Often even more strongly linked to past than prior to the increment.
Selection environment	Powerful market	Powerful market. Signals more meaningful than prior to the increment.

accrue during periods when the network is in a normal pattern, even though the foundation for this market success may have been a risky "investment" in an earlier transformation or transition.

Incremental innovations along an established trajectory are characterized by technological changes that deliver enhanced performance. For example, the innovations may deliver *greater* speed, *more* precision, *higher* operating temperatures, *more diverse* applications, *lower* production costs, etc. By contrast, the designs of both the product and process technologies remain basically the same before and after an incremental innovation.

Similarly, the networks that carry out the innovation remain basically the same before and after the innovation. There may be some changes in the network membership, but these modifications usually take the form of changes in suppliers of complementary assets. Table 10.1 summarizes typical technological and organizational changes within the normal pattern.

Enhancing existing core capabilities

Innovations within the normal pattern generally enhance established core capabilities. The emphasis is on improving existing performance rather than expanding into entirely new areas.[3] Faced with the challenges of innovating complex technologies, most networks gradually enlarge the diversity of their capabilities, but their capability profile remains relatively stable.[4] Deepening and broadening existing capabilities by internal learning and by accessing an ever wider array of complementary assets is the normal route to incremental innovation. Core capabilities are often enhanced through the changing utilization of complementary assets and the associated reconfiguration of the network. This process of augmenting core capabilities incrementally has been termed "creative accumulation."[5]

As established networks and technologies coevolve along an established trajectory, core capabilities tend to become more fixed as the "core" of the technology. However, even in the most mature trajectories, new tacit knowledge and know-how continue to develop as incremental innovations occur. One area in which this is often evident is in an increasing mastery of systems integration, architectural knowledge, and the capacity to synthesize previously separate knowledge and complementary assets.[6] Many observers emphasize the particular importance of tacit knowledge to the continual improvement of process technologies (e.g. engineering design, concurrent engineering) during the later stages of a trajectory.[7] The blend of tacit and explicit process knowledge acquired from incremental innovations has been the foundation for much of the success with lean or agile production described in Chapter 3.[8]

The exploitation role of complementary assets

In the normal pattern, complementary assets are used to *exploit* established core capabilities. Some established assets acquire a higher priority over time and some may even become core capabilities. New complementary assets are often added to networks during normal innovation. As a normal trajectory evolves, however, there is often a growing distinction between specialized and generic assets. Alternatively, the boundary between the most important specialized complementary assets and the network's core capabilities becomes blurred.

Organizational indicators of this blurring process include higher levels of trust between the holders of core capabilities and holders of critical complementary assets. As the normal pattern unfolds, many networks manifest nearly seamless relationships between "first-tier" complementary asset suppliers, priority users, and the holders of core capabilities. Second-tier asset holders, by comparison, tend to evolve toward more formal, arm's length relationships with the holders of core capabilities.[9] But even with more distant second-tier suppliers, the network must retain enough knowledge (e.g. design expertise) to be able to access and use their assets. The holders of core capabilities must, as Andrea Prencipe says, maintain an "intelligent customership" for complementary assets.[10]

Local learning

Organizational learning in the normal pattern is predominately internal, and it tends to become more focused with each incremental advance. As network routines and heuristics become well developed, learning becomes ever more dependent upon what has been done in the past. Thus, as problems emerge established networks know where to go for solutions. This makes problem solving a less risky process than it is when more wide-ranging, exploratory learning is required.[11] The local learning in successful networks is highly dynamic and seldom involves just reusing past experiences. Adaptive local learning entails breaking with the past in small but significant ways. Often this involves integrating new knowledge from a variety of projects occurring along the same trajectory, or it may take advantage of synergies emerging from entirely different trajectories. In general, the more significant the incremental innovation, the more difficult it is to recognize the similarities to previous experiences.[12]

Strong path dependence

Local learning is inherently path dependent because of its reliance on an accumulated technological base. Knowing how to solve particular problems in particular ways tends to shape and define new problems. Anders Lundgren summarizes the path dependence dynamic:

> It is a cumulative process in the traditional sense that it is a consequence of incremental technological change and gradual learning, and it is as much a question of retaining previous experience, combining it with the prevailing circumstances, as it is of developing novel solutions ... Technological development unfolds in sequences of problem-solving, where problems lead on to problems and where the solutions to these drive the technological frontier along a particular path.[13]

Powerful market selection

Once a network, technology, and trajectory are well established, market forces usually play a significant selection role. At the beginning of the normal pattern, the tradeoffs between alternative incremental innovations may be understood by only a few lead-users and first-tier suppliers. Thus, market-demand signals may be mixed and conflicting. Markets also develop a good deal of path dependence as they coevolve with the trajectory. Well defined market segments and the relationships between the network and a wider array of users and suppliers usually develop only after extensive incremental learning and adaptation.[14]

Eventually, the relative stability of the normal pattern enhances the importance of markets because a consensus develops concerning technological expectations. These expectations, in conjunction with the collection of demonstrated capabilities and embedded routines, provide a relatively solid framework within which market signals can be read and evaluated.

An example: the GE turbine blade

Aspects of the turbine blade case illustrate the normal pattern. Recall that General Electric (GE) entered the turbine blade business at the initiative of the US Army Air Corps. GE initially held the core capabilities for blade design, development, and use, as well as many of the complementary assets. For several decades GE maintained the capability to produce turbine blades entirely in house. Its goal in maintaining this capacity was to be able to measure the performance of outside complementary asset suppliers (e.g. casting companies). Over the past two decades, GE has systematically divested itself of most in-house complementary assets, and its core capabilities now focus on the design of turbine blades. In carrying out the design function, GE has modified its relationship with the casting companies, in a number of ways. First, because of incremental innovations in computer-aided design, GE must now work closely with the casting companies in the early design stages. One result has been the conversion of a substantial amount of tacit knowledge held by the casting companies into explicit knowledge. GE has established new contractual relationships with the casting companies in which the latter pay their own development costs but are given production contracts at the time design begins. Thus, the casting companies have become first-tier holders of specialized complementary assets.

The evolution of the GE network has been further facilitated by the US Air Force's creation of a new supplier of complementary assets. The Air Force underwrote the creation of a software company that could test early blade prototypes by running computer simulations. The goal was to speed up the innovation process and thereby reduce costs. This effort has led to close cooperation between GE and its major competitor, Pratt and Whitney, which also uses the new complementary assets created by the Air Force.

The evolution of GE's role in the innovation of turbine blades has paralleled its movement toward a focus on two core capabilities: systems integration, and the "hot side" of the jet engine (e.g. combustion chamber, high pressure turbine). GE's core capabilities with regard to blades now focus on the design of the blade and its integration into the engine. The other activities are the responsibility of complementary asset suppliers.

GE's changing focus on core capabilities has also triggered major adaptations in its network. In recent years GE has created "centers of excellence" organized around specific jet engine subsystems. These centers have integrated responsibilities for everything from research to contracting with suppliers. GE is now intimately integrated at the subsystem level with specialized asset suppliers. These organizational adaptations reflect new kinds of longer-term, trust-based relationships. All the network modifications, however, have taken place within well established technological boundaries that are highly path dependent. These boundaries reflect, for example, the expectation that improvements in the alloys used in the turbine blades will occur in increments of about 50° F (about 28° C) and that improved airflow designs for blades will be the primary route through which advances in performance will be achieved.

The transition pattern

Innovations that occur within the transition pattern create new technologies and networks as a result of major changes in what previously existed. Transitional innovations are often distinguished by major advances in performance, as well as qualitative changes in design. Major innovations commonly modify an established technology in ways that overcome what were thought to be major constraints on development, enabling the technology to perform beyond what was thought possible. Often the basic technology remains, but there is enough design modification to enable movement across a previously insurmountable threshold. Frequently a transition pattern arises from modifications in the overall design of a product or production process that results from integrating a new subsystem. One illustration is the transition from propeller to jet aircraft. In this case, the airplane crossed a previously constraining aerodynamic boundary. In the process, a major redesign of airplanes resulted.[15] After the transition, the airplane was not only faster; it took a new shape.

Networks that carry out transitions become new networks. Often new organizations that provide major new product or process subsystems are added to the existing network. Major innovations also add new core capabilities, which may be either held by new participant organizations or developed by the holders of the old network's core capabilities. Significantly restructured network linkages are integral to all such changes in core capabilities and complementary assets.

When transitions occur, networks face significant uncertainty about the design characteristics of the technology and about what the innovation will cost and when it will occur. Nonetheless, major innovations can usually rely on a reservoir of knowledge that has been accumulated while carrying out the incremental innovations associated with previous trajectories. Thus, a new network resulting from a trajectory transition can have a reasonable level of confidence in its ability to solve these transition issues by modifying the learning approaches, heuristics, and routines developed in the past.

Transitions may be generated by problems, opportunities, or a combination of both. The most common context for a problem-generated transition is migration of a network from an established technology to a new technological base. Exhausting the possibilities of the established technology or encountering a technological barrier or discontinuity along the established trajectory can induce this kind of transition. For instance, the networks moving along the various semiconductor trajectories may be approaching a transition because their ability to continue integrating more and more transistors onto one chip at ever lower costs seems to be confronting impassable technical barriers (e.g. the need for more advanced materials). Concerns about an impending transition have nagged the semiconductor industry for years:

> In stark contrast to what would seem to be implied by the dependable doubling of transistor densities, the route that led to today's chips was anything but smooth. It was more like a harrowing obstacle course that repeatedly required chipmakers to overcome significant limitations in their equipment and production processes. None of these problems turned out to be the dreaded showstopper whose solution would be so costly that it would slow or even halt the pace of advances in semiconductors and, therefore, the growth of the industry. Successive roadblocks, however, have become increasingly imposing, for reasons tied to the underlying technologies of semiconductor manufacturing.[16]

In other cases, the identification of new opportunities may be the primary incentive to undertake a transition; for example, when an alternative technology offers major performance improvements. The Boeing network undertook such a transition in its incorporation of new engineering design and manufacturing capabilities in the innovation of the 777 aircraft:

> A complete overhaul of the old management process and development tools support process was instituted involving a re-invention of not just the airplane, but the company. The team organization, involving joint development with international vendors and customers, is a massive concurrent engineering exercise based on a paperless development and factory process and computer tools.[17]

Frequently opportunities manifest themselves when technologies are taken into another sector. A highly visible example of a transition generated by a cross-sectoral movement of technology was Sony's innovation of digital electronic imaging as a challenge to the photochemical processes used in cameras.[18] A cross-sectoral transition may appear as a transformation to networks operating in the sector entered by the new technology, although it represents a transition for the network responsible for introducing the innovation. Thus, digital imaging may have seemed transformational to the Kodak network, while it was transitional for the new Sony-centered network.

When networks that have been innovating technologies like semiconductors or advanced materials find broader applications, the technologies can sweep over broad areas of the technological landscape (e.g. into automobiles and manufacturing

Table 10.2 Typical technological and organizational changes in the transition pattern

Network resources and constraining and focusing factors	Before a transition innovation	After a transition innovation
Core capabilities	Established	Partly new, due to some combination of: • adapting existing capabilities by modifying problem solving approaches and routines; • adding new capabilities (e.g. cross-sector spillovers); • eliminating outdated capabilities.
Complementary assets	Established	Partly new; specialized complementary assets are often added.
Organizational learning	Local	Regional. Broadening rather than deepening. Altered heuristics, experimentation.
Path dependence	Strong	Medium. Influence of past depends on whether transition arises from and depends on past.
Market selection	Powerful	Moderately powerful. Institutions become as important as markets.

processes), with major transitional consequences. Increasingly, the competition triggered by these cross-sectoral opportunities emerges in the form of networks that have been called "invisible enemies"[19] or "invading technologies."[20] Whatever the particular factors leading to trajectory transitions, they are never easy.[21]

When impending transitions are widely recognized, there are substantial incentives for previously competing networks to cooperate. The great uncertainty associated with transitions is a powerful inducement to establish strategic alliances and other forms of cooperation. As part of the transition to a new trajectory, even the most entrenched competitor networks are increasingly engaging in collaborative activities.[22] One factor that encourages cooperation is the belief that limiting the number of transition pathways through the use of voluntary standards setting has advantages for all the networks involved.[23]

As with the normal pattern, the transition pattern has characteristic changes in organizational behavior and technology, which are explored more fully below. Table 10.2 provides a summary of some of the changes typical of a transition pattern.

Expanding and eliminating core capabilities

Trajectory transitions involve some new core capabilities. In most cases, only a portion of the capabilities integral to the former dominant technology becomes obsolete. Part of the prior core capabilities remains useful. The most common transition pattern we observed involves linking some prior capabilities with core capabilities developed in another sector to provide a new source of competitive advantage. As this occurs, some capabilities that once were essential may become irrelevant, while previously marginal competencies may become important.[24] This highly uncertain set of developments contributes to competitors' interest in cooperating during a transition.

One way to expand and adapt capabilities is to create new and more dynamic network routines that promote different approaches to problem solving. Another way is to combine older routines in new ways. Although new routines are critical to new networks, they are difficult to develop because they depend so heavily on experience and so often require tacit knowledge. For these reasons there are powerful tendencies to continue using old routines. One point appears clear: in most transitions the changing of routines is inseparable from the process of developing the new network.[25]

When a transition requires the acquisition of new core capabilities, the need for speed typically means that network learning involves either acquiring explicit knowledge or adding new members to the network. Tacit knowledge integral to new core capabilities generally takes too long to develop internally, so some expansion of the network's organizational boundaries is required.[26]

The exploration role of complementary assets

As with core capabilities, a trajectory transition can either enhance complementary assets or make them obsolete. In most cases new assets are needed, and they need to be linked to existing assets, as well as to the core capabilities. Because specialized assets are most likely to be made obsolete by a transition, the search for or development of new specialized complementary assets becomes particularly important. Integral to that search process is the development of the new network.

Regional learning

Organizational learning during a trajectory transition is usually characterized by moving from a narrow but deep knowledge base to one that is broader. Networks expand their scope beyond the local learning of the normal pattern to engage in more exploratory, *regional* learning. There is a shift to search and discovery activities that are more external and longer term, but they normally remain in the same broad technological area, or "region." This shift in learning is particularly difficult. Because the problems encountered in transitions tend to be ambiguous, learning heuristics and routines must be repeatedly modified or restructured. Absent a defined technological community, it is hard to know where to go for relevant problem solving knowledge. A network in this situation must embrace more risky trial-and-error experimentation. Given the greater uncertainty of experiments during a transition, mistakes become an especially important source of feedback.[27]

Medium path dependence

Path dependence erodes during a trajectory transition, but the needed exploratory learning is always constrained by the contexts from which the new network arose. The persistence of path dependence during a transition can be both an advantage and a liability. On the positive side, once a network has developed learning experience along a trajectory, it is well equipped to screen its environment to identify technological changes consistent with its underlying capabilities. In effect, path dependence that has focused the capacity for organizational learning can position the network to search for ways to modify its competence base and successfully complete a transition. On the negative side, path dependence may severely limit the exploratory learning that is undertaken, just when breadth of learning is needed to make a successful transition possible.[28]

Ultimately, the impact of path dependence on the transition pattern depends on what Durand calls the principle of *competence relatedness*: success or failure rests on how much distance there is between the competencies required for the transition and the competencies that exist.[29]

Moderate market selection

In a transitional pattern, stability and predictability erode. One consequence is that the market provides unclear signals. When the process of innovation is highly exploratory, the networks that are being modified are less responsive to economic signals because the market has little knowledge about the new performance capabilities being developed. In such situations, linkages to institutions (e.g. relationships with other networks or government) matter more than market processes because they provide some stability and some limited foundations upon which decisions can be based.[30]

An example: cardio-imaging

The trajectory transition from cardio-imaging technology based on ultrasound to an MRI-based technology resulted from at least three developments. One was the search by HP for new markets. The second was the development of technical capabilities that would allow the cardio-imaging technology to replace invasive diagnostic techniques with non-invasive techniques. The third was the set of routines that drove the network to keep innovating when faced with the absence of a clear target for incremental innovation.

The potential benefits of substituting an MRI base for ultrasound were part of a developing set of expectations within the broader cardio-imaging community. MRI was a developed technology in widespread use for other kinds of diagnosis. However, HP did not have state-of-the-art MRI capabilities in-house or within any of its existing networks. For HP, the choice was to either develop its own MRI expertise or link with another network. Although HP had no doubt that it could develop the MRI expertise, doing so would involve a heavily empirical learning process because some of the knowledge needed was tacit and existed in the form of routines and heuristics. A key part of this tacit knowledge concerned developing the links necessary to synthesize the MRI technology product and process designs and debug them. For HP this would have meant developing a new network, which would then need to be synthesized with its existing cardio-imaging network.

HP chose to find a partner with MRI expertise because it did not want to spend the time required to develop its own new network. Following discussions with several companies, HP linked with Philips primarily because the two companies' cultures were believed to be compatible. Both sides assumed there would be many problems to overcome, but believed they could develop a sufficient level of trust to carry out the innovation rapidly. This confidence was reflected in the fact that the two companies signed a "statement of principles," which specified that they would evaluate their relative contributions to the innovation after it was on the market and divide the profits based on that evaluation, and would continue to do that with each follow-on incremental innovation.

The HP–Philips linkage involved the integration of two established networks to create a new network. HP held the core capabilities in specialized electronics and signal processing; Philips held the core capabilities in magnets and the systems integration of the MRI base. The network learning associated with the innovation involved developing effective links between the HP-centered and Philips-centered networks. In addition, the innovation required working closely with various lead-users in research hospitals and medical schools. The new network successfully demonstrated the new technology, but at the point that it was to be taken to the market, HP withdrew and turned the technology over to Philips. This decision was made as part of a redefinition of priorities within HP, even though the innovation was a success and became commercially available and successful.

The MRI-based cardio-imaging system benefited from the path dependencies of the previous two networks. Those path dependencies did not become constraints on learning because active involvement by top managers helped overcome culture differences that might have been barriers. For example, the different routines of the two networks (e.g. need-to-know information sharing in Philips and open information sharing in HP) were dealt with by quick action by top managers of the two companies.

The transformation pattern

The transformation pattern is the most chaotic of the three. Its innovations involve fundamental changes in technology or fundamentally new technologies, so the coevolution process entails that new networks be formed. The transformation pattern has pervasive and unavoidable uncertainty.[31] Major surprises and discontinuities are frequently encountered, and everything is subject to change, including the economic competitiveness of the network.

The fundamental changes associated with transformational innovations are distinguished by the development of product and process designs that differ from anything that existed before. The new designs usually deliver both different and increased performance. For example, the Clinac radiation therapy technology substituted artificial energy for the natural energy of cobalt, and provided two kinds of energy: X-ray and electron. Thus, it is useful to think of transforming innovations as doing more than overcoming some existing boundaries. Fundamental innovations involve establishing a previously unavailable technology path.

Technologies that involve fundamentally different designs are always produced by networks that have new core capabilities and some new specialized complementary assets. The basic design of a technology in a transformational innovation is usually only marginally dependent on and linked to any preceding technology product trajectory.

Breakthroughs, fusion, and other sources of transformational innovations are not common. But when they occur, great turmoil and uncertainty results. Innovations that fall within the transformation pattern frequently spell the death knell for preceding trajectories and their networks. For example, in the 1970s Japanese machine tool makers developed numerically controlled machines, which drove many of the British, French, and American machine tool companies out of business. The Western producers could not handle the synthesis of numeric controls and machine tools. Similarly, most US electronic vacuum tube companies did not have the

Table 10.3 Typical technological and organizational changes in the transformation pattern

Network resources and constraining and focusing factors	Before a transformation innovation	After a transformation innovation
Core capabilities	Established (or none)	Mostly new. Some uses for existing capabilities, but highly unpredictable.
Complementary assets	Established (or none)	Mostly new. Role for hybrid or fused complementary assets.
Organizational learning	Local or regional (or none)	Cosmopolitan. Broad expansion of search and discovery processes.
Path dependence	Strong or medium (or none)	Weak. Past development of innovation context somewhat important.
Selection environment	Powerful or moderately powerful (or none)	Strong institutional role; limited market role.

technical capabilities to enter the semiconductor industry.[32] Table 10.3 is a summary of the changes typical of a transformation.

Creating core capabilities

Transformational innovations require new core capabilities. These new capabilities may be transferred from some other technical community or technology sector, or they may be created from whole cloth either by fusing previously separate technologies or by tapping into new technology waves. In the arena of complex technologies, commercial opportunities seldom flow directly and immediately from scientific breakthroughs. Synthesizing new scientific discoveries into commercial technologies is most often an uncertain process, which frequently occurs in unexpected ways. Thus the identification and development of entirely new core capabilities is a risky trial-and-error process. Recall the decision by IBM to focus on systems integration when it developed the personal computer. The valuable core capabilities turned out to be microprocessors and software. Not only did IBM fail to anticipate what would happen, so did Intel. An alternative example is provided by Sumitomo Electric's experience with the fundamentally new fiber optics technology. In this case Sumitomo turned out to have a core capability advantage by synthesizing its established cable-coating capabilities with the new technology in a way that allowed it to become a leader in the transformational innovation of fiber optics.[33]

Thus, although transformational innovations require new core capabilities, those capabilities are themselves often the product of complex synthesis. That synthesis often uses and benefits from established core capabilities. In the realm of fundamental change, however, the development and utilization of core capabilities is a highly uncertain process.

The diversification role of complementary assets

Transformation patterns of innovation require new complementary assets. These range from new suppliers to new distribution channels.[34] Established networks are unlikely to hold many of these assets internally, so gaining access to the right combination of external assets is critical to commercial success in a transformation pattern.

To the degree that a transformation can be anticipated, networks often seek to diversify their search for complementary assets in ways that allow them to explore, experiment, and learn about a broad range of technological developments. David Lei suggests that networks increasingly develop "fused" or "hybrid" capabilities and assets (e.g. coupling biotechnology with plastics to give rise to "environmentally friendly" packaging) to lay the groundwork for technological fusion opportunities. The key in many cases is investing in capabilities and assets that are "seemingly unrelated."[35]

Cosmopolitan learning

Learning in areas that are unrelated to past learning requires that a network learn to "be at home anywhere"; it must become cosmopolitan. In the transformation pattern, learning boundaries expand and become blurred. No potential source of usable knowledge can be ruled out.[36] Success is usually associated with a general openness to redefining organizational strategy and structure, as well as existing routines and decision making procedures.[37] For any particular firm or other organization, undertaking cosmopolitan learning may require memberships in multiple networks cutting across different industries, sectors, and economies.

Weak path dependence

Technological transformations represent breaks with the past. They therefore have the weakest path dependence of the three innovation patterns. Yet even in the most radical innovation, such as those triggered by scientific breakthroughs, there is path dependence of a broad social and economic type. Nathan Rosenberg makes the point as follows:

> It can be argued that precisely because new scientific knowledge opens up new paths, such knowledge creates discontinuities that loosen the influence of the otherwise heavy hand of the past. In this sense, scientific research is a disrupter of technologically-generated, path dependent phenomena.
>
> I believe that this is, at best, only partially true ... This is because the ability to *exploit* new scientific knowledge in a commercial context will depend directly and heavily upon the technological capabilities that are available within an economy. Consider the great excitement all over the world concerning the recent remarkable breakthroughs in superconductivity. As a purely scientific breakthrough, the excitement is well justified. Nevertheless, it may be decades before this is actually translated into better computers, magnetically levitated trains, the transmission of electricity without loss, or the storage of electricity. Achieving these outcomes is not primarily a matter of scientific research, although progress toward their achievement may draw very heavily upon scientific knowledge. Designing new products that exploit the knowledge of high-temperature superconductors, and then designing and making the technology that can produce these new products, are activities that draw primarily upon existing technological capabilities.[38]

Rosenberg's quote is especially compelling in the context of complex technologies. The introduction to this chapter made the point that all complex technologies have roots in predecessor technologies. Faced with a lack of understanding of how to innovate complex technologies and the associated high risk, the networks involved typically seek the minimum change necessary to carry out the transformation. A powerful societal routine in the arena of complex technologies is to stay with what you know as much as possible. The Japanese approach to innovation represents this most clearly. A Japanese network will do everything it can to avoid "betting the farm" during a risky transformation.

Limited market selection

Transformation patterns tend to emerge in the absence of powerful market selection forces. Most radical innovations have never been seen before and have no clearly defined initial market.[39] By definition, fundamentally new technologies must face a market in which there is little user knowledge of what is being introduced. This may lead potential customers to discount the new technology's possibilities. Low user interest may, in turn, reduce the incentives for networks to develop markets aggressively enough. Even when well defined markets do emerge, it can take a long time (often more than a decade).[40] The weakness of market forces is often cited as a reason why many potential competitors opt out of pursuing an innovation pathway that turns out to be transformational. For example, negative analysis of the market potential of early xerography technology appears to have been a key factor in the decision by IBM managers not to pursue the innovation of copiers.[41]

As the influence of market forces wanes during a transformation, the relative weight networks assign to the existing institutional structure of the national innovation system increases. Institutions provide the stability necessary for fundamental technical change. Supportive institutions make it possible to allocate more creative resources to high risk activities. It is society's institutions, including public policy, that provide the innovative foundation needed during periods of transformational change.

An example: the Sony CD

The transformational change from the analog magnetic tape trajectory to the CD trajectory (see Figure 2.1) resulted from at least two developments. First, the market for 8-millimeter audio tape systems was reaching saturation. Second, a fundamentally new technology wave, digital electronics, had been developing rapidly. Opportunities for digital electronics were exploding, but none of the companies in the audio sector felt confident that, by themselves, they could keep up with such rapidly moving technology.

The pervasiveness of the digital technology wave meant that all the major participants in the audio industry recognized that a trajectory change was imminent. In response, over 50 companies joined together in 1977 to establish the *ad hoc* Digital Audio Disc (DAD) Committee for the purpose of exchanging information about the technological state of the art. DAD's creation, supported by the Japanese Ministry for International Trade and Industry (MITI), was driven by the desire to reduce the risks and uncertainties associated with the forthcoming transformation by exchanging information.

A turning point came in 1979 when Philips and Sony joined forces for roughly two years to develop the design standards for a CD audio system. The joint venture addressed four issues that were necessary to expand the two firms' core capabilities: quantization, sample frequency, error correction, and channel coding. Philips contributed heavily in the area of optics and lasers. Sony provided experience from video and audio tape technology. The two companies sought to achieve state-of-the-art core capabilities by developing the industry's CD design standards. In sum, the joint venture sought to establish the key boundaries for the path of the new technology. Using the capabilities that developed during this collaborative process, each company agreed in advance that it would create its own network to compete in the incremental innovation that would occur when a new normal pattern emerged.

In the course of carrying out the design work, Sony and Philips created linkages with a diverse set of complementary asset providers. Among the most important of these were companies in the music recording business, particularly Polygram and CBS Records. But Philips and Sony also retained linkages with the DAD Committee. The learning that occurred in conjunction with this joint venture featured an active and open exchange between two companies that held the core capabilities of two competing networks for producing audio tapes within a preceding normal pattern. Both Sony and Philips accessed the diverse learning available within their respective networks. They also sought to learn from external sources, especially those within digital electronics.

The decision to make the Sony–Philips design the single industry standard was ultimately made by the DAD Committee, which also considered two other designs (offered by JVC and Telefunken). The committee's function evolved from exchanging information to making a key technology decision because none of DAD's members wanted to take the risks associated with leaving the design selection to the market.

Once the design was established, Sony entered a crash program to bring the CD technology to market. This effort entailed substantial in-house work, but it also meant building a network that could provide five key technological components: the laser diode, the optical pickup system, the disc, the large-scale integrated circuits, and systems integration. Sony at first attempted to develop its own laser diode but was unsuccessful and had to use a diode produced by Sharp. Sony began by using an optical pickup system provided by Olympus, but later developed its own. A disc production technology provided by CBS was incorporated into the Sony network. The large-scale integrated circuits and the systems integration were provided from within Sony.

The initial introduction of the CD into the market was a success, but within a year demand dropped substantially. At that point, Sony contacted Philips to discuss cutting the sales price by nearly 50 percent, even though the two firms were now active competitors. This marketing agreement triggered enough demand for the CD to be installed as the dominant audio technology. Sony's strategy stimulated widespread adoption of the technology. Sony was willing to take a loss in the initial period because the objective was to capture market share and postpone profit taking until the process of incremental innovation that followed. This turned out to be a prescient decision.

In the CD case, the fundamental change was associated with one component of a modular audio system. The CD underwent a transformation, but the broader audio system did not.

Conclusions

The primary need, and the primary pressure, for changes in strategy and policy occurs when there is movement from one innovation pattern to another. During these periods of more rapid and more radical change, network participants need to review what is occurring with regard to core capabilities, complementary assets, learning, path dependence, and the selection environment. The next chapter looks at ways of identifying pattern changes and the implications of those changes for strategy. As a conclusion to the preceding characterization of the three patterns, it is useful to look at how these patterns have manifested themselves in a particular sector, specifically the sector for radiation therapy technology.

Before we look at the case, however, it is important to emphasize that whether one sees an innovation as involving a transition or transformation depends on the vantage point. In every case we have used the vantage point of the network undergoing the change.

The transformation from a cobalt-60 trajectory to the linear accelerator based Clinac trajectory produced a fundamental change in technologies. It occurred primarily because a new opportunity was recognized by a lead-user, a physician at the Stanford University medical school. Within a transformation pattern, a technology developed for physics research was transferred to the field of cancer treatment. The prototype technology and the initial core capabilities were developed in a laboratory associated with the Stanford physics department. A network of complementary asset suppliers was developed, ranging from a British company that supplied the magnetron energy source to the lead-user physicians. The prototype treatment machine benefited from accumulated learning in both the linear accelerator community and the cancer treatment community. There was no established path dependence. The market was uncertain. Even so, tests of the prototype convinced all of those involved of the efficacy of what was to become the Clinac radiation therapy technology.

The trajectory launched by the prototype Clinac machine quickly moved into the normal pattern of incremental innovations. The core capabilities developed in the physics laboratory at Stanford were moved to the Varian Corporation. A network was developed to link Varian with what became an established, relatively stable set of complementary asset suppliers. The Clinac replaced the cobalt-60 technology rather rapidly, in part because its artificial energy source provided better control of the radiation beam. It did not experience the continual energy erosion of a cobalt-60 source, and unlike a cobalt-60 source, the accelerator could be shut off when not being used for treatment.

As the Clinac network and technology coevolved along its normal trajectory, repeated performance improvements resulted from incremental innovations. Those improvements were of two general types: ever more precise control of the amounts and kinds of energy applied to tumors and an ever more precise ability to apply the energy only to the tumor and not to surrounding healthy tissue. The learning that made the improvements possible came primarily from within the network; it was predominately local. A well established path dependence developed, bounded by hardware improvements that offered better beam control. Over time a predictable market developed for the ever improving technology. In fact the network established a number of ways to determine what improvements the users wanted. This link to the market was facilitated by the fact that a technically sophisticated community of medical physicists and physicians (radiation oncologists) were the buyers and users of the Clinac.

The change from a normal pattern to a transition pattern for the Clinac network and technology occurred with a major innovation that synthesized the established (hardware) technology with computers. This innovation occurred in response to a problem and an opportunity. The problem was a growing recognition that the market for Clinacs in the United States was saturated as a result of two circumstances. First, every major medical facility had acquired linear accelerator based radiation therapy technology. The second circumstance was the consolidation and increased cost-consciousness in the US health care system, exemplified by the rapid growth of health maintenance organizations.

The opportunity for a transition came from the growing sophistication of computers, particularly of application software. Synthesizing computers and treatment hardware allowed not only greater precision but also more efficient use by both increasing the number of treatments in a given period and linking the Clinacs into an institutional user's broader medical information system (medical records and billing).

To add these computerized control and reporting capabilities to the technology product required the integration of a new core capability (i.e. software) into the network. Integrating the Clinac's operations with the broader medical information system required additional complementary assets. The result of this major change in the knowledge base was a move to a new network. The search process associated with accessing and developing appropriate software required moving outside the old network to conduct a regional search. Boundaries that were previously associated with the powerful path dependence of normal incremental innovations were crossed. There was a painful search for new routines, as the previously hardware-focused network sought to develop procedures that would allow inclusion of software producers. The market was uncertain. Neither the Clinac network nor the health care community understood how to link the new technology to their information systems. The network did not know whether to market itself as a service provider that would provide and run the new information system or to remain a technology provider.

The implications of the changes from one pattern to another posed major challenges for company strategy and public policy at every point. For example, should Varian's strategy be to remain an equipment supplier or become a service provider? How should public policy deal with the implications of the innovation produced in the transition pattern, which had the capability to design a treatment regime that might be superior to what could be provided by a physician specialist? That is, with the characteristics of the cancer as input information, the computer could use knowledge-based reasoning methods to deduce the most effective treatment. Under these conditions, where would legal liability lie when inappropriate treatment occurred? The following chapter investigates these questions in greater detail.

Notes

1.   Ellinor Ehrnberg, "On the Definition and Measurement of Technological Discontinuities," *Technovation*, Vol. 15, No. 7, September 1995, pp. 437–52.
2.   Ritta Smeds, "Radical Change through Incremental Innovations: Generic Principles and

Cultural Differences in Evolution Management," *International Journal of Technology Management*, Vol. 14, No. 1, 1997, pp. 146–7.

3. Kumiko Miyazaki, *Building Competences in the Firm: Lessons from Japanese and European Optoelectronics*, New York: St Martin's Press, 1995, pp. 27–8.

4. Pari Patel and Keith Pavitt, "The Technological Competencies of the World's Largest Firms: Complex and Path Dependent, but Not Much Variety," *Research Policy*, Vol. 26, No. 2, May 1997, pp. 141–56.

5. Ove Granstrand, Pari Patel, and Keith Pavitt, "Multi-technology Corporations: Why They Have 'Distributed' Rather than 'Distinctive Core' Competences," *California Management Review*, Vol. 39, No. 4, Summer 1997, p. 13.

6. Andrea Prencipe, "Technological Competencies and Product's Evolutionary Dynamics: a Case Study from the Aero-engine Industry," *Research Policy*, Vol. 25, No. 8, January 1997, p. 1265.

7. E. B. Grant and M. J. Gregory, "Tacit Knowledge, the Life Cycle and International Manufacturing Transfer," *Technology Analysis and Strategic Management*, Vol. 9, No. 2, 1997, pp. 149–61.

8. Joseph C. Montgomery, "The Agile Production System," in Joseph C. Montgomery and Lawrence O. Levine, eds, *The Transition to Agile Manufacturing: Staying Flexible for Competitive Advantage*, Milwaukee, WI: ASQC Press, 1996, pp. 1–27.

9. Rajan R. Kamath and Jeffrey K. Liker, "A Second Look at Japanese Product Development," *Harvard Business Review*, Vol. 72, No. 6, November/December 1994, pp. 154–70.

10. Prencipe, "Technological Competencies and Product's Evolutionary Dynamics," p. 1273.

11. Daniel Levinthal, "Three Faces of Organizational Learning: Wisdom, Inertia, and Discovery," in Raghu Garud, Praveen R. Nayyar, and Zur B. Shapira, eds, *Technological Innovation: Oversights and Foresights*, New York: Cambridge University Press, 1997, p. 172.

12. Emilio Bartezzaghi, Mariano Corso, and Roberto Verganti, "Continuous Improvement and Inter-project Learning in New Product Development," *International Journal of Technology Management*, Vol. 14, No. 1, 1997, p. 122.

13. Anders Lundgren, *Technological Innovation and Network Evolution*, New York: Routledge, 1995, p. 91.

14. Roberto Mazzoleni, "Learning and Path-dependence in the Diffusion of Innovations: Comparative Evidence on Numerically Controlled Machine Tools," *Research Policy*, Vol. 26, Nos 4/5, December 1997, p. 424.

15. Edward W. Constant II, *The Origins of the Turbojet Revolution*, Baltimore: Johns Hopkins University Press, 1980, pp. 99–117.

16. G. Dan Hutcheson and Jerry D. Hutcheson, "Technology and Economics in the Semiconductor Industry," *Scientific American*, Vol. 274, No. 1, January 1996, p. 54.

17. L. Ken Keys, "Management and Organizational Challenges to Technology (Paradigm) S-Curve Change Management," *International Journal of Technology Management*, Vol. 14, Nos. 2/3/4, 1997, p. 271.

18. James M. Utterback, *Managing the Dynamics of Innovation*, Boston: Harvard Business School Press, 1994, p. 180.

19. Fumio Kodama, "Changing Global Perspective: Japan, the USA and the New Industrial Order," *Science and Public Policy*, Vol. 18, No. 6, December 1991, p. 390.

20. Utterback, *Mastering the Dynamics of Innovation*, pp. 158–65.

21. C. Jay Lambe and Robert E. Spekman, "Alliances, External Technology Acquisition, and Discontinuous Technological Change," *Journal of Product Innovation Management*, Vol. 14, No. 2, March 1997, pp. 102–16.

22. Kulwant Singh, "The Impact of Technological Complexity and Interfirm Cooperation on Business Survival," *Academy of Management Journal*, Vol. 40, No. 2, April 1997, p. 334.

23. Chris DeBresson and Fernand Amesse, "Networks of Innovators: a Review and Introduction to the Issue," *Research Policy*, Vol. 20, No. 5, October 1991, p. 368.

24. Prencipe, "Technological Competencies and Product's Evolutionary Dynamics," p. 1264.
25. David J. Teece, Gary Pisano, and Amy Shuen, "Dynamic Capabilities and Strategic Management," *Strategic Management Journal*, Vol. 18, No. 7, August 1997, p. 519.
26. Lambe and Spekman, "Alliances, External Technology Acquisition, and Discontinuous Technological Change," p. 111.
27. Daryl McKee, "An Organizational Learning Approach to Product Innovation," *Journal of Product Innovation Management*, Vol. 9, No. 3, July 1992, pp. 239–41.
28. David T. Lei, "Competence-building, Technology Fusion and Competitive Advantage: the Key Roles of Organizational Learning and Strategic Alliances," *International Journal of Technology Management*, Vol. 22, Nos 2, 3 and 4, 1997, p. 212.
29. Thomas Durand, "Dual Technological Trees: Assessing the Intensity and Strategic Significance of Technological Change," *Research Policy*, Vol. 21, No. 4, August 1992, p. 378.
30. Giovanni Dosi, "Institutions and Markets in a Dynamic World," *Manchester School of Economic and Social Studies*, Vol. 56, No. 2, June 1988, p. 128.
31. Christopher Freeman, "Critical Survey: the Economics of Technological Change," *Cambridge Journal of Economics*, Vol. 18, No. 5, November 1994, pp. 474–88.
32. Durand, "Dual Technological Trees," p. 376.
33. Miyazaki, *Building Core Competencies in the Firm*, p. 29.
34. US Congress, Office of Technology Assessment, *Innovation and Commercialization of Emerging Technologies*, Washington: Government Printing Office, September 1995, p. 57.
35. Lei, "Competence-building, Technology Fusion and Competitive Advantage," p. 227.
36. John W. Slocum, Jr, Michael McGill, and David T. Lei, "The New Learning Strategy: Anytime, Anything, Anywhere," *Organizational Dynamics*, Vol. 23, No. 2, Autumn 1994, pp. 33–47.
37. Patricia W. Meyers, "Non-linear Learning in Large Technological Firms: Period Four Implies Chaos," *Research Policy*, Vol. 19, No. 2, April 1990, p. 100.
38. Nathan Rosenberg, *Exploring the Black Box: Technology, Economics, and History*, New York: Cambridge University Press, 1994, p. 18.
39. Donald N. Frey, "The New Dynamism: Part I," *Interfaces*, Vol. 24, No. 2, March/April 1994, pp. 87–91.
40. Gary S. Lynn, Joseph G. Morone, and Albert S. Paulson, "Marketing and Discontinuous Innovation: the Probe and Learn Process," *California Management Review*, Vol. 38, No. 3, Spring 1996, p. 10.
41. Lambe and Spekman, "Alliances, External Technology Acquisition, and Discontinuous Technological Change," p. 109.

CHAPTER ELEVEN

Adaptive Network Strategies

Company strategies that foster innovation must begin with the recognition that networks are the innovators of complex commercial technologies. Only networks can provide access to the diverse knowledge that is required; and only self-organizing networks can provide the intimate interactions among organizational participants that make synthesis possible.[1] The repeated innovations that are essential to commercial success require that networks embody the coevolution of a range of core capabilities, complementary assets, and learning activities.

Network flexibility and renewal are essential as the search for knowledge and synthesis is carried out.[2] Thus, the starting point for managers seeking to foster the innovation of complex technologies must be the realization that organizational adaptability is critical. The adaptation that is necessary involves a process of network self-organization that is proactive. Successful network adaptation requires more than just responding to external changes, more than just responding to the demands of the market.[3] Networks that seek commercial technological success must develop and maintain the ability not only to adapt to highly competitive environments, but also to adapt in ways that influence that environment.[4]

The sources of innovation for complex technologies are multiple, and the importance of the various sources changes over time. For instance, our case studies support the large body of anecdotal evidence that indicates that knowledge derived from R&D often plays a larger role when trajectories are being launched. Alternatively, market demands frequently play a greater role once trajectories are established and a consensus exists on the desired technical performance to be delivered by the next incremental innovation. But while these sources of knowledge are evident, the more general characteristic of complex technologies that dominates in every pattern of innovation is the synthesis of multiple factors such as R&D, production learning, intersectoral transfers, intellectual property protection, and market demands.

Because so many ingredients go into synthetic innovation, all networks live with, and strategy must be continuously sensitive to, uncertainty.[5] Uncertainty within the normal innovation pattern is of two primary kinds. First, there is always the uncertainty associated with not knowing how to accomplish the next incremental innovation. Second, there is the uncertainty that flows from the ever present threat that the normal pattern can be disrupted quickly and unexpectedly by transitional or transformational innovations.

Networks have three primary ways of dealing with uncertainty: maintain state-of-the-art core capabilities and other resources, maintain continuous and broad-based search proficiency (e.g. monitoring relevant external technologies), and maintain the

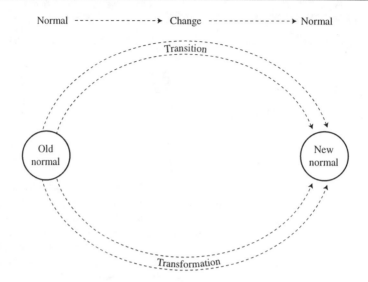

Figure 11.1 Changes in innovation patterns

capacity for rapid self-organization (e.g. be prepared to integrate knowledge in new ways and create new networks).[6]

Since innovation in the normal pattern usually involves small changes, strategic adaptations tend to be minor. When networks and technical communities are faced with changes in innovation patterns, however, major adaptations in strategic thinking and action are required.[7] It is to the identification of and responses to the need for major strategy adaptations that we now turn.

Mapping changes in patterns

When mapped in a way that shows their interactions, the normal, transitional, and transformational patterns can provide useful insights for those formulating company strategies. Figure 11.1 provides a map that shows links among the patterns; specifically, it indicates that the transitional and transformational patterns represent changes from old to new normal patterns, or in rare instances the transformational pattern may involve a first of a kind launching of a new trajectory. Transitional and transformational patterns are, metaphorically, bridges between old and new normal patterns.

Although innovations in all the patterns are heavily dependent on cumulative learning derived from solving problems through trial and error processes, that which occurs within the transitional and transformational patterns involves the greatest amount of problem solving and the greatest uncertainty. These two patterns also require the most significant organizational adaptation. Thus, in the transitional and transformational patterns there is a particularly tight web of interdependence among: (a) strategy; (b) network adaptation; and (c) the ability to access, create, and synthesize the knowledge needed to carry out innovations.

Since by definition complexity means that managers cannot know in advance what detailed network adaptations will be successful, these adaptations must be discovered during the course of the coevolutionary process of innovation. A rule of thumb for managers is that developing effective strategy in the midst of the ongoing innovation processes is a difficult activity in any event, but within the transitional and transformational patterns strategic actions are likely to be especially turbulent and messy. This rule of thumb serves as a constraint on the powerful impulses to adopt strategies aimed at maintaining managerial control and organizational stability. The managerial control impulse is all too often the enemy of the learning and technical creativity needed for successful self-organization and network migration among the various innovation options.[8]

The ability to accept instability and evolve effective strategies in unpredictable situations is enhanced by a capacity to anticipate pattern changes and appreciate their characteristics. The value of being able to identify and gain insight into pattern changes makes the development of indicators of change important. Indicators provide an opportunity to take Brian Arthur's advice. That is, during pattern changes, managers have the opportunity to use strategy "oars" to punt the network "boat" from one "eddy" to another.[9]

Effective "rowing" aimed at fostering the innovation of complex commercial technologies has, among others, one of two goals. Within the transitional and transformational patterns the goal is establishment of a normal pattern. Within the normal pattern the goal is to carry out incremental innovations more rapidly than the competition and to stay in the normal pattern as long as rapid innovation is possible.

In Figure 11.1 the two change patterns are represented by the double lines between the two normal patterns. Each involves a different route from an old normal pattern to a new normal pattern. In the case of transformation patterns there may be no single dominant predecessor trajectory as appears to be the case, for example, with the Internet; instead, in such instances the roots of the change in trajectory are in multiple predecessor trajectories (e.g. computers, telecommunications).

Figure 11.1 offers a lens that can be used to monitor the innovation patterns of technologies. Used in conjunction with appropriate indicators, presented in the following section, the relationship outlined in the figure offers those involved in formulating strategy the possibility of early warning of pattern changes and some appreciation of what those changes mean for networks.

Indicators of pattern changes

The highest risk for networks and technical communities exists when a pattern change is under way without managers recognizing it. This is most likely when path dependencies are strong and the network and technical community are overly optimistic about emerging opportunities or overestimate their ability to overcome emerging technological problems.[10] The unidentified change may come in the form of either the transitional or transformational pattern. The desire to anticipate pattern changes can, however, generate its own costs. This occurs when a network or group of networks expends major resources on an anticipated pattern change that does not occur. This happened, for example, when Japan's television manufacturers, with government support, focused major resources on the development of an analog high definition television (HDTV) trajectory. The Europeans, determined not to lose out on what they believed was the next major consumer electronic product, then launched their own initiative.[11] In the end the analog technology was not successful, and a digital HDTV design was later adopted as the world standard. A different illustration occurred when some semiconductor companies, based on believing that optical lithography was only suitable for dimensions greater than one micron, launched efforts to develop alternatives. This initiative was based on the belief that a major advance in miniaturization could be had by developing X-ray technology as a substitute for traditional lithography.[12] In fact, additional incremental innovations of the established design proved to be more attractive and to date the major efforts focused on X-ray have not paid off.[13]

There is no fully reliable way to determine when a pattern change is under way or will begin, but any enhanced identification capability is beneficial because of the speed with which pattern changes can take place. Like most changes in complex systems, pattern changes commonly have both deep roots and short time frames between their appearance and the establishment of a new normal pattern. The process is analogous to the change from hot to boiling water, where a single degree, after a long period of heating, makes the difference.

No single or simple indicators of pattern changes are adequate. It is useful in conceptualizing the search for indicators of pattern changes to view each technological trajectory as a single boat cruising on a bay full of other cruising boats (i.e. trajectories). To reach the desired port (i.e. continued competitiveness) it is necessary to monitor not only one's own boat's performance, but also that of the other boats, plus the general environment of the bay. The search for indicators is like the process of innovation itself: it requires the synthesis of diverse knowledge.

There appear to be at least four conditions that individually or in combination often serve as indicators of pattern changes. These four conditions are appropriately labeled: technical community disintegration, foreign invaders, new technological waves, and climate changes.

Technical community disintegration

- Lack of consensus on the next incremental innovation.
- Consensus on the lack of an attractive incremental innovation.

Technical communities and networks share and in significant part are held together by the common knowledge, heuristics, and routines that are essential to innovation success.[14] Shared knowledge, heuristics, and routines are major contributors to the condition we consistently found to exist as part of the normal patterns in each of the case studies. That is, in the normal pattern the cases all exhibited general agreement within their technical communities concerning the performance characteristics of the next incremental innovation. When technical communities no longer share a common view of what comes next, there is a likelihood that a pattern change will take place or is occurring.[15] A lack of consensus on the next innovation is especially likely to portend a pattern change when the community has had a long history of consensus on the next incremental innovation. This is a distinctive characteristic of trajectories that have developed very strong path dependence.

Sometimes a community will reach general agreement that no attractive incremental innovations are available within the existing shared knowledge, heuristics, and routines. There are repeated examples of technical communities that have developed a consensus that their technology has "run out its string." Several interviewees suggested that this was the condition that existed within the audio technology community immediately prior to the pattern change that produced the CD.

Foreign invaders

- New syntheses.
- Integration of new subsystems.
- Invasions from other technology sectors.

Probably the most common condition indicating changes in innovation patterns is that involving foreign invaders; that is, where different technologies and organizations are integrated into established trajectories. The distinguishing characteristic of foreign invaders is that they have knowledge and capabilities that make it possible to breach the boundaries of the established path. Although foreign invaders cause major changes in the existing networks and technologies, it is nonetheless the case that the general parameters of the previous trajectory remain identifiable after the invasion. Thus, foreign invaders tend not to totally destroy existing trajectories, but to modify and extend them in major ways.[16]

Although foreign invaders may appear in many forms, three of the most common conditions involve: major modifications in the synthesis process; integration of new subsystems; and movement of capabilities from one technology sector to another (e.g. by fusion).[17] Modifications in the synthesis process are illustrated by the development of lean production by Toyota. Lean production systems allowed Toyota to achieve efficiencies comparable to those of US companies with smaller scale and improved quality and flexibility.[18] The movement of turbine blade manufacture from forged to cast processes also represented a new synthesis.

The integration of a new subsystem into established technologies is happening at an accelerating rate. Replacement of the electronic vacuum tube by the transistor and then the integrated circuit is a visible example. Finally, the pattern of networks originating in one technology sector taking their capabilities into another sector is what occurred when the linear accelerator was taken into the radiation therapy sector. Often new networks emerge from another national economy. Many have their roots in developing countries. The dominant examples have been in the rapidly developing nations of East Asia.[19] Because these transnational entries usually embody unique cultural characteristics, their appearance is an especially strong indicator of dramatic pattern change.

New technology waves

- New technologies offer new or better products and processes across a wide range of sectors.

The development of new technology waves is a condition that indicates a wide set of pattern changes. Technology waves exist when different technologies become available that offer the possibility of providing marketable products with distinctly different and better performance and/or cost characteristics. Examples of these waves include digital electronics and biotechnology.[20] New technology waves usually have broad impacts on a wide range of established technological processes and products. For example, most of the technologies included in the 30 most valuable manufactures exports discussed in Chapter 1 have been significantly affected by the digital electronics wave, especially the impacts of semiconductors and software.

Although new technology waves are widely recognized as the sources of potential innovation pattern changes, existing networks often have difficulty identifying precisely how the new technology will be integrated into an established trajectory or how it will be used to launch a new trajectory. It is this uncertainty that has led competitor networks increasingly to cooperate in designing and establishing standards for how the new technology wave will be integrated. The example we have used repeatedly is the transition from the analog tape to the CD.

It is important to recognize that new technology waves in the era of complex technologies pose quite different challenges than those generated historically by such big breakthrough ideas as solid state electronics. For example, recall that the vacuum tube makers failed to move to transistors because they did not recognize the new technology's potential long-term performance and cost advantages. Transistors stimulated a whole new industry, one in which not a single major vacuum tube maker was successful.[21]

By comparison, new technology waves in the era of complex technologies are often integrated into already complex systems to launch new trajectories. Even the biotechnology wave appears to be in the process of being synthesized into existing medical, pharmaceutical, chemical, and agricultural sectors.[22] This means that selection of technical standards and concern with compatibility are often integral to the development of the new technology's capabilities for commercial purposes. Integrating a new technology wave into a technology trajectory or creating a new trajectory involves a process of synthesis that normally requires major changes in the networks involved and thus in company strategies. It was precisely this mix of factors that led to the creation of the DAD Committee preceding the transition from the analog magnetic tape technology to the CD.

Climate change

- Market change.
- Policy change.
- Social change.

Pattern changes may be indicated by conditions that develop in the general climate that affects the selection environment for technologies. Climate can be usefully thought of as reflecting the interaction of the market, public policy, and the broader social system (including, but not limited to, the national innovation system).

Market changes may manifest themselves in a variety of ways. Market saturation is perhaps the easiest change to identify. The difficulties encountered in advancing the incremental state of the art fast enough to avoid glutting a market may indicate that a network has encountered an especially difficult bottleneck or discontinuity, and thus a pattern shift may be on the horizon. Confusion arising from unexpected shifts in market size can also indicate that unexpected shifts are taking place in the climate. For example, decisions made as part of the evolving relationships between government and financial institutions can shrink or expand markets in ways that are difficult to anticipate and to gauge. In the case of the Varian Clinac, the assessment of the future market at the time of the transition to a computer controlled technology was made more difficult because of the changing structure of the US health care system, specifically the effort of new health delivery organizations to increase utilization of existing equipment.

Public policies may generate climate changes in a wide variety of ways. Broad governmental efforts to enhance the capacity of the national innovation system (e.g. infrastructure investments) or to modify appropriability regimes (e.g. changes in the terms of patent protection) are examples. Other, more focused policies have a stated intent to alter the innovation climate for specific established technologies; for example, the US Department of Defense support for Sematech. Alternatively, some government support for research is undertaken with the objective of inducing radical change and generating specific new trajectories; research on solar energy is such an example.[23]

Climate change of a social character can be induced by organizations and institutions that are not normally part of the technical community or the national innovation system. Organizations such as consumer and environmental groups and institutions such as the media can and do influence the climate for innovation.[24] The identification of significant environmental or consumer risks associated with a particular product or process often sets in motion highly turbulent social events, often multiplied by media exposure, that displace existing trajectories and introduce new innovation patterns. The emergence of "environmentally conscious manufacturing" initiatives and pollution prevention programs in most developed countries can be attributed to social climate change.[25]

Strategic guidance

The strategic benefits of being able to identify when pattern changes are approaching and to characterize at least some of the attributes of those changes are great.[26] In Chapter 7 we argued that the overarching strategic objective of networks is attaining a mutually reinforcing fit among resources (capabilities, assets, and learning) that provides a unique competitive position. In order to achieve such a position, the organizations involved must make it a strategic priority to establish effective communication links to sources of knowledge about the possible paths of potentially relevant technologies and their coevolving organizations. Successful strategic coordination among network members involves cooperation in monitoring a wide range of technological movements and incorporating the intelligence collected into the process of selecting the next competitive position. For example, successful strategic coordination can provide for standard setting processes that reduce risks and costs by reducing or eliminating the need for market competition in determining the design of the next trajectory's technology.[27]

The trajectory metaphor has great strategic value. A trajectory may be regarded as a set of technological and organizational patterns on which strategies are targeted. Thus, a technology strategy corresponds to a choice of position on a trajectory. Every strategic decision can be related to a position on a trajectory and to a desired change in that position:

> Formulating a technology strategy means defining the 'trajectory' by which technological resources are accumulated, acquired and used. The matter is to understand how a certain step in a technology strategy is linked with the previous ones, opens opportunities and creates options for future investments along a defined trajectory.[28]

Choosing a future trajectory position is a matter of *strategic intent* – a shared vision about the future direction of innovation within which self-organization can take place.[29] Strategic efforts to learn from supporting R&D provide a good example. Investing in R&D with an exploration orientation (e.g. long term, high risk) can be seen as strategic intent to create new capabilities in an attempt to develop a technological breakthrough and move the network to a new trajectory. On the other hand, undertaking R&D of a more exploitive nature can be viewed as a strategic intent to focus on an incremental advance on an established trajectory. In either case, the network's moves along the trajectory are not imposed from the outside. The self-organizing network is able to use the vision embedded in the shared strategic intent to manage its change in position.[30]

In order for networks to link strategies to desired trajectory positions, they must engage in sophisticated scanning and search initiatives. Besides the often abundant technological opportunities that shape progress along an existing trajectory, many networks are becoming aware of the extensive potential for tapping into opportunities in related and as yet unknown fields and sectors. Andreas Pyka summarizes the complexity of trajectory relationships as follows:

> The different technological trajectories and their technological opportunities do not co-exist unrelatedly, but are connected by several influencing devices and feedbacks. Therefore, a single technology cannot be explained in isolation but should be understood in a broader framework. Improvements in one technology can create totally different applications in other technologies or even totally new technological opportunities. Accordingly, nearly exhausted trajectories can be influenced by other innovations and technology fields which open up new opportunities.[31]

These feedbacks and linkages are a major reason why even well established trajectories are not linear in character, but often manifest "zig-zagging movements" as established technologies are combined with emerging capabilities and complementary assets to exploit some specific competitive advantage. And new technological opportunities have shapes and dynamics that often are only partly visible. Therefore, continuous monitoring and trend analysis have become key elements of network strategy.[32]

Most countries with knowledge-based economies recognize the need for early recognition of technological opportunities worldwide. Networks and firms in these countries repeatedly identify the need for intelligence about international technology and markets. But intelligence is expensive, and thus government agencies and other elements of the national innovation system need to share the financial and other costs with business.[33]

One aspect of strategic scanning and intelligence gathering that seems especially valuable to industrial sectors, networks, and governments alike is the generation of *technology roadmaps*. These roadmaps, such as those generated by the semiconductor industry, generally represent a collective vision of technological futures, and they serve as broad templates for ways to integrate resources in the context of evolving selection environments. Roadmaps also facilitate open debates about alternative technological pathways, strategies, and public policies.[34] We have more to say on the public policy implications of roadmaps in the next chapter.

Beyond search, scanning, and monitoring of opportunities, strategy is enhanced when managers view uncertainty and instability as the expected condition, view failures as essential to learning, and adapt rapidly – that is, quickly pursue new options and quickly move away from options that don't work. Given the legacy in the United States of viewing management as a discipline whose theories and rules are heavily linear, rational, analytic/reductionist, weighted toward financial and economic factors, and applicable regardless of what is being managed, this kind of strategic adaptability is often difficult to create and maintain.[35]

This is not to say that traditional management approaches have no use. But, during pattern changes, managerial instinct and judgment based on deep knowledge of and experience with the technologies involved become critical. The extraordinary demands that complexity places on management put a premium on "decision making that results from an exploratory, experimental process based on intuition and reasoning by analogy."[36]

It is especially important that there be an appreciation of the routines, heuristics, and general tacit knowledge that the involved organizations have accumulated over their histories. Managers must balance accumulated knowledge with knowledge located outside the established trajectory.

In the transitional and transformational patterns technical and network changes involve a process of coevolution that often requires strategies that facilitate learning based on broad searches for knowledge that is in part group-based and tacit. Managing tacit knowledge is a significant challenge, as Dorothy Leonard and Sylvia Sensiper point out:

> The marvelous capacity of the human mind to make sense of a lifetime's collection of experience and to connect patterns from the past to the present and future is, by its very nature, hard to capture. However, it is essential to the innovation process. The management of tacit knowledge is relatively unexplored – particularly when compared to the work on explicit knowledge. Moreover, while individual creativity is important, exciting, and even crucial to business, the creativity of groups is equally important. The creation of today's complex systems of products and services requires the merging of knowledge from diverse national, disciplinary, and personal skill-based perspectives. Innovation – whether it be revealed in new products and services, new processes, or new organizational forms – is rarely an individual undertaking. Creative cooperation is critical.[37]

Searching and learning strategically involves the capacity to rapidly link to and decouple from diverse organizations. Especially during periods of pattern change, those in networks must be willing to follow their hunches, and this willingness reinforces the need to have strategies that make failure a learning opportunity.[38]

Faced with a pattern change and its identification as either transitional or transformational, managers should look for strategic guidance by seeking answers to or at least insight into three questions. What is there in the environment (i.e. innovation climate) that facilitates or impedes successfully making a pattern change? What search patterns will provide the knowledge needed for the innovations? What network characteristics and thus what organizational adaptations are necessary to a successful pattern change?

Ralph Stacey offers important insights for managers faced with pattern transitions and thus with responding to the above questions. His beginning point is that control in complex systems rests in groups and is inseparable from group learning. The challenge for managers is to appreciate that self-organization produces control even though no one is in control. Groups are most effective at self-organization when they discover their own objectives. Managers are especially valuable when they help articulate and support group objectives. It is very important, given the ever present opportunity and threat of pattern changes, that counter cultures be maintained in networks innovating within the normal pattern. The pressure for speed and thus minimum information make it very important that managers actively create and support counter cultures. Maintenance of counter cultures within networks can only exist if personnel, financial, and organizational slack is provided. Achieving perfect efficiency is the enemy of the slack needed to access and create the knowledge that will facilitate pattern changes.[39]

Surely one of the most important roles of managers and of strategy involves influencing the degree to which networks focus on internal versus external learning. During periods of rapid innovation along established trajectories, too much emphasis on external learning can slow down the learning needed for the next innovation. These are the times when the benefits of minimum information strategies are great. Alternatively, during times of pattern change, the reverse appears to be the case.

When faced with a pattern change there is another challenge. It is to determine whether the primary search for knowledge will be regional or cosmopolitan, whether the change pattern is transitional or transformational. Making these judgments requires diverse knowledge of both tacit and explicit kinds. Appreciating the character of the change pattern, and thus the general boundaries of the search needed, enhances the prospects of a fruitful search process.

The probability that managers will be able to formulate appropriate strategies is often influenced by the broader environment within which networks operate. That environment in turn can be significantly affected either negatively or positively by public policy. As technologies become ever more complex, the need for adaptations in public policy warrant increasing attention. It is to an investigation of possible policy adaptations that we turn in the next chapter.

Notes

1. Stephen Chen, "A New Paradigm for Knowledge-based Competition: Building an Industry Through Knowledge Sharing," *Technology Analysis and Strategic Management*, Vol. 9, No. 4, December 1997, pp. 437–52; Giovanni Dosi, "Opportunities, Incentives and the Collective Patterns of Technological Change," *Economic Journal*, Vol. 107, No. 444, September 1997, pp. 1530–47.
2. James F. Moore, "The Rise of a New Corporate Form," *Washington Quarterly*, Vol. 21, No.1, Winter 1997, pp. 167–81.
3. Margaret Wheatley and Myron Keliner–Rogers, "Self-organization: the Irresistible Future of Organizing," *Strategy and Leadership*, Vol. 24, No. 4, July/August 1996, pp. 18–24.
4. Michael D. McMaster, *The Intelligence Advantage: Organizing for Complexity*, Boston: Butterworth–Heinemann, 1996, p. 113.
5. Ron Sanchez, "Strategic Management at the Point of Inflection: Systems, Complexity and Competence Theory," *Long Range Planning*, Vol. 30, No. 6, December 1997, p. 940.
6. David T. Lei, "Competence-Building, Technology Fusion and Competitive Advantage: the Key Roles of Organizational Learning and Strategic Alliances," *International Journal of Technology Management*, Vol. 14, Nos 2/3/4, 1997, pp. 208–37.
7. Leo Wildeman, "Alliances and Networks: the Next Generation," *International Journal of Technology Management*, Vol. 15, Nos 1/2, 1998, pp. 96–108.
8. Ralph Stacey, "Management and Science of Complexity: if Organizational Life Is Nonlinear, Can Business Strategy Survive?" *Research-Technology Management*, Vol. 39, No. 3, May/June 1996, pp. 8–10.
9. Quoted in M. Mitchell Waldrop, *Complexity: the Emerging Science at the Edge of Order and Chaos*, New York: Simon and Schuster, 1992, p. 330.

10. Giovanni Dosi and Dan Lovallo, "Rational Entrepreneurs or Optimistic Martyrs? Some Considerations on Technological Regimes, Corporate Entities, and the Evolutionary Role of Decision Biases," in Raghu Garud, Praveen R. Nayyar, and Zur B. Shapira, eds, *Technological Innovation: Oversights and Foresights*, New York: Cambridge University Press, 1997, pp. 41–68.

11. Laura D. Tyson, *Who's Bashing Whom: Trade Conflict in High-technology Industries*, Washington, DC: Institute for International Economics, 1992, pp. 237–44.

12. G.L.-T. Chiu and J. M. Shaw, "Optical Lithography: Introduction," *IBM Journal of Research and Development*, Vol. 41, Nos 1/2, 1997, p. 1.

13. Andrew S. Grove, *Only The Paranoid Survive: How to Exploit the Crisis Points that Challenge Every Company and Career*, New York: Doubleday, 1996, p. 101.

14. Leonard H. Lynn, Mohan Reddy, and John D. Aram, "Linking Technology and Institutions: the Innovation Community Framework," *Research Policy*, Vol. 25, No. 1, January 1996, pp. 99–100; Andrew H. Van de Ven, "A Community Perspective on the Emergence of Innovations," *Journal of Engineering and Technology Management*, Vol. 10, Nos 1/2, June 1993, pp. 34–6.

15. Rau Garud, Praveen Nayyar, and Zur Shapira, "Beating the Odds: towards a Theory of Technological Innovation," in Garud, Nayyar, and Shapira, eds, *Technological Innovation: Oversights and Foresights*, pp. 345–54.

16. Birgitte Andersen, "The Evolution of Technological Trajectories, 1890–1990," *Structural Change and Economic Dynamics*, Vol. 9, No. 1, 1998, p. 32.

17. C. K. Prahalad, "Managing Discontinuities: the Emerging Challenge," *Research-Technology Management*, Vol. 41, No. 3, May/June 1998, p. 16.

18. Christer Karlsson and Par Ahlstrom, "The Difficult Path to Lean Product Development," *Journal of Product Innovation Management*, Vol. 13, No. 4, July 1996, pp. 283–85.

19. Linsu Kim, *Imitation to Innovation: the Dynamics of Korea's Technological Learning*, Boston: Harvard Business School Press, 1997, pp. 191–243.

20. Paul Saffo, "Sensors: The Next Wave of Innovation," *Communications of the ACM*, Vol. 40, No. 2, February 1997, pp. 92–7.

21. Thomas Durand, "Dual Technological Trees: Assessing the Intensity and Strategic Significance of Technological Change," *Research Policy*, Vol. 21, No. 4, August 1992, p. 376.

22. Office of Science and Technology Policy, Executive Office of the President, *National Critical Technologies Report*, Washington, DC: Government Printing Office, March 1995, pp. 69–87.

23. J. Stanley Metcalfe, *Evolutionary Economics and Creative Destruction*, New York: Routledge, 1998, pp. 115–22.

24. Paul Windrum and Chris Birchenhall, "Is Product Life Cycle Theory a Special Case? Dominant Designs and the Emergence of Market Niches through Coevolutionary-learning," *Structural Change and Economic Dynamics*, Vol. 9, No. 1, 1998, p. 114.

25. Joseph Sarkis, "Manufacturing Strategy and Environmental Consciousness," *Technovation*, Vol. 15, No. 3, March 1995, pp. 79–97; Deanna J. Richards and Ann B. Fullerton, eds, *Industrial Ecology: US–Japan Perspectives*, Washington, DC: National Academy Press, 1994.

26. Pier P. Saviotti, "Technology Mapping and the Evaluation of Technical Change," *International Journal of Technology Management*, Vol. 10, Nos 4/5/6, 1995, p. 423.

27. Charles W. L. Hill, "Establishing a Standard: Competitive Strategy and Technological Standards in Winner-take-all Industries," *Academy of Management Executive*, Vol. 11, May 1997, pp. 12–14.

28. Vittorio Chiesa and Raffaella Manzini, "Towards a Framework for Dynamic Technology Strategy," *Technology Analysis and Strategic Management*, Vol. 10, No. 1, March 1998, p. 115.

29. McMaster, *The Intelligence Advantage*, pp. 118–20; Gary Hamel and C. K. Prahalad,

Competing for the Future, Cambridge, MA: Harvard Business School Press, 1994, p. 290.

30. Pascal Bye and Jean-Jacques Chanaron, "Technology Trajectories and Strategies," *International Journal of Technology Management*, Vol. 10, No. 1, 1995, p. 50.

31. Andreas Pyka, "Informal Networking," *Technovation*, Vol. 17, No. 4, April 1997, p. 208.

32. Alexander Gerybadze, "Technology Forecasting as a Process of Organisational Intelligence," *R&D Management*, Vol. 24, No. 2, April 1994, pp. 131–40.

33. Alain Albagli, Peter Dawson, and Sadiq Hasnain, "Competitive Science and Technology Intelligence," *International Journal of Technology Management*, Vol. 12, No. 3, 1996, pp. 320–8; Ellinor Ehrnberg and Staffan Jacobson, "Managing Technological Discontinuities – a Tentative Framework," *International Journal of Technology Management*, Vol. 11, Nos 3/4, 1996, pp. 452–69.

34. Lewis M. Branscomb and James H. Keller, *Investing in Innovation: Creating a Research and Innovation Policy that Works*, Cambridge, MA: The MIT Press, 1998, ppp. 477–8; Peter A. Koen, "Technology Maps: Choosing the Right Path," *Engineering Management Journal*, Vol. 9, No. 4, December 1997, pp. 7–11.

35. Kenyon B. DeGreene, "Nonlinear Management in Technologically-induced Fields," *Systems Research*, Vol. 7, No. 3, 1990, pp. 162–6.

36. Ralph D. Stacey, *Managing the Unknowable: Strategic Boundaries between Order and Chaos in Organizations*, San Francisco: Jossey-Bass Publishers, 1992, p. 14.

37. Dorothy Leonard and Sylvia Sensiper, "The Role of Tacit Knowledge in Group Innovation," *California Management Review*, Vol. 40, No. 3, Spring 1998, p. 112.

38. John W. Slocum, Jr, Michael McGill, and David T. Lei, "The New Learning Strategy: Anytime, Anything, Anywhere," *Organizational Dynamics*, Vol. 23, No. 2, Autumn 1994, pp. 39–41.

39. Ralph Stacey "Strategy as Order Emerging from Chaos", *Long Range Planning*, Vol. 26, No. 1, February 1993, pp. 16–17.

CHAPTER TWELVE

Adaptive Public Policies

A continuous theme throughout this book has been that those who make public policy aimed at fostering the innovation of complex technologies face the same daunting challenges as private sector managers. Continuous learning and repeated adaptations are givens for policy makers. Complexity means that the learning involved is always incomplete; thus, neither successes nor failures can be understood in detail. Policy adaptation, like network adaptation, is always a trial-and-error process. Indeed, the challenges facing policy makers may be even greater than those facing managers because national innovation systems (NIS) are much more complex than networks or firms. One thing is certain, company or network strategies and public policies are intertwined; over any significant period of time they are inseparable. It is a postulate of this chapter that an evolving NIS is critical to the capacity to innovate, and that public policy is critical to the successful evolution of the NIS.[1]

With the accelerating growth in the economic importance of complex technologies has come an accelerating growth in the importance of organizational networks. Given the importance of networks, no area of public policy deserves greater attention than that which facilitates or impedes the ability of companies to link and decouple from each other; that is, join networks and depart from them. Data on what is happening in the US NIS concerning organizational adaptation are limited but instructive. A recent survey shows over 20,000 corporate alliances were formed during the period 1988–92, and that there has been an annual US growth rate in alliances of 25 percent since 1985.[2] As complexity increases this pattern seems certain to continue, but the rate and characteristics of the alliances and organizational linkages will be significantly affected by public policy. A central question that will be continuously faced by US policy makers concerns the appropriate role of policy in fostering greater self-organizing adaptation among not only networks but also firms, government agencies, universities and other core actors, and work groups.[3]

In an era of complex technologies, and that will surely be the dominant characteristic of the early part of the twenty-first century, public policies, like network and company strategies, will need to facilitate learning and be ever more adaptable. Public policies aimed at facilitating innovation will need to be as synthetic as the innovation process itself.[4]

As with synthetic innovation, synthetic policy making is fraught with uncertainty. There is no way to be assured of successful policy in advance of trying it. Like the innovation of complex technologies, the formulation of successful policy is unknowable in a detailed sense.[5] Thus, specific policy prescriptions developed in the absence of the specific context of innovation are as dangerous as they are tempting. The following discussion of policy proceeds with that danger in mind. Thus, no specific prescriptions are offered. Rather, the discussion follows Keith Smith's advice that: *it is important to think of innovation policy in broad conceptual ways because specific policy problems and issues can only be addressed within the context of agreed upon general concepts about, for example, how sociotechnical systems (e.g. networks, the NIS) are related.*[6]

The following discussion of policy focuses on and uses the United States as its example. The general findings, however, are probably applicable to policies focused on complex technologies in most countries. The policy categories, guidelines, and suggestions used in the following have been selected with the goal of gaining insight into how existing US national policies might be adapted to take into account the patterns of innovation defined in Chapter 10 and the strategic management issues raised by movement among patterns discussed in Chapter 11. Before looking at technology policy, however, it is useful to delineate the broader policy landscape regarding the innovation of complex commercial technologies.

Government's role in innovation

Much of the acrimonious debate in the United States regarding the appropriate role of government in technological innovation arises because of fundamental conceptual differences. The debate generally is framed around an ideological formation: there is no role for government in assisting in the innovation process because if government is involved it will control or dominate the process and that will result in failure. Thus, even those who support an activist technology policy in the United States are usually compelled to characterize their proposals as exceptions to the norm. In practice, this formulation does not fit with the experience in the United States or most other countries. An examination of the technology policy activities of governments in advanced countries indicates that they commonly participate in or carry out four functions: (a) climate setting; (b) surveying; (c) coordinating; and (d) gap filling.[7]

Climate setting

As used here, *climate refers to the environment within which networks carry out innovation.* It is useful to view climate as encompassing not only the selection environment but also culture (i.e. shared norms and values) and the more formalized institutional governance rules (e.g. laws, regulations, best practice standards) that influence relationships among various actors in all types of sociotechnical systems. At any point in time climate both enhances and impedes innovation. Within limits, however, policy can be used to modify climate in ways that facilitate innovation.

There is an extensive literature on the influence of *national culture* on the innovation of technologies.[8] To suggest the differences in national cultures, Richard Adams summarized the body of research with regard to the United States and Japan as follows. Americans have a mechanistic view of the universe, a reductionist approach to learning, a preference for explicit knowledge, and a tendency to trust in individuals and competition. Japanese have an organic view of the universe, an integrated/synthetic approach to learning, a preference for tacit knowledge, and a tendency to trust in groups and cooperation.[9] As we have pointed out, the Japanese cultural characteristics that assign high value to group interactions appear to have been advantageous in building long-term, trust-based relationships among suppliers and manufacturers that have enabled the rapid generation, sharing, and conversion of tacit knowledge. Alternatively, the US penchant for valuing individualism seems to have been a strength in developing and transferring explicit knowledge through scientific research. Both sets of strengths have been reinforced repeatedly by national policies (e.g. heavy US public subsidies for fundamental research, Japanese government support for process technologies).

Similarly, national cultural characteristics that impede the innovation of complex technologies (e.g. adversarial relations between the public and private sectors in the USA) may be at least partially compensated for by policy (e.g. efforts to link the US national laboratories with American corporations through cooperative research and development agreements).

In every country, different laws, regulations, standards, and other *governance rules* bound the way sociotechnical systems are structured and how they behave.[10] To illustrate, the institutional set-up of the US financial system gives major impetus to company strategies that emphasize relatively short-term performance, in part because the financial system ensures that capital is raised in the equity market and banks are not allowed to be major owners of the companies to which they loan money. The situation is just the opposite in Japan. Distinctive organizational practices also comprise an important part of the innovation climate. For instance, the organizing of work varies considerably among countries. Differences in labor–management relations and factory operating procedures have been identified as major factors affecting, for example, the adoption of automation in the workplace.[11] Policies designed to modify governance rules occupy much of the technology policy agenda of governments. In the USA, controversies about the merits and liabilities flowing from modification in antitrust and patent law, to cite two of the most contentious examples, show no signs of abating.[12]

Both culture and governance rules are intertwined with the selection environment. This helps explain why, despite the growing internationalization of markets, companies and networks tend to retain most of their innovative capabilities in their home country.[13] A selection environment influenced by noncommercial considerations like unique national antitrust laws or a long history of labor–management tensions regarding the introduction of new process technologies into the workplace can affect the nature and location of innovative activities. For instance, most of the actual production of technology, including the critical systems integration normally essential for the high value-added synthesis associated with complex technologies, tends to be carried out in specific regions of the home countries of the companies that hold network core capabilities. One reason why this happens is that:

> studies of technological change demonstrate that technological capabilities develop in conjunction with production. In other words, they cannot be acquired simply by purchasing a product; rather they are "hands-on" or tacit capabilities that depend on actual involvement in the production process. A nation that sacrifices a particular high technology industry will gradually lose many of the local technological capabilities nurtured by it.[14]

For example, the decision by US companies to withdraw from video innovation when televisions became commodity products contributed to the inability of American firms to participate in the later innovation of flat panel displays. When this later became a concern, public policy was the only hope for catalyzing a new US industry.[15]

Surveying

Intelligence about commercial technologies has been gathered and disseminated by national governments everywhere for some time, but as knowledge has become more central to the innovation of complex technologies, this policy role has acquired greater significance. Markets alone do not seem capable of delivering accurate information about the multiple interdependencies between existing and emerging technologies, or about changes taking place in industrial organization (e.g. network formation and evolution). Thus, the management of the flows of knowledge, through monitoring and forecasting international technological trends, may have become as important for government agencies as management of R&D funding. For example, Martin Fransman raises what he calls the "MITI paradox": How can MITI be the most powerful Japanese ministry in the area of technology if it only controls 13 percent of the government's total science and technology budget? His answer is that:

> MITI continues to have political "clout" including the science and technology area where its influence far exceeds its share of the Japanese government's budget. However, MITI's influence comes, not only from the important role it continues to play in Japanese industry and trade, but also from the substantial global information network that it controls. The "nodes" in this network extend out from MITI to include the formal and informal advisory and consultative committees that the ministry has established; the industry associations that have been established, often under MITI's guidance, in the sectors over which MITI has jurisdiction and which, as noted, are the most dynamic in the Japanese economy; the links MITI has forged with other ministries and agencies, often through the secondment of MITI staff; and the activities of JETRO [Japan External Trade Research Organization] which provides detailed information on industry, technology, and markets abroad.
>
> MITI's global information network has given the ministry unparalleled high-quality information regarding both Japan and the rest of the global economy. This information, *crossing* countries, technologies, companies, industrial sectors and markets, has given MITI's decision-makers an enormously broad "vision" on the basis of which to identify the strengths, weaknesses, and opportunities facing the Japanese manufacturing sector. While this information network has not necessarily been particularly expensive to run, it has put MITI's bureaucrats in a strong position to identify what needs to be done and how (although MITI officials do not always "get it right").[16]

The close linking of intelligence, forecasting, planning, and technology development is a hallmark of Japanese government, and while other nations have not gone as far with the surveying role,[17] even the USA, with its cultural aversion to many of these activities, has begun to employ modest intelligence-gathering and dissemination policies (e.g. critical technology assessments, technology "road maps" and competitive benchmarks).[18]

Coordinating

National governments are uniquely able to ensure that the various organizations within the NIS know of each other and can interact. This coordination role is most visible where policy takes on the task of fostering the creation of networks.

Government-supported networks have often focused on the need to integrate specific sets of core actors in the NIS. Thus, at various times policy in the USA has emphasized interfirm cooperation, collaboration between government laboratories and firms, and linkages between firms and universities. Sometimes US government-coordinated networks are limited to national firms and other core actors (often under the guise of national security), but many involve international participation. Governmental coordination has supported networks involved in everything from basic research to "precompetitive" R&D to joint production of new products and processes.[19] Public policy has also helped organize network relationships that are not directly involved in the innovation process. In the USA, for example, the National Institute of Standards and Technology has a long track record of coordinating industrial standards setting networks (e.g. consortia pursuing test methods for integrated circuits).[20]

Gap filling

Public policy is often established because some capability needed for technological innovation is missing or deficient and is not likely to be generated by other actors in the NIS. Jack Gibbons a former Director of the White House Office of Science and Technology Policy (OSTP), has pointed out perhaps the most obvious gap in the US national innovation system:

> If you look at Japan and Germany, we're ending up as the low man on the totem pole. That's a kind of warning signal that says we're becoming more dependent on other countries for our knowledge base. So one thing to set right there is to figure out why we have so many good ideas in basic research here that go off over there and get turned into products and jobs. Part of that comes from what I call the gap – it is a gap between the bench, where they create the ideas, and the companies that turn those ideas into products. This administration feels that gap is a challenge to the private sector to come upstream toward the researchers. We're moving downstream in terms of policies – opening up the federal laboratories, running programs like the Advanced Technology Program and the Cooperative Research and Development Agreements with the labs. These attract industry and the labs to each other.[21]

Gap filling is the most open-ended and thus the most controversial government technology policy role. Because filling gaps tends to focus on unique cases, in the United States these policies often generate the cry that government is "picking winners." The Advanced Technology Program (ATP) that Gibbons refers to typifies this problem. Designed to promote cost-shared R&D partnerships between government and companies to accelerate development of high-risk technologies that promise significant commercial payoffs, ATP has been attacked by opponents in Congress as "corporate welfare" for industry.[22] In fact, gap filling has been a fixture in US policy throughout the country's history. A particularly striking example was the provision of wind tunnels in the early days of the airplane industry.[23]

Policy guidelines

A starting point for the search for policy guidelines is to step outside the analytical debates of the past and look for insights from the vantage point of the science of complexity and evolutionary economics. One way to begin this process is to examine recent US technology policy initiatives through the lens of the framework for self-

Table 12.1 Public policies for complex technological innovation

Network resources
● Targeted education programs (e.g. science, engineering).
● Aid for worker training and upgrading skills (e.g. manufacturing extension).
● Direct subsidies for development of firm, network, or sector capabilities (e.g. flat panel displays).

Learning opportunities, potential capabilities, assets, and path dependencies
● Research and development funding.
● Sponsorship of cooperative activities (e.g. Sematech).
● Transfer of defense science and technology (e.g. dual-use systems) to civilian sectors.
● Surveying, trend analysis, and diffusion of knowledge (e.g. critical technologies assessments).
● Infrastructure investments (e.g. information "superhighway").

Selection environment
● Intellectual property protection (e.g. non-profit organizations can have title to government-sponsored patents).
● Antitrust enforcement and exemptions (e.g. joint production among firms).
● Government procurement and standards setting (e.g. greater flexibility and simplification in military purchasing).
● Taxation and regulation designed to encourage innovation (e.g. R&D tax credits).
● Import barriers and export incentives.

Sources: Board on Science, Technology, and Economic Policy, National Research Council, *Conflict and Cooperation in National Competition for High-technology Industry*, Washington, DC: National Academy Press, 1996, pp. 39–40; US Congress, Office of Technology Assessment, *Innovation and Commercialization of Emerging Technologies*, Washington, DC: Government Printing Office, September 1995, pp. 61–96; Rose M. Ham and David C. Mowery, "Enduring Dilemmas in US Technology Policy," *California Management Review*, Vol. 37, No. 4, Summer 1995, pp. 94–5; Eugene B. Skolnikoff, "Evolving US Science and Technology Policy in a Changing International Environment," *Science and Public Policy*, Vol. 22, No. 2, April 1995, pp. 74–84; Stephen J. Kline and Don E. Kash, "Government Technology Policy: What Should It Do?" *The Bridge*, Vol. 22, No. 1, Spring 1992, pp. 12–18.

organization elaborated in Chapter 6. Table 12.1 provides that perspective by arraying categories of policy according to their relevance to the elements of self-organization: network resources and constraining and focusing forces. To reflect the policy realities in the USA, we have divided constraining and focusing forces into two parts: (a) learning opportunities, potential core capabilities and complementary assets, and path dependencies; and (b) the selection environment.

Table 12.1 highlights several generalizations that are worth noting. First, while there have been some policy initiatives related to each of the three sets of self-organization factors, *by far the least attention has been paid to network resources.* Federal policies in the United States relevant to education, worker training, or direct enhancement of network capabilities, assets, and learning have been limited and contradictory. The policies listed as examples in Table 12.1 are typical of the tentative efforts that are in part a reflection of the US ideological predisposition against a significant national government role in these areas. This pattern of tentative policy exists despite the fact that it has now become almost conventional wisdom in Washington that broadly based human resources policies are critical to the future of American innovative capacity. Dr. Gibbons of OSTP summarizes the emerging view:

Upon departing the formal system of education, students must make the transition to the workforce and be prepared to contribute to US productivity. What skills will one need to enter the 21st century workforce directly upon completion of high school or after two years of post-secondary education? How will these needs differ from the "retooling" of people whose skills require refreshing as what constitutes "appropriate training" for various jobs is redefined? This need for retraining or "lifelong learning" (and for some, re-entry to the workforce) is one vexing but predictable feature of scientific and technological progress ... The current distribution of resources for S&T tends to favor those pursuing academic careers in research, but interventions at the level of K-12 and undergraduate levels will likely be more influential in the long run on not only the size and composition of the future pool of scientists and engineers but also the workforce in general. If the future S&T workforce needs to be broader-gauged and geared to other sectors and work activities, then readjustments are warranted in resource allocation and priorities.[24]

Similar perspectives are held by at least a few members of Congress. Representative George Brown, a Democrat from California and ranking minority member of the House Science Committee, has proposed an "investment budget" that establishes budgetary growth rates and identifies ways to enforce them for three major categories of public spending: R&D, capital infrastructure (e.g. transportation systems), and *education and training*. On the last, Congressman Brown says: "The goal is to produce a workforce that can be integrated into the overall growth in the economy that technology and transportation investments will bring."[25]

A major shift in national priorities seems long overdue because nothing would be more useful for networks moving from one innovation pattern to another than an NIS capacity for appropriate education and training. Appropriate training and retraining of personnel that provides continuous upgrading of needed skills would contribute to the workforce's ability to adjust to changes in technology.[26] *Human resource competencies are inseparable from network core capabilities.*[27] To the extent that public policy can help provide worker skills and know-how, networks will be able to make rapid adjustment to changes in trajectories.

Direct US policy interventions designed to develop capabilities at the firm, network, or sector level have been as rare as human resource initiatives. Governmental support for companies to develop their capabilities in flat panel displays is an obvious exception. The logic for government funding in this case was defined largely in terms of defense requirements, but the fundamental need is to build core capabilities in US firms. As Michael Borrus and Jeffrey Hart have pointed out, the broader policy issue is:

Should we be concerned about the shifts in the sourcing and production of electronics technology and know-how? Don't technologies and the capabilities they embody diffuse rapidly across national borders in a relatively open world economy? If diffusion were perfect and instantaneous, then there would be little cause for worry. But, of course, diffusion is not perfect because not all relevant know-how is internationally accessible through market and nonmarket mechanisms. Nor is diffusion instantaneous, since the ability to absorb new capabilities depends in part on the available mix of old capabilities. Technology diffusion, like technology development, is a path-dependent process of learning in which today's ability to exploit technology grows out of yesterday's experience and practices. For example, because the demise of the American consumer electronics industry brought with it a sharp decline in corresponding skills, there is today little US capability to competitively produce liquid crystal displays (LCDs) in high volume – *even though the basic technology is internationally available.*[28]

That activist resource development policies like the flat panel display program have been attacked as industrial policy that "picks winners," and defended most aggressively as a dual-use exception to the general rule of no government involvement, only points out the US preoccupation with the concepts and language of an earlier era.[29] Nonetheless, Richard Nelson's point is persuasive when he argues that technology policy ought to have a broader industry focus than the relatively narrow flat panel initiative. Not only are the politics of broader programs more ideologically and politically palatable in the USA, but more effective public–private governance mechanisms appear easier to develop when industry-wide technological issues are being addressed.[30]

A second broad generalization in the United States is that *by far the most policy attention has been given to the selection environment.* In itself, this would not be a problem. But US policy has tended to focus on only one dimension of the selection environment, markets, to the relative exclusion of the other institutions that comprise the national innovation system. Emphasis on intellectual property rights, antitrust protection, and the like ignores the fact that without coherent national systems of innovation, markets collapse.[31]

The American policy fascination with market dynamics reflects an overemphasis on factors such as patents as guarantors of appropriability and drivers of technological innovation. Many more factors appear to be involved in inducing innovation than market forces, including firm, network, and sectoral differences in core capabilities and technological opportunities.[32] Markets are, therefore, only part of the puzzle, and to the extent that US technology policy focuses on single variable solutions, such as the international harmonization of intellectual property regimes as a quick fix for chronic balance of trade difficulties, the result is certain to be failure and frustration.

Approaching policy toward the selection environment more holistically is part of the solution to assisting networks in making changes in trajectories, and this means taking the idea of a national innovation system seriously. Crucial to this shift in thinking and in policy making is the recognition that innovation takes place through both market and nonmarket transactions and that the latter involve not only businesses but also public organizations that exercise considerable influence over broader institutions (e.g. regulatory regimes).[33]

Non-market interactions are powerful forces in the selection process, as the literature on standards setting and regulation clearly indicates. Outside the marketplace, networks seeking to enhance the selection of their innovations frequently find themselves involved in what Jacqueline Senker, in her study of the industrial biotechnology sector, refers to as "institutional engineering," the process of "negotiating with, convincing or placating regulatory authorities, the legal system, and the medical profession."[34] In the United States only the national government is capable of affecting these market and non-market relationships and interconnections in any systematic way.

The third generalization is that *many of the most important changes in US technology policy are related to learning opportunities, potential core capabilities, complementary assets, and path dependencies.* Efforts to enhance network learning through government-sponsored collaborative activities have proliferated in recent years, and they seem to be headed in the right direction. *The unit of organization in technology policy has in an increasing number of cases changed from the firm to the network.* This change in policy focus should facilitate effective interaction and self-organization of all actors. Public policy should focus major attention on ways to maintain open channels of access to networks by new actors with diverse and potentially useful core capabilities and complementary assets.

Access to cooperative arrangements can be particularly important both for networks migrating among innovation patterns and for networks seeking to remain on a trajectory in the normal pattern. The Sematech collaboration as it has evolved appears to be a successful example of the latter.[35]

R&D funding must continue to be a high priority of governments, but *the primacy given to R&D is a problem for the innovation of complex technologies.* Too much rhetoric and analysis continues to assume that support for R&D, sometimes only the "R", is synonymous with national technology policy.[36] Congressman Brown calls this "an excessive faith in the creation of new knowledge as an engine of economic growth and a neglect of the processes of knowledge diffusion and application."[37] Support of R&D certainly creates learning opportunities, but, as we saw in Chapter 8, there are many learning avenues that have little or nothing to do with either research or development. Similarly, the emphasis on R&D skews the generation of capabilities targeted by policy, as a recent analysis of the European Union's efforts pointed out:

> By far the largest proportion devoted to technology policy, in the European Union and elsewhere, falls into two categories: expenditure on the provision of what we have called the research and technology infrastructure, and expenditure on research subsidies. There are, of course, persuasive economic justifications for this, but it is certainly at odds with what this study suggests are the most urgent needs with regard to technology management on the part of the firms. *It could be argued that these types of support – and research support for firms in particular – are relied on partly because of a lack of politically and operationally credible ways of supporting other (non-technical) competences directly.*[38]

In other words, R&D support is easy for governments to justify, but it is not necessarily what companies, networks, and the NIS always need. Often what are needed are new or enhanced organizational capabilities that facilitate development of tacit know-how and skills, integrated production process improvements, and ways to synthesize and integrate the talents and expertise of individuals into work groups and teams.[39] These organizational "black arts" are not usually a part of national R&D agendas, but if the complexity challenge is to be met, policy will need to be flexible enough to incorporate them as well as other non-traditional ideas.

A twenty-first-century policy perspective

The dominant engine driving the economy of the twenty-first century will be the capacity of networks and national innovation system to synthesize repeated innovations of complex technologies. If policy is to be adapted in ways that foster the needed innovation, policy makers and other participants in the policy process will need to develop new perspectives. In Chapter 2 we identified three characteristics whose recognition is essential to the needed perspective. First, networks offer, through their capacity to carry out synthesis, a capability for innovating almost anything on demand; but it is not possible for individuals to understand the processes of innovation in detail. The reality is that policy must be made without any capability for understanding in a detailed sense what will work.

Second, traditional boundaries will be of less and less use to those making policy. The blurred boundary phenomenon applies across the spectrum, from the public/private sector boundary to the product/process boundary to the tacit/explicit knowledge boundary. Third, continuous coevolution between organizations and technologies will be the norm: the aggregate change will be composed of the continuous emergence of small incremental organizational and technological adaptations. Complexity will continue to emerge silently.

The great challenge facing policy makers is to find an accommodation between the set of analytical ideas and concepts that are the currency of contemporary policy formulation and debate, and a reality that has moved beyond that currency and is incompatible with it. The United States enters the twenty-first century as a society whose policy rhetoric is dominated by a model of "analytic governance," but whose reality is dominated by "complex synthetic technologies."[40] The tensions between an analytic conceptual system and a synthetic reality will likely increase because, by definition, the increasing importance of complex technologies experiencing repeated innovations means that policy will have great difficulty in dealing effectively with reality. It is unlikely that a policy that is only reactive will be adequate. The twenty-first century will demand adaptive policy. It will require policy makers who can act in the absence of understanding. In truth, the most successful policy will be that which pursues adaptation through trial and error.

Although policy must be made without detailed understanding, it does not follow that knowledge and information are of little or no value. To the contrary, the most successful policy making will usually be that which is best informed. Being informed in the era of complex technologies will require accessing tacit as well as explicit knowledge. This means that there are compelling reasons for addressing the problems posed by the existence of high walls of separation between the public and private sectors and the high walls that exist within the US federal government. Only policy that is informed by state-of-the-art knowledge of the repeated nonlinear changes occurring in the various sectors of technology can be appropriately adaptive. The views that are presently dominant in the United States concerning the importance of "walls of separation" and protections against "conflicts of interest" will need to be adapted if policies are to be formulated that most effectively foster innovation. Arm's length relationships between the public and private sectors are likely to result in ill-informed policies, because only those who are intimately involved in the innovation of complex technologies can provide state-of-the-art knowledge about what is happening.

Perhaps the most important perspective involves an explicit recognition by policy makers that most economically successful innovations are incremental and are carried out by self-organizing networks; they are innovations that occur within the normal pattern. Further, even the innovations that result in pattern changes most often involve synthesis; that is, the fusion of existing technologies. The key point is that the coevolution associated with most economically successful innovation involves small steps. Policy that is sensitive to this process of adaptation and thus policy that adapts rapidly and in small steps is likely to be most effective.

One of the consequences of a reality driven by repeated innovations of complex technologies is that repeated unanticipated consequences become a given; they are a permanent phenomenon that will require repeated policy adaptations. Complexity science communicates no message more clearly than that even small events have unanticipated consequences, and one of its most dramatic messages is that sometimes small events have dramatic unanticipated consequences. In the socio-technical systems represented by NIS there are multiple interactions, so that technical changes generate consequences for policy, but the reverse is also the case.

Thus, the interaction between technical, network, and policy adaptions must be taken as a starting point in the formulation of policy. Although small adaptations can have dramatic unanticipated consequences, it seems plausible that major adaptions will have a greater probability of major unanticipated consequences. Because of this interdependence and because both successful policy and innovation rely heavily on trial and error, it is generally the case that policy adaptions that occur in small steps and incrementally are attractive. That is, they are most likely to result in economic success. Similarly, it seems plausible that incremental policy making offers the greatest prospect of rapid and appropriate adaptation to the inevitable negative unanticipated consequences that are a continuing output of a system that has the innovation of complex technologies as its main reason for being.

Conclusions

The fascination with technical, explicit, and product-oriented R&D to the exclusion of more organizational and process-related concerns is an example of what public policy should avoid in the future. Simple responses to the complexities of technological innovation are always seductive and usually wrong. But what *should* public policy do? Our general response is that policy making must focus on pattern-based learning and adaptation. More specific policy guidance is not yet feasible, in large part because we have not developed an appropriate policy language. We need new synthetic policy metaphors to replace the outdated images of the mass manufacturing era. Fortunately, programs are now in place at research centers like the Santa Fe Institute to undertake this task. One researcher who has been involved in such efforts argues that a key objective is to develop metaphors that help with "the delicate conversion of conflict into cooperation."[41] Given the importance of policy that facilitates network formation and evolution, this kind of thinking is promising. We hope this book contributes both to the development of a useful language and to strategy and policy that focus major attention on network formation and evolution.

Notes

1. Paul N. Doremus, William W. Keller, Louis W. Pauly, and Simon Reich, *The Myth of the Global Corporation*, Princeton, NJ: Princeton University Press, 1998, pp. 144–9.
2. Stephen Chen, "A New Paradigm for Knowledge-based Competition: Building an Industry through Knowledge Sharing," *Technology Analysis and Strategic Management*, Vol. 9, No. 4, December 1997, p. 442.
3. Bent Dalum, Bjorn Johnson, and Bengt-Ake Lundvall, "Public Policy in the Learning Society," in Bengt-Ake Lundvall, ed., *National Systems of Innovation: towards a Theory of Innovation and Interactive Learning*, New York: Pinter, 1992, p. 308.
4. J. S. Metcalfe, "Evolutionary Economics and Technology Policy," *Economic Journal*, Vol. 104, No. 425, July 1994, p. 933.
5. Steven Durlauf, "What Should Policymakers Know about Economic Complexity?" *Washington Quarterly*, Vol. 21, No. 1, Winter 1998, p. 164.
6. Keith Smith, "Innovation Policy in an Evolutionary Context," in P. Paolo Saviotti and J. Stanley Metcalfe, eds, *Evolutionary Theories of Economic and Technological Change:*

Present Status and Future Prospects, Reading, PA: Harwood Academic Publishers, 1991, p. 257.

7. Stephen J. Kline and Don E. Kash, "Government Technology Policy: What Should It Do?" *The Bridge*, Vol. 22, No. 1, Spring 1992, pp. 12–18.

8. Francis Fukuyama, *Trust: the Social Virtues and the Creation of Prosperity*, New York: Free Press, 1995; Lane Kenworthy, *In Search of National Economic Success: Balancing Competition and Cooperation*, London: Sage Publications, 1995, pp. 154–96; Richard R. Nelson, "Technical Change as Cultural Evolution," in Ross Thomason, ed., *Learning and Technological Change*, New York: St. Martin's Press, 1993, pp. 9–23; Stewart R. Clegg and S. Gordon Redding, eds, *Capitalism in Contrasting Cultures*, New York: Walter de Gruyter, 1990.

9. Richard C. Adams, *Culture, Policy, and Technology Innovation: US and Japanese Performance in Electro/Mechanical Technologies*, PhD Dissertation, Fairfax, VA: George Mason University, 1995, pp. 64–87.

10. US Congress, Office of Technology Assessment, *Innovation and Commercialization of Emerging Technologies*, Washington: Government Printing Office, September 1995, pp. 62–3.

11. Giovanni Dosi and Bruce Kogut, "National Specificities and the Context of Change: the Coevolution of Organization and Technology," in Bruce Kogut, ed., *Country Competitiveness: Technology and the Organizing of Work*, New York: Oxford University Press, 1993, pp. 249–62; Marcie J. Tyre, "Managing the Introduction of New Process Technology: International Differences in a Multi-plant Network," *Research Policy*, Vol. 20, No. 1, February 1991, pp. 57–76.

12. Eugene B. Skolnikoff, "Evolving US Science and Technology Policy in a Changing International Environment," *Science and Public Policy*, Vol. 22, No. 2, April 1995, pp. 75–7.

13. Doremus, Keller, Pauly, and Reich, *The Myth of the Global Corporation*, p. 86–137.

14. Laura D. Tyson, *Who's Bashing Whom? Trade Conflict in High-technology Industries*, Washington, DC: Institute for International Economics, 1992, pp. 9–10.

15. Kenneth S. Flamm, "Flat-panel Displays: Catalyzing a US Industry," *Issues in Science and Technology*, Vol. 11, No. 1, Fall 1994, pp. 27–32.

16. Martin Fransman, "Is National Technology Policy Obsolete in a Globalized World? The Japanese Response," *Cambridge Journal of Economics*, Vol. 19, No. 1, February 1995, pp. 117–18.

17. B. Bowonder and M. Miyake, "Technology Forecasting in Japan," *Futures*, Vol. 25, No. 7, September 1993, pp. 757–77.

18. Executive Office of the President, *Technology for Economic Growth: President's Progress Report*, Washington, DC: Executive Office of the President, November 1993, pp. 18–19.

19. Rose M. Ham and David C. Mowery, "Enduring Dilemmas in US Technology Policy," *California Management Review*, Vol. 37, No. 4, Summer 1995, p. 93.

20. Gregory Tassey, "The Roles of Standards as Technology Infrastructure," in Richard W. Hawkins, Robin Mansell, and Jim Skea, eds, *Standards, Innovation and Competitiveness: The Politics and Economics of Standards in Natural and Technical Environments*, Brookfield, VT: Edward Elgar, 1995, p. 166.

21. Gene Koprowski, "Does High-tech Need Fed Funds?" *Forbes ASAP*, April 10, 1995, p. 91.

22. David J. Hanson, "Advanced Technology Program: Victim of Congressional Fervor?" *Chemical and Engineering News*, August 21, 1995, p. 27.

23. Edward W. Constant II, *The Origins of the Turbojet Revolution*, Baltimore: Johns Hopkins University Press, 1980.

24. John H. Gibbons and William G. Wells, Jr, "Science, Technology and Government in the United States: Toward the Year 2000," *Technology in Society*, Vol. 19, Nos 3/4, 1997, pp. 580–1.

25. George E. Brown, Jr, "An Investment Budget," *Issues in Science and Technology*, Vol. 13, No. 4, Summer 1997, p. 28.

26. Henry Ergas, "Does Technology Policy Matter?" in Bruce R. Guile and Harvey Brooks, eds,

Technology and Global Industry: Companies and Nations in the World Economy, Washington, DC: National Academy Press, 1987, p. 233.

27. Ken Kamoche, "Strategic Human Resource Management within a Resource-capability View of the Firm," *Journal of Management Studies*, Vol. 33, No. 2, March 1996, pp. 213–33.

28. Michael Borrus and Jeffrey A. Hart, "Display's the Thing: the Real Stakes in the Conflict over High-resolution Displays," *Journal of Policy Analysis and Management*, Vol. 13, No. 1, Winter 1994, p. 22.

29. Flamm, "Flat-panel Displays," pp. 27–32.

30. Richard R. Nelson, "Why Should Managers Be Thinking about Technology Policy?" *Strategic Management Journal*, Vol. 16, No. 8, November 1995, pp. 585–6.

31. Doremus, Keller, Pauly, and Reich, *The Myth of the Global Corporation*, pp. 1–10.

32. Giovanni Dosi, "Opportunities, Incentives and the Collective Patterns of Technological Change," *Economic Journal*, Vol. 107, No. 444, September 1997, p. 1533.

33. Daniele Archibugi and Jonathan Michie, "Technological Globalisation or National Systems of Innovation?" *Futures*, Vol. 29, No. 2, March 1997, pp. 121–37.

34. Jacqueline Senker, "National Systems of Innovation, Organizational Learning and Industrial Biotechnology," *Technovation*, Vol. 16, No. 5, May 1996, p. 225.

35. Larry D. Browning, Janice M. Beyer, and Judy C. Shetler, "Building Cooperation in a Competitive Industry: Sematech and the Semiconductor Industry," *Academy of Management Journal*, Vol. 38, No. 1, February 1995, pp. 113–51.

36. Linda R. Cohen and Roger G. Noll, "Privatizing Public Research," September 1994, pp. 72–7; Deborah Shapley, "Clintonizing Science Policy," December 1993, pp. 39–43.

37. George E. Brown, Jr, "Rational Science, Irrational Reality: A Congressional Perspective on Basic Research and Society," *Science*, Vol. 258, No. 5080, October 9, 1992, p. 200.

38. William Cannell, "Conclusion: Technology Management in the European Union and Its Policy Implications," in William Cannell and Ben Dankbaar, eds, *Technology Management and Public Policy in the European Union*, New York: Oxford University Press, 1996, p. 172.

39. E. B. Grant and M. J. Gregory, "Tacit Knowledge, the Life Cycle and International Manufacturing Transfer," *Technology Analysis and Strategic Management*, Vol. 9, No. 2, 1997, pp. 149–60.

40. Don E. Kash and Robert W. Rycroft, "Synthetic Technology – Analytic Governance: the 21st Century Challenge," *Technological Forecasting and Social Change*, Vol. 54, 1997, pp. 17–27.

41. Michael Lissack, "Mind Your Metaphors: Lessons from Complexity Science," *Long Range Planning*, Vol. 30, No. 2, April 1997, p. 294.

Data and Methodology for Classifying Simple and Complex Technologies

This analysis divides exported technologies into two broad categories: simple and complex. Complex technologies are defined as follows:

> A technology is complex if it cannot be understood in detail by an individual expert and communicated precisely among experts across time and distance.

Simple technologies are defined as follows:

> A simple technology is one that can be understood in detail by an individual expert and communicated precisely among experts across time and distance.

Technologies were classified as simple or complex by experts familiar with the products and processes used to produce them. We sought out experts from industry, academic institutions, and government agencies, including those interviewed for the case studies supporting this book. Being careful not to misuse the complex classification, our bias was always toward the simple classification. That is, if anyone said simple, the technology was classified as simple.

Using this definition, products were grouped using the simple/complex distinction. The technological processes used to produce these goods were similarly grouped. We analyzed export and trade balance performance for these products from 1970 to 1995, at five year intervals, and for every year in the 1990s. We examined several sources of trade data, but chose the United Nations' *Yearbook of International Trade Statistics, Trade by Commodity and Country* volumes as our data source. The annual UN publications report trade statistics for the past five years (i.e. current year and previous four years). Typically, the current year data are revised in subsequent yearbooks as updated data are received. In order to capture complete data for all commodities and countries for our study, yearbooks other (later) than the current year were selected as follows:

Data for year(s)	Taken from UN Yearbook
1970	1974
1975	1976
1980	1980
1985	1986
1990	1991
1991–95	1995

There were a few exceptions to this, and they are noted in the following tables.

Our database ultimately included balance of trade performance for the following 22 countries, consisting of major industrialized countries, newly developed industrialized countries, and a handful of others that appeared to reflect changes in export trends over this time period:

Argentina	Australia	Brazil	Canada
Chile	China	France	Germany
India	Indonesia	Italy	Japan
Malaysia	Mexico	Netherlands	Republic of Korea
Spain	Sweden	Thailand	United Kingdom
United States	Venezuela		

For this appendix we chose to report trade balance performance for only the United States and Japan, since the case studies supporting this book involved technological products from these two countries.

The following series of tables summarize data for the top 30 highest value export products for the years 1970, 1975, 1980, 1985, 1990, and 1995. We settled on 30 products since this number represents almost one-half of world exports (the top 30 three-digit SITC (Standard International Trade Classification) categories represent between 42 and 56 percent of all goods exports in the years between 1970 and 1995). We also segmented the export data into all goods (all SITC codes) and manufactured only goods (SITC codes 500 through 800). Manufactured goods seemed a better basis to examine changes in product and process complexity since they exclude raw material exports such as crude petroleum products. Six data tables are provided for each year:

- top 30 goods exports traded globally;
- top 30 goods exports traded globally, grouped by complex/simple classification;
- top 30 manufactured goods exports traded globally (SITC codes 500 through 800);
- top 30 manufactured goods exports traded globally (SITC codes 500 through 800), grouped by complex/simple classification;
- United States balance of trade for top 30 manufactured goods exports traded globally;
- Japan balance of trade for top 30 manufactured goods exports traded globally.

Top 30 goods exports traded globally, 1995

Rank	SITC	Commodity	Value (million US$)	Classification Product	Process
1	781	Pass. motor vehicles exc. buses	230,631	Complex	Complex
2	333	Crude petroleum	185,801	Simple	Simple
3	776	Transistors, valves, etc.	179,492	Complex	Complex
4	752	Automatic data processing eqpt	123,840	Complex	Complex
5	784	Motor vehicle parts, acces. NES	120,103	Complex	Complex
6	764	Telecom eqpt, parts, acces. NES	115,970	Complex	Complex
7	759	Office, adp. machine parts, acces.	90,503	Complex	Complex
8	334	Petroleum products refined	79,869	Simple	Complex
9	778	Electrical machinery NES	76,972	Complex	Complex
10	641	Paper and paperboard	75,720	Simple	Complex
11	583	Polymerization, etc., products	74,395	Simple	Complex
12	541	Medicinal, etc., products	71,590	Simple	Complex
13	792	Aircraft, etc.	70,316	Complex	Complex
14	772	Switchgear, etc., parts NES	62,704	Complex	Complex
15	728	Other machinery for special indus.	59,881	Complex	Complex
16	749	Non-elec. machine parts, acces. NES	56,637	Simple	Complex
17	713	Internal combustion piston engine	54,786	Complex	Complex
18	674	Iron, steel univ., plate, sheet	53,421	Simple	Complex
19	874	Measuring, controlling eqpt	52,980	Complex	Complex
20	893	Articles of plastic NES	48,300	Simple	Complex
21	782	Lorries, spcl mtr vehicles NES	46,526	Complex	Complex
22	821	Furniture, parts thereof	44,881	Simple	Simple
23	684	Aluminum	41,376	Simple	Simple
24	843	Women's outerwear nonknit	40,530	Simple	Simple
25	851	Footwear	40,409	Simple	Simple
26	667	Pearl, prec., semi-p. stone	40,391	Simple	Simple
27	894	Toys, sporting goods, etc.	38,737	Simple	Simple
28	011	Meat fresh, chilled, frozen	37,718	Simple	Simple
29	741	Heating, cooling eqpt	37,272	Simple	Complex
30	699	Base metal mfrs NES	36,101	Simple	Simple
		Top 30 subtotal	2,287,852		
		World exports	4,925,668		
		% of total	46.4		

Note: in all appendix tables, NES = not elsewhere specified.

Top 30 goods exports traded globally, grouped by complex/simple classification, 1995

Rank	SITC	Commodity	Value (million US$)	Product	Process	% of total
2	333	Crude petroleum	185,801	Simple	Simple	
22	821	Furniture, parts thereof	44,881	Simple	Simple	
23	684	Aluminum	41,376	Simple	Simple	
24	843	Women's outerwear nonknit	40,530	Simple	Simple	
25	851	Footwear	40,409	Simple	Simple	
26	667	Pearl, prec., semi-p. stone	40,391	Simple	Simple	
27	894	Toys, sporting goods, etc.	38,737	Simple	Simple	
28	011	Meat fresh, chilled, frozen	37,718	Simple	Simple	
30	699	Base metal mfrs NES	36,101	Simple	Simple	
		Subtotal simple/simple	505,944			22.1
8	334	Petroleum products refined	79,869	Simple	Complex	
10	641	Paper and paperboard	75,720	Simple	Complex	
11	583	Polymerization, etc., products	74,395	Simple	Complex	
12	541	Medicinal, etc., products	71,590	Simple	Complex	
16	749	Non-elec. machine parts, acces. NES	56,637	Simple	Complex	
18	674	Iron, steel univ., plate, sheet	53,421	Simple	Complex	
20	893	Articles of plastic NES	48,300	Simple	Complex	
29	741	Heating, cooling eqpt	37,272	Simple	Complex	
		Subtotal simple/complex	497,204			21.7
1	781	Pass. motor vehicles exc. buses	230,631	Complex	Complex	
3	776	Transistors, valves, etc.	179,492	Complex	Complex	
4	752	Automatic data processing eqpt	123,840	Complex	Complex	
5	784	Motor vehicle parts, acces. NES	120,103	Complex	Complex	
6	764	Telecom eqpt, parts, acces. NES	115,970	Complex	Complex	
7	759	Office, adp. machine parts, acces.	90,503	Complex	Complex	
9	778	Electrical machinery NES	76,972	Complex	Complex	
13	792	Aircraft, etc.	70,316	Complex	Complex	
14	772	Switchgear, etc., parts NES	62,704	Complex	Complex	
15	728	Other machinery for special indus.	59,881	Complex	Complex	
17	713	Internal combustion piston engine	54,786	Complex	Complex	
19	874	Measuring, controlling eqpt	52,980	Complex	Complex	
21	782	Lorries, spcl mtr vehicles NES	46,526	Complex	Complex	
		Subtotal complex/complex	1,284,704			56.2
		Top 30 subtotal	2,287,852			

**Top 30 manufactured goods exports traded globally, 1995
(SITC codes 500 through 800)**

Rank	SITC	Commodity	Value (million US$)	Classification Product	Process
1	781	Pass. motor vehicles exc. buses	230,631	Complex	Complex
2	776	Transistors, valves, etc.	179,492	Complex	Complex
3	752	Automatic data processing eqpt	123,840	Complex	Complex
4	784	Motor vehicle parts, acces. NES	120,103	Complex	Complex
5	764	Telecom eqpt, parts, acces. NES	115,970	Complex	Complex
6	759	Office, adp. machine parts., acces.	90,503	Complex	Complex
7	778	Electrical machinery NES.	76,972	Complex	Complex
8	641	Paper and paperboard	75,720	Simple	Complex
9	583	Polymerization, etc., products	74,395	Simple	Complex
10	541	Medicinal, etc., products	71,590	Simple	Complex
11	792	Aircraft, etc.	70,316	Complex	Complex
12	772	Switchgear, etc., parts NES	62,704	Complex	Complex
13	728	Other machinery for special indus.	59,881	Complex	Complex
14	749	Non-elec. machine parts, acces. NES	56,637	Simple	Complex
15	713	Internal combustion piston engine	54,786	Complex	Complex
16	674	Iron, steel univ., plate, sheet	53,421	Simple	Complex
17	874	Measuring, controlling eqpt	52,980	Complex	Complex
18	893	Articles of plastic NES	48,300	Simple	Complex
19	782	Lorries, spcl mtr vehicles NES	46,526	Complex	Complex
20	821	Furniture, parts thereof	44,881	Simple	Simple
21	684	Aluminum	41,376	Simple	Simple
22	843	Women's outerwear nonknit	40,530	Simple	Simple
23	851	Footwear	40,409	Simple	Simple
24	667	Pearl, prec., semi-p. stone	40,391	Simple	Simple
25	894	Toys, sporting goods, etc.	38,737	Simple	Simple
26	741	Heating, cooling eqpt	37,272	Simple	Complex
27	699	Base metal mfrs NES	36,101	Simple	Simple
28	793	Ships and boats, etc.	36,009	Complex	Complex
29	598	Miscel. chemical products NES	34,899	Simple	Complex
30	744	Mechanical handling eqpt	33,756	Simple	Complex
		Top 30 Subtotal	2,089,128		

**Top 30 manufactured goods exports traded globally, 1995
(SITC codes 500 through 800): Grouped by complex/simple classification**

Rank	SITC	Commodity	Value (million US$)	Product	Process	% of total
20	821	Furniture, parts thereof	44,881	Simple	Simple	
21	684	Aluminum	41,376	Simple	Simple	
22	843	Women's outerwear nonknit	40,530	Simple	Simple	
23	851	Footwear	40,409	Simple	Simple	
24	667	Pearl, prec., semi-p. stone	40,391	Simple	Simple	
25	894	Toys, sporting goods, etc.	38,737	Simple	Simple	
27	699	Base metal mfrs NES	36,101	Simple	Simple	
		Subtotal simple/simple	282,425			13.5
8	641	Paper and paperboard	75,720	Simple	Complex	
9	583	Polymerization, etc., products	74,395	Simple	Complex	
10	541	Medicinal, etc., products	71,590	Simple	Complex	
14	749	Non-elec. machine parts, acces. NES	56,637	Simple	Complex	
16	674	Iron, steel univ., plate, sheet	53,421	Simple	Complex	
18	893	Articles of plastic NES	48,300	Simple	Complex	
26	741	Heating, cooling eqpt	37,272	Simple	Complex	
29	598	Miscel. chemical products NES	34,899	Simple	Complex	
30	744	Mechanical handling eqpt	33,756	Simple	Complex	
		Subtotal simple/complex	485,990			23.3
1	781	Pass. motor vehicles exc. buses	230,631	Complex	Complex	
2	776	Transistors, valves, etc.	179,492	Complex	Complex	
3	752	Automatic data processing eqpt	123,840	Complex	Complex	
4	784	Motor vehicle parts, acces. NES	120,103	Complex	Complex	
5	764	Telecom eqpt, parts, acces. NES	115,970	Complex	Complex	
6	759	Office, adp. machine parts, acces.	90,503	Complex	Complex	
7	778	Electrical machinery NES	76,972	Complex	Complex	
11	792	Aircraft, etc.	70,316	Complex	Complex	
12	772	Switchgear, etc., parts NES	62,704	Complex	Complex	
13	728	Other machinery for special indus.	59,881	Complex	Complex	
15	713	Internal combustion piston engine	54,786	Complex	Complex	
17	874	Measuring, controlling eqpt	52,980	Complex	Complex	
19	782	Lorries, spcl mtr vehicles NES	46,526	Complex	Complex	
28	793	Ships and boats, etc.	36,009	Complex	Complex	
		Subtotal complex/complex	1,320,713			63.2
		Top 30 subtotal	2,089,128			

United States 1995 balance of trade (million US$) on top 30 manufactured goods traded globally

SITC	Commodity	Exports	Imports	Trade balance
667	Pearl, prec., semi-p. stone	2,471	6,687	−4,216
684	Aluminum	3,814	5,948	−2,134
699	Base metal mfrs NES	4,521	5,207	−686
821	Furniture, parts thereof	3,806	9,128	−5,322
843	Women's outerwear nonknit	0	11,346	−11,346
851	Footwear	0	12,177	−12,177
894	Toys, sporting goods, etc.	4,231	13,900	−9,669
	Subtotal simple/simple	18,843	64,393	−45,550
541	Medicinal, etc., products	6,554	5,605	949
583	Polymerization, etc., products	8,766	4,786	3,980
598	Miscel. chemical products NES	6,717	2,563	4,154
641	Paper and paperboard	7,221	11,512	−4,291
674	Iron, steel univ., plate, sheet	0	4,528	−4,528
741	Heating, cooling eqpt	5,656	2,755	2,901
744	Mechanical handling eqpt	4,667	4,243	424
749	Non-elec. machine parts, acces. NES	5,403	2,479	2,924
893	Articles of plastic NES	5,394	6,196	−802
	Subtotal simple/complex	50,378	44,667	5,711
713	Internal combustion piston engine	8,833	11,437	−2,604
728	Other machinery for special indus.	9,392	6,704	2,688
752	Automatic data processing eqpt	23,078	35,423	−12,345
759	Office, adp. machine parts., acces.	17,768	23,954	−6,186
764	Telecom eqpt, parts, acces. NES	17,842	18,647	−805
772	Switchgear, etc., parts NES	8,319	9,699	−1,380
776	Transistors, valves, etc.	35,711	40,957	−5,246
778	Electrical machinery NES	9,352	10,542	−1,190
781	Pass. motor vehicles exc. buses	16,799	66,127	−49,328
782	Lorries, spcl mtr vehicles NES	5,318	10,193	−4,875
784	Motor vehicle parts, acces. NES	23,817	21,156	2,661
792	Aircraft, etc.	25,613	6,387	19,226
793	Ships and boats, etc.	1,244	0	1,244
874	Measuring, controlling eqpt	13,485	7,345	6,140
	Subtotal complex/complex	216,571	268,571	−52,000
	Top 30 goods subtotal	285,792	377,631	−91,839

Japan 1995 balance of trade (million US$) on top 30 manufactured goods traded globally

SITC	Commodity	Exports	Imports	Trade balance
667	Pearl, prec., semi-p. stone	0	3,365	−3,365
684	Aluminum	0	5,620	−5,620
699	Base metal mfrs NES	2,377	1,157	1,220
821	Furniture, parts thereof	0	3,155	−3,155
843	Women's outerwear nonknit	0	4,556	−4,556
851	Footwear	0	2,747	−2,747
894	Toys, sporting goods, etc.	2,097	3,510	−1,413
	Subtotal simple/simple	4,474	24,110	−19,636
541	Medicinal, etc., products	1,844	4,917	−3,073
583	Polymerization, etc., products	4,952	1,099	3,853
598	Miscel. chemical products NES	3,085	1,983	1,102
641	Paper and paperboard	1,729	1,925	−196
674	Iron, steel univ., plate, sheet	9,671	1,574	8,097
741	Heating, cooling eqpt	5,618	1,184	4,434
744	Mechanical handling eqpt	4,850	0	4,850
749	Non-elec. machine parts, acces. NES	9,979	1,553	8,426
893	Articles of plastic NES	1,757	1,740	17
	Subtotal simple/complex	43,485	15,975	27,510
713	Internal combustion piston engine	13,119	0	13,119
728	Other machinery for special indus.	11,260	1,709	9,551
752	Automatic data processing eqpt	17,163	10,429	6,734
759	Office, adp. machine parts., acces.	16,349	5,305	11,044
764	Telecom eqpt, parts, acces. NES	18,212	5,814	12,398
772	Switchgear, etc., parts NES	11,435	1,739	9,696
776	Transistors, valves, etc.	40,847	12,260	28,587
778	Electrical machinery NES	14,431	2,987	11,444
781	Pass. motor vehicles exc. buses	41,674	9,993	31,681
782	Lorries, spcl mtr vehicles NES	9,616	0	9,616
784	Motor vehicle parts, acces. NES	19,656	1,454	18,202
792	Aircraft, etc.	0	2,768	−2,768
793	Ships and boats, etc.	10,932	0	10,932
874	Measuring, controlling eqpt	7,629	3,391	4,238
	Subtotal complex/complex	232,323	57,849	174,474
	Top 30 goods subtotal	280,282	97,934	182,348

Top 30 goods exports traded globally, 1990

Rank	SITC	Commodity	Value (million US$)	Classification Product	Process
1	781	Pass. motor vehicles exc. buses	168,722	Complex	Complex
2	333	Crude petroleum	148,822	Simple	Simple
3	784	Motor vehicle parts, acces. NES	83,681	Complex	Complex
4	334	Petroleum products refined	76,894	Simple	Complex
5	752	Automatic data processing eqpt	71,203	Complex	Complex
6	776	Transistors, valves, etc.	63,968	Complex	Complex
7	792	Aircraft, etc.	63,638	Complex	Complex
8	764	Telecom eqpt, parts, acces. NES	58,934	Complex	Complex
9	641	Paper and paperboard	51,086	Simple	Complex
10	759	Office, adp. machine parts., acces.	49,910	Complex	Complex
11	583	Polymerization, etc., products	48,921	Simple	Complex
12	728	Other machinery for special indus.	38,363	Complex	Complex
13	778	Electrical machinery NES	38,146	Complex	Complex
14	674	Iron, steel univ., plate, sheet	37,809	Simple	Complex
15	874	Measuring, controlling eqpt	37,540	Complex	Complex
16	782	Lorries, spcl mtr vehicles NES	37,529	Complex	Complex
17	749	Non-elec. machine parts, acces. NES	37,378	Simple	Complex
18	541	Medicinal, etc., products	37,261	Simple	Complex
19	713	Internal combustion piston engine	36,488	Complex	Complex
20	772	Switchgear, etc., parts NES	36,341	Complex	Complex
21	667	Pearl, prec., semi-p. stone	31,220	Simple	Simple
22	821	Furniture, parts thereof	30,279	Simple	Simple
23	684	Aluminum	30,037	Simple	Simple
24	893	Articles of plastic NES	29,080	Simple	Complex
25	851	Footwear	28,859	Simple	Simple
26	793	Ships and boats, etc.,	28,666	Complex	Complex
27	843	Women's outerwear nonknit	28,165	Simple	Simple
28	845	Outerwear knit non-elastic	26,629	Simple	Simple
29	011	Meat fresh, chilled, frozen	26,388	Simple	Simple
30	736	Metalworking machine tools	25,060	Complex	Complex
		Top 30 subtotal	1,507,017		
		World exports	3,426,665		
		% of total	44.0		

Top 30 goods exports traded globally, grouped by complex/simple classification, 1990

Rank	SITC	Commodity	Value (million US$)	Product	Process	% of total
2	333	Crude petroleum	148,822	Simple	Simple	
21	667	Pearl, prec., semi-p. stone	31,220	Simple	Simple	
22	821	Furniture, parts thereof	30,279	Simple	Simple	
23	684	Aluminum	30,037	Simple	Simple	
25	851	Footwear	28,859	Simple	Simple	
27	843	Women's outerwear nonknit	28,165	Simple	Simple	
28	845	Outerwear knit non-elastic	26,629	Simple	Simple	
29	011	Meat fresh, chilled, frozen	26,388	Simple	Simple	
		Subtotal simple/simple	350,399			23.3
4	334	Petroleum products refined	76,894	Simple	Complex	
9	641	Paper and paperboard	51,086	Simple	Complex	
11	583	Polymerization, etc., products	48,921	Simple	Complex	
14	674	Iron, steel univ., plate, sheet	37,809	Simple	Complex	
17	749	Non-elec. machine parts, acces. NES	37,378	Simple	Complex	
18	541	Medicinal, etc., products	37,261	Simple	Complex	
24	893	Articles of plastic NES	29,080	Simple	Complex	
		Subtotal simple/complex	318,429			21.1
1	781	Pass. motor vehicles exc. buses	168,722	Complex	Complex	
3	784	Motor vehicle parts, acces. NES	83,681	Complex	Complex	
5	752	Automatic data processing eqpt	71,203	Complex	Complex	
6	776	Transistors, valves, etc.	63,968	Complex	Complex	
7	792	Aircraft, etc.	63,638	Complex	Complex	
8	764	Telecom eqpt, parts, acces. NES	58,934	Complex	Complex	
10	759	Office, adp. machine parts., acces.	49,910	Complex	Complex	
12	728	Other machinery for special indus.	38,363	Complex	Complex	
13	778	Electrical machinery NES	38,146	Complex	Complex	
15	874	Measuring, controlling eqpt	37,540	Complex	Complex	
16	782	Lorries, spcl mtr vehicles NES	37,529	Complex	Complex	
19	713	Internal combustion piston engine	36,488	Complex	Complex	
20	772	Switchgear, etc., parts NES	36,341	Complex	Complex	
26	793	Ships and boats, etc.	28,666	Complex	Complex	
30	736	Metalworking machine tools	25,060	Complex	Complex	
		Subtotal complex/complex	838,189			55.6
		Top 30 subtotal	1,507,017			

Top 30 manufactured goods exports traded globally, 1990 (SITC codes 500 through 800)

Rank	SITC	Commodity	Value (million US$)	Classification Product	Classification Process
1	781	Pass. motor vehicles exc. buses	168,722	Complex	Complex
2	784	Motor vehicle parts, acces. NES	83,681	Complex	Complex
3	752	Automatic data processing eqpt	71,203	Complex	Complex
4	776	Transistors, valves, etc.	63,968	Complex	Complex
5	792	Aircraft, etc.	63,638	Complex	Complex
6	764	Telecom eqpt, parts, acces. NES	58,934	Complex	Complex
7	641	Paper and paperboard	51,086	Simple	Complex
8	759	Office, adp. machine parts., acces.	49,910	Complex	Complex
9	583	Polymerization, etc., products	48,921	Simple	Complex
10	728	Other machinery for special indus.	38,363	Complex	Complex
11	778	Electrical machinery NES	38,146	Complex	Complex
12	674	Iron, steel univ., plate, sheet	37,809	Simple	Complex
13	874	Measuring, controlling eqpt	37,540	Complex	Complex
14	782	Lorries, spcl mtr vehicles NES	37,529	Complex	Complex
15	749	Non-elec. machine parts, acces. NES	37,378	Simple	Complex
16	541	Medicinal, etc., products	37,261	Simple	Complex
17	713	Internal combustion piston engine	36,488	Complex	Complex
18	772	Switchgear, etc., parts NES	36,341	Complex	Complex
19	667	Pearl, prec., semi-p. stone	31,220	Simple	Simple
20	821	Furniture, parts thereof	30,279	Simple	Simple
21	684	Aluminum	30,037	Simple	Simple
22	893	Articles of plastic NES	29,080	Simple	Complex
23	851	Footwear	28,859	Simple	Simple
24	793	Ships and boats, etc.	28,666	Complex	Complex
25	843	Women's outerwear nonknit	28,165	Simple	Simple
26	845	Outerwear knit non-elastic	26,629	Simple	Simple
27	736	Metalworking machine tools	25,060	Complex	Complex
28	651	Textile yarn and thread	24,746	Simple	Simple
29	744	Mechanical handling eqpt	24,358	Simple	Complex
30	894	Toys, sporting goods, etc.	24,254	Simple	Simple
		Top 30 subtotal	1,328,271		

**Top 30 manufactured goods exports traded globally, 1990
(SITC codes 500 through 800): grouped by complex/simple classification**

Rank	SITC	Commodity	Value (million US$)	Product	Process	% of total
19	667	Pearl, prec., semi-p. stone	31,220	Simple	Simple	
20	821	Furniture, parts thereof	30,279	Simple	Simple	
21	684	Aluminum	30,037	Simple	Simple	
23	851	Footwear	28,859	Simple	Simple	
25	843	Women's outerwear nonknit	28,165	Simple	Simple	
26	845	Outerwear knit non-elastic	26,629	Simple	Simple	
28	651	Textile yarn and thread	24,746	Simple	Simple	
30	894	Toys, sporting goods, etc.	24,254	Simple	Simple	
		Subtotal simple/simple	224,189			16.9
7	641	Paper and paperboard	51,086	Simple	Complex	
9	583	Polymerization, etc., products	48,921	Simple	Complex	
12	674	Iron, steel univ., plate, sheet	37,809	Simple	Complex	
15	749	Non-elec. machine parts, acces. NES	37,378	Simple	Complex	
16	541	Medicinal, etc., products	37,261	Simple	Complex	
22	893	Articles of plastic NES	29,080	Simple	Complex	
29	744	Mechanical handling eqpt	24,358	Simple	Complex	
		Subtotal simple/complex	265,893			20.0
1	781	Pass. motor vehicles exc. buses	168,722	Complex	Complex	
2	784	Motor vehicle parts, acces. NES	83,681	Complex	Complex	
3	752	Automatic data processing eqpt	71,203	Complex	Complex	
4	776	Transistors, valves, etc.	63,968	Complex	Complex	
5	792	Aircraft, etc.	63,638	Complex	Complex	
6	764	Telecom eqpt, parts, acces. NES	58,934	Complex	Complex	
8	759	Office, adp. machine parts., acces.	49,910	Complex	Complex	
10	728	Other machinery for special indus.	38,363	Complex	Complex	
11	778	Electrical machinery NES	38,146	Complex	Complex	
13	874	Measuring, controlling eqpt	37,540	Complex	Complex	
14	782	Lorries, spcl mtr vehicles NES	37,529	Complex	Complex	
17	713	Internal combustion piston engine	36,488	Complex	Complex	
18	772	Switchgear, etc., parts NES	36,341	Complex	Complex	
24	793	Ships and boats, etc.	28,666	Complex	Complex	
27	736	Metalworking machine tools	25,060	Complex	Complex	
		Subtotal complex/complex	838,189			63.1
		Top 30 subtotal	1,328,271			

United States 1990 balance of trade (million US$, 1995 equivalent) on top 30 manufactured goods traded globally

SITC	Commodity	Exports	Imports	Trade balance
651	Textile yarn and thread	1,293	0	1,293
667	Pearl, prec., semi-p. stone	1,802	4,631	−2,829
684	Aluminum	2,868	2,928	−60
821	Furniture, parts thereof	1,933	5,509	−3,576
843	Women's outerwear nonknit	0	8,221	−8,221
845	Outerwear knit non-elastic	0	7,097	−7,097
851	Footwear	0	9,570	−9,570
894	Toys, sporting goods, etc.	2,208	9,493	−7,285
	Subtotal simple/simple	10,104	47,449	−37,345
	In 1995 $	11,609	54,519	−42,909
541	Medicinal, etc., products	4,177	2,540	1,637
583	Polymerization, etc., products	5,431	2,521	2,910
641	Paper and paperboard	3,852	8,282	−4,430
674	Iron, steel univ., plate, sheet	0	3,714	−3,714
744	Mechanical handling eqpt	3,089	2,878	211
749	Non-elec. machine parts, acces. NES	3,309	4,604	−1,295
893	Articles of plastic NES	2,904	3,849	−945
	Subtotal simple/complex	22,762	28,388	−5,626
	In 1995 $	26,154	32,618	−6,464
713	Internal combustion piston engine	5,755	7,286	−1,531
728	Other machinery for special indus.	4,588	3,886	702
736	Metalworking machine tools	1,903	3,010	−1,107
752	Automatic data processing eqpt	15,682	15,757	−75
759	Office, adp. machine parts., acces.	11,185	8,988	2,197
764	Telecom eqpt, parts, acces. NES	8,388	11,840	−3,452
772	Switchgear, etc., parts NES	5,724	6,099	−375
776	Transistors, valves, etc.	13,991	13,139	852
778	Electrical machinery NES	5,033	6,036	−1,003
781	Pass. motor vehicles exc. buses	10,811	46,871	−36,060
782	Lorries, spcl mtr vehicles NES	3,163	8,680	−5,517
784	Motor vehicle parts, acces. NES	14,982	16,604	−1,622
792	Aircraft, etc.	30,549	6,428	24,121
793	Ships and boats, etc.	1,299	0	1,299
874	Measuring, controlling eqpt	9,033	4,203	4,830
	Subtotal complex/complex	142,086	158,827	−16,741
	In 1995 $	163,257	182,492	−19,235
	Top 30 goods subtotal	174,952	234,664	−59,712
	In 1995 $	201,020	269,629	−68,609

Japan 1990 balance of trade (million US$, 1995 equivalent) on top 30 manufactured goods traded globally

SITC	Commodity	Exports	Imports	Trade balance
651	Textile yarn and thread	1,162	1,201	−39
667	Pearl, prec., semi-p. stone	0	3,379	−3,379
684	Aluminum	0	4,771	−4,771
821	Furniture, parts thereof	0	1,485	−1,485
843	Women's outerwear nonknit	0	1,894	−1,894
845	Outerwear knit non-elastic	0	2,002	−2,002
851	Footwear	0	1,283	−1,283
894	Toys, sporting goods, etc.	1,516	1,819	−303
	Subtotal simple/simple	2,678	17,834	−15,156
	In 1995 $	3,077	20,491	−17,414
541	Medicinal, etc., products	879	2,836	−1,957
583	Polymerization, etc., products	2,676	785	1,891
641	Paper and paperboard	1,540	1,039	501
674	Iron, steel univ., plate, sheet	6,389	997	5,392
744	Mechanical handling eqpt	3,035	0	3,035
749	Non-elec. machine parts, acces. NES	5,090	1,082	4,008
893	Articles of plastic NES	935	799	136
	Subtotal simple/complex	20,544	7,538	13,006
	In 1995 $	23,605	8,661	14,944
713	Internal combustion piston engine	6,400	0	6,400
728	Other machinery for special indus.	4,620	1,111	3,509
736	Metalworking machine tools	4,317	793	3,524
752	Automatic data processing eqpt	12,172	2,950	9,222
759	Office, adp. machine parts., acces.	8,764	2,171	6,593
764	Telecom eqpt, parts, acces. NES	15,161	1,982	13,179
772	Switchgear, etc., parts NES	5,412	1,013	4,399
776	Transistors, valves, etc.,	13,347	3,310	10,037
778	Electrical machinery NES	7,389	1,440	5,949
781	Pass. motor vehicles exc. buses	41,348	6,189	35,159
782	Lorries, spcl mtr vehicles NES	8,502	0	8,502
784	Motor vehicle parts, acces. NES	11,288	777	10,511
792	Aircraft, etc.	0	3,261	−3,261
793	Ships and boats, etc.	5,566	0	5,566
874	Measuring, controlling eqpt	3,819	2,293	1,526
	Subtotal complex/complex	148,105	27,290	120,815
	In 1995 $	170,173	31,356	138,816
	Top 30 goods subtotal	171,327	52,662	118,665
	In 1995 $	196,855	60,509	136,346

Top 30 goods exports traded globally, 1985

Rank	SITC	Commodity	Value (million US$)	Classification	
				Product	Process
1	333	Crude petroleum	170,755	Simple	Simple
2	781	Pass. motor vehicles exc. buses	82,487	Complex	Complex
3	334	Petroleum products refined	73,405	Simple	Complex
4	784	Motor vehicle parts, acces. NES	42,097	Complex	Complex
5	341	Gas, natural and manufactured	29,471	Simple	Simple
6	792	Aircraft, etc.	28,504	Complex	Complex
7	752	Automatic data processing eqpt	26,020	Complex	Complex
8	764	Telecom eqpt, parts, acces. NES	24,650	Complex	Complex
9	782	Lorries, spcl mtr vehicles NES	23,007	Complex	Complex
10	776	Transistors, valves, etc.	22,515	Complex	Complex
11	641	Paper and paperboard	22,260	Simple	Complex
12	759	Office, adp. machine parts., acces.	20,991	Complex	Complex
13	793	Ships and boats, etc.	19,284	Complex	Complex
14	874	Measuring, controlling eqpt	18,950	Complex	Complex
15	674	Iron, steel univ., plate, sheet	18,528	Simple	Complex
16	583	Polymerization, etc., products	17,913	Simple	Complex
17	713	Internal combustion piston engine	17,811	Complex	Complex
18	541	Medicinal, etc., products	15,834	Simple	Complex
19	728	Other machinery for special indus.	15,818	Complex	Complex
20	778	Electrical machinery NES	15,622	Complex	Complex
21	749	Non-elec. machine parts, acces. NES	14,831	Simple	Complex
22	772	Switchgear, etc., parts NES	14,767	Complex	Complex
23	651	Textile yarn and thread	14,018	Simple	Simple
24	678	Iron, steel tubes, pipes, etc.	13,780	Simple	Complex
25	684	Aluminum	12,923	Simple	Simple
26	041	Wheat, etc., unmilled	12,856	Simple	Simple
27	011	Meat fresh, chilled, frozen	12,853	Simple	Simple
28	723	Civil eng. & cont. plant & eqpt	12,797	Simple	Simple
29	071	Coffee	12,624	Simple	Simple
30	673	Iron and steel shapes	12,612	Simple	Complex
		Top 30 subtotal	839,983		
		World exports	1,943,169		
		% of total	43.2		

Top 30 goods exports traded globally, grouped by complex/simple classification, 1995

Rank	SITC	Commodity	Value (million US$)	Product	Process	% of total
1	333	Crude petroleum	170,755	Simple	Simple	
5	341	Gas, natural and manufactured	29,471	Simple	Simple	
23	651	Textile yarn and thread	14,018	Simple	Simple	
25	684	Aluminum	12,923	Simple	Simple	
26	041	Wheat, etc., unmilled	12,856	Simple	Simple	
27	011	Meat fresh, chilled, frozen	12,853	Simple	Simple	
28	723	Civil eng. & cont. plant & eqpt	12,797	Simple	Simple	
29	071	Coffee	12,624	Simple	Simple	
		Subtotal simple/simple	278,297			33.1
3	334	Petroleum products refined	73,405	Simple	Complex	
11	641	Paper and paperboard	22,260	Simple	Complex	
15	674	Iron, steel univ., plate, sheet	18,528	Simple	Complex	
16	583	Polymerization, etc., products	17,913	Simple	Complex	
18	541	Medicinal, etc., products	15,834	Simple	Complex	
21	749	Non-elec. machine parts, acces. NES	14,831	Simple	Complex	
24	678	Iron, steel tubes, pipes etc.	13,780	Simple	Complex	
30	673	Iron and steel shapes	12,612	Simple	Complex	
		Subtotal simple/complex	189,163			22.5
2	781	Pass. motor vehicles exc. buses	82,487	Complex	Complex	
4	784	Motor vehicle parts, acces. NES	42,097	Complex	Complex	
6	792	Aircraft, etc.	28,504	Complex	Complex	
7	752	Automatic data processing eqpt	26,020	Complex	Complex	
8	764	Telecom eqpt, parts, acces. NES	24,650	Complex	Complex	
9	782	Lorries, spcl mtr vehicles NES	23,007	Complex	Complex	
10	776	Transistors, valves, etc.	22,515	Complex	Complex	
12	759	Office, adp. machine parts., acces.	20,991	Complex	Complex	
13	793	Ships and boats, etc.	19,284	Complex	Complex	
14	874	Measuring, controlling eqpt	18,950	Complex	Complex	
17	713	Internal combustion piston engine	17,811	Complex	Complex	
19	728	Other machinery for special indus.	15,818	Complex	Complex	
20	778	Electrical machinery NES	15,622	Complex	Complex	
22	772	Switchgear, etc., parts NES	14,767	Complex	Complex	
		Subtotal complex/complex	372,523			44.3
		Top 30 subtotal	839,983			

Top 30 manufactured goods exports traded globally, 1985
(SITC codes 500 through 800)

Rank	SITC	Commodity	Value (million US$)	Classification	
				Product	Process
1	781	Pass. motor vehicles exc. buses	82,487	Complex	Complex
2	784	Motor vehicle parts, acces. NES	42,097	Complex	Complex
3	792	Aircraft, etc.	28,504	Complex	Complex
4	752	Automatic data processing eqpt	26,020	Complex	Complex
5	764	Telecom eqpt, parts, acces. NES	24,650	Complex	Complex
6	782	Lorries, spcl mtr vehicles NES	23,007	Complex	Complex
7	776	Transistors, valves, etc.	22,515	Complex	Complex
8	641	Paper and paperboard	22,260	Simple	Complex
9	759	Office, adp. machine parts., acces.	20,991	Complex	Complex
10	793	Ships and boats, etc.	19,284	Complex	Complex
11	874	Measuring, controlling eqpt	18,950	Complex	Complex
12	674	Iron, steel univ., plate, sheet	18,528	Simple	Complex
13	583	Polymerization, etc., products	17,913	Simple	Complex
14	713	Internal combustion piston engine	17,811	Complex	Complex
15	541	Medicinal, etc., products	15,834	Simple	Complex
16	728	Other machinery for special indus.	15,818	Complex	Complex
17	778	Electrical machinery NES	15,622	Complex	Complex
18	749	Non-elec. machine parts, acces. NES	14,831	Simple	Complex
19	772	Switchgear, etc., parts NES	14,767	Complex	Complex
20	651	Textile yarn and thread	14,018	Simple	Simple
21	678	Iron, steel tubes, pipes, etc.	13,780	Simple	Complex
22	684	Aluminum	12,923	Simple	Simple
23	723	Civil eng. & cont. plant & eqpt	12,797	Simple	Simple
24	673	Iron and steel shapes	12,612	Simple	Complex
25	667	Pearl, prec., semi-p. stone	12,261	Simple	Simple
26	763	Video & audio eqpt & unrec. med.	11,343	Complex	Complex
27	843	Women's outerwear nonknit	11,222	Simple	Simple
28	851	Footwear	10,900	Simple	Simple
29	682	Copper	10,833	Simple	Simple
30	741	Heating, cooling eqpt	10,102	Simple	Complex
		Top 30 subtotal	594,680		

**Top 30 manufactured goods exports traded globally, 1985
(SITC codes 500 through 800): grouped by complex/simple classification**

Rank	SITC	Commodity	Value (million US$)	Product	Process	% of total
20	651	Textile yarn and thread	14,018	Simple	Simple	
22	684	Aluminum	12,923	Simple	Simple	
23	723	Civil eng. & cont. plant & eqpt	12,797	Simple	Simple	
25	667	Pearl, prec., semi-p. stone	12,261	Simple	Simple	
27	843	Women's outerwear nonknit	11,222	Simple	Simple	
28	851	Footwear	10,900	Simple	Simple	
29	682	Copper	10,833	Simple	Simple	
		Subtotal simple/simple	84,954			14.3
8	641	Paper and paperboard	22,260	Simple	Complex	
12	674	Iron, steel univ., plate, sheet	18,528	Simple	Complex	
13	583	Polymerization, etc., products	17,913	Simple	Complex	
15	541	Medicinal, etc., products	15,834	Simple	Complex	
18	749	Non-elec. machine parts, acces. NES	14,831	Simple	Complex	
21	678	Iron, steel tubes, pipes etc.	13,780	Simple	Complex	
24	673	Iron and steel shapes	12,612	Simple	Complex	
30	741	Heating, cooling eqpt	10,102	Simple	Complex	
		Subtotal simple/complex	125,860			21.2
1	781	Pass. motor vehicles exc. buses	82,487	Complex	Complex	
2	784	Motor vehicle parts, acces. NES	42,097	Complex	Complex	
3	792	Aircraft, etc.	28,504	Complex	Complex	
4	752	Automatic data processing eqpt	26,020	Complex	Complex	
5	764	Telecom eqpt, parts, acces. NES	24,650	Complex	Complex	
6	782	Lorries, spcl mtr vehicles NES	23,007	Complex	Complex	
7	776	Transistors, valves, etc.	22,515	Complex	Complex	
9	759	Office, adp. machine parts., acces.	20,991	Complex	Complex	
10	793	Ships and boats, etc.	19,284	Complex	Complex	
11	874	Measuring, controlling eqpt	18,950	Complex	Complex	
14	713	Internal combustion piston engine	17,811	Complex	Complex	
16	728	Other machinery for special indus.	15,818	Complex	Complex	
17	778	Electrical machinery NES	15,622	Complex	Complex	
19	772	Switchgear, etc., parts NES	14,767	Complex	Complex	
26	763	Video & audio eqpt & unrec. med.	11,343	Complex	Complex	
		Subtotal complex/complex	383,866			64.5
		Top 30 subtotal	594,680			

United States 1985 Balance of Trade (million US$, 1995 equivalent) on top 30 manufactured goods traded globally

SITC	Commodity	Exports	Imports	Trade balance
651	Textile yarn and thread	637	0	637
667	Pearl, prec., semi-p. stone	663	3,645	−2,982
682	Copper	0	1,203	−1,203
684	Aluminum	931	2,066	−1,135
723	Civil eng. & contractors' plant & eqpt	739	1,937	−1,198
843	Women's outerwear nonknit	0	5,182	−5,182
851	Footwear	0	6,104	−6,104
	Subtotal simple/simple	2,970	20,137	−17,167
	In 1995 $	4,072	27,608	−23,536
541	Medicinal, etc., products	2,843	1,718	1,125
583	Polymerization, etc., products	1,899	0	1,899
641	Paper and paperboard	1,760	5,657	−3,897
673	Iron and steel shapes	0	1,946	−1,946
674	Iron, steel univ., plate, sheet	0	4,508	−4,508
678	Iron, steel tubes, pipes, etc.	540	2,671	−2,131
741	Heating, cooling eqpt	1,813	0	1,813
749	Non-electric machine parts, acces. NES	1,578	2,195	−617
	Subtotal simple/complex	10,433	18,695	−8,262
	In 1995 $	14,304	25,631	−11,327
713	Internal combustion piston engine	4,299	5,224	−925
728	Other machinery for special indus.	2,866	2,472	394
752	Automatic data processing eqpt	7,392	4,117	3,275
759	Office, adp. machine parts., acces.	7,817	5,327	2,490
763	Video & audio eqpt & unrec. med.	0	6,037	−6,037
764	Telecom eqpt, parts, acces. NES	3,870	8,068	−4,198
772	Switchgear, etc., parts NES	2,294	2,344	−50
776	Transistors, valves, etc.	5,319	6,294	−975
778	Electrical machinery NES	2,638	3,627	−989
781	Pass. motor vehicles exc. buses	6,154	39,089	−32,935
782	Lorries, spcl mtr vehicles NES	2,317	7,558	−5,241
784	Motor vehicle parts, acces. NES	10,863	10,639	224
792	Aircraft, etc.	14,498	3,600	10,898
793	Ships and boats, etc.	553	0	553
874	Measuring, controlling eqpt	5,567	2,356	3,211
	Subtotal complex/complex	76,447	106,752	−30,305
	In 1995 $	104,809	146,357	−41,548
	Top 30 goods subtotal	89,850	145,584	−55,734
	In 1995 $	123,184	199,596	−76,411

Japan 1985 Balance of Trade (million US$, 1995 equivalent) on top 30 manufactured goods traded globally

SITC	Commodity	Exports	Imports	Trade balance
651	Textile yarn and thread	1,025	834	191
667	Pearl, prec., semi-p. stone	0	759	−759
682	Copper	585	592	−7
684	Aluminum	615	1,861	−1,246
723	Civil eng. & contractors' plant & eqpt	2,002	0	2,002
843	Women's outerwear nonknit	0	273	−273
851	Footwear	0	391	−391
	Subtotal simple/simple	4,227	4,710	−483
	In 1995 $	5,795	6,457	−662
541	Medicinal, etc., products	0	1,292	−1,292
583	Polymerization, etc., products	1,425	340	1,085
641	Paper and paperboard	836	500	336
673	Iron and steel shapes	2,345	0	2,345
674	Iron, steel univ., plate, sheet	5,209	346	4,863
678	Iron, steel tubes, pipes, etc.	4,029	0	4,029
741	Heating, cooling eqpt	1,841	0	1,841
749	Non-elec. machine parts, acces. NES	2,113	421	1,692
	Subtotal simple/complex	17,798	2,899	14,899
	In 1995 $	24,401	3,975	20,427
713	Internal combustion piston engine	2,861	0	2,861
728	Other machinery for special indus.	2,132	373	1,759
752	Automatic data processing eqpt	4,625	1,024	3,601
759	Office, adp. machine parts, acces.	2,106	502	1,604
763	Video & audio eqpt & unrec. med.	8,704	0	8,704
764	Telecom eqpt, parts, acces. NES	7,299	445	6,854
772	Switchgear, etc., parts NES	2,280	427	1,853
776	Transistors, valves, etc.	4,753	1,016	3,737
778	Electrical machinery NES	3,413	590	2,823
781	Pass. motor vehicles exc. buses	25,402	539	24,863
782	Lorries, spcl mtr vehicles NES	8,184	0	8,184
784	Motor vehicle parts, acces. NES	5,366	0	5,366
792	Aircraft, etc.	0	1,497	−1,497
793	Ships and boats, etc.	5,929	286	5,643
874	Measuring, controlling eqpt	1,751	1,022	729
	Subtotal complex/complex	84,805	7,721	77,084
	In 1995 $	116,268	10,585	105,682
	Top 30 goods subtotal	106,830	15,330	91,500
	In 1995 $	146,464	21,017	125,447

Top 30 goods exports traded globally, 1980

Rank	SITC	Commodity	Value (million US$)	Classification Product	Classification Process
1	333	Crude petroleum	275,933	Simple	Simple
2	334	Petroleum products refined	69,139	Simple	Complex
3	781	Pass. motor vehicles exc. buses	58,881	Complex	Complex
4	784	Motor vehicle parts, acces. NES	32,835	Complex	Complex
5	792	Aircraft, etc.	25,025	Complex	Complex
6	341	Gas, natural and manufactured	24,858	Simple	Simple
7	782	Lorries, spcl mtr vehicles NES	21,779	Complex	Complex
8	641	Paper and paperboard	20,684	Simple	Complex
9	674	Iron, steel univ., plate, sheet	20,391	Simple	Complex
10	667	Pearl, prec., semi-p. stone	19,263	Simple	Simple
11	583	Polymerization, etc., products	17,832	Simple	Complex
12	764	Telecom eqpt, parts, acces. NES	17,651	Complex	Complex
13	749	Non-elec. machine parts, acces. NES	15,866	Simple	Complex
14	011	Meat fresh, chilled, frozen	14,994	Simple	Simple
15	678	Iron, steel tubes, pipes etc.	14,922	Simple	Complex
16	041	Wheat, etc., unmilled	14,904	Simple	Simple
17	728	Other machinery for special indus.	14,853	Complex	Complex
18	874	Measuring, controlling eqpt	14,837	Complex	Complex
19	713	Internal combustion piston engine	14,778	Complex	Complex
20	673	Iron and steel shapes	14,327	Simple	Complex
21	778	Electrical machinery NES	14,190	Complex	Complex
22	793	Ships and boats, etc.	14,055	Complex	Complex
23	541	Medicinal, etc., products	13,790	Simple	Complex
24	682	Copper	13,502	Simple	Simple
25	776	Transistors, valves, etc.	13,465	Complex	Complex
26	287	Base metal, ores, conc., etc.	13,331	Simple	Simple
27	651	Textile yarn and thread	13,213	Simple	Simple
28	684	Aluminum	12,742	Simple	Simple
29	772	Switchgear, etc., parts NES	12,663	Complex	Complex
30	752	Automatic data processing eqpt	12,620	Complex	Complex
		Top 30 subtotal	857,323		
		World exports	2,020,539		
		% of total	42.4		

Top 30 goods exports traded globally grouped by complex/simple classification, 1980

Rank	SITC	Commodity	Value (million US$)	Product	Process	% of total
1	333	Crude petroleum	275,933	Simple	Simple	
6	341	Gas, natural and manufactured	24,858	Simple	Simple	
10	667	Pearl, prec., semi-p. stone	19,263	Simple	Simple	
14	011	Meat fresh, chilled, frozen	14,994	Simple	Simple	
16	041	Wheat, etc., unmilled	14,904	Simple	Simple	
24	682	Copper	13,502	Simple	Simple	
26	287	Base metal, ores, conc., etc.	13,331	Simple	Simple	
27	651	Textile yarn and thread	13,213	Simple	Simple	
28	684	Aluminum	12,742	Simple	Simple	
		Subtotal simple/simple	402,740			47.0
2	334	Petroleum products refined	69,139	Simple	Complex	
8	641	Paper and paperboard	20,684	Simple	Complex	
9	674	Iron, steel univ., plate, sheet	20,391	Simple	Complex	
11	583	Polymerization, etc., products	17,832	Simple	Complex	
13	749	Non-elec. machine parts, acces. NES	15,866	Simple	Complex	
15	678	Iron, steel tubes, pipes, etc.	14,922	Simple	Complex	
20	673	Iron and steel shapes	14,327	Simple	Complex	
23	541	Medicinal, etc., products	13,790	Simple	Complex	
		Subtotal simple/complex	186,951			21.8
3	781	Pass. motor vehicles exc. buses	58,881	Complex	Complex	
4	784	Motor vehicle parts, acces. NES	32,835	Complex	Complex	
5	792	Aircraft, etc.	25,025	Complex	Complex	
7	782	Lorries, spcl mtr vehicles NES	21,779	Complex	Complex	
12	764	Telecom eqpt, parts, acces. NES	17,651	Complex	Complex	
17	728	Other machinery for special indus.	14,853	Complex	Complex	
18	874	Measuring, controlling eqpt	14,837	Complex	Complex	
19	713	Internal combustion piston engine	14,778	Complex	Complex	
21	778	Electrical machinery NES	14,190	Complex	Complex	
22	793	Ships and boats, etc.	14,055	Complex	Complex	
25	776	Transistors, valves, etc.	13,465	Complex	Complex	
29	772	Switchgear, etc., parts NES	12,663	Complex	Complex	
30	752	Automatic data processing eqpt	12,620	Complex	Complex	
		Subtotal complex/complex	267,632			31.2
		Top 30 subtotal	857,323			

**Top 30 manufactured goods exports traded globally, 1980
(SITC codes 500 through 800)**

Rank	SITC	Commodity	Value (million US$)	Product	Process
				Classification	
1	781	Pass. motor vehicles exc. buses	58,881	Complex	Complex
2	784	Motor vehicle parts, acces. NES	32,835	Complex	Complex
3	792	Aircraft, etc.	25,025	Complex	Complex
4	782	Lorries, spcl mtr vehicles NES	21,779	Complex	Complex
5	641	Paper and paperboard	20,684	Simple	Complex
6	674	Iron, steel univ., plate, sheet	20,391	Simple	Complex
7	667	Pearl, prec., semi-p. stone	19,263	Simple	Simple
8	583	Polymerization, etc., products	17,832	Simple	Complex
9	764	Telecom eqpt, parts, acces. NES	17,651	Complex	Complex
10	749	Non-elec. machine parts, acces. NES	15,866	Simple	Complex
11	678	Iron, steel tubes, pipes, etc.	14,922	Simple	Complex
12	728	Other machinery for special indus.	14,853	Complex	Complex
13	874	Measuring, controlling eqpt	14,837	Complex	Complex
14	713	Internal combustion piston engine	14,778	Complex	Complex
15	673	Iron and steel shapes	14,327	Simple	Complex
16	778	Electrical machinery NES	14,190	Complex	Complex
17	793	Ships and boats, etc.	14,055	Complex	Complex
18	541	Medicinal, etc., products	13,790	Simple	Complex
19	682	Copper	13,502	Simple	Simple
20	776	Transistors, valves, etc.	13,465	Complex	Complex
21	651	Textile yarn and thread	13,213	Simple	Simple
22	684	Aluminum	12,742	Simple	Simple
23	772	Switchgear, etc., parts NES	12,663	Complex	Complex
24	752	Automatic data processing eqpt	12,620	Complex	Complex
25	681	Silver, platinum, etc.	11,720	Simple	Simple
26	744	Mechanical handling eqpt	11,423	Simple	Complex
27	598	Miscel. chemical products NES	11,282	Simple	Complex
28	736	Metalworking machine tools	11,206	Complex	Complex
29	741	Heating, cooling eqpt	11,166	Simple	Complex
30	699	Base metal mfrs NES	10,774	Simple	Simple
		Top 30 subtotal	511,735		

**Top 30 manufactured goods exports traded globally, 1980
(SITC codes 500 through 800): grouped by complex/simple classification**

Rank	SITC	Commodity	Value (million US$)	Product	Process	% of total
7	667	Pearl, prec., semi-p. stone	19,263	Simple	Simple	
19	682	Copper	13,502	Simple	Simple	
21	651	Textile yarn and thread	13,213	Simple	Simple	
22	684	Aluminum	12,742	Simple	Simple	
25	681	Silver, platinum, etc.	11,720	Simple	Simple	
30	699	Base metal mfrs NES	10,774	Simple	Simple	
		Subtotal simple/simple	81,214			15.9
5	641	Paper and paperboard	20,684	Simple	Complex	
6	674	Iron, steel univ., plate, sheet	20,391	Simple	Complex	
8	583	Polymerization, etc., products	17,832	Simple	Complex	
10	749	Non-elec. machine parts, acces. NES	15,866	Simple	Complex	
11	678	Iron, steel tubes, pipes, etc.	14,922	Simple	Complex	
15	673	Iron and steel shapes	14,327	Simple	Complex	
18	541	Medicinal, etc., products	13,790	Simple	Complex	
26	744	Mechanical handling eqpt	11,423	Simple	Complex	
27	598	Miscel. chemical products NES	11,282	Simple	Complex	
29	741	Heating, cooling eqpt	11,166	Simple	Complex	
		Subtotal simple/complex	151,683			29.6
1	781	Pass. motor vehicles exc. buses	58,881	Complex	Complex	
2	784	Motor vehicle parts, acces. NES	32,835	Complex	Complex	
3	792	Aircraft, etc.	25,025	Complex	Complex	
4	782	Lorries, spcl mtr vehicles NES	21,779	Complex	Complex	
9	764	Telecom eqpt, parts, acces. NES	17,651	Complex	Complex	
12	728	Other machinery for special indus.	14,853	Complex	Complex	
13	874	Measuring, controlling eqpt	14,837	Complex	Complex	
14	713	Internal combustion piston engine	14,778	Complex	Complex	
16	778	Electrical machinery NES	14,190	Complex	Complex	
17	793	Ships and boats, etc.	14,055	Complex	Complex	
20	776	Transistors, valves, etc.	13,465	Complex	Complex	
23	772	Switchgear, etc., parts NES	12,663	Complex	Complex	
24	752	Automatic data processing eqpt	12,620	Complex	Complex	
28	736	Metalworking machine tools	11,206	Complex	Complex	
		Subtotal complex/complex	278,838			54.5
		Top 30 subtotal	511,735			

United States 1980 Balance of Trade (million US$, 1995 equivalent) on top 30 manufactured goods traded globally

SITC	Commodity	Exports	Imports	Trade balance
651	Textile yarn and thread	760	0	760
667	Pearl, prec., semi-p. stone	1,113	2,719	−1,606
681	Silver, platinum, etc.	1,703	2,500	−797
682	Copper	0	1,535	−1,535
684	Aluminum	1,995	987	1,008
699	Base metal mfrs NES	1,396	1,194	202
	Subtotal simple/simple	6,967	8,935	−1,968
	In 1995 $	12,408	15,913	−3,505
541	Medicinal, etc., products	2,036	803	1,233
583	Polymerization, etc., products	2,173	0	2,173
598	Miscel. chemical products NES	2,057	0	2,057
641	Paper and paperboard	2,189	3,447	−1,258
673	Iron and steel shapes	0	1,556	−1,556
674	Iron, steel univ., plate, sheet	939	2,657	−1,718
678	Iron, steel tubes, pipes, etc.	1,103	2,441	−1,338
741	Heating, cooling eqpt	2,344	0	2,344
744	Mechanical handling eqpt	2,557	607	1,950
749	Non-elec. machine parts, acces. NES	1,822	1,347	475
	Subtotal simple/complex	17,220	12,858	4,362
	In 1995 $	30,669	22,900	7,769
713	Internal combustion piston engine	3,717	2,075	1,642
728	Other machinery for special indus.	2,296	1,120	1,176
736	Metalworking machine tools	1,275	1,666	−391
752	Automatic data processing eqpt	4,616	572	4,044
764	Telecom eqpt, parts, acces. NES	2,750	3,212	−462
772	Switchgear, etc., parts NES	1,780	1,159	621
776	Transistors, valves, etc.	4,056	3,653	403
778	Electrical machinery NES	2,326	1,515	811
781	Pass. motor vehicles exc. buses	4,245	18,017	−13,772
782	Lorries, spcl mtr vehicles NES	2,142	2,093	49
784	Motor vehicle parts, acces. NES	7,597	5,510	2,087
792	Aircraft, etc.	12,894	2,298	10,596
793	Ships and boats, etc.	754	0	754
874	Measuring, controlling eqpt	4,539	1,043	3,496
	Subtotal complex/complex	54,987	43,933	11,054
	In 1995 $	97,932	78,245	19,687
	Top 30 goods subtotal	79,174	65,726	13,448
	In 1995 $	141,009	117,058	23,951

Japan 1980 balance of trade (million US$, 1995 equivalent) on top 30 manufactured goods traded globally

SITC	Commodity	Exports	Imports	Trade balance
651	Textile yarn and thread	0	1,231	−1,231
667	Pearl, prec., semi-p. stone	0	440	−440
681	Silver, platinum, etc.	997	151	846
682	Copper	224	294	−70
684	Aluminum	664	0	664
699	Base metal mfrs NES	2,579	752	1,827
	Subtotal simple/simple	4,464	2,868	1,596
	In 1995 $	7,950	5,108	2,842
541	Medicinal, etc., products	0	1,074	−1,074
583	Polymerization, etc., products	1,253	0	1,253
598	Miscel. chemical products NES	418	610	−192
641	Paper and paperboard	716	384	332
673	Iron and steel shapes	3,004	0	3,004
674	Iron, steel univ., plate, sheet	5,388	187	5,201
678	Iron, steel tubes, pipes, etc.	4,749	0	4,749
741	Heating, cooling eqpt	1,685	0	1,685
744	Mechanical handling eqpt	1,313	0	1,313
749	Non-elec. machine parts, acces. NES	1,835	0	1,835
	Subtotal simple/complex	20,361	2,255	18,106
	In 1995 $	36,263	4,016	32,247
713	Internal combustion piston engine	1,783	0	1,783
728	Other machinery for special indus.	1,179	0	1,179
736	Metalworking machine tools	1,568	0	1,568
752	Automatic data processing eqpt	542	732	−190
764	Telecom eqpt, parts, acces. NES	3,771	292	3,479
772	Switchgear, etc., parts NES	1,629	0	1,629
776	Transistors, valves, etc.	2,307	713	1,594
778	Electrical machinery NES	2,264	334	1,930
781	Pass. motor vehicles exc. buses	16,115	452	15,663
782	Lorries, spcl mtr vehicles NES	6,434	0	6,434
784	Motor vehicle parts, acces. NES	2,168	0	2,168
792	Aircraft, etc.	0	1,000	−1,000
793	Ships and boats, etc.	4,682	575	4,107
874	Measuring, controlling eqpt	895	747	148
	Subtotal complex/complex	45,337	4,845	40,492
	In 1995 $	80,745	8,629	72,116
	Top 30 goods subtotal	70,162	9,968	60,194
	In 1995 $	124,959	17,753	107,206

Top 30 goods exports traded globally, 1975

Rank	SITC	Commodity	Value (million US$)	Classification Product	Process
1	331	Crude petroleum etc.*	112,079	Simple	Simple
2	732	Road motor vehicles	55,342	Complex	Complex
3	719	Machines NES non-electric	37,219	Simple	Complex
4	332	Petroleum products	31,549	Simple	Simple
5	735	Ships and boats	15,046	Complex	Complex
6	729	Electrical machinery NES	14,554	Complex	Complex
7	841	Clothing not of fur	13,384	Simple	Simple
8	711	Power machinery non-electric	12,957	Complex	Complex
9	724	Telecom equipment	12,936	Complex	Complex
10	512	Organic chemicals	12,771	Simple	Complex
11	718	Machines for special industries	12,691	Complex	Complex
12	678	Iron, steel tubes, pipes, etc.	12,293	Simple	Simple
13	061	Sugar and honey*	11,086	Simple	Simple
14	674	Iron, steel univ., plate, sheet	10,680	Simple	Simple
15	041	Wheat etc., unmilled	10,616	Simple	Simple
16	581	Plastic materials, etc.	10,475	Simple	Complex
17	641	Paper and paperboard	9,640	Simple	Simple
18	722	Elec. power machinery, switchgear	9,561	Complex	Complex
19	734	Aircraft	9,086	Complex	Complex
20	714	Office machines	8,973	Complex	Complex
21	861	Instruments, apparatus	8,718	Complex	Complex
22	653	Woven textiles noncotton	8,046	Simple	Simple
23	673	Iron and steel shapes	7,388	Simple	Simple
24	321	Coal, coke, briquettes	7,361	Simple	Simple
25	712	Agricultural machinery	7,318	Complex	Complex
26	044	Maize	6,828	Simple	Simple
27	011	Meat fresh, chilled, frozen	6,770	Simple	Simple
28	599	Chemicals NES	6,573	Simple	Complex
29	541	Medicinal, etc., products	6,563	Simple	Complex
30	651	Textile yarn and thread	6,322	Simple	Simple
		Top 30 subtotal	494,825		
		World exports	877,061		
		% of total	56.4		

*Source: 1977 Yearbook

Top 30 goods exports traded globally grouped by complex/simple classification, 1975

Rank	SITC	Commodity	Value (million US$)	Product	Process	% of total
1	331	Crude petroleum, etc.*	112,079	Simple	Simple	
4	332	Petroleum products	31,549	Simple	Simple	
7	841	Clothing not of fur	13,384	Simple	Simple	
12	678	Iron, steel tubes, pipes, etc.	12,293	Simple	Simple	
13	061	Sugar and honey*	11,086	Simple	Simple	
14	674	Iron, steel univ., plate, sheet	10,680	Simple	Simple	
15	041	Wheat, etc., unmilled	10,616	Simple	Simple	
17	641	Paper and paperboard	9,640	Simple	Simple	
22	653	Woven textiles noncotton	8,046	Simple	Simple	
23	673	Iron and steel shapes	7,388	Simple	Simple	
24	321	Coal, coke, briquettes	7,361	Simple	Simple	
26	044	Maize	6,828	Simple	Simple	
27	011	Meat fresh, chilled, frozen	6,770	Simple	Simple	
30	651	Textile yarn and thread	6,322	Simple	Simple	
		Subtotal simple/simple	254,042			51.3
3	719	Machines NES non-electric	37,219	Simple	Complex	
10	512	Organic chemicals	12,771	Simple	Complex	
16	581	Plastic materials, etc.	10,475	Simple	Complex	
28	599	Chemicals NES	6,573	Simple	Complex	
29	541	Medicinal, etc., products	6,563	Simple	Complex	
		Subtotal simple/complex	73,601			14.9
2	732	Road motor vehicles	55,342	Complex	Complex	
5	735	Ships and boats	15,046	Complex	Complex	
6	729	Electrical machinery NES	14,554	Complex	Complex	
8	711	Power machinery non-electric	12,957	Complex	Complex	
9	724	Telecom equipment	12,936	Complex	Complex	
11	718	Machines for special industries	12,691	Complex	Complex	
18	722	Elec. power machinery, switchgear	9,561	Complex	Complex	
19	734	Aircraft	9,086	Complex	Complex	
20	714	Office machines	8,973	Complex	Complex	
21	861	Instruments, apparatus	8,718	Complex	Complex	
25	712	Agricultural machinery	7,318	Complex	Complex	
		Subtotal complex/complex	167,182			33.8
		Top 30 subtotal	494,825			

*Source: 1977 Yearbook

**Top 30 manufactured goods exports traded globally, 1975
(SITC codes 500 through 800)**

Rank	SITC	Commodity	Value (million US$)	Classification Product	Process
1	732	Road motor vehicles	55,342	Complex	Complex
2	719	Machines NES non-electric	37,219	Simple	Complex
3	735	Ships and boats	15,046	Complex	Complex
4	729	Electrical machinery NES	14,554	Complex	Complex
5	841	Clothing not of fur	13,384	Simple	Simple
6	711	Power machinery non-electric	12,957	Complex	Complex
7	724	Telecom equipment	12,936	Complex	Complex
8	512	Organic chemicals	12,771	Simple	Complex
9	718	Machines for special industries	12,691	Complex	Complex
10	678	Iron, steel tubes, pipes, etc.	12,293	Simple	Simple
11	674	Iron, steel univ., plate, sheet	10,680	Simple	Simple
12	581	Plastic materials, etc.	10,475	Simple	Complex
13	641	Paper and paperboard	9,640	Simple	Simple
14	722	Elec. power machinery, switchgear	9,561	Complex	Complex
15	734	Aircraft	9,086	Complex	Complex
16	714	Office machines	8,973	Complex	Complex
17	861	Instruments, apparatus	8,718	Complex	Complex
18	653	Woven textiles noncotton	8,046	Simple	Simple
19	673	Iron and steel shapes	7,388	Simple	Simple
20	712	Agricultural machinery	7,318	Complex	Complex
21	599	Chemicals NES	6,573	Simple	Complex
22	541	Medicinal, etc., products	6,563	Simple	Complex
23	651	Textile yarn and thread	6,322	Simple	Simple
24	715	Metalworking machinery	6,239	Complex	Complex
25	717	Textile, leather machinery	6,198	Simple	Simple
26	682	Copper	5,817	Simple	Simple
27	667	Pearl, prec., semi-p. stone	5,680	Simple	Simple
28	561	Fertilizers, manufactured	5,162	Simple	Simple
29	698	Metal manufactures NES	4,660	Simple	Simple
30	629	Rubber articles, NES	4,602	Simple	Complex
		Top 30 subtotal	346,894		

**Top 30 manufactured goods exports traded globally, 1975
(SITC codes 500 through 800): grouped by complex/simple classification**

Rank	SITC	Commodity	Value (million US$)	Product	Process	% of total
5	841	Clothing not of fur	13,384	Simple	Simple	
10	678	Iron, steel tubes, pipes, etc.	12,293	Simple	Simple	
11	674	Iron, steel univ., plate, sheet	10,680	Simple	Simple	
13	641	Paper and paperboard	9,640	Simple	Simple	
18	653	Woven textiles noncotton	8,046	Simple	Simple	
19	673	Iron and steel shapes	7,388	Simple	Simple	
23	651	Textile yarn and thread	6,322	Simple	Simple	
25	717	Textile, leather machinery	6,198	Simple	Simple	
26	682	Copper	5,817	Simple	Simple	
27	667	Pearl, prec., semi-p. stone	5,680	Simple	Simple	
28	561	Fertilizers, manufactured	5,162	Simple	Simple	
29	698	Metal manufactures NES	4,660	Simple	Simple	
		Subtotal simple/simple	95,270			27.5
2	719	Machines NES non-electric	37,219	Simple	Complex	
8	512	Organic chemicals	12,771	Simple	Complex	
12	581	Plastic materials, etc.	10,475	Simple	Complex	
21	599	Chemicals NES	6,573	Simple	Complex	
22	541	Medicinal, etc., products	6,563	Simple	Complex	
30	629	Rubber articles, NES	4,602	Simple	Complex	
		Subtotal simple/complex	78,203			22.5
1	732	Road motor vehicles	55,342	Complex	Complex	
3	735	Ships and boats	15,046	Complex	Complex	
4	729	Electrical machinery NES	14,554	Complex	Complex	
6	711	Power machinery non-electric	12,957	Complex	Complex	
7	724	Telecom equipment	12,936	Complex	Complex	
9	718	Machines for special industries	12,691	Complex	Complex	
14	722	Elec. power machinery, switchgear	9,561	Complex	Complex	
15	734	Aircraft	9,086	Complex	Complex	
16	714	Office machines	8,973	Complex	Complex	
17	861	Instruments, apparatus	8,718	Complex	Complex	
20	712	Agricultural machinery	7,318	Complex	Complex	
24	715	Metalworking machinery	6,239	Complex	Complex	
		Subtotal complex/complex	173,421			50.0
		Top 30 subtotal	346,894			

United States 1975 Balance of Trade (million US$, 1995 equivalent) on top 30 manufactured goods traded globally

SITC	Commodity	Exports	Imports	Trade balance
561	Fertilizers, manufactured	1,084	557	527
641	Paper and paperboard	1,136	1,582	−446
651	Textile yarn and thread	300	130	170
653	Woven textiles noncotton	391	442	−51
667	Pearl, prec., semi-p. stone	397	851	−454
673	Iron and steel shapes	183	942	−759
674	Iron, steel univ., plate, sheet	328	1,728	−1,400
678	Iron, steel tubes, pipes, etc.	1,427	1,040	387
682	Copper	336	419	−83
698	Metal manufactures NES	583	599	−16
717	Textile, leather machinery	497	521	−24
841	Clothing not of fur	395	2,536	−2,141
	Subtotal simple/simple	7,057	11,347	−4,290
	In 1995 $	17,988	28,924	−10,935
512	Organic chemicals	2,392	1,084	1,308
541	Medicinal, etc., products	876	0	876
581	Plastic materials, etc.	1,177	0	1,177
599	Chemicals NES	1,237	0	1,237
629	Rubber articles, NES	420	591	−171
719	Machines NES non-electric	7,626	1,977	5,649
	Subtotal simple/complex	13,728	3,652	10,076
	In 1995 $	34,993	9,309	25,684
711	Power machinery non-electric	3,595	1,665	1,930
712	Agricultural machinery	2,108	872	1,236
714	Office machines	2,674	1,067	1,607
715	Metalworking machinery	933	368	565
718	Machines for special industries	3,650	555	3,095
722	Elec. power machinery, switchgear	1,724	557	1,167
724	Telecom equipment	1,630	2,098	−468
729	Electrical machinery NES	3,562	1,697	1,865
732	Road motor vehicles	10,096	11,417	−1,321
734	Aircraft	6,194	519	5,675
735	Ships and boats	329	0	329
861	Instruments, apparatus	1,821	737	1,084
	Subtotal complex/complex	38,316	21,552	16,764
	In 1995 $	97,667	54,936	42,731
	Top 30 goods subtotal	59,101	36,551	22,550
	In 1995 $	150,648	93,168	57,480

Japan 1975 Balance of Trade (million US$, 1995 equivalent) on top 30 manufactured goods traded globally

SITC	Commodity	Exports	Imports	Trade balance
561	Fertilizers, manufactured	601	0	601
641	Paper and paperboard	361	94	267
651	Textile yarn and thread	587	198	389
653	Woven textiles noncotton	1,738	349	1,389
667	Pearl, prec., semi-p. stone	0	358	−358
673	Iron and steel shapes	1,576	0	1,576
674	Iron, steel univ., plate, sheet	3,241	0	3,241
678	Iron, steel tubes, pipes, etc.	3,315	0	3,315
682	Copper	206	293	−87
698	Metal manufactures NES	379	0	379
717	Textile, leather machinery	784	93	691
841	Clothing not of fur	332	503	−171
	Subtotal simple/simple	13,120	1,888	11,232
	In 1995 $	33,443	4,813	28,630
512	Organic chemicals	0	1,231	−1,231
541	Medicinal, etc., products	0	440	−440
581	Plastic materials, etc.	997	151	846
599	Chemicals NES	224	294	−70
629	Rubber articles, NES	664	0	664
719	Machines NES non-electric	2,579	752	1,827
	Subtotal simple/complex	4,464	2,868	1,596
	In 1995 $	11,379	7,311	4,068
711	Power machinery non-electric	0	1,231	−1,231
712	Agricultural machinery	0	440	−440
714	Office machines	997	151	846
715	Metalworking machinery	224	294	−70
718	Machines for special industries	664	0	664
722	Elec. power machinery, switchgear	2,579	752	1,827
724	Telecom equipment	1,630	2,098	−468
729	Electrical machinery NES	3,562	1,697	1,865
732	Road motor vehicles	10,096	11,417	−1,321
734	Aircraft	6,194	519	5,675
735	Ships and boats	329	0	329
861	Instruments, apparatus	1,821	737	1,084
	Subtotal complex/complex	28,096	19,336	8,760
	In 1995 $	71,617	49,287	22,329
	Top 30 goods subtotal	45,680	24,092	21,588
	In 1995 $	116,438	61,411	55,028

Top 30 goods exports traded globally, 1970

Rank	SITC	Commodity	Value (million US$)	Classification Product	Process
1	732	Road motor vehicles	20,756	Complex	Complex
2	331	Crude petroleum, etc.	15,033	Simple	Simple
3	719	Machines NES non-electric	13,111	Simple	Complex
4	332	Petroleum products	7,709	Simple	Simple
5	682	Copper	5,745	Simple	Simple
6	729	Electrical machinery NES	5,570	Complex	Complex
7	674	Iron, steel univ., plate, sheet	5,155	Simple	Simple
8	841	Clothing not of fur	5,106	Simple	Simple
9	711	Power machinery non-electric	4,781	Complex	Complex
10	724	Telecom equipment	4,712	Complex	Complex
11	512	Organic chemicals	4,401	Simple	Complex
12	641	Paper and paperboard	4,396	Simple	Simple
13	718	Machines for special industries	4,354	Complex	Complex
14	714	Office machines	4,226	Complex	Complex
15	734	Aircraft	4,128	Complex	Complex
16	653	Woven textiles noncotton	3,967	Simple	Simple
17	581	Plastic materials, etc.	3,949	Simple	Complex
18	735	Ships and boats	3,868	Complex	Complex
19	283	Nonferrous base metal ore, conc.	3,386	Simple	Simple
20	722	Elec. power machinery, switchgear	3,382	Complex	Complex
21	861	Instruments, apparatus	3,336	Complex	Complex
22	651	Textile yarn and thread	3,296	Simple	Simple
23	011	Meat fresh, chilled, frozen	3,242	Simple	Simple
24	071	Coffee	3,205	Simple	Simple
25	673	Iron and steel shapes	3,043	Simple	Simple
26	717	Textile, leather machinery	2,855	Simple	Simple
27	041	Wheat, etc., unmilled	2,713	Simple	Simple
28	541	Medicinal, etc., products	2,687	Simple	Complex
29	251	Pulp and waste paper	2,531	Simple	Simple
30	061	Sugar and honey	2,526	Simple	Simple
		Top 30 subtotal	157,169		
		World exports	313,913		
		% of total	50.1		

Top 30 goods exports traded globally grouped by complex/simple classification, 1970

Rank	SITC	Commodity	Value (million US$)	Product	Process	% of total
2	331	Crude petroleum, etc.	15,033	Simple	Simple	
4	332	Petroleum products	7,709	Simple	Simple	
5	682	Copper	5,745	Simple	Simple	
7	674	Iron, steel univ., plate, sheet	5,155	Simple	Simple	
8	841	Clothing not of fur	5,106	Simple	Simple	
12	641	Paper and paperboard	4,396	Simple	Simple	
16	653	Woven textiles noncotton	3,967	Simple	Simple	
19	283	Nonferrous base metal ore, conc.	3,386	Simple	Simple	
22	651	Textile yarn and thread	3,296	Simple	Simple	
23	011	Meat fresh, chilled, frozen	3,242	Simple	Simple	
24	071	Coffee	3,205	Simple	Simple	
25	673	Iron and steel shapes	3,043	Simple	Simple	
26	717	Textile, leather machinery	2,855	Simple	Simple	
27	041	Wheat, etc., unmilled	2,713	Simple	Simple	
29	251	Pulp and waste paper	2,531	Simple	Simple	
30	061	Sugar and honey	2,526	Simple	Simple	
		Subtotal simple/simple	73,908			47.0
3	719	Machines NES non-electric	13,111	Simple	Complex	
11	512	Organic chemicals	4,401	Simple	Complex	
17	581	Plastic materials, etc.	3,949	Simple	Complex	
28	541	Medicinal, etc., products	2,687	Simple	Complex	
		Subtotal simple/complex	24,148			15.4
1	732	Road motor vehicles	20,756	Complex	Complex	
6	729	Electrical machinery NES	5,570	Complex	Complex	
9	711	Power machinery non-electric	4,781	Complex	Complex	
10	724	Telecom equipment	4,712	Complex	Complex	
13	718	Machines for special industries	4,354	Complex	Complex	
14	714	Office machines	4,226	Complex	Complex	
15	734	Aircraft	4,128	Complex	Complex	
18	735	Ships and boats	3,868	Complex	Complex	
20	722	Elec. power machinery, switchgear	3,382	Complex	Complex	
21	861	Instruments, apparatus	3,336	Complex	Complex	
		Subtotal complex/complex	59,113			37.6
		Top 30 subtotal	157,169			

Top 30 manufactured goods exports traded globally, 1970
(SITC codes 500 through 800)

Rank	SITC	Commodity	Value (million US$)	Classification Product	Process
1	732	Road motor vehicles	20,756	Complex	Complex
2	719	Machines NES non-electric	13,111	Simple	Complex
3	682	Copper	5,745	Simple	Simple
4	729	Electrical machinery NES	5,570	Complex	Complex
5	674	Iron, steel univ., plate, sheet	5,155	Simple	Simple
6	841	Clothing not of fur	5,106	Simple	Simple
7	711	Power machinery non-electric	4,781	Complex	Complex
8	724	Telecom equipment	4,712	Complex	Complex
9	512	Organic chemicals	4,401	Simple	Complex
10	641	Paper and paperboard	4,396	Simple	Simple
11	718	Machines for special industries	4,354	Complex	Complex
12	714	Office machines	4,226	Complex	Complex
13	734	Aircraft	4,128	Complex	Complex
14	653	Woven textiles noncotton	3,967	Simple	Simple
15	581	Plastic materials, etc.	3,949	Simple	Complex
16	735	Ships and boats	3,868	Complex	Complex
17	722	Elec. power machinery, switchgear	3,382	Complex	Complex
18	861	Instruments, apparatus	3,336	Complex	Complex
19	651	Textile yarn and thread	3,296	Simple	Simple
20	673	Iron and steel shapes	3,043	Simple	Simple
21	717	Textile, leather machinery	2,855	Simple	Simple
22	541	Medicinal, etc., products	2,687	Simple	Complex
23	599	Chemicals NES	2,497	Simple	Complex
24	715	Metalworking machinery	2,460	Complex	Complex
25	667	Pearl, prec., semi-p. stone	2,431	Simple	Simple
26	678	Iron, steel tubes, pipes, etc.	2,393	Simple	Simple
27	712	Agricultural machinery	2,208	Complex	Complex
28	684	Aluminum	2,160	Simple	Simple
29	698	Metal manufactures NES	1,754	Simple	Simple
30	851	Footwear	1,641	Simple	Simple
		Top 30 subtotal	134,368		

Top 30 manufactured goods exports traded globally, 1970
(SITC codes 500 through 800): grouped by complex/simple classification

Rank	SITC	Commodity	Value (million US$)	Product	Process	% of total
3	682	Copper	5,745	Simple	Simple	
5	674	Iron, steel univ., plate, sheet	5,155	Simple	Simple	
6	841	Clothing not of fur	5,106	Simple	Simple	
10	641	Paper and paperboard	4,396	Simple	Simple	
14	653	Woven textiles noncotton	3,967	Simple	Simple	
19	651	Textile yarn and thread	3,296	Simple	Simple	
20	673	Iron and steel shapes	3,043	Simple	Simple	
21	717	Textile, leather machinery	2,855	Simple	Simple	
25	667	Pearl, prec., semi-p. stone	2,431	Simple	Simple	
26	678	Iron, steel tubes, pipes, etc.	2,393	Simple	Simple	
28	684	Aluminum	2,160	Simple	Simple	
29	698	Metal manufactures NES	1,754	Simple	Simple	
30	851	Footwear	1,641	Simple	Simple	
		Subtotal simple/simple	43,942			32.7
2	719	Machines NES non-electric	13,111	Simple	Complex	
9	512	Organic chemicals	4,401	Simple	Complex	
15	581	Plastic materials, etc.	3,949	Simple	Complex	
22	541	Medicinal, etc., products	2,687	Simple	Complex	
23	599	Chemicals NES	2,497	Simple	Complex	
		Subtotal simple/complex	26,645			19.8
1	732	Road motor vehicles	20,756	Complex	Complex	
4	729	Electrical machinery NES	5,570	Complex	Complex	
7	711	Power machinery non-electric	4,781	Complex	Complex	
8	724	Telecom equipment	4,712	Complex	Complex	
11	718	Machines for special industries	4,354	Complex	Complex	
12	714	Office machines	4,226	Complex	Complex	
13	734	Aircraft	4,128	Complex	Complex	
16	735	Ships and boats	3,868	Complex	Complex	
17	722	Elec. power machinery, switchgear	3,382	Complex	Complex	
18	861	Instruments, apparatus	3,336	Complex	Complex	
24	715	Metalworking machinery	2,460	Complex	Complex	
27	712	Agricultural machinery	2,208	Complex	Complex	
		Subtotal complex/complex	63,781			47.5
		Top 30 subtotal	134,368			

United States 1970 balance of trade (million US$, 1995 equivalent) on top 30 manufactured goods traded globally

SITC	Commodity	Exports	Imports	Trade balance
641	Paper and paperboard	528	1,039	−511
651	Textile yarn and thread	146	223	−77
653	Woven textiles noncotton	154	498	−344
667	Pearl, prec., semi-p. stone	199	487	−288
673	Iron and steel shapes	118	486	−368
674	Iron, steel univ., plate, sheet	336	906	−570
678	Iron, steel tubes, pipes, etc.	227	349	−122
682	Copper	359	532	−173
684	Aluminum	360	238	122
698	Metal manufactures NES	258	224	34
717	Textile, leather machinery	278	361	−83
841	Clothing not of fur	202	1,263	−1,061
851	Footwear	11	629	−618
	Subtotal simple/simple	3,176	7,235	−4,059
	In 1995 $	11,173	25,453	−14,280
512	Organic chemicals	1,072	355	717
541	Medicinal, etc., products	422	87	335
581	Plastic materials, etc.	654	123	531
599	Chemicals NES	553	85	468
719	Machines NES non-electric	3,013	736	2,277
	Subtotal simple/complex	5,714	1,386	4,328
	In 1995 $	20,102	4,876	15,226
711	Power machinery non-electric	1,425	782	643
712	Agricultural machinery	628	264	364
714	Office machines	1,556	505	1,051
715	Metalworking machinery	402	164	238
718	Machines for special industries	1,141	206	935
722	Elec. power machinery, switchgear	616	247	369
724	Telecom equipment	675	1,102	−427
729	Electrical machinery NES	1,475	598	877
732	Road motor vehicles	3,573	5,481	−1,908
734	Aircraft	2,671	274	2,397
735	Ships and boats	152	47	105
861	Instruments, apparatus	868	356	512
	Subtotal complex/complex	15,182	10,026	5,156
	In 1995 $	53,410	35,271	18,139
	Top 30 goods subtotal	24,072	18,647	5,425
	In 1995 $	84,685	65,600	19,085

Japan 1970 balance of trade (million US$, 1995 equivalent) on top 30 manufactured goods traded globally

SITC	Commodity	Exports	Imports	Trade balance
641	Paper and paperboard	127	27	100
651	Textile yarn and thread	426	37	389
653	Woven textiles noncotton	940	118	822
667	Pearl, prec., semi-p. stone	45	122	−77
673	Iron and steel shapes	350	7	343
674	Iron, steel univ., plate, sheet	1,552	0	1,552
678	Iron, steel tubes, pipes, etc.	522	6	516
682	Copper	141	484	−343
684	Aluminum	39	139	−100
698	Metal manufactures NES	143	20	123
717	Textile, leather machinery	327	113	214
841	Clothing not of fur	462	89	373
851	Footwear	134	8	126
	Subtotal simple/simple	5,208	1,170	4,038
	In 1995 $	18,322	4,116	14,206
512	Organic chemicals	399	227	172
541	Medicinal, etc., products	66	216	−150
581	Plastic materials, etc.	427	73	354
599	Chemicals NES	57	180	−123
719	Machines NES non-electric	727	359	368
	Subtotal simple/complex	1,676	1,055	621
	In 1995 $	5,896	3,711	2,185
711	Power machinery non-electric	237	154	83
712	Agricultural machinery	72	40	32
714	Office machines	329	322	7
715	Metalworking machinery	116	168	−52
718	Machines for special industries	198	106	92
722	Elec. power machinery, switchgear	297	93	204
724	Telecom equipment	1,400	53	1,347
729	Electrical machinery NES	45	290	−245
732	Road motor vehicles	1,874	81	1,793
734	Aircraft	34	249	−215
735	Ships and boats	1,410	61	1,349
861	Instruments, apparatus	498	115	383
	Subtotal complex/complex	6,510	1,732	4,778
	In 1995 $	22,902	6,093	16,809
	Top 30 goods subtotal	13,394	3,957	9,437
	in 1995 $	47,120	13,921	33,199

Glossary

coevolution the simultaneous process of evolution along a path or innovation trajectory involving the technologies and the organizational networks that produce and use them.

complementary assets skills, capabilities, or equipment, when combined with core capabilities, comprise the major network resources underpinning the self-organization required for complex technological innovation.

complex technology process or product that cannot be understood in full detail by an individual expert sufficiently to communicate all the details of the process or product across time and distance to other experts. (A simple process or product is one that can be understood and communicated by one individual.)

complexity the notion that processes, products, and entire systems are gradually becoming more difficult to understand due to increased scale and scope – a common measure of complexity is the number of component parts per system.

complexity science a growing research program and body of literature commonly associated with the Santa Fe Institute that attempts to explain the phenomenon of increasing complexity through unconventional – typically nonlinear – models.

core capabilities interrelated sets of expertise, skills, and understanding embodied in an organization's evolving structure and behavior that provide distinct organizational identity.

craft production involves highly skilled workers making customized products for individual consumers – the traditional production method based upon the individual craftworker's skill and simple but flexible tools that augment and expand the worker's capacity for productive expression.

culture the set of key values, beliefs, and norms shared by members of a society or organization.

emergence the unpredicted appearance of new characteristics or phenomena in the course of biological or social evolution.

evolutionary economics founded on the principles of Austrian economist Joseph Schumpeter, evolutionary economics views the notion of equilibrium as more the exception than the rule and considers technological innovation as central to economic growth.

explicit knowledge knowledge that is formally and easily transferred through written communication.

fundamental (transformational) innovation the development of new product and process designs that differ from anything that existed before, usually delivering both different and increased performance – fundamental innovations involve establishing a previously unavailable technology path.

heuristics any methods, procedures, or techniques used to discover, learn, or understand.

increasing returns economic principle that the change in outputs increases at a greater rate than a change of inputs along a range of outputs (i.e. exponential increase in outputs resulting from a linear increase in inputs).

incremental (normal) innovation product or process innovation involving an established technology and established network along an existing trajectory.

industrial (mass) production involves the division of a product into its component parts, which are standardized, and then making and assembling the parts under conditions where efficiency increases with scale.

innovation pattern basic model or structure that characterizes a particular path of innovation – three forms are labeled normal, transition, and transformation.

innovation trajectory a dominant pattern of complex technological innovation involving a given technology and organizational network(s), typically expressed as an S-shaped curve.

learning organization an organization engaged in identifying and solving problems, enabling the organization to continuously experiment, improve, and increase its capability through integrating explicit and tacit knowledge and skills, embedding them in equipment and applying them to problem solving, experimentation, and commercial innovation.

lock-in associated with path dependence, the possibility that an inferior or less optimal alternative may be chosen by forces other than the "invisible hand" of market competition.

major (transitional) innovation innovations often distinguished by major advances in performance as well as qualitative changes in design, commonly modifying an established technology in ways that overcome what were thought to be major constraints on development, enabling the technology to perform beyond what was thought possible.

modular technology involves systems composed of subsystems and components that can be designed independently and that, when put together, produce a functioning whole.

Moore's Law the notion that semiconductor devices will double in circuit density and capability on a regular basis, about every 18 months (posited by Gordon Moore in 1965).

national innovation system (NIS) connects sociotechnical complexes, networks, core actors, and work groups with broad sets of social institutions (e.g. educational systems, labor–management relations) that provide the most general context for all technological innovation.

network resources   strengths and advantages held by an organizational network, including existing core capabilities, complementary assets, and organizational learning.

nonlinear change   a change that occurs in an irregular and often unpredictable fashion.

normal innovation pattern   the coevolution of an established network and technology along an established trajectory.

organic organizational structure   an organizational structure that is free flowing, has few rules and regulations, encourages employee teamwork, and decentralizes decision making.

organizational learning   the process by which organizations increase their knowledge, skills, and capabilities through the collective and cumulative learning of individual members; characterized as local learning – what is learned is in part unique to those involved because it is based on previous accumulated learning that is partly tacit.

organizational network   the assemblage of individuals and groups, both internal and external (e.g. suppliers, users) to an organization, for the purpose of technological innovation – the network is the dominant sociotechnical system.

path dependence   the economics concept that a seemingly small advantage or inconsequential lead for some technology, product, or standard can have important and sometimes irreversible influences on the ultimate market allocation of resources.

pattern change   process brought about by a significant change in the technology or organizational network of an established innovation trajectory; occurs as either transitional (major) or transformational (fundamental).

phase transition   a term used by many students of complexity science to describe generic changes in the nature of the real world involving changes in substance, and particularly in the organizational and technological substance of human production systems.

positive feedback   the economics concept that increased use of outputs is communicated (fed back) to the production process and help reinforce an increase in production and output.

seamless (connectual) technology   any technology that requires the adaptation of the whole system in an interactive or synthetic way.

selection environment   the constraining and focusing force that determines which technology is selected for use (e.g. markets).

self-organization   the concept that an organization self-determines its structure and identity by focusing on its core competencies and adapting quickly to new opportunities and threats because it is not locked into the rigid boundaries of pre-established structures.

simple technology   process or product that can be understood and communicated by one individual.

sociotechnical system   the idea that technologies and the organizations involved in developing and using them are inseparable, and thus interrelate in a systematic fashion.

synergy   the condition that exists when the organization's parts interact to produce a joint effort that is greater than the sum of the parts acting alone.

synthetic production   involves teams of multiskilled people using flexible, increasingly automated machines to design and make a large variety and relatively high volume of products on the same production line.

system   a set of interrelated parts that function as a whole to achieve a common purpose.

tacit knowledge   knowledge obtained through informal learning methods (e.g. learning by doing and trial and error) – as such difficult to transfer and communicate to others.

technological community   any combination of organizational networks that share a common interest in the research, development, or use of a given technology.

technological innovation   creative activities involved with introducing new ideas, practices, or objects to a market or a community.

transformation innovation pattern   the launching of a new trajectory by a new coevolving network and technology – the most chaotic of the three innovation patterns, transformational innovations involve fundamental changes in technology or fundamentally new technologies.

transition innovation pattern   the coevolutionary movement to a new trajectory by an established network and technology.

Bibliography

Complexity science

Allen, Peter M. "Coherence, Chaos and Evolution in the Social Context," *Futures*, Vol. 26, No. 6, July/August 1994, pp. 583–97.

Anderson, Philip W., "Complexity II: The Santa Fe Institute," *Physics Today*, Vol. 45, No. 6, June 1992, pp. 9–11.

—— "Is Complexity Physics? Is It Science? What Is It?" *Physics Today*, Vol. 44, No. 7, July 1991, pp. 9–11.

Arthur, W. Brian, "Complexity in Economic Theory: Inductive Reasoning and Bounded Rationality," *American Economic Association Papers and Proceedings*, Vol. 84, No. 2, May 1994, pp. 406–11.

—— "Why Do Things Become More Complex?" *Scientific American*, Vol. 268, No. 5, May 1993, p. 144.

—— "Pandora's Marketplace," *New Scientist*, Vol. 137, No. 1859 (Complexity Supplement), February 6, 1993, pp. 6–8.

Bak, Per and Maya Paczuski, "Complexity, Contingency, and Criticality," *Proceedings of the National Academy of Sciences of the United States of America*, Vol. 92, No. 15, July 18, 1995, pp. 6689–96.

Bechtel, William and Robert C. Richardson, *Discovering Complexity: Decomposition and Localization as Strategies in Scientific Research*, Princeton, NJ: Princeton University Press, 1993.

Cambel, A. B., *Applied Chaos Theory: a Paradigm for Complexity*, New York: Academic Press, 1993.

Casti, John L., *Complification: Explaining a Paradoxical World through the Science of Surprise*, New York: HarperCollins, 1994.

Cheetham, Tom, "The Forms of Life: Complexity, History, and Actuality," *Environmental Ethics*, Vol. 15, No. 4, Winter 1993, pp. 293–311.

Cohen, Jack and Ian Stewart, *The Collapse of Chaos: Discovering Simplicity in a Complex World*, New York: Viking Penguin, 1994.

Cooper, William W., Kingshuk K. Sinha, and Robert S. Sullivan, "Measuring Complexity in High-technology Manufacturing: Indexes for Evaluation," *Interfaces*, Vol. 22, No. 4, July/August 1992, pp. 38–48.

Costanza, Robert, Lisa Wainger, Carl Folk, and Karl-Goran Maler, "Modeling Complex Ecological Economic Systems: toward a Dynamic Understanding of People and Nature," *Bioscience*, Vol. 43, No. 8, September 1993, pp. 545–55.

Coveney, Peter and Roger Highfield, *Frontiers of Complexity: the Search for Order in a Chaotic World*, New York: Fawcett Columbine, 1995.

De Greene, Kenyon B., "Can System Dynamics Be Theoretically Improved, and if So, Does It Matter Practically?" *Systems Research*, Vol. 11, No. 3, 1994, pp. 3–21.

—— "Nonlinear Management in Technologically-induced Fields," *Systems Research*, Vol. 7, No. 3, 1990, pp. 159–68.

Dooley, Kevin J., Timothy L. Johnson, and David H. Bush, "TQM, Chaos, and Complexity," *Human Systems Management*, Vol. 14, No. 4, 1995, pp. 287–302.

Dyke, C., "Expectation and Strategy in a Nonlinear World," *Systems Research*, Vol. 7, No. 2, 1990, pp. 117–25.

Fichant, F. Y., "Be Complex, Not Complicated," *Across the Board*, January 1994, pp. 56–7.

Fivaz, Roland, "The Nature of Order in Complex Systems," *Systems Research*, Vol. 11, No. 3, 1994, pp. 43–65.

Flood, R. L., "Complexity: a Definition by Construction of a Conceptual Framework," *Systems Research*, Vol. 4, No. 3, 1987, pp. 177–85.

Funtowicz, Silvio and Jerome R. Ravetz, "Emergent Complex Systems," *Futures*, Vol. 26, No. 6, July/August 1994, pp. 568–82.

Gell-Mann, Murray, *The Quark and the Jaguar: Adventures in the Simple and the Complex*, New York: W. H. Freeman, 1994.

Hagel, John III, "Managing Complexity," *McKinsey Quarterly*, Spring 1998, pp. 2–23.

Harvey, David L. and Michael Reed, "Social Science as the Study of Complex Systems," in L. Douglas Kiel and Euel Elliott, eds, *Chaos Theory in the Social Sciences: Foundations and Applications*, Ann Arbor, MI: University of Michigan Press, 1996, pp. 295–323.

Holland, John H., *Hidden Order: How Adaptation Builds Complexity*, Reading, MA: Addison-Wesley, 1995.

—— "Complex Adaptive Systems," *Daedalus*, Vol. 121, No. 1, Winter 1992, pp. 17–30.

Holling, C. S., "Simplifying the Complex: the Paradigms of Ecological Function and Structure," *Futures*, Vol. 26, No. 6, July/August 1994, pp. 598–609.

Holt, D. Lynn and R. Glynn Holt, "Regularity in Nonlinear Dynamical Systems," *British Journal for the Philosophy of Science*, Vol. 44, December 1993, pp. 711–27.

Horgan, John, "From Complexity to Perplexity," *Scientific American*, Vol. 272, No. 6, June 1995, pp. 104–9.

Ibarra, Eduardo C., "Strategic Analysis of Organizations: a Model from the Complexity Paradigm," *Human Systems Management*, Vol. 14, No. 1, 1995. pp. 51–70.

Jervis, Robert, "Complexity and the Analysis of Political and Social Life," *Political Science Quarterly*, Vol. 112, No. 4, Winter 1997–8, pp. 569–93.

Kauffman, Stuart, A., *At Home in the Universe: the Search for Laws of Self-organization and Complexity*, New York: Oxford University Press, 1995.

—— "Principals of Adaptation in Complex Systems," in Daniel L. Stein, ed., *Lectures in the Sciences of Complexity*, Redwood City, CA: Addison-Wesley, 1989, pp. 619–712.

Kesting, W. Roy, "Product Development and the Science of Chaos," *Technology Transfer*, Winter/Spring 1993, pp. 22–31.

Kiel, L. Douglas, *Managing Chaos and Complexity in Government: a New Paradigm for Managing Change, Innovation and Organizational Renewal*, San Francisco: Jossey-Bass, 1994.

—— "The Nonlinear Paradigm: Advancing Paradigmatic Progress in the Policy

Sciences," *Systems Research*, Vol. 9, No. 2, 1992, pp. 27–42.

—— "Lessons from the Nonlinear Paradigm: Applications of the Theory of Dissipative Structures in the Social Sciences," *Social Science Quarterly*, Vol. 72, No. 3, September 1991, pp. 431–42.

Kline, Stephen J., *Conceptual Foundations for Multidisciplinary Thinking*, Stanford, CA: Stanford University Press, 1995 pp. 49–97.

Krugman, Paul R., "Complexity and Emergent Structure in the International Economy," in Jim Leinsohn, Alan V. Densdorff, and Robert M. Stern, eds, *New Dimensions in Trade Theory*, Ann Arbor, MI: University of Michigan Press, 1995, pp. 23–46.

Langlois, Richard N. and Michael J. Everett, "Complexity, Genuine Uncertainty, and the Economics of Organization," *Human Systems Management*, Vol. 11, No. 2, 1992, pp. 67–75.

Leach, Lawrence P., "TQM, Reengineering, and the Edge of Chaos," *Quality Progress*, February 1996, pp. 85–90.

Lemonick, Michael D., "Life, the Universe and Everything," *Time*, Vol. 141, No. 8, February 22, 1993, pp. 62–3.

Levy, David, "Chaos Theory and Strategy: Theory, Application, and Managerial Implications," *Strategic Management Journal*, Vol. 15, Summer 1994, pp. 167–78.

Lewin, Roger, "A Simple Matter of Complexity," *New Scientist*, Vol. 141, No. 1911, February 5, 1994, pp. 37–40.

—— "Order for Free," *New Scientist* (Complexity Supplement), Vol. 137, No. 1860, February 13, 1993, pp. 10–11.

—— "The Right Connections," *New Scientist* (Complexity Supplement), Vol. 137, No. 1859, February 6, 1993, pp. 4–5.

—— *Complexity: Life at the Edge of Chaos*, New York: Macmillan, 1992.

Loye, David and Riane Eisler, "Chaos and Transformation: Implications of Nonequilibrium Theory for Social Science and Society," *Behavioral Science*, Vol. 32, No. 1, January 1987, pp. 53–65.

McGlade, Jacqueline, "Alternative Ecologies," *New Scientist* (Complexity Supplement), Vol. 137, No. 1860, February 13, 1993, pp. 14–16.

Mitchell, Melanie, "Imitation of Life," *New Scientist* (Complexity Supplement), Vol. 137, No. 1860, February 13, 1993, pp. 12–13.

Moore, James F., "The Rise of a New Corporate Form," *Washington Quarterly*, Vol. 21, No. 1, Winter 1998, pp. 167–81.

Morris, Charles R., "It's Not the Economy Stupid," *Atlantic Monthly*, Vol. 272, No. 1, July 1993, pp. 49–62.

Nicolis, Gregoire and Ilya Prigogine, *Exploring Complexity: An Introduction*, New York: W. H. Freeman, 1989.

O'Conner, Martin, "Complexity and Coevolution: Methodology for a Positive Treatment of Indeterminacy," *Futures*, Vol. 26, No. 6, July/August 1994, pp. 610–15.

Pagels, Heinz R., *The Dreams of Reason: the Computer and the Rise of the Sciences of Complexity*, New York: Simon and Schuster, 1988.

Peak, David and Michael Frame, *Chaos Under Control: the Art and Science of Complexity*, New York: W. H. Freeman, 1994.

Prigogine, Ilya and Isabelle Stengers, *Order Out of Chaos: Man's New Dialogue With Nature*, New York: Bantam Books, 1984, pp. 177–209.

Resnick, Mitchel, "Changing the Centralized Mind," *Technological Review*, Vol. 97, No. 5, July 1994, pp. 32–40.

Ruthen, Russell, "Adapting to Complexity: Trends in Nonlinear Dynamics," *Scientific American*, Vol. 268, No. 1, January 1993, pp. 130–40.

Sanchez, Ron, "Strategic Management at the Point of Inflection: Systems, Complexity and Competence Theory," *Long Range Planning*, Vol. 30, No. 6, December 1997, pp. 939–45.

Sardar, Ziauddin and Jerome R. Ravetz, "Complexity: Fad or Future?" *Futures*, Vol. 26, No. 6, July/August 1994, pp. 563–7.

Schneider, Eric D. and James J. Kay, "Complexity and Thermodynamics: towards a New Ecology," *Futures*, Vol. 26, No. 6, July/August 1994, pp. 626–47.

Sedgwick, John, "The Complexity Problem," *Atlantic Monthly*, Vol. 271, March 1993, pp. 96–100.

Serra, Roberto and Gianni Zanarini, "Complexity in Natural and Cultural Systems," *Systems Research*, Vol. 4, No. 2, 1987, 111–17.

Shackley, Simon, Brian Wynne and Claire Waterton, "Imagine Complexity: the Past, Present and Future Potential of Complex Thinking," *Futures*, Vol. 28, No. 3, April 1996, pp. 201–25.

Stacey, Ralph D., *Complexity and Creativity in Organizations*, San Francisco: Berrett-Koehler Publishers, 1996.

—— "Management and the Science of Complexity: If Organizational Life Is Nonlinear, Can Business Strategies Prevail?" *Research-Technology Management*, May/June 1996, pp. 8–10.

—— "Emerging Strategies for a Chaotic Environment," *Long Range Planning*, Vol. 29, No. 2, April 1996, pp. 182–9.

—— "The Science of Complexity: an Alternative Perspective for Strategic Change Processes," *Strategic Management Journal*, Vol. 16, Special Issue, Summer 1995, pp. 477–95.

—— "Strategy as Order Emerging from Chaos," *Long Range Planning*, Vol. 26, No. 1, February 1993, pp. 10–17.

—— *Managing the Unknowable: Strategic Boundaries Between Order and Chaos in Organizations*, San Francisco: Jossey-Bass, 1992.

Stewart, Ian, *Nature's Numbers: the Unreal Reality of Mathematical Imagination*, New York: Basic Books, 1995.

—— "A New Order," *New Scientist* (Complexity Supplement), Vol. 137, No. 1859, February 6, 1993, pp. 2–3.

—— and Jack Cohen, "Why Are There Simple Rules in a Complicated Universe?" *Futures*, Vol. 26, No. 6, July/August 1994, pp. 648–64.

Stites, Janet, "Complexity," *Omni*, Vol. 16, No. 8, May 1994, pp. 42–52.

Traub, Joseph H. and Henryk Wozniakowski, "Breaking Intractability," *Scientific American*, Vol. 270, No. 1, January 1994, pp. 102–7.

Wahlstrom, Bjorn, "Avoiding Technological Risks: the Dilemma of Complexity," *Technological Forecasting and Social Change*, Vol. 42, No. 4, December 1992, pp. 351–65.

Waldrop, M. Mitchell, *Complexity: the Emerging Science at the Edge of Order and Chaos*, New York: Simon and Schuster, 1992.

Warfield, John N., "Complexity and Cognitive Equilibrium: Experimental Results and Their Implications," *Human Systems Management*, Vol. 10, No. 3, 1991, pp. 195–202.

Westhoff, Frank H., Beth V. Yarborough, and Robert M. Yarborough, "Complexity, Organization, and Stuart Kaufmann's *The Origins of Order*," *Journal of Economic Behavior and Organization*, Vol. 29, January 1996, pp. 1–25.

Wulff, Peter, "More Large Accidents through Complexity?" *Risk Analysis*, Vol. 11, No. 2, June 1991, pp. 249–53.

Evolutionary economics

Allen, Peter M., "Why the Future Is Not What It Was: New Models of Evolution," *Futures*, Vol. 22, No. 6, July/August 1990, pp. 555–70.

—— "Towards a New Science of Human Systems, "*International Social Science Journal*, Vol. 41, No. 1, February 1989, pp. 81–91.

—— "Evolution, Innovation and Economics," in Giovanni Dosi, Gerald Silverberg, and Luc Soete, eds, *Technical Change and Economic Theory*, New York: Pinter Publishers, 1988, pp. 95–119.

Andersen, Esben S., *Evolutionary Economics: Post-Schumpeterian Contributions*, New York: Pinter Press, 1994, pp. 1–25.

Arthur W. Brian, "Self-reinforcing Mechanisms in Economics," in Philip W. Anderson, Kenneth J. Arrow, and David Pines, eds, *The Economy as an Evolving Complex System*, Redwood City, CA: Addison-Wesley, 1988, pp. 9–31.

Blauwhof, Gertrud and Loet Leydesdorff, "New Developments in Technology Studies: Evolutionary Economics and Chaos Theory," *Science and Public Policy*, Vol. 20, No. 6, December 1993, pp. 417–23.

Bush, Paul D., "The Theory of Institutional Change," *Journal of Economic Issues*, Vol. 21, No. 3, September 1987, pp. 1075–116.

Clark, Norman, "Organization and Information in the Evolution of Economic Systems," in P. Paolo Saviotti and J. Stanley Metcalfe, eds., *Evolutionary Theories of Economic and Technological Change*, Reading, PA: Harwood Academic Publishers, 1991, pp. 88–107.

Colander, David, "New Institutionalism, Old Institutionalism , and Distribution Theory," *Journal of Economic Issues*, Vol. 30, No. 2, June 1996, pp. 433–42.

Day, Richard H., "Nonlinear Dynamics and Evolutionary Economics," in Richard H. Day and Ping Chen, eds, *Nonlinear Dynamics and Evolutionary Economics*, New York: Oxford University Press, 1993, pp. 18–41.

Dopfer, Kurt, "How Economic Institutions Emerge: Industrial Entrepreneurs and Behavioral Seeds," in Yuichi Shionoya and Mark Perlman, eds, *Innovation in Technology, Industries, and Institutions: Studies in Schumpeterian Perspectives*, Ann Arbor, MI: University of Michigan Press, 1994, pp. 299–329.

Dosi, Giovanni, "Performances, Interactions and Evolution in the Theory of Industrial Organization," in Alfredo Del Monte, ed., *Recent Developments in the Theory of Industrial Organization*, Ann Arbor, MI: University of Michigan Press, 1992, pp. 34–57.

—— "Perspectives on Evolutionary Theory," *Science and Public Policy*, Vol. 18, No. 6, December 1991, pp. 353–61.

—— "Economic Change and Its Interpretation, or, Is There a 'Schumpeterian Approach?'," in Arnold Heertje and Mark Perlman, eds, *Evolutionary Technology and Market Structure: Studies in Schumpeterian Economics*, Ann Arbor, MI: University of Michigan Press, 1990, pp. 335–41.

—— Institutions and Markets in a Dynamic World," *Manchester School of Economic and Social Studies*, Vol. 56, No. 2, June 1988, pp. 119–46.

—— and Y. Kaniovski, "On Badly Behaved Dynamics: Some Applications of Generalized Urn Schemes to Technological and Economic Change," *Journal of Evolutionary Economics*, Vol. 4, No. 2, 1994, pp. 93–123.

—— and Richard R. Nelson, "Introduction to Evolutionary Theories in Economics," *Journal of Evolutionary Economics*, Vol. 4, No. 3, 1994, pp. 153–72.

—— Keith Pavitt and Luc Soete, *The Economics of Technical Change and International Trade*, New York: New York University Press, 1990.

"Evo-economics: Biology Meets the Dismal Science," *The Economist*, Vol. 329, No. 7843, December 25, 1993, pp. 93–5.

Foster, John and Phillip Wild, "Economic Evolution and the Science of Synergetics, "*Journal of Evolutionary Economics*, Vol. 6, No. 3, 1996, pp. 239–60.

Foxall, Gordon R. and John R. Fawn, "An Evolutionary Model of Technological Innovation as a Strategic Management Process," *Technovation*, Vol. 12, No. 2, April 1992, pp. 191–202.

Freeman, Christopher, "Critical Survey: the Economics of Technical Change," *Cambridge Journal of Economics*, Vol. 18, No. 5, November 1994, pp. 463–514.

Hall, Peter, *Innovation, Economics and Evolution: Theoretical Perspectives on Changing Technology in Economic Systems*, New York: Harvester Wheatsheaf, 1994.

Hodgson, Geoffrey M., *Economics and Evolution: Bring Life Back into Economics*, Cambridge, MA: Polity Press, 1993.

—— "Theories of Economic Evolution: a Preliminary Taxonomy," *Manchester School of Economic and Social Studies*, Vol. 61, No. 2, June 1993, pp. 125–43.

—— "The Mecca of Alfred Marshall," *Economic Journal*, Vol. 103, No. 417, March 1993, pp. 406–15.

Jensen, Hans E., "The Theory of Human Nature," *Journal of Economic Issues*, Vol. 21, No. 3, September 1987, pp. 1039–73.

Kemp, Rene and Luc Soete, "The Greening of Technological Progress: an Evolutionary Perspective," *Futures*, Vol. 24, No. 5, June 1992, pp. 437–57.

Koselka, Rita, "Evolutionary Economics: Nice Guys Don't Finish Last," *Forbes*, Vol. 152, No. 8, October 11, 1993, pp. 110–14.

Lazlo, Ervin, "Evolution: the New Paradigm," *World Futures*, Vol. 23, November 1987, pp. 151–60.

Leydesdorff, Loet, "New Models of Technological Change: New Theories for Technology Studies?" in Loet Leydesdorff and Peter Van den Besselaar, eds, *Evolutionary Economics and Chaos Theory: New Directions in Technology Studies*, New York: St Martin's Press, 1994, pp. 180–92.

Lower, Milton D., "The Concept of Technology within the Institutionalist Perspective," *Journal of Economic Issues*, Vol. 21, No. 3, September 1987, pp. 1147–76.

Mannermaa, Mika, "In Search of an Evolutionary Paradigm for Futures Research," *Futures*, Vol. 23, No. 4, May 1991, pp. 349–72.

Nelson, Richard R., "Recent Evolutionary Theorizing about Economic Change," *Journal of Economic Literature*, Vol. 33, No. 1, March 1995, pp. 48–90.

—— "What Has Been the Matter with Neoclassical Growth Theory?," in Gerald Silverberg and Luc Soete, eds, *The Economics of Growth and Technical Change: Technologies, Nations, Agents*, Brookfield, VT: Edward Elgar, 1994, pp. 290–324.

—— "Technical Change as Cultural Evolution," in Ross Thomson, ed., *Learning and Technological Change*, New York: St Martin's Press, 1993, 9–23.

—— "The Role of Firm Differences in an Evolutionary Theory of Technical Advance," *Science and Public Policy*, Vol. 18, No. 6, December 1991, pp. 347–52.

—— and Sidney G. Winter, *An Evolutionary Theory of Economic Change*, Cambridge, MA: Harvard University Press, 1982.

Poirot, C. S., Jr, "Institutions and Economic Evolution," *Journal of Economic Issues*, Vol. 27, No. 3, September 1993, pp. 887–907.

Pryor, Frederick L., *Economic Evolution and Structure: the Impact of Complexity on the US Economic System*, New York: Cambridge University Press, 1996.

Radzicki, Michael J., "Institutional Dynamics: an Extension of the Institutionalist Approach to Socioeconomic Analysis," *Journal of Economic Issues*, Vol. 22, No. 3, September 1988, pp. 633–65.

Smith, John K., "Thinking about Technological Change: Linear and Evolutionary Models," in Ross Thomson, ed., *Learning and Technological Change*, New York: St Martin's Press, 1993, pp. 65–79.

Tisdell, Clem, "Evolutionary Economics and Research and Development," in Steve Dowrick, ed., *Economic Approaches to Innovation*, Brookfield, VT: Edward Elgar, 1995, pp. 120–44.

Self-organization

Allen, Peter M., "Self-organization in the Urban System," in William C. Schieve and Peter M. Allen, eds, *Self-organization and Dissipative Structures: Applications in the Physical and Social Sciences*, Austin: University of Texas Press, 1982, pp. 132–58.

Auger, Pierre M., "Self-organization in Hierarchically Organized Systems" *Systems Research*, Vol. 7, No. 4, 1990, pp. 221–36.

Bak, Per and Kan Chen, "Self-organized Criticality," *Scientific American*, Vol. 264, No. 1, January 1991, pp. 46–53.

—— and Michael Creutz, "Self-organized Criticality in the 'Game of Life'," *Nature*, Vol. 342, No. 6251, December 14, 1989, pp. 780–2.

Benton, Caroline F. and Kyoichi Kijima, "Maintaining Foreign Subsidiaries' Ability to Self-organize in the Japanese Market," *Systems Research*, Vol. 13, No. 4, December 1996, pp. 447–56.

Corning, Peter A., "Synergy and Self-organization in the Evolution of Complex Systems," *Systems Research*, Vol. 12, No. 2, June 1995, pp. 89–121.

De Vany Arthur, "Information Chance, and Evolution: Alchian and the Economics of Self-organization," *Economic Inquiry*, Vol. 34, No. 3, July 1996, pp. 427–43.

Foster, John, "Economics and the Self-organisation Approach: Alfred Marshall Revisited?" *Economic Journal*, Vol. 103, No. 419, July 1993, pp. 975–91.

Kaplan, Marvin L. and Netta R. Kaplan, "The Self-organization of Human Psychological Functioning," *Behavioral Science*, Vol. 36, No. 3, July 1991, pp. 161–78.

Krugman, Paul R., *The Self-organization Economy*, Cambridge, MA: Blackwell Publishers, 1996.

Lee, Mary E., "The Evolution of Technology: a Model of Socio-ecological Self-organization," in Loet Leydesdorff and Peter Van den Besselaar, eds, *Evolutionary Economics and Chaos Theory: New Directions in Technology Studies*, New York: St. Martin's Press, 1994, pp. 167–79.

Lesourne, Jacques, "Self-organization as a Process in the Evolution of Economic Systems," in Richard H. Day and Ping Chen, eds, *Nonlinear Dynamics and Evolutionary Economics*, New York: Oxford University Press, 1993, 150–66.

Morgan, Gareth, *Images of Organization*, Beverly Hills, CA: Sage Publications, 1986, pp. 77–109, 223–72.

Nelson, Richard, R.. "Why Do Firms Differ, and How Does It Matter?," *Strategic Management Journal*, Vol. 12, Special Issue, Winter 1991, pp. 61–74.

Nonaka, Ikujiro and Teruo Yamanouchi, "Managing Innovation as a Self-renewing Process," *Journal of Business Venturing*, Vol. 4, No. 5, September 1989, 299–315.

Peters, Tom, "A Paean to Self-organization," *Forbes ASAP*, October 10, 1994, pp. 154–6.

Prigogine, Ilya and Peter M. Allen, "The Challenge of Complexity," in William C. Shieve and Peter M. Allen, eds, *Self-organization and Dissipative Structures: Applications in the Physical and Social Sciences*, Austin: University of Texas Press, 1982, pp. 3–39.

Radzicki, Michael J., "Institutional Dynamics, Deterministic Chaos, and Self-organizing Systems," *Journal of Economic Issues*, Vol. 24, No. 1, March 1990, pp. 57–102.

Richter, Frank-Jurgen, "The Emergence of Corporate Alliance Networks – Conversion to Self-organization," *Human Systems Management*, Vol. 13, No. 1, 1994, pp. 19–26.

Romme, A. Georges L., "The Process of Self-renewal by Management Teams," *Human Systems Management*, Vol. 13, No. 1, 1994, pp. 49–55.

—— "The Formation of Firm Strategy as Self-organization," in Christopher Freeman and Luc Soete, eds, *New Explorations in the Economics of Technological Change*, New York: Pinter Publishers, 1990, pp. 38–54.

Scheinkman, Jose A. and Michael Woodford, "Self-organized Criticality and Economic Fluctuations," *American Economic Association Papers and Proceedings*, Vol. 84, No. 2, May 1994, pp. 417–21.

Silverberg, Gerald, Giovanni Dosi, and Luigi Orsenigo, "Innovation, Diversity and Diffusion: a Self-organisation Model," *Economic Journal*, Vol. 98, December 1988, pp. 1032–54.

Smith, Charles, "Self-organization in Human Systems – a Paradigm of Ethics?," *Systems Research*, Vol. 7, No. 4, 1990, 237–44.

van Olffen, Woody and A. Georges L. Romme, "The Role of Hierarchy in Self-organizing Systems," *Human Systems Management*, Vol. 14, No. 3, 1995, pp. 199–206.

Watts, Diane L., "Disorder and Contradiction: an Empirical Perspective on Self-organization," *Human Systems Management*, Vol. 9, No. 4, 1990, pp. 239–48.

Wheatley, Margaret J., *Leadership and the New Science: Learning about Organization from an Orderly Universe*, San Francisco: Berrett-Koehler Publishers, 1992, pp. 75–99.

—— and Myron Kellner-Rogers, "Self-organization: the Irresistible Future of Organizing," *Strategy and Leadership*, Vol. 24, No. 4, July/August 1996, pp. 18–24.

Witt, Ulrich, "Self-organization and Economics – What Is New?" *Structural Change and Economic Dynamics*, Vol. 8, No. 4, October 1997, pp. 489–507.

Zuijderhoudt, Robert W. L., "Chaos and the Dynamics of Self-organization," *Human Systems Management*, Vol. 9, No. 4, 1990, pp. 225–38.

Organizational learning

Adler, Paul S. and Robert E. Cole, "Designed for Learning: a Tale of Two Auto Plants," *Sloan Management Review*, Vol. 35, No. 4, Spring 1993, pp. 85–94.

Alasoini, Tuomo, "A Learning Factory: Experimenting with Adaptable Production in Finnish Engineering Workshops," *International Journal of Human Factors in Manufacturing*, Vol. 6, No. 1, Winter 1996, pp. 3–19.

Allen, Peter M., "Evolution: Persistent Ignorance from Continual Learning," in Richard H. Day and Ping Chen, eds, *Nonlinear Dynamics and Evolutionary Economics*, New York: Oxford University Press, 1993, pp. 101–12.

Argote, Linda, "Organizational Learning Curves: Persistence, Transfer and Turnover," *International Journal of Technology Management*, Vol. 11, Nos 7/8, 1996, Special Issue on Unlearning and Learning for Technological Innovation, pp. 759–69.

—— and Dennis Epple, "Learning Curves in Manufacturing," *Science*, Vol. 247, No. 4945, February 23, 1990, pp. 920–4.

Bahlmann, Tineke, "The Learning Organization in a Turbulent Environment," *Human Systems Management*, Vol. 9, No. 3, 1990, pp. 195–202.

Barrett, Frank J., "Creating Appreciative Learning Cultures," *Organizational Dynamics*, Vol. 24, No. 2, Autumn 1995, pp. 36–49.

Bartezzaghi, Emilio, Mariano Corso, and Roberto Verganti, "Continuous Improvement and Inter-project Learning in New Product Development," *International Journal of Technology Management*, Vol. 14, No. 1, 1997, pp. 116–38.

Benson, Tracy E., "The Learning Organization: Heading toward Places Unimaginable," *Industry Week*, Vol. 242, No. 1, January 4, 1993, pp. 35–8.

Bessant, John, "The Lessons of Failure: Learning to Manage New Manufacturing Technology," *International Journal of Technology Management*, Vol. 8, Nos 2/3/4, Special Issue on Manufacturing Technology: Diffusion, Implementation and Management, 1993, pp. 197–214.

Bettis, Richard A. and C.K Prahalad, "The Dominant Logic: Retrospective and Extension," *Strategic Management Journal*, Vol. 16, No. 1, January 1995, pp. 5–14.

Boisot, Max H., "Is Your Firm as Creative Destroyer? Competitive Learning and Knowledge Flows in the Technological Strategies of Firms," *Research Policy*, Vol. 24, No. 4, July 1995, pp. 489–506.

Brown, John S. and Paul Duguid, "Organizing Knowledge," *California Management Review*, Vol. 40, No. 3, Spring 1998, pp. 90–111.

Callahan, John and Peter Diedrich, "Organizational Learning across Critical Linkages: the Case of Captive ASIC Design and Manufacturing," *Technovation*, Vol. 12, No. 7, November 1992, pp. 433–46.

Chiaromonte, Francesca, Giovanni Dosi, and Luigi Orsenigo, "Innovative Learning and Institutions in the Process of Development: on the Microfoundation of Growth Regimes," in Ross Thomson, ed., *Learning and Technological Change*, New York: St. Martin's Press, 1993, pp. 117–49.

Cohen, Wesley M. and Daniel A. Levinthal, "Innovation and Learning: the Two Faces of R&D," *Economic Journal*, Vol. 99, No. 397, September 1989, pp. 569–96.

Fagerberg, Jan, "User–Producer Interaction, Learning and Comparative Advantage," *Cambridge Journal of Economics*, Vol. 19, No. 1, February 1995, pp. 243–56.

Fiol, C. Marlene, "Consensus, Diversity, and Learning in Organizations," *Organizational Science*, Vol. 5, No. 3, August 1994, pp. 403–20.

Fleck, James, "Learning by Trying: the Implementation of Configurational Technology," *Research Policy*, Vol. 23, No. 6, November 1994, pp. 637–52.

Florida, Richard, "Toward the Learning Region," *Futures*, Vol. 27, No. 5, June 1995, pp. 527–36.

Garvin, David A., "Building a Learning Organization," *Harvard Business Review*, Vol. 71, No. 4, July/August 1993, pp. 78–91.

Habermeier, Karl F., "Product Use and Product Improvement," *Research Policy*, Vol. 19, No. 3, June 1990, pp. 271–83.

Hodgetts, Richard M., Fred Luthans, and Sang M. Lee, "New Paradigm Organizations: from Total Quality to Learning to World-class," *Organizational Dynamics*, Vol. 22, No. 3, Winter 1994, pp. 5–19.

Inkpen, Andrew C., "Creating Knowledge through Collaboration," *California Management Review*, Vol. 35, No. 1, Fall 1996, pp. 123–40.

Kim, Daniel H., "The Link between Individual and Organizational Learning," *Sloan Management Review*, Vol. 35, No. 1, Fall 1993, pp. 37–50.

Kofman, Fred and Peter M. Senge, "Communities of Commitment: the Heart of Learning Organizations," *Organizational Dynamics*, Vol. 22, No. 2, Autumn 1993, pp. 5–23.

Lazonick, William, "Learning and the Dynamics of International Competitive Advantage," in Yuichi Shionoya and Mark Perlman, eds, *Innovation in Technology, Industries, and Institutions: Studies in Schumpeterian Perspectives*, Ann Arbor: University of Michigan Press, 1994, pp. 189–211.

Leonard-Barton, Dorothy, "The Factory as a Learning Laboratory," *Sloan Management Review*, No. 34, No. 1, Fall 1992, pp. 23–38.

Levinson, Nanette, S. and Minoru Asahi, "Cross-national Alliances and Inter-organizational Learning," *Organizational Dynamics*, Vol. 24, No. 2, Autumn 1995, pp. 50–63.

McKee, Daryl, "An Organizational Learning Approach to Product Innovation," *Journal of Product Innovation Management*, Vol. 9, No. 3, 1992, pp. 232–45.

Malerba, Franco, "Learning by Firms and Incremental Technical Change," *Economic Journal*, Vol. 102, No. 413, July 1992, 845–59.

Mathews, John, "Organizational Foundations of Economic Learning," *Human Systems Management*, Vol. 15, 1996, pp. 113–24.

Meyers, Patricia W., "Non-linear Learning in Large Technological Firms: Period Four Implies Chaos," *Research Policy*, Vol. 19, No. 2, April 1990, pp. 97–115.

Mody, Ashoka, "Learning through Alliances," *Journal of Economic Behavior and Organization*, Vol. 20, February 1993, pp. 151–70.

—— "Firm Strategies for Costly Engineering Learning," *Management Science*, Vol. 35, No. 4, April 1989, pp. 496–514.

Nonaka, Ikujiro, "Dynamic Theory of Organizational Knowledge Creation," *Organization Science*, Vol. 5, No. 1, February 1994, pp. 14–37.

—— "The Knowledge-creating Company," *Harvard Business Review*, Vol. 69, No. 6, November/December 1991, pp. 96–104.

—— and Hirotaka Takeuchi, *The Knowledge-creating Company: How Japanese Companies Create the Dynamics of Innovation*, New York: Oxford University Press, 1995.

Pennings, Johannes M., Harry Barkema and Sytse Douma, "Organizational Learning and Diversification," *Academy of Management Journal*, Vol. 37, No. 3, June 1994, pp. 608–40.

Pisano, Gary P., "Knowledge, Integration, and the Locus of Learning: an Empirical Analysis of Process Development," *Strategic Management Journal*, Vol. 15, Special Issue, Winter 1994, pp. 85–100.

Senker, Jacqueline, "National Systems of Innovation, Organizational Learning and Industrial Biotechnology," *Technovation*, Vol. 16, No. 5, May 1996, pp. 219–29.

—— and Margaret Sharp, "Organizational Learning in Cooperative Alliances: Some Case Studies in Biotechnology," *Technology Analysis and Strategic Management*, Vol. 9, No. 1, 1997, pp. 35–51.

Silverberg, Gerald and Bart Verspagen, "Collective Learning, Innovation and Growth in a Boundedly Rational, Evolutionary World," *Journal of Evolutionary Economics*, Vol. 4, No. 3, 1994, pp. 207–26.

Slaughter, Sarah, "Innovation and Learning During Implementation: a Comparison of User and Manufacturer Innovations," *Research Policy*, Vol. 22, No. 1, February 1993, pp. 81–95.

Slocum, John W., Jr, Michael McGill and David T. Lei, "The New Learning Strategy: Anytime, Anything, Anywhere," *Organizational Dynamics*, Vol. 23, No. 2, Autumn 1994, pp. 33–47.

Starbuck, William H., "Unlearning Ineffective or Obsolete Technologies," *International Journal of Technology Management*, Special Issue on Unlearning and Learning for Technological Innovation, Vol. 11, Nos 7/8, 1996, pp. 725–37.

Teece, David J., Richard Rumelt, Giovanni Dosi, and Sidney Winter, "Understanding Corporate Coherence: Theory and Evidence," *Journal of Economic Behavior and Organization*, Vol. 23, No. 1, January 1994, pp. 1–30.

Tyre, Marcie J. and Wanda J. Orlikowski, "The Episodic Process of Learning by Using," *International Journal of Technology Management*, Vol. 11, Nos 7/8, 1996, Special Issue on Unlearning and Learning for Technological Innovation, p. 790–8.

Tyre, Marcie J. and Eric von Hippel. "The Situated Nature of Adaptive Learning in Organizations," *Organization Science*, Vol. 8, No. 1, January/February 1997, pp. 71–81.

Vincenti, Walter, *What Engineers Know and How They Know It: Analytical Studies from Aeronautical History*, Baltimore: John Hopkins University Press, 1991.

Von Hippel, Eric and Maurice J. Tyre, "How Learning by Doing Is Done: Problem Identification in Novel Process Equipment," *Research Policy*, Vol. 24, No. 1, January 1995, pp. 1–12.

Networks

Baba, Yasunori and Ken-ichi Imai, "A Network View of Innovation and Entrepreneurship: the Case of Evolution of the VCR Systems," *International Social Science Journal*, Vol. 45, No. 1, February 1993, pp. 23–24.

Bleeker, Samuel E., "The Virtual Organization, *Futurist*, March/April 1994, pp. 9–14.

Bush, John B., Jr. and Alan L. Frohman, "Communication in a 'Network' Organization," *Organizational Dynamics*, Vol. 20, No. 2, Autumn 1991, pp. 23–36.

DeBresson, Chris and Fernand Amesse, "Networks of Innovators: a Review and Introduction to the Issue," *Research Policy*, Vol. 20, No. 5, October 1991, pp. 363–79.

Elzen, Boelie, Bert Enserink and Wim A. Smit, "Socio-technical Networks: How a Technology Studies Approach May Help to Solve Problems Related to Technical Change," *Social Studies of Science*, Vol. 26, No. 1, February 1996, pp. 95–141.

Freeman, C., "Networks of Innovators: a Synthesis of Research Issues," *Research Policy*, Vol. 20, No. 5, October 1991, pp. 499–514.

Fruin, W. Mark and Toshihiro Nishiguchi, "Supplying the Toyota Production System: Intercorporate Organizational Evolution and Supplier Subsystems," in Bruce Kogut, ed., *Country Competitiveness: Technology and the Organizing of Work*, New York: Oxford University Press, 1993, pp. 225–56.

Gerlach, Michael L. and James R. Lincoln, "The Organization of Business Networks in the United States and Japan," in Nitin Nohria and Robert G. Eccles, eds, *Networks and Organizations: Structure, form, and Action*, Boston: Harvard Business School Press, 1992, pp. 491–520.

Grandori, Anna and Giuseppe Soda, "Inter-firm Networks: Antecedents, Mechanisms and Forms," *Organization Studies*, Vol. 16, No. 2, 1995, pp. 183–214.

Hagedoorn, John, "Strategic Technology Partnering during the 1980s: Trends, Networks and Corporate Patterns in Non-core Technologies," *Research Policy*, Vol. 24, No. 2, March 1995, pp. 207–31.

―― "Global Strategies in Innovation: Networks of Research and Production," *International Journal of Technology Management*, Special Publication on the Role of Technology in Corporate Policy, 1991, pp. 81–94.

―― and Jos Schakenraad, "Inter-firm Partnerships for Generic Technologies – The Case of New Materials," *Technovation*, Vol. 11, No. 7, 1991, pp. 429–444.

Kreiner, Kristian and Majken Schultz, "Informal Collaboration in R&D: the Formation of Networks across Organizations," *Organization Studies*, Vol. 14, No. 2, 1993, pp. 189–209.

Langlois, Richard N. and Paul L. Robertson, "Networks and Innovation in a Modular System: Lessons from the Microcomputer and Stereo Component Industries," *Research Policy*, Vol. 21, No. 4, August 1992, pp. 297–313.

Larsson, Stig, "New Dimensions in Organizing Industrial Networks," *International Journal of Technology Management*, Vol. 8, Nos 1/2, Special Issue on 'New Technological Foundations of Strategic Management,' 1993, pp. 39–58.

Lorenzoni, Gianni and Charles Baden-Fuller, "Creating a Strategic Center to Manage a Web of Partners," *California Management Review*, Vol. 37, No. 3, Spring 1995, pp. 146–63.

Lundgren, Anders, *Technological Innovation and Network Evolution*, New York: Routledge, 1995, pp. 77–104.

Malecki, Edward J. and Deborah M. Tootle, "The Role of Networks in Small Firm Competitiveness," *International Journal of Technology Management*, Vol. 11, Nos 1/2, Special Issue on Informal Information Flow, 1996, pp. 43–57.

Medcof, John W., "Challenges in Managing Technology in Transnational Multipartner Networks," *Business Horizons*, Vol. 39, No. 1, January/February 1996, pp. 47–54.

Midgley, David F., Pamela Morrison and John H. Roberts, "The Effect of Network Structure in Industrial Diffusion Processes," *Research Policy*, Vol. 21, No. 6, December 1992, pp. 533–52.

Miles, Raymond E. and Charles C. Snow, "The New Network Form: a Spherical Structure Built on a Human Investment Philosophy," *Organizational Dynamics*, Vol. 23, No. 4, Spring 1995, pp. 4–18.

Miller, Roger, "Global R&D Networks and Large-scale Innovation: the Case of the Automobile Industry," *Research Policy*, Vol. 23, No. 1, January 1994, pp. 27–46.

Osborn, Richard N. and John Hagedoorn, "The Institutionalization and Evolutionary Dynamics of Interorganizational Alliances and Networks," *Academy of Management Journal*, Vol. 40, No. 2, April 1997, 261–78.

Pyka, Andreas, "Informal Networking," *Technovation*, Vol. 17, No. 4, April 1997, pp. 207–20.

Reich, Robert B., *The Work of Nations: Preparing Ourselves for 21st Century Capitalism*, New York: Alfred A. Knopf, 1991, pp. 87–97.

Robertson, Paul L. and Richard N. Langlois, "Innovation, Networks, and Vertical Integration," *Research Policy*, Vol. 24, No. 4, July 1995, pp. 543–62.

Snow, Charles C., Raymond E. Miles, and Henry J. Coleman, Jr, "Managing 21st Century Network Organizations," *Organizational Dynamics*, Vol. 20, No. 3, Winter 1992, pp. 5–20.

Sorenson, Knut H. and Nora Levold, "Tacit Networks, Heterogeneous Engineers, and Embodied Knowledge," *Science, Technology, and Human Values*, Vol. 17, No. 1, Winter 1992, pp. 13–35.

Stewart, Thomas A., "The Search for the Organization of the Future," *Fortune*, Vol. 125, No. 10, May 18, 1992, pp. 92–8.

Wildeman, Leo, "Alliances and Networks: the Next Generation," *International Journal of Technology Management*, Vol. 15, Nos 1/2, 1998, pp. 96–108.

Ziman, John, "A Neutral Net Model of Innovation," *Science and Public Policy*, Vol. 18, No. 1, February 1991, pp. 65–75.

Cooperation

Aldrich, Howard E. and Toshihiro Sasaki, "R&D Consortia in the United States and Japan," *Research Policy*, Vol. 24, No. 2, March 1995, pp. 301–16.

Bolton, Michele K., Roger Malmrose, and William G. Ouchi, "The Organization of Innovation in the United States and Japan: Neoclassical and Relational Contracting," *Journal of Management Studies*, Vol. 31, No. 5, September 1994, pp. 653–79.

Borrus, Michael and Jeffrey A. Hart, "Display's the Thing: the Real Stakes in the Conflict over High-resolution Displays," *Journal of Policy Analysis and Management*, Vol. 13, No. 1, Winter 1994, pp. 21–54.

Browning, Larry D., Janice M. Beyer, and Judy C. Shelter, "Building Cooperation in a Competitive Industry: Sematech and the Semiconductor Industry," *Academy of Management Journal*, Vol. 38, No. 1, February 1995, pp. 113–51.

Coombs, Rod, Albert Richards, Pier P. Saviotti, and Vivien Walsh, "Introduction: Technological Collaboration and Networks of Alliances in the Innovation Process," in Rod Coombs, Albert Richards, Pier P. Saviotti, and Viven Walsh, eds, *Technological Collaboration: The Dynamics of Cooperation in Industrial Innovation*, Brookfield, VT: Edward Elgar, 1996, pp. 1–17.

Dickson, Keith, "How Informal Can You Be? Trust and Reciprocity within Co-operative and Collaborative Relationships," *International Journal of Technology Management*, Vol. 11, Nos 1/2, Special Issue on Informal Information Flow, 1996, pp. 129–39.

Duysters, Geert and John Hagedoorn, "Internationalization of Corporate Technology through Strategic Partnering: an Empirical Investigation," *Research Policy*, Vol. 25, No. 1, January 1996, pp. 1–12.

Ferguson, Charles H., "Computers and the Coming of the US Keiretsu," *Harvard Business Review*, Vol. 68. No. 4, July/August 1990, pp. 55–70.

Flamm, Kenneth, S., "Flat-panel Displays: Catalyzing a US Industry," *Issues in Science and Technology*, Vol. 11, No. 1, Fall 1994, pp. 27–32.

Freeman, Chris and John Hagedoorn, "Convergence and Divergence in the Internationalization of Technology," in John Hagedoorn, ed., *Technical Change and the World Economy: Convergence and Divergence in Technology Strategies*, Brookfield, VT: Edward Elgar, 1995, pp. 34–57.

Gibson, David V. and Everett M. Rogers, *R&D Collaboration on Trial: the Microelectronics and Computer Technology Corporation*, Boston: Harvard Business School Press, 1994, pp. 467–553.

Grindley, Peter, David C. Mowery, and Byron Silverman, "SEMATECH and Collaborative Research: Lessons in the Design of High-technology Consortia," *Journal of Policy Analysis and Management*. Vol. 13, No. 4, 1994, pp. 723–58.

Hansen, Niles, "Competition, Trust, and Reciprocity in the Development of Innovative Regional Milieux," *Papers in Regional Science*, Vol. 71, No. 2, 1992, pp. 95–105.

Kamath, Rajan R. and Jeffrey K. Liker, "A Second Look at Japanese Product Development," *Harvard Business Review*, Vol. 72, No. 6, November/December 1994, pp. 154–70.

Kenworthy, Lane, *In Search of National Economic Success: Balancing Competition and Cooperation*, London: Sage Publications, 1995, pp. 154–96.

Kogut, Bruce, "Joint Ventures: Theoretical and Empirical Perspectives," *Strategic Management Journal*, Vol. 9, No. 4, July/August 1988, pp. 319–32.

Lane, Christel and Reinhard Bachmann, "The Social Constitution of Trust: Supplier Relations in Britain and Germany," *Organization Studies*, Vol. 17, Issue 3, 1996, pp. 365–95.

Lazonick, William, *Business Organization and the Myth of the Market Economy*, New York: Cambridge University Press, 1991.

—— "Organizational Integration in Three Industrial Revolutions," in Arnold Heertje and Mark Perlman, eds, *Evolving Technology and Market Structure: Studies in Schumpeterian Economics*, Ann Arbor: University of Michigan Press, 1990, 77–97.

Mangematin, Vincent, "The Simultaneous Shaping of Organization and Technology within Cooperative Agreements," in Rod Coombs, Albert Richards, Pier P. Saviotti, and Vivien Walsh, eds, *Technological Collaboration: The Dynamics of Cooperation in Industrial Innovation*, Brookfield, VT: Edward Elgar, 1996, pp. 119–41.

Miyata, Yukio, "An Analysis of Cooperative R&D in the United States, "*Technovation*, Vol. 16, No. 3, 1996, pp. 123–31.

Rothwell, Roy, "Issues in User–Producer Relations in the Innovation Process: the Role of Government," *International Journal of Technology Management*, Vol. 9, Nos 5/6/7, Special Issue on Technological Responses to Increasing Competition, 1994, pp. 629–49.

Schott, Thomas, "Collaboration in the Invention of Technology: Globalization, Regions, and Centers," *Social Science Research*, Vol. 23, No. 1, March 1994, pp. 23–56.

"Sematech's Evolving Role: an Interview with William J. Spencer," *Issues in Science and Technology*, Vol. 10, No. 2, Winter 1993, pp. 63–8.

Singh, Kulwant, "The Impact of Technological Complexity and Interfirm Cooperation on Business Survival," *Academy of Management Journal*, Vol. 40, No. 2, April 1997, pp. 339–67.

Spencer, William J. and Peter Grindley, "SEMATECH after Five Years: High-technology Consortia and US Competitiveness," *California Management Review*, Vol. 35, No. 4, Summer 1993, pp. 9–32.

Subramanian, S. K. and Yeswanth Subramanian, "Managing Technology Fusion through Synergy Circles in Japan," *Journal of Engineering and Technology Management*, Vol. 8, No. 4, December 1991, pp. 313–37.

Tucker, Jonathan B., "Partners and Rivals: a Model of International Collaboration in Advanced Technology," *International Organization*, Vol. 45, No. 1, Winter 1991, pp. 83–120.

Tylecote, Andrew, "Managerial Objectives and Technological Collaboration: the Role of National Variations in Cultures and Structures," in Rod Coombs, Albert Richards, Pier P. Saviotti, and Vivien Walsh, eds, *Technological Collaboration: the Dynamics of Cooperation in Industrial Innovation*, Brookfield, VT: Edward Elgar, 1996, pp. 35–53.

"Winning through Cooperation: an Interview with William Spencer," *Technology Review*, Vol. 100, No. 1, January 1997, pp. 22–7.

Yamamoto, Hisatoshi, "Complementary Competition in Japan," *Research Technology Management*, Vol. 37, No. 2, March/April 1994, pp. 49–54.

Metaphors of technology, organization, and evolution

Champlin, Dell and Paulette Olson, "Post-industrial Metaphor: Understanding Corporate Restructuring and the Economic Environment of the 1990s," *Journal of Economic Issues*, Vol. 28, No. 2, June 1994, pp. 449–59.

Diehl-Callaway, Linda, "Is Capitalism Kaput?" *American Economist*, Vol. 36, No. 1, Spring 1992, pp. 71–6.

Dunn, Steven, "Root Metaphor in the Old and New Industrial Relations," *British Journal of Industrial Relations*, Vol. 28, No. 1, March 1990, pp. 1–30.

Garud, Raghu and Suresh Kotha, "Using the Brain as a Metaphor to Model Flexible Production Systems," *Academy of Management Review*, Vol. 19, No. 4, October 1994, pp. 671–98.

Hodgson, Geoffrey M., "The Economy as an Organism – Not a Machine," *Futures*, Vol. 25, No. 2, May 1993, pp. 392–403.

Joerges, Bernward, "Images of Technology in Sociology: Computer as Butterfly and Bat," *Technology and Culture*, Vol. 31, No. 2, April 1990, pp. 203–27.

Judge, Anthony J. N., "Metaphor and the Language of Futures," *Futures*, Vol. 25, No. 3, April 1993, pp. 275–85.

Lissack, Michael, "Mind Your Metaphors: Lessons from Complexity Science," *Long Range Planning*, Vol. 30, No. 2, April 1997, pp. 294–8.

Marshak, Robert J., "Managing the Metaphors of Change," *Organizational Dynamics*, Vol. 22, No. 1, Summer 1993, pp. 44–56.

Michael, Donald N., "Governing by Learning: Boundaries, Myths and Metaphors," *Futures*, Vol. 25, No. 1, February 1993, pp. 81–9.

Morgan, Gareth, "More on Metaphors: Why We Cannot Control Tropes in Administrative Science," *Administrative Science Quarterly*, Vol. 28, No. 4, December 1983, pp. 601–7.

Pearce, Craig L. and Charles P. Osmond, "Metaphors for Change: the ALPs Model of Change Management," *Organizational Dynamics*, Vol. 24, No. 3, Winter 1996, pp. 23–35.

Tepper, August, "Controlling Technology by Shaping Visions," *Policy Sciences*, Vol. 29, No. 1, February 1996, pp. 29–44.

Tsoukas, Haridimos, "The Missing Link: a Transformational View of Metaphors in Organizational Science," *Academy of Management Review*, July 1991, pp. 566–85.

Human know-how, skills, and expertise

Cappelli, Peter and Anne Crocker-Hefter, "Distinctive Human Resources Are Firms' Core Competencies," *Organizational Dynamics*, Vol. 24, No. 1, Winter 1996, pp. 1–21.

Dunlop, John T., "The Challenge of Human Resource Development," *Industrial Relations*, Vol. 31, No. 1, Winter 1992, pp. 50–5.

Harrison, Bennett, "The Dark Side of Flexible Production," *Technology Review*, Vol. 97, No. 4, May/June 1994, pp. 38–45.

Johnson, Joanne, John R. Baldwin, and Brent Diverty, "The Implications of Innovation for Human Resource Strategies," *Futures*, Vol. 28, No. 2, March 1996, pp. 103–19.

Kamoche, Ken, "Strategic Human Resource Management within a Resource-capability View of the Firm," *Journal of Management Studies*, Vol. 33, No. 2, March 1996, pp. 213–33.

Karwowski, W., *et al.*, "Integrating People, Organization, and Technology in Advanced Manufacturing: a Position Paper Based on the Joint View of Industrial Managers, Engineers, Consultants, and Researchers," *International Journal of Human Factors in Manufacturing*, Vol. 4, No. 1, January 1994, pp. 1–19.

Marshall, Ray, "The Future Role of Government in Industrial Relations," *Industrial Relations*, Vol. 31, No. 1, Winter 1992, pp. 31–49.

Reich, Robert B., "Training a Skilled Work Force: Why US Corporations Neglect Their Workers," *Dissent*, Vol. 39, No. 1, Winter 1992, pp. 42–6.

Sadler-Smith, Eugene and Beryl Badger, "Cognitive Style, Learning, and Innovation," *Technology Analysis and Strategic Management*, Vol. 10, No. 2, June 1998, pp. 247–65.

Sobol, Marion G. and David Lei, "Environment, Manufacturing Technology, and Embedded Knowledge," *International Journal of Human Factors in Manufacturing*, April 1994, pp. 167–89.

Warner, Malcolm, "Innovation and Training," in Mark Dodgson and Roy Rothwell, eds, *The Handbook of Industrial Innovation*, Brookfield, VT: Edward Elgar, 1994, pp. 348–54.

Core capabilities and complementary assets

Bercovitz, Janet E. L., John M. de Figueiredo, and David J. Teece, "Firm Capabilities and Managerial Decision Making: a Theory of Innovation Biases," in Raghu Garud, Praveen R. Nayyar, and Zur B. Shapira, eds, *Technological Innovation: Oversights and Foresights*, New York: Cambridge University Press, 1997, pp. 233–59.

Chiesa, Vittorio and Raffaella Manzini, "Towards a Framework for Dynamic Technology Strategy," *Technology Analysis and Strategic Management*, Vol. 10, No. 1, March 1998, pp. 111–29.

Christensen, Jens F., "Asset Profiles for Technological Innovation," *Research Policy*, Vol. 24, No. 5, September 1995, pp. 727–45.

Coombs, Rod, "Core Competencies and the Strategic Management of R&D," *R&D Management*, Vol. 26, No. 4, October 1996, pp. 345–55.

Dosi, Giovanni and Luigi Marengo, "Some Elements of an Evolutionary Theory of Organizational Competences," in Richard W. England, ed., *Evolutionary Concepts in Contemporary Economics*, Ann Arbor, MI: University of Michigan Press, 1994, pp. 147–78.

Gallon, Mark R., Harold M. Stillman, and David Coates, "Putting Core Competency Thinking into Practice," *Research-Technology Management*, Vol. 38, No. 3, May/June 1995, pp. 20–8.

Granstrand, Ove, Pari Patel, and Keith Pavitt, "Multi-technology Corporations: Why They Have 'Distributed' Rather than 'Distinctive Core' Competencies," *Californian Management Review*, Vol. 39, No. 4, Summer 1997, pp. 8–25.

Grant, Robert M., "Prospering in Dynamically-competitive Environments: Organizational Capability as Knowledge Integration," *Organization Science*, Vol. 7, No. 4, July/August 1996, pp. 375–87.

Hamel, Gary, "Competition for Competence and Inter-partner Learning within International Strategic Alliances," *Strategic Management Journal*, Vol. 12, Special Issue, 1991, pp. 83–103.

Lei, David T., "Competence-building, Technology Fusion and Competitive Advantage: the Key Roles of Organizational Learning and Strategic Alliances," *International Journal of Technology Management*, Vol. 14, Nos 2/3/4, 1997, pp. 208–37.

—— Michael A. Hitt, and Richard Bettis, "Dynamic Core Competences through Meta-learning and Strategic Context," *Journal of Management*, Vol. 22, No. 4, 1996, pp. 549–69.

Leonard-Barton, Dorothy, *Wellsprings of Knowledge: Building and Sustaining the Sources of Innovation*, Boston: Harvard Business School Press, 1995, pp. 3–28.

Miyazaki, Kumiko, *Building Competences in the Firm: Lessons from Japanese and European Optoelectronics*, New York: St. Martin's Press, 1995, pp. 11–38.

Patel, Pari and Keith Pavitt, "The Technological Competencies of the World's Largest Firms: Complex and Path Dependent, but Not Much Variety," *Research Policy*, Vol. 26, No. 2, May 1997, pp. 141–56.

Prencipe, Andrea, "Technological Competencies and Product's Evolutionary Dynamics: a Case Study from the Aero-engine Industry," *Research Policy*, Vol. 25, No. 8, January 1997, pp. 1261–76.

Steensma, H. Kevin, "Acquiring Technological Competencies through Inter-organizational Collaboration: an Organizational Learning Perspective," *Journal of Engineering Technology and Management*, Vol. 12, No. 4, January 1996, pp. 267–86.

Taylor, Peter and Julian Lowe, "Are Functional Assets or Knowledge Assets the Basis of New Product Development Performance?," *Technology Analysis and Strategic Management*, Vol. 9, No. 4, December 1997, pp. 473–88.

Teece, David J., "Competition, Cooperation, and Innovation: Organizational Arrangements for Regimes of Rapid Technological Progress," *Journal of Economic Behavior and Organization*, Vol. 18, April 1992, pp. 1–25.

Winter, Sidney G., "Knowledge and Competence as Strategic Assets," in David J. Teece, ed., *The Competitive Challenge: Strategies for Industrial Innovation and Renewal*, Cambridge, MA: Ballinger Publishing Company, 1987, pp. 160–84.

Technological communities and trajectories

Andrsen, Birgitte, "The Evolution of Technological Trajectories 1890–1900," *Structural Change and Economic Dynamics*, Vol. 9, No. 1, 1998, pp. 5–34.

Bye, Pascal, "Technology Trajectories and Strategies," *International Journal of Technology Management*, Vol. 10, No. 1, 1995, pp. 45–66.

Cimoli, Mario and Giovanni Dosi, "Technological Paradigms, Patterns of Learning and Development: an Introductory Roadmap," *Journal of Evolutionary Economics*, Vol. 5, No. 3, 1995, pp. 243–268.

Dosi, Giovanni and Dan Lovallo, "Rational Entrepreneurs or Optimistic Martyrs? Some Considerations on Technological Regimes, Corporate Entities, and the Evolutionary Role of Decision Biases," in Raghu Garud, Praveen R. Nayyar, and Zur B. Shapira, eds, *Technological Innovation: Oversights and Foresights*, New York: Cambridge University Press, 1997, pp. 44–68.

Durand, Thomas, "Dual Technological Trees: Assessing the Intensity and Strategic Significance of Technological Change," *Research Policy*, Vol. 21, No. 4, August 1992, pp. 361–80.

Kim, Dong-Jae, "Technological Platforms and Diversification," *Organization Science*, Vol. 7, No. 3, May/June 1996, pp. 283–301.

Koen, Peter A., "Technology Maps: Choosing the Right Path," *Engineering Management Journal*, Vol. 9, No. 4, December 1997, pp. 7–11.

Lynn, Leonard H., John D. Aram, and N. Mohan Reddy, "Technology Communities and Innovation Communities," *Journal of Engineering and Technology Management*, Vol. 14, No. 2, June 1997, pp. 129–45.

Lynn, Leonard H., N. Mohan Reddy, and John D. Aram, "Linking Technology and Institutions: The Innovation Community Framework," *Research Policy*, Vol. 25, No. 1, January 1996, pp. 91–106.

Saviotti, Pier P., "Technology Mapping and the Evaluation of Technical Change," *International Journal of Technology Management*, Vol. 10, Nos 4/5/6, 1995, pp. 407–25.

Van de Ven, Andrew, "A Community Perspective on the Emergence of Innovations," *Journal of Engineering and Technology Management*, Vol. 10, Nos 1/2, June 1993, pp. 23–51.

Wade, James, "Dynamics of Organizational Communities and Technological Bandwagons: an Empirical Investigation of Community Evolution in the Microprocessor Market," *Strategic Management Journal*, Vol. 16, Special Issue, Summer 1995, pp. 111–33.

Innovation

Aram, John D., Leonard H. Lynn, and N. Mohan Reddy, "Institutional Relationships and Technology Commercialization: Limitations of Market-Based Policy," *Research Policy*, Vol. 21, No. 5, June 1992, pp. 409–21.

Archibugi, Daniele and Johnathan Michie, "Technological Globalisation or National Systems of Innovation?" *Futures*, Vol. 29, No. 2, March 1997, pp. 121–37.

—— "The Globalization of Technology: a Taxonomy," *Cambridge Journal of Economics*, Vol. 19, No. 1, February 1995, pp. 121–40.

Ashton, W. Bradford, Bruce R. Kinzey, and Marvin E. Gunn, Jr, "A Structured Approach for Monitoring Science and Technology Developments," *International Journal of Technology Management*, Vol. 6, Nos 1/2, 1991, pp. 91–111.

Ayres, Robert U., "Toward a Non-linear Dynamics of Technological Progress," *Journal of Economic Behavior and Organization*, Vol. 24, June 1994, pp. 35–69.

Bowonder, B. and T. Miyake, "Globalization, Alliances, Diversification and Innovation: a Case Study from Hitachi Ltd," *Creativity and Innovation Management*, Vol. 3, No. 1, 1994, pp. 11–28.

—— "Technology Forecasting in Japan," *Futures*, Vol. 25, No. 7, September 1993, pp. 757–77.

—— "Japanese Innovations in Advanced Technologies: an Analysis of Functional Integration," *International Journal of Technology Management*, Vol. 8, Nos 1/2, 1993, pp. 135–56.

Brooks, Harvey, "The Relationship between Science and Technology," *Research Policy*, Vol. 23, No. 5, September 1994, pp. 477–86.

Chen, Stephen, "A New Paradigm for Knowledge-based Competition: Building an Industry through Knowledge Sharing," *Technology Analysis and Strategic Management*, Vol. 9, No. 4, December 1997, pp. 437–52.

Chesbrough, Henry W. and David J. Teece, "When Is Virtual Virtuous? Organizing for Innovation," *Harvard Business Review*, Vol. 74, No. 1, January/February 1996, pp. 65–73.

Dasgupta, Partha and Paul A. David, "Toward a New Economics of Science," *Research Policy*, Vol. 23, No.5, September 1994, pp. 487–521.

De Bondt, Raymond, "Spillovers and Innovative Activities," *International Journal of Industrial Organization*, Vol. 15, No. 1, February 1997, pp. 1–28.

Dosi, Giovanni, "Sources, Procedures, and Microeconomic Effects of Innovation," *Journal of Economic Literature*, Vol. 26, No. 3, September 1988, pp. 1120–71.

Eliasson, Gunnar, "Spillovers, Integrated Production and the Theory of the Firm," *Journal of Evolutionary Economics*, Vol. 6, No. 2, 1996, pp. 125–40.

Fagerberg, Jan, "Technology and International Differences in Growth Rates," *Journal of Economic Literature*, Vol. 32, No. 3, September 1994, pp. 1147–75.

Faulkner, Wendy, "Conceptualizing Knowledge Used in Innovation: a Second Look at the Science-Technology Distinction and Industrial Innovation," *Science, Technology, and Human Values*, Vol. 19, No. 4, Autumn 1994, pp. 425–58.

Florida, Richard, "The New Industrial Revolution," *Futures*, Vol. 23, No. 6, July/August 1991, pp. 559–76.

Fransman, Martin, "The Japanese Innovation System: How Does It Work?" in Mark Dodgson and Roy Rothwell, eds, *The Handbook of Industrial Innovation*, Brookfield, VT: Edward Elgar, 1994, pp. 67–77.

Freeman, Chris, "The 'National System of Innovation' in Historical Perspective," *Cambridge Journal of Economics*, Vol. 19, No. 1, February 1995, pp. 5–24.

Frey, Donald N., "The New Dynamism: Part I," *Interfaces*, Vol. 24, No. 2, March/April 1994, pp. 87–91.

Henry, Nick, Doreen Massey, and David Weld, "Along the Road: R&D, Society, and Space," *Research Policy*, Vol. 24, No. 5, September 1995, pp. 707–26.

Hobday, Mike, "Product Complexity, Innovation and Industrial Organisation," *Research Policy*, Vol. 26, No. 6, February 1998, pp. 689–710.

Hutcheson, G. Dan and Jerry D. Hutcheson, "Technology and Economics in the Semiconductor Industry," *Scientific American*, Vol. 274, No. 1, January 1996, pp. 54–62.

Imai, Ken-ichi, "The Japanese Pattern of Innovation and Its Evolution," in Nathan Rosenberg, Ralph Landau, and David C. Mowery, eds, *Technology and the Wealth of Nations*, Stanford, CA: Stanford University Press, 1992, pp. 225–46.

Jorde, Thomas M. and David J. Teece, "Innovation and Cooperation: Implications for Competition and Antitrust," *Journal of Economic Perspectives*, Summer 1990, pp. 75–96.

Karlsson, Christer and Par Ahlstrom, "The Difficult Path to Lean Product Development," *Journal of Product Innovation Management*, Vol. 13, No. 4, July 1996, pp. 283–95.

Kemp, Rene, "Technology and the Transition to Environmental Sustainability," *Futures*, Vol. 26, No. 10, December 1994, pp. 1023–46.

Kiely, Tom, "Innovation Congregations," *Technology Review*, Vol. 97, No. 3, April 1994, pp. 55–60.

Klevorick, Alvin K., Richard C. Levin, Richard R. Nelson, and Sidney G. Winter, "On the Sources and Significance of Interindustry Differences in Technological Opportunities," *Research Policy*, Vol. 24, No. 2, March 1995, pp. 185–205.

Kline, Stephen J., *Innovation Styles in Japan and the United States: Cultural Bases: Implications for Competitiveness*, Palo Alto, CA: Department of Mechanical Engineering, Stanford University, 1989.

—— "Innovation is not a Linear Process," *Research Management*, Vol. 28, No. 4, July/August 1985, pp. 36–45.

Kodama, Fumio, "Technology Fusion and the New R&D," *Harvard Business Review*, Vol. 70, No. 4, July/August 1992, pp. 70–8.

—— "Changing Global Perspective: Japan, the USA and the New Industrial Order," *Science and Public Policy*, Vol. 18, No. 6, December 1991, pp. 385–92.

Leonard, Dorothy and Sylvia Sensiper, "The Role of Tacit Knowledge in Group Innovation," *California Management Review*, Vol. 40, No. 3, Spring 1998, pp. 112–32.

Levin, Richard C., Alvin K. Klevorick, Richard R. Nelson, and Sidney G. Winter, "Appropriating the Returns from Industrial Research and Development," *Brookings Papers on Economic Activity*, No. 3, 1987, pp. 783–820.

Lundvall, Bengt-Ake, "Standards in an Innovative World," in Richard W. Hawkins, Robin Mansell, and Jim Skea, eds, *Standards, Innovation and Competitiveness: The Politics and Economics of Standards in Natural and Technical Environments*, Brookfield, VT: Edward Elgar, 1995, pp. 7–12.

Mansell, Robin, "Standards, Industrial Policy and Innovation," in Richard W. Hawkins, Robin Mansell, and Jim Skea, eds, *Standards, Innovation and Competitiveness: The Politics and Economics of Standards in Natural and Technical Environments*, Brookfield, VT: Edward Elgar, 1995, pp. 213–27.

Mansfield, Edwin, "Academic Research Underlying Industrial Innovations: Sources, Characteristics, and Financing," *Review of Economics and Statistics*, Vol. 77, No. 1, February 1995, pp. 55–65.

—— "Academic Research and Industrial Innovation," *Research Policy*, Vol. 20, No. 1, February 1991, pp. 1–12.

Marceau, Jane, "Clusters, Chains and Complexes: Three Approaches to Innovation with a Public Policy Perspective," in Mark Dodgson and Roy Rothwell, eds, *The Handbook of Industrial Innovation*, Brookfield, VT: Edward Elgar, 1994, pp. 3–12.

Merrifield, D. Bruce, "Measurements of Productivity: Key to Survival," *International Journal of Technology Management*, Vol. 9, Nos 5/6/7, 1994, pp. 771–83.

—— "Value-added: the Dominant Factor in Industrial Competitiveness," *International Journal of Technology Management*, Special Publication on the Role of Technology in Corporate Policy, 1991, pp. 226–35.

—— "What Is Private and What Is Public about Technology?" *Science, Technology, and Human Values*, Vol. 14, No. 3, Summer 1989, pp. 229–41.

—— and Gavin Wright, "The Rise and Fall of American Technological Leadership: the Postwar Era in Historical Perspective," *Journal of Economic Literature*, Vol. 30, No. 4, December 1992, pp. 1931–64.

Nonaka, Ikujiro and Martin Kenney, "Towards a New Theory of Innovation Management: a Case Study Comparing Canon, Inc. and Apple Computer, Inc.," *Journal of Engineering and Technology Management*, Vol. 8, June 1991, pp. 67–83.

Parayil, Govindan, "Models of Technological Change: a Critical Review of Current Knowledge," *History and Technology*, Vol. 10, No. 2, 1993, pp. 105–26.

Patel, Pari, "Localized Production of Technology for Global Markets," *Cambridge Journal of Economics*, Vol. 19, No. 1, February 1995, pp. 141–53.

—— and Keith Pavitt, "Divergence in Technological Development Among Countries and Firms," in John Hagedoorn, ed., *Technical Change and the World Economy: Convergence and Divergence in Technological Strategies*, Brookfield, VT: Edward Elgar, 1995, pp. 147–81.

Pavitt, Keith, "What Makes Basic Research Economically Valuable?" *Research Policy*, Vol. 20, No. 2, April 1991, pp. 109–19.

Porter, Michael E., "What Is Strategy?" *Harvard Business Review*, Vol. 74, No. 6, November/December 1996, pp. 61–78.

Rosenberg, Nathan and Richard R. Nelson, "American Universities and Technical Advance in Industry," *Research Policy*, Vol. 23, No. 3, May 1994, pp. 323–48.

Rothwell, Roy, "The Changing Nature of the Innovation Process: Implications for SMEs," in Ray Oakley, ed., *New Technology-Based Firms in the 1990s*, New York: Paul Chapman Publishing, 1994, pp. 11–21.

—— "The Changing Nature of the Innovation Process," *Technovation*, Vol. 13, No. 1, January 1993, pp. 1–2.

—— "Successful Industrial Innovation: Critical Factors for the 1990s," *R&D Management*, Vol. 22, No. 3, July 1992, pp. 221–39.

Saint-Onge, Hubert, "Tacit Knowledge: the Key to the Strategic Alignment of Intellectual Capital," *Strategy and Leadership*, Vol. 24, No. 2, April 1996, pp. 10–14.

Tassey, Gregory, "The Roles of Standards as Technology Infrastructure," in Richard W. Hawkins, Robin Mansell, and Jim Skea, eds, *Standards, Innovation and Competitiveness: the Politics and Economics of Standards in Natural and Technical Environments*, Brookfield, VT: Edward Elgar, 1995, pp. 161–71.

—— "The Functions of Technology Infrastructure in a Competitive Economy," *Research Policy*, Vol. 20, No. 4, August 1991, pp. 345–61.

Teece, David J., "Capturing Value from Knowledge Assets: the New Economy, Markets for Know-how, and Intangible Assets," *California Management Review*, Vol. 40, No. 3, Spring 1998, pp. 55–79.

—— "Inter-organizational Requirements of the Innovation Process," *Managerial and Decision Economics*, Vol. 10, Special Issue on Competitiveness, Technology, and Productivity, Spring 1989, pp. 35–42.

—— "Profiting from Technological Innovation: Implications for Integration, Collaboration, Licensing and Public Policy," *Research Policy*, Vol. 15, No. 6, October 1986, pp. 285–305.

US Congress, Office of Technology Assessment, *Innovation and Commercialization of Emerging Technologies*, Washington, DC: Government Printing Office, September 1995.

Patterns of technological change

Brown, Shona L. and Kathleen M. Eisenhardt, "The Art of Continuous Change: Linking Complexity Theory and Time-paced Evolution in Relentlessly Shifting Organizations," *Administrative Science Quarterly*, Vol. 42, No. 1, March 1997, pp. 1–34.

Bessant, John and Sarah Caffyn, "High-involvement Innovation through Continuous Improvement," *International Journal of Technology Management*, Vol. 14, No. 1, 1997, pp. 7–28.

Ehrnberg, Ellinor, "On the Definition and Measurement of Technological Discontinuities," *Technovation*, Vol. 15, No. 7, September 1995, pp. 437–52.

—— and Staffan Jacobsson, "Managing Technological Discontinuities – A Tentative Framework," *International Journal of Technology Management*, Vol. 11, Nos 3/4, 1996, pp. 452–69.

Lambe, C. Jay and Robert E. Spekman, "Alliances, External Technology Acquisition, and Discontinuous Technological Change," *Journal of Product Innovation Management*, Vol. 14, No. 2, May 1997, pp. 102–16.

Lynn, Gary S., Joseph G. Morone, and Albert S. Paulson, "Marketing and Discontinuous Innovation: the Probe and Learn Process," *California Management Review*, Vol. 38, No. 3, Spring 1996, pp. 8–37.

Malerba, Franco and Luigi Orsenigo, "Schumpeterian Patterns of Innovation Are Technology-specific," *Research Policy*, Vol. 25, No. 3, May 1996, pp. 451–78.

—— "Schumpeterian Patterns of Innovation," *Cambridge Journal of Economics*, Vol. 19, No. 1, February 1995, pp. 47–66.

Prahalad, C. K., "Managing Discontinuities: the Emerging Challenges," *Research-Technology Management*, Vol. 41, No. 3, May/June 1998, pp. 14–22.

Smeds, Rita, "Radical Change Through Incremental Innovations: Generic Principles and Cultural Differences in Evolution Management," *International Journal of Technology Management*, Vol. 14, No. 1, 1997, pp. 146–162.

Windrum, Paul and Chris Birchenhall, "Is Product Life Cycle Theory a Special Case? Dominant Designs and the Emergence of Market Niches through Coevolutionary-learning," *Structural Change and Economic Dynamics*, Vol. 9, No. 1, 1998, pp. 109–34.

Manufacturing

Alic, John A., "Computer-assisted Everything? Tools and Techniques for Design and Production," *Technological Forecasting and Social Change*, Vol. 44, 1993, pp. 359–74.

—— "Who Designs Work? Organizing Production in an Age of High Technology," *Technology in Society*, Vol. 12, No. 3, 1990, pp. 301–17.

Ayres, Robert U., "CIM: a Challenge to Technology Management," *International Journal of Technology Management*, Vol. 7, Nos 1/2/3, Special Issue on Strengthening Corporate and National Competitiveness Through Technology, 1992, pp. 17–39.

—— and Duane C. Butcher, "The Flexible Factory Revisited," *American Scientist*, Vol. 81, September/October 1993, pp. 448–59.

Benders, Jos, "Leaving Lean? Recent Changes in the Production Organization of Some Japanese Car Plants," *Economic and Industrial Democracy*, Vol. 17, 1996, pp. 9–38.

Bianchi, Patrizio, "Structural Change and Strategic Behavior: Moving from Mass-production to Flexibility," *International Journal of Technology Management*, Special Publication on the Role of Technology in Corporate Policy, 1991, pp. 21–39.

Bowen, H. Kent, Kim B. Clark, Charles A. Holloway, and Steven C. Wheelwright, "Development Projects: the Engine of Renewal," *Harvard Business Review*, Vol. 72, No. 5, September/October 1994, pp. 110–20.

Busby, J. S. and I.-S. Fan, "The Extended Manufacturing Enterprise: Its Nature and Its Needs," *International Journal of Technology Management*, Vol. 8, Nos 3/4/5, Special Issue on Manufacturing Technology: Diffusion, Implementation and Management, 1993, pp. 294–308.

Clark, Kim B. and Takahiro Fujimoto, "The Power of Product Integrity," *Harvard Business Review*, November/December 1990, pp. 107–17.

Cusumano, Michael A., "Shifting Economies: from Craft Production to Flexible Systems and Software Factories," *Research Policy*, Vol. 21, October 1992, pp. 453–80.

—— and Kentaro Nobeoka, "Strategy, Structure and Performance in Product Development: Observations from the Auto Industry," *Research Policy*, Vol. 21, June 1992, pp. 265–93.

Drucker, Peter E., "The Emerging Theory of Manufacturing," *Harvard Business Review*, May/June 1990, pp. 94–102.

Florida, Richard and Martin Kenney, "The New Age of Capitalism: Innovation-mediated Production," *Futures*, Vol. 25, July/August 1993, pp. 637–51.

Gertler, Meric S., "'Being There': Proximity, Organization, and Culture in the Development and Adoption of Advanced Manufacturing Technologies," *Economic Geography*, January 1995, pp. 1–26.

Goldman, Steven L. and Roger N. Nagel, "Management, Technology and Agility: the Emergence of a New Era in Manufacturing," *International Journal of Technology Management*, 1993, p. 18–38.

Grant, E. B. and M. J. Gregory, "Tacit Knowledge, the Life Cycle and International Manufacturing Transfer," *Technology Analysis and Strategic Management*, Vol. 9, No. 2, 1997, pp. 149–61.

Hayes, Robert H. and Gary P. Pisano, "Beyond World Class: the New Manufacturing Strategy," *Harvard Business Review*, Vol. 72, No. 1, January/February 1994, pp. 77–86.

Henderson, Rebecca M. and Kim B. Clark, "Architectural Innovation: the Reconfiguration of Existing Product Technologies and the Future of Established Firms," *Administrative Science Quarterly*, Vol. 35, March 1990, pp. 9–30.

Hill, Christopher T., "New Manufacturing Paradigms – New Manufacturing Policies?" *The Bridge*, Summer 1991, pp. 15–24.

Kaplan, Gadi, ed., "Manufacturing à la Carte: Agile Assembly Lines, Faster Development Cycles," *IEEE Spectrum*, Special Issue/Manufacturing, September 1993, pp. 24–85.

Kumar, Nirmalya, "The Power of Trust in Manufacturer–Retailer Relationships," *Harvard Business Review*, Vol. 74, No. 6, November/December 1996, pp. 92–106.

Leonard-Barton, Dorothy, H. Kent Bowen, Kim B. Clark, Charles A. Holloway, and Steven C. Wheelwright, "How to Integrate Work and Deepen Expertise," *Harvard Business Review*, September/October 1994, pp. 121–30.

Montgomery, Joseph C., "The Agile Production System," in Joseph C. Montgomery and Lawrence O. Levine, eds, *The Transition to Agile Manufacturing: Staying Flexible for Competitive Advantage*, Milwaukee, WI: ASQC Quality Press, 1996, pp. 1–27.

Morris, Charles R. and Charles H. Ferguson, "How Architecture Wins Technology Wars," *Harvard Business Review*, March/April 1993, pp. 86–96.

Mueller, Frank, "Flexible Working Practices in Engine Plants: Evidence from the European Automobile Industry," *Industrial Relations Journal*, Autumn 1992, pp. 191–204.

Nagel, Roger and Rick Dove, *21st Century Manufacturing Enterprise Strategy: an Industry-led View, Volume 1*, Bethlehem, PA: Iaocca Institute, Lehigh University, 1991.

Nell, Edward J., "Transformational Growth and Learning: Developing Craft Technology into Scientific Mass Production," in Ross Thomson, ed., *Learning and Technological Change*, New York: St. Martin's Press, 1993, pp. 217–42.

O'Hara, Joseph P., Howard E. Evans, and Terry F. Hayden, "Developing New Manufacturing Processes: a Case Study and Model," *Journal of Engineering and Technology Management*, Vol. 10, 1993, pp. 285–306.

Rosenblatt, Alfred and George F. Watson, "Concurrent Engineering," *IEEE Spectrum*, July 1991, pp. 22–37.

Sheridan, John H., "Agile Manufacturing: Stepping Beyond Lean Production," *Industry Week*, April 19, 1993, pp. 30–46.

Swink, Morgan L., Christopher Sandvig, and Vincent A. Mabert, "Customizing Concurrent Engineering Processes: Five Case Studies," *Journal of Product Innovation Management*, Vol. 13, May 1996, pp. 229–44.

Tyre, Marcie J., "Managing the Introduction of New Process Technology: International Differences in a Multi-plant Network," *Research Policy*, February 1991, pp. 57–76.

—— and Wanda J. Orlikowski, "Windows of Opportunity: Temporal Patterns of Technological Adaptation in Organizations," *Organization Science*, February 1994, pp. 98–118.

—— "Exploring Opportunities for Technological Improvement in Organizations," *Sloan Management Review*, Fall 1993, pp. 13–25.

Wheelwright, Steven C. and Kim B. Clark, "Creating Project Plans to Focus Product Development," *Harvard Business Review*, March/April 1992, pp. 70–82.

Womack, James P. and Daniel T. Jones, "From Lean Production to the Lean Enterprise," *Harvard Business Review*, Vol. 72, No. 2, March/April 1994, pp. 93–103.

Competitiveness

Belohlav, James A., "The Evolving Competitive Paradigm," *Business Horizons*, Vol. 39, No. 2, March/April 1996, pp. 11–19.

Bettis, Richard A. and Michael A. Hitt, "The New Competitive Landscape," *Strategic Management Review*, Vol. 16, Special Issue, Summer 1995, pp. 7–19.

Bosworth, Barry P. "Growing Pains: Trade Frictions Corrode US-Asian Relationship," *Brookings Review*, Winter 1996, pp. 4–9.

Boulton, William R., Michael R. Dowling, and Jurgen Loymeyer, "Technology Development Strategies in Japan, Europe, and the United States," *Technovation*, Vol. 12, No. 2, 1992, pp. 99–118.

Burton, Daniel F., Jr, "Competitiveness: Here to Stay," *Washington Quarterly*, Vol. 17, No. 4, Autumn 1994, pp. 99–109.

Franko, Lawrence G., "The Japanese Juggernaut Rolls On," *Sloan Management Review*, Vol. 37, No. 2, Winter 1996, pp. 103–9.

Hayes, Robert H., "US Competitiveness: 'Resurgence' Versus Reality," *Challenge*, Vol. 39, No. 2, March/April 1996, pp. 36–44.

Krugman, Paul, "America the Boastful," *Foreign Affairs*, Vol. 77, No. 3, May/June 1998, pp. 32–45.

—— "Competitiveness: a Dangerous Obsession," *Foreign Affairs*, Vol. 73, No. 2, March/April 1994, pp. 28–44.

—— "Myths and Realities of US Competitiveness," *Science*, November 8, 1991, pp. 811–15.

Lim, Linda Y. C., "Whose 'Model' Failed? Implications of the Asian Economic Crisis," *Washington Quarterly*, Vol. 21, No. 3, Summer 1998, pp. 25–36.

Office of Technology Policy, US Department of Commerce, *International Science and Technology: Emerging Trends in Government Policies and Expenditures*, Washington, DC: Department of Commerce, 1996.

Papadakis, Maria, "The Delicate Task of Linking Industrial R&D to National Competitiveness," *Technovation*, Vol. 15, No. 9, November 1995, pp. 569–83.

—— "Did (or Does) the United States Have a Competitiveness Crisis?," *Journal of Policy Analysis and Management*, Vol. 13, No. 1, Winter 1994, pp. 1–20.

"The Fight over Competitiveness: a Zero Sum Debate?" *Foreign Affairs*, Vol. 73, No. 4, July/August 1994, pp. 186–203.

Path dependence

Arthur, W. Brian, "Urban Systems and Historical and Path Dependence," in R. Herman and J. Ausubel, eds, *Urban Systems and Infrastructure*, Washington, DC: National Academy Press, 1987, pp. 85–97.

Balmann, Alfons, Martin Odening, Hans-Peter Weikard, and Wilhelm Brandes, "Path-dependence without Increasing Returns to Scale and Network Externalities," *Journal of Economic Behavior and Organization*, Vol. 29, January 1996, pp. 159–72.

Cowan, Robin and Philip Gunby, "Sprayed to Death: Path Dependence, Lock-in and Pest Control Strategies," *Economic Journal*, Vol. 106, No. 436, May 1996, pp. 521–42.

David, Paul A., "Path-dependence and Predictability in Dynamic Systems with Local Network Externalities: a Paradigm for Historical Economies," in Dominique Foray and Christopher Freeman, eds, *Technology and the Wealth of Nations: the Dynamics of Constructive Advantage*, New York: Pinter Publishers, 1996, pp. 208–31.

—— and Julie A. Bunn, "The Economics of Gateway Technologies and Network Evolution," *Information Economics and Policy*, Vol. 3, 1988, pp. 165–202.

—— and Dominique Foray, "Dynamics of Competitive Technology Diffusion through Local Network Structures: the Case of EDI Document Standards," in Loet Leydesdorff and Peter Van den Besselaar, eds, *Evolutionary Economics and Chaos Theory: New Directions in Technology Studies*, New York: St. Martin's Press, 1994, pp. 63–78.

—— "Understanding the Economics of QWERTY: the Necessity of History," in W.

N. Parker, ed., *Economic History and the Modern Economist*, New York: Basil Blackwell, 1986, pp. 30–49.

—— "Clio and the Economics of QWERTY," *Economic History*, May 1985, pp. 332–7.

—— and Shane Greenstein, "The Economics of Compatibility Standards: an Introduction to Recent Research," *Economics of Innovation and New Technologies*, Vol. 1, 1990, pp. 3–41.

Dopfer, Kurt, "Toward a Theory of Economic Institutions: Synergy and Path Dependence," *Journal of Economic Issues*, Vol. 25, No. 2, June 1991, pp. 535–50.

Dosi, Giovanni, "Opportunities, Incentives, and the Collective Patterns of Technological Change," *Economic Journal*, Vol. 107, No. 444, September 1997, pp. 1530–47.

Farrell, Joseph and Garth Saloner, "Standardization, Compatibility, and Innovation," *Rand Journal of Economics*, Vol. 16, No. 1, Spring 1985, pp. 70–83.

Greenstein, Shane, "Did Installed Base Give an Incumbent Any (Measurable) Advantages in Federal Computer Procurement?," *Rand Journal of Economics*, Vol. 24, No. 1, Spring 1993, pp. 1–39.

Mazzoleni, Roberto, "Learning and Path Dependence in the Diffusion of Innovations: Comparative Evidence on Numerically Controlled Machine Tools," *Research Policy*, Vol. 26, Nos 4/5, December 1997, pp. 405–28.

Rosenberg, Nathan, *Exploring the Black Box: Technology, Economics, and History*, New York: Cambridge University Press, 1994, pp. 9–23.

Ruttan, Vernon W., "Induced Innovation, Evolutionary Theory and Path Dependence: Sources of Technological Change," *Economic Journal*, Vol. 107, No. 444, September 1997, pp. 1520–9.

Vega-Redondo, Fernando, "Technological Change, Path Dependence, and Growth: a Graph-theoretic Approach," in Jan Fagerberg, Bart Verspagen, and Nick von Tunzelmann, eds, *The Dynamics of Technology, Trade and Growth*, Brookfield, VT: Edward Elgar, 1994, pp. 145–67.

—— "Technological Change and Path Dependence: a Co-evolutionary Model on a Directed Graph," *Journal of Evolutionary Economics*, No. 1, 1994, pp. 59–80.

Wright, Gavin, "Towards a More Historical Approach to Technological Change," *Economic Journal*, Vol. 107, No. 444, September 1997, pp. 1560–6.

Increasing returns and lock-in

Arthur, W. Brian, "Increasing Returns and the New World of Business," *Harvard Business Review*, Vol. 74, No. 4, July/August 1996, pp. 100–9.

—— ed., *Increasing Returns and Path Dependency in the Economy*, Ann Arbor, MI: University of Michigan Press, 1994.

—— "Positive Feedbacks in the Economy," *Scientific American*, Vol. 262, No. 2, February 1990, pp. 92–9.

—— "Competing Technologies, Increasing Returns, and Lock-in by Historical Events," *Economic Journal*, Vol. 99, No. 394, March 1989, pp. 116–31.

Cimoli, Mario, "Lock-in and Specialization (Dis)Advantages in a Structuralist Growth Model," in Jan Fagerberg, Bart Verspagen, and Nick von Tunzelmann, eds, *The Dynamics of Technology, Trade and Growth*, Brookfield, VT: Edward Elgar, 1994, pp. 123–44.

Cowan, Robin, "Tortoises and Hares: Choice among Technologies of Unknown Merit," *Economic Journal*, Vol. 101, No. 407, July 1991, pp. 801–14.

—— "Nuclear Power Reactors: a Study in Technological Lock-in," *Journal of Economic History*, Vol. 50, No. 3, September 1990, pp. 541–67.

Hill, Charles W. L., "Establishing a Standard: Competitive Strategy and Technological Standards in Winner-take-all Industries," *Academy of Management Executive*, Vol. 11, No. 2, May 1997, pp. 7–25.

Krugman, Paul, "Complex Landscapes and Economic Geography," *American Economic Association Papers and Proceedings*, Vol. 84, No. 2, May 1994, pp. 412–16.

—— "Increasing Returns and Economic Geography," *Journal of Political Economy*, Vol. 99, No. 3, July 1991, pp. 483–99.

Metcalfe, J. S., "Competition, Fisher's Principle and Increasing Returns in the Selection Process," *Journal of Evolutionary Economics*, No. 4, 1994, pp. 327–46.

Vandermerwe, Sandra, "Increasing Returns: Competing for Customers in the Global Market," *Journal of World Business*, Vol. 32, No. 4, Winter 1997, pp. 333–50.

Coevolution and emergence

Crutchfield, James P., "Is Anything Ever New? Considering Emergence," in George A. Cowan, David Pines, and David Meltzer, eds, *Complexity: Metaphors, Models, and Reality*, Reading, MA: Addison-Wesley, 1994, pp. 515–33.

Dosi, Giovanni and Bruce Kogut, "National Specificities and the Context of Change: the Coevolution of Organization and Technology," in Bruce Kogut, ed., *Country Competitiveness: Technology and the Organization at Work*, New York: Oxford University Press, 1993, pp. 249–62.

Gowdy, John M., *Coevolutionary Economics: the Economy, Society and the Environment*, Boston: Kluwer Academic, 1995, pp. 131–54.

Inayatullah, Sohail, "Life, the Universe and Emergence," *Futures*, Vol. 26, No. 6, July/August 1994, pp. 683–96.

Nelson, Richard R., "The Coevolution of Technologies and Institutions," in Richard W. England, ed., *Evolutionary Concepts in Contemporary Economics*, Ann Arbor: University of Michigan Press, 1994, pp. 139–56.

—— "Economic Growth via the Coevolution of Technology and Institutions," in Loet Leydesdorff and Peter Van den Besselaar, eds, *Evolutionary Economics and Chaos Theory: New Directions in Technology Studies*, New York: St. Martin's Press, 1994, pp. 21–32.

Science and technology policy

Cannell, William, "Technology Management in the European Union and Its Policy Implications," in William Cannell and Ben Dankbaar, eds, *Technology Management and Public Policy in the European Union*, New York: Oxford University Press, 1996, pp. 158–78.

Clinton, President William J. and Vice President Albert Gore, Jr, *Science in the National Interest*, Washington, DC: Executive Office of the President, August 1994.

—— *Technology for America's Economic Growth: a New Direction to Build Economic Strength*, Washington, DC: Executive Office of the President, February 22, 1993.

Cohen, Linda R. and Roger G. Noll, "Privatizing Public Research," *Scientific American*, September 1994, pp. 72–7.

Crow, Michael M., "Science and Technology Policy in the United States: Trading in the

1950 Model," *Science and Public Policy*, Vol. 21, No. 4, August 1994, pp. 202–12.

Dalum, Bent, Bjorn Johnson, and Bengt-Ake Lundvall, "Public Policy in the Learning Society," in Bengt-Ake Lundvall, ed., *National Systems of Innovation: towards a Theory of Innovation and Interactive Learning*, New York: Pinter Press, 1992, pp. 296–317.

de Bandt, Jacques, "Alternative Approaches to Developing National Technological Policies," *International Journal of Technology Management*, Special Issue on the Increasing Role of Technology in Corporate Policy, 1991, pp. 14–44.

Durlauf, Steven N., "What Should Policymakers Know about Economic Complexity?" *Washington Quarterly*, Vol. 21, No. 1, Winter 1998, pp. 157–65.

Ergas, Henry, "Does Technology Policy Matter?," in Bruce R. Guile and Harvey Brooks, eds, *Technology and Global Industry: Companies and Nations in the World Economy*, Washington, DC: National Academy Press, 1978, pp. 191–245.

Executive Office of the President, *Technology for Economic Growth: President's Progress Report*, Washington, DC: Executive Office of the President, November 1993.

Florida, Richard, "Technology Policy for a Global Economy," *Issues in Science and Technology*, Spring 1995, pp. 49–56.

Fransman, Martin, "Is National Technology Policy Obsolete in a Globalized World: the Japanese Response," *Cambridge Journal of Economics*, Vol. 19, No. 1, February 1995, pp. 95–120.

Gibbons, John H. and William G. Wells, Jr, "Science, Technology and Government in the United States: toward the Year 2000," *Technology in Society*, Vol. 19, Nos 3/4, 1997, pp. 561–85.

Graham, Otis L., Jr, *Losing Time: the Industrial Policy Debate*, Cambridge, MA: Harvard University Press, 1992, pp. 173–206.

Ham, Rose M. and David C. Mowery, "Enduring Dilemmas in US Technology Policy," *California Management Review*, Vol. 37, No. 4, Summer 1995, pp. 89–107.

Kline, Stephen J. and Don E. Kash, "Government Technology Policy: What Should It Do?" *The Bridge*, Vol. 22, No. 1, Spring 1992, pp. 12–18.

Koprowski, Gene, "Does High Technology Need Fed Funds?" *Forbes ASAP*, April 10, 1995, pp. 88–89, 91.

Metcalfe, J. Stanley, *Evolutionary Economics and Creative Destruction*, New York: Routledge, 1998, pp. 107–23.

—— "Technology Systems and Technology Policy in an Evolutionary Framework," *Cambridge Journal of Economics*, February 1995, pp. 25–46.

—— "Technology Policies and Small Firms: an Evolutionary Perspective," in Ray Oakey, ed., *New Technology-based Firms in the 1990s*, New York: Paul Chapman Publishing, 1994, pp. 157–68.

—— "Evolutionary Economics and Technology Policy," *Economic Journal*, Vol. 104, No. 425, July 1994, pp. 931–44.

Nelson, Richard R., "Why Should Managers Be Thinking about Technology Policy?," *Strategic Management Journal*, Vol. 16, No. 8, November 1995, pp. 581–8.

—— and Paul M. Romer, "Science, Economic Growth, and Public Policy," *Challenge*, Vol. 39, No. 2, March/April 1996, pp. 9–21.

Ostry, Sylvia and Richard R. Nelson, *Techno-nationalism and Techno-globalism: Conflict and Cooperation*, Washington, DC: Brookings Institution, 1995.

Shapley, Deborah, "Clintonizing Science Policy," *Bulletin of the Atomic Scientists*, December 1993, pp. 39–43.

Skolnikoff, Eugene B., "Evolving US Science and Technology Policy in a Changing International Environment," *Science and Public Policy*, Vol. 22, No. 2, April 1995, pp. 74–84.

Smith, Keith, "Innovation Policy in an Evolutionary Context," in P. Paolo Saviotti and J. Stanley Metcalfe, eds, *Evolutionary Theories of Economic and Technological Change: Present Status and Future Prospects*, Reading, PA: Harwood Academic Publishers, 1991, pp. 256–75.

Tonelson, Alan, "The Perils of Techno-globalism," *Issues in Science and Technology*, Summer 1995, pp. 31–8.

Index